Collaborative Land Use Management

Collaborative Land Use Management

The Quieter Revolution in Place-Based Planning

Robert J. Mason

Rowman & Littlefield Publishers, Inc.
Lanham • Boulder • New York • Toronto • Plymouth, UK

ROWMAN & LITTLEFIELD PUBLISHERS, INC.

Published in the United States of America
by Rowman & Littlefield Publishers, Inc.
A wholly owned subsidary of The Rowman & Littlefield Publishing Group, Inc.
4501 Forbes Boulevard, Suite 200, Lanham, Maryland 20706
www.rowmanlittlefield.com

Estover Road, Plymouth PL6 7PY, United Kingdom

Copyright © 2008 by Rowman & Littlefield Publishers, Inc.

British Library Cataloguing in Publication Information Available

Library of Congress Cataloging-in-Publication Data

Mason, Robert J., 1955–
  Collaborative land use management : the quieter revolution in place-based planning /
Robert J. Mason.
    p. cm.
  Includes bibliographical references.
  ISBN-13: 978-0-7425-4700-1 (hbk. : alk. paper)
  ISBN-10: 0-7425-4700-0 (hbk. : alk. paper)
  ISBN-13: 978-0-7425-4701-8 (hbk. : alk. paper)
  ISBN-10: 0-7425-4701-9 (hbk. : alk. paper)
    1. Land use—United States—Planning. 2. Regional planning—Environmental
aspects—United States. 3. Public-private sector cooperation—United States. I. Title.
  HD205.M355 2008
  333.730973—dc22   2007015235

Printed in the United States of America

♾™ The paper used in this publication meets the minimum requirements of American
National Standard for Information Sciences—Permanence of Paper for Printed Library
Materials, ANSI/NISO Z39.48-1992.

CONTENTS

CHAPTER ONE   Introducing the Quieter Revolution 1

CHAPTER TWO   Lead-up to the Revolution 17

CHAPTER THREE   The Politics of Place 43

CHAPTER FOUR   Protecting Regional Landscapes 79

CHAPTER FIVE   Slowing Sprawl, Saving Spaces 149

CHAPTER SIX   Let a Thousand Local Initiatives Bloom 199

CHAPTER SEVEN   Counterrevolutionaries 235

CHAPTER EIGHT   Evaluating the Revolution 261

CHAPTER NINE   A Quieter Future? 279

References 297
Index 347

CHAPTER ONE

INTRODUCING THE QUIETER REVOLUTION

I am here today to announce a bold new initiative . . . that will help us build more livable communities in which to raise our families, places where young and old can walk, bike, and play together; places where we not only protect historic old neighborhoods, but where farms, green spaces, and forests can add life and beauty to the newest of suburbs; places where we can work competitively, and still spend less time in traffic and more time, that most precious of commodities for the families we really are, with our children, our spouses, our friends. (Vice President Al Gore, "Livability Announcement," January 11, 1999)

Who could possibly take issue with such a glorious, holistic, sustainable vision? Probably very few would—until we begin descending from Al Gore's stratospheric ideals to actions on the ground. Implementing the vision means planning, redistribution of resources, and—at least for some—personal sacrifice. Because Americans place such exceptional value on their personal freedoms, the mere mention of centralized oversight can provoke spirited reaction. To many, it would seem, land use planning is like medication—sometimes necessary, but hardly desirable. We are highly skeptical of claims made by planners and their allies, and extraordinarily fearful of distant governments intruding into what are seen as essentially private matters. Indeed, this is why *locally* based restrictions—the ones that have been so effective in sorting us by race, class, and income—are as widely accepted as they are (Weigel, Fairbank, and Metz 2004). By contrast, comprehensive regional, state, and

1

federal planning—designed ideally to take into account efficient use of resources, environmental protection, and social and economic equity—is much more elusive and contested.

Yet, over the past two decades or so, a new approach has emerged, one that seems altogether fitting for an era of diminished government. The command-and-control model—where central government establishes specific, legally binding requirements, implemented through regulations—is institutionalized in many of our air and water pollution control laws. But land use laws, especially supralocal ones, have tended to be more flexible all along, in recent years trending toward an even "quieter" tack. This softer, gentler approach embraces many state-of-the-art concepts and terms, among them "smart growth," "environmental stewardship," "place-based planning," "collaborative management," and "new regionalism."

Federal and state governments retain important, but tempered, roles in this new land-management world. One of those roles is provider of funds, technical resources, incentives, and disincentives. Another role, in which agencies are more directly engaged, is as equal partners with—or perhaps even lesser players than—nonprofit organizations, private landowners, and local governments. Governments are collaborators and partners, acting more as facilitators than commanders in chief. As the federal regulatory presence has shrunk, state- and local-level innovation has flourished. Wherever future political and economic circumstances take us, these diverse and devolved approaches will likely remain with us. Granted, this evolutionary process is far more complex, nuanced, and historically rooted than this brief description would imply . . . and that is what makes it such a compelling and fascinating theme for this book.

The backdrop for all this—and the inspiration for the book's title—is what Fred Bosselman and David Callies (1971) characterized more than three decades ago as the "quiet revolution in land use control." What they were describing was the proliferation of state and regional land use regulatory programs of the early 1970s. Local zoning was seen as woefully inadequate, and becoming more so, at a time when demands on the nation's land base were rapidly escalating. From the California coast to New York's Adirondack Mountains, new plans, procedures, and restrictions were being put into place. Federal legislation was proposed as well, though Congress never did quite manage to enact a national land use law. In the heady environmental days of the early 1970s, it probably was not too presumptuous to look toward a future of much greater central control over land use decisions. But things did not work out that way. Not only did the national law falter; so, too, did state and regional initiatives. Long before diffusing to its full national potential, the planning innovation wave crested and broke.

But environmental and land use innovation did not come to a dead stop after the mid-1970s. While Ronald Reagan and, to a lesser degree, George H. W. Bush may have wanted to scale back our environmental regulatory infrastructure, they were constrained by Democratic Congresses and a concerned American public (Dunlap 1992, 2002; Bosso and Guber 2006). And indeed, even some new federal laws and mandates—directed mostly toward guiding local and state land use decisions—would come to pass (Popper 1988). States and localities themselves continued developing programs, though not with the same fervor as during the "quiet revolution." New Jersey's Pinelands Plan (New Jersey Pinelands Commission 1980; Mason 1992a) and State Development and Redevelopment Plan (New Jersey State Planning Commission 2001), for example, came on line during the 1980s. While the Clinton era did not, as some had at first anticipated, bring dramatic environmental progress at the federal level, the 1990s and the turn of the century did witness a reemergence of organized land use activity—but in a much gentler, less-intrusive, more locally oriented form than what had preceded it in the early 1970s.

This is the "quieter revolution" in land use management. Today the emphasis is on place-based, public-private, multistakeholder approaches that treat the human occupants of valued places inclusively and respectfully. These approaches are supported by federal and state grants, subsidies, and beneficial tax treatment for land trusts, watershed conservancies, and other nongovernmental organizations (NGOs). The quieter revolution is adaptive, attuned, and adjusted to a political climate much more constrained and conservative than that of the 1970s. Thirty-five years ago, more federal environmental funding was available and decisions regarding environmental impact assessment, law enforcement, and "taking" of private lands for public purposes gave rather greater weight to environmental interests than is the case today (Echeverria and Zeidler 1999; Bosso 2005; Sabatier et al. 2005).

The quieter revolution is filling the gaps and reshaping the American landscape in its own ways. From many an environmentalist's or planner's perspective, it may not be doing nearly enough to confront sprawl, protect habitats, or face down a resurgent property rights movement—but it is still making a meaningful mark in a multitude of places. While the changes may not be especially consistent, comprehensive, or well coordinated, each is consequential in its own right, and their connectedness and cumulative impacts are growing. Indeed, the quieter revolution holds much potential, as it is building infrastructure that can help us respond, in a serious way, to looming petroleum dependency and climate crises.

Key quieter revolution elements, then, are:

Scale: Most activity at local and regional levels; often bioregional; state and federal "infrastructural" support (policies, frameworks, funds, incentives, technical expertise)

Organizations and individuals: Land trusts, watershed conservancies, government agencies with environmental and planning portfolios, mainstream environmental organizations and their local branches, stakeholders representing diverse interests (residential, recreational, small-business, corporate, educational, etc.)

Methods: Multistakeholder, collaborative decision making; conventional local and regional planning; habitat conservation planning; land and easement acquisitions; transfer of development rights programs; subsidy payments and tax breaks; federal and state targeted laws and policies (infrastructure development, planning enabling legislation experiments); federal and state regulatory threats to deter unsustainable actions and rewards for sustainable actions; adaptive planning

Funding sources: Ballot questions, federal and state bonds, government and foundation grants and loans, tax breaks, development fees, pollution taxes, legal settlements, corporate funding programs

A New Politics of Place

While the quieter revolution reaches across many spatial scales, there is a premium on the local. In an increasingly homogenized, speed-of-light, Wal-Marted world, we are witnessing a countercurrent, in the form of renewed public concern about local places—indeed, what we might regard as a new "politics of place." It is reflected in the remarkable growth of watershed associations, land trusts, environmental ballot questions, and place-based education and service-learning programs. Is all this activity simply therapeutic relief, satisfying the scattered and sentimental yearnings of an aging population hoping to reinhabit a time when America's communities were prosperous, human-scale, pedestrian-friendly, and aesthetically pleasing? Perhaps this new politics of place will eventually give way to the hard realities of a prolonged economic downturn, chronic deflation, or sustained high rates of unemployment. Another critical dimension is social equity: Are place-based politics an elitist enterprise that unifies well-to-do citizens across the political spectrum but excludes and fails to excite those of lesser means? Or are place-based politics evolving toward greater diversity and inclusiveness? These are some of the questions considered in following chapters.

As the idea for this book was first taking shape, an era of Clinton/Gore-inspired collaborative land use planning seemed to be in the offing. Starting with the Northwest Forest Plan (DellaSala and Williams 2006) and culminating in a nationwide network of livable communities (chapter 5) and Habitat Conservation Plans (chapter 6), this would be a kinder, gentler era for environmental and land use planning. Gone would be the days of confrontational environmentalism, with environmentalists reflexively engaging with a host of enemies on issues ranging from water quality to urban environmental justice. In its place would be a collaborative, "win-win" form of environmentalism, embracing and bringing new benefits to very diverse constituencies. At least, that is one anticipatory telling of the tale.

For a time it seemed as if the "smart growth" agenda, with its emphasis on urban revitalization and more livable, energy-efficient suburbs, might become a flagship Gore administration theme. Of course, to be tempered and realistic about all this, adversarialism would hardly cease to exist; indeed, the Northwest Forest Plan itself was the outcome of an incredibly contentious process. In the broader win-win future, federal and state regulators would still feel compelled to boast that laws and regulations are implemented and enforced without fear or favor, and the environmental community might do very well to position itself as watchdog first, cooperative stakeholder second. Trust, but verify! Watch out for those who would co-opt the collaborative process and find ways to blunt existing environmental laws and programs. But the overall trend would be toward a quieter and gentler—and more "livable"—environmental future.

Yet during the height of the 2000 campaign, the smart growth theme never did get the play that many had anticipated. Of course, if Al Gore had occupied the White House, land use and growth management might by now be highly placed on the national agenda, despite being short-shrifted in the campaign. Gore probably would have emphasized partnership approaches more than new regulatory schemes—and this is probably what we should expect from the next administration, whether Democratic or Republican. George W. Bush's ascension to the presidency meant diminished attention not only to environmental initiatives generally but even to quieter approaches to land use management. Still, the era of collaborative planning—especially land use planning—has been with us for some time now, and it is here to stay. Indeed, even the Bush administration embraces the rhetoric of collaborative land use planning, if not much of its framers' original intent. And beyond this, states, localities, and NGOs will continue to support cooperative efforts, even when the general climate for environmental and land use innovation is not especially supportive. Indeed, in an era of restricted fiscal and political options, cooperative approaches are tremendously valuable in enabling both government and nongovernment actors to expand their capacity and reach (Van de Ven and Ferry 1980; Endicott 1993; McNeely 1995; Yaffee et al. 1996; Michaels, Mason, and Solecki 1999; Koontz et al. 2004; Sabatier et al. 2005).

The Bush administration's limited interest in land use planning is in some ways a deterrent, but in other ways a stimulus for state and local efforts. Indeed, states and localities are today's leading environmental policy laboratories. Moreover, the post–September 11 era may be bringing renewed appreciation of local places. Increased concern about homeland security may trickle down to thinking about how to make our localities better-planned places—though admittedly this thinking is rather speculative. Despite heightened awareness of place following the September 11 attacks and Hurricane Katrina, there has been modest official interest, at best, in deploying land use strategies to make our communities more ecologically and socially resilient. Indeed, with the Bush administration's reluctance to embrace far-reaching environmental goals, the stage for renewed adversarialism has been set. The environmental community believes the environment is under siege and that progress made over the past three decades is now recklessly endangered. Environmentalists are at least as angry as they were when Ronald Reagan was elected in 1980. Yet we may now be at a tipping point, with the 2006 election of a Democratic Congress and renewed interest from both political parties in environmental and energy sustainability.

Environmental justice and property rights issues, both critical to the quieter revolution's fortunes, emerged in a big way in the early 1990s. The wise use/property rights movements—which were energized by the 1994 Republican revolution but seemed to be in retreat by the late 1990s—is receiving something of a boost in the new millennium. Property rights advocates have been emboldened by the Bush administration's brand of environmentalism, combined with a dozen years of Republican congressional majorities. At the same time, the receptive political climate may have enabled them to let their guard down, at least a bit. But, as we shall see in chapter 7, it is not quite this simple. Various events—among them a Supreme Court decision supporting controversial uses of eminent domain power, along with a raft of pro–property rights legislation and ballot measures, exemplified by Oregon's Measure 37—have reshaped and energized the wise use/property rights forces. A full depiction of the resurgent movement is not a principal objective for this book; instead, its changing influence and significance with respect to specific place-based planning efforts, and place-based planning as a whole, are taken up in chapter 7.

Today, environmental justice issues receive far less federal attention than they did through the Clinton years and even the first Bush era. Just as with wise use/property rights, a full assessment is not in order here. But what is significant is the perception of increased environmental injustices. Indeed, this may provoke victims and their allies toward more assertive political action. And this is likely to play out in various place-based planning contexts. Environmental equity cannot, for example, be separated from smart growth. Because it calls for urban revitalization, brownfields remediation, and affordable housing, the smart growth agenda seemingly is attuned to environmental justice issues. But is smart growth really advancing the environmental justice cause or simply using it as a divisive and exclusionary means to promote suburban growth control agendas? The truth—if there is truth to be had here—probably is somewhere in between.

Both environmental justice and property rights issues are profoundly affected by economic conditions. Slow economic growth may heighten property rights and environmental justice conflicts and more generally act to dampen down calls for increased environmental regulation. This could favor collaborative approaches, even in a political climate not nurturing of environmental innovation. Regardless of economic influences, collaboration might well be the best way to go in such political circumstances. Indeed, former secretary of the interior Gale Norton—no friend to the environmental community—embraced cooperative planning for wetlands protection. As this example suggests, collaborative approaches are likely to enjoy continued support across the political spectrum.

The emerging politics of place has made itself evident in a variety of forms, and at many different spatial scales. Nonprofit land trusts, for example, are active locally, buying land and easements in order to protect particular places. Every year, voters approve dozens of open-space ballot measures, most of them authorizing funds for local open-space acquisitions. New Jersey voters, in 1998, approved a billion-dollar statewide open-space fund, and they may be voting on a new funding measure in 2007. Abandoned rail rights-of-way and towpaths are being turned into greenways for hiking, biking, and other recreational pursuits. River corridors and other heritage sites are gaining federal recognition and receiving federal, state, and local grant funds. Maryland and Oregon are leaders in nurturing smart growth, while Pennsylvania is actively promoting multi-municipal planning. Government agencies are seeking to curtail sprawl by directing public infrastructure investments toward areas already developed or immediately adjacent to developed lands. Commercial and residential redevelopment of abandoned industrial sites—brownfields—is strongly promoted by the U.S. Environmental Protection Agency and other federal agencies, as well as by many state governments.

These examples begin to show us that place-based environmentalism works at multiple, overlapping scales. To illustrate more specifically, let us briefly consider the New York/New Jersey Highlands (chapter 4). While the much larger Appalachian ecoregion's contours are broadly familiar to the general public as well as the specialists, a Highlands subregion was not widely recognized until the 1990s (Mitchell 1992). As the U.S. Forest Service's recent comprehensive regional research report (Phelps and Hoppe 2002) acknowledges, a compelling physiographic case can be made for recognizing a more extensive highlands subregion that encompasses parts of Pennsylvania and Connecticut. A federal study spanning this larger area is now under way (USDA Forest Service, Northeastern Area 2007). But the reasons for separating out the New York/New Jersey subregion in the first place are as much about pressures from recreation use, transportation corridors, burgeoning residential and commercial development, and consequent availability of federal support for the project area as defined, as they are about physiography. And individual state political cultures are even more relevant; in 2004, New Jersey adopted a quiet revolution planning scheme for its slice of the Highlands region (New Jersey Department of Environmental Protection [NJDEP] 2007a). Highlands planning, then, is not ecoregional planning with a strictly ecoregional basis, but rather critical area planning, where the critical region is a construct based as much on recent demographic, social, and political trends as it is on natural features.

In addition to such newly minted regions as the Highlands, we have many traditional physical regions, among them New York's Adirondack Park, the Chesapeake Bay and its watershed, the Great Basin, and the Great Lakes Basin. This is not to imply that boundary delineation in these cases is physiographically simple and historically consistent; indeed, regional definitions of even these long-recognized areas often involve contentious negotiations. Other regions now promoting place-based approaches, such as metropolitan Pittsburgh and Atlanta, are political rather than ecoregional constructs. And then there are the land use programs not confined to any one local region but that instead span entire states or even the nation. State-level smart growth initiatives, such as Maryland's, or state planning, as in New Jersey, apply over a great multitude of local places. This is just the message that New Jersey sought to convey in titling its state plan, "Communities of Place" (New Jersey State Planning Commission 2001).

This all begins to add up to an elaborate assortment of places, plans, and programs—of all types, shapes, and sizes—across the country. The emerging map is something of a crazy quilt, with its great diversity of patches and pieces. The quiltmakers, if they can be called that, have sewn smaller bits over larger pieces and larger patches over smaller ones. And while many of the individual pieces may be very well planned and managed, administrative coordination across multiple and overlapping scales is at best a very challenging and highly elusive proposition.

While some would argue that scale is important only insofar as the largest possible wild areas must be protected or restored (Terborgh and Soulé 1999; Locke 2000; Klyza 2001), others—many bioregionalists among them (Sale 1985; Mason, Solecki, and Lotstein 1987; McGinnis 1999; Thomas 2003)—put principal emphasis on the very local. What, then, are the appropriate scales for various quieter revolution initiatives—and in what degree is this to be determined, respectively and in combination, by such dimensions as physiography, economics, politics, public perceptions of place, and other relevant factors? How do we develop "planning ecologies"—to use Godschalk's (2004) terminology—across several spatial scales? At a very basic level, we must reckon with subwatersheds contained within larger watersheds, small mountain ranges that are part of larger physiographic regions, and neighborhoods within metropolitan areas. As we begin to deal with the fuller array of social, cultural, and political factors that shape regions, we must determine if a particular planning scale is appropriate simply because it can be made to "work." And as place-based planning becomes more commonplace, we need to ask ourselves if we have actually moved toward greater watershed consciousness and bioregional understanding than was typical three or four decades ago.

Another critical place-based planning dimension is evaluation. How do we assess effectiveness? Of course, not all programs should be subject to the same set of evaluation criteria. But sufficient and appropriate criteria can be developed for each situation, or category of cases. Unfortunately, this is where many current efforts fall short, sometimes distressingly short. To date, systematic attempts to evaluate place-based planning programs, such as those by Yaffee et al. (1996) and Sabatier et al. (2005), are few and far between.

Ecological criteria, such as biodiversity and water quality indicies, comprise one measure and form the basis for some comprehensive regional assessments (U.S. Environmental Protection Agency 1997). Proponents of collaborative planning often are content with cooperation itself; if stakeholders work together, then the process has succeeded. Other important dimensions often are neglected or underplayed—among them economic costs/benefits/effectiveness, cultural resources management, and environmental justice and equity. Of course, when it comes to quantification and data availability, these elements are more complex and elusive than are basic physical criteria. Moreover, different stakeholders will adopt varying methods of evaluation, depending on their needs and interests. In the end, we are left without clear protocols for evaluation and assessment. And at least to a certain extent, this is as it should be. Place-based planning is meant to be adaptive and accommodating—but, as a result, bottom-line assessment becomes all the more elusive. Still, it behooves quieter revolution proponents to work toward more consistent, comparable means for making contextual sense of the many and varied programs that come under its umbrella.

One overriding contextual frame is environmental justice. Conceivably, environmental justice implications would occupy a central place in the design and evaluation of place-based planning initiatives. But thus far they have received rather scant attention. While we can find notable exceptions—and at least one huge exception, if we regard concerns about property rights infringements as environmental justice matters—concern overall has been limited indeed. Particularly when it comes to the smart growth agenda—which plays into a host of class, race, and power issues involving individual mobility and household choice—environmental justice should be front and center. In fact, equity issues are only just beginning to be addressed.

These are the broad issues addressed in subsequent chapters, as we navigate various types and examples of place-based land use planning. The book's general plan is outlined below, chapter by chapter.

Overview of Subsequent Chapters

Chapter 2 is a selective overview of historical and more recent developments, of the past three to four decades, in American land use policy. Though land use is the main focus, broader environmental and nature protection frameworks are regarded as contextual backdrop. Recent debates about presentation and interpretation of environmental history—especially those involving relative importance of ecological protection versus human health and urban environmental issues—help place contemporary environmental and land use trends in perspective.

The "quiet revolution in land use control" of the early 1970s—the inspiration for the book's title—is discussed at some length in chapter 2. Its significance and aftermath are examined, and this leads into a general discussion of recent land use policy developments. Evidence of sustained environmental concern over the past three decades, accompanied by rather low issue salience, is presented. Growing recent alarm at the consequences of suburban sprawl, farmland loss, and threats to natural lands are discussed, and quieter revolution responses are outlined. Their collective significance to the future of American environmentalism and land use management is then considered.

Chapter 3 deals more specifically with the "politics of place." While we have witnessed a broad decline in civic engagement in America—as described and analyzed in Robert Putnam's (2000) *Bowling Alone*—we also have seen a proliferation of local and regional, place-based environmental planning projects. While these initiatives do not necessarily herald a civic environmental revival, they do represent a deepening of engagement in specific places, around specific concerns. But beyond deeper civic engagement, how do these efforts affect the physical environment, social and environmental justice, and cost-effectiveness of environmental planning programs?

Chapter 3 also provides a brief history of civic environmentalism, highlighting the shift from agency-led public participation programs toward collaborative, multistakeholder processes, which often are initiated or led by nongovernment organizations. Broad questions about public participation in civic and environmental affairs are raised, among them the desirability and fairness of interest group versus demographic representation, as well as legally mandated participation versus genuine grassroots initiatives. Motivations for participation are considered; for example, land protection efforts in rapidly growing suburban areas may be inspired as much or more by exclusionary, even racist, tendencies as by environmental concerns. Biocentrists, by contrast, may want to remove or substantially reduce human populations in ecologically critical areas. Yet other participants may be driven by amenity or economic concerns. In some instances, environmentalists refuse to collaborate; to do so, they argue, would be to weaken the existing environmental management system.

Representation issues are central to place-based, multistakeholder planning projects. So, too, are process and outcome questions, especially as they guide evaluations of the quieter revolution's civic dimensions. And the pervasive matter of spatial scale also comes up in chapter 3. Several leading examples of place-based, collaborative projects are briefly, but critically, reviewed. Finally, the future of quieter revolution civic engagement is considered.

Chapter 4 looks at regional land use planning in a variety of contexts. Quiet revolution initiatives are briefly reviewed, followed by a segue into the "quieter" revolution. We begin with continental-scale approaches, which are big on ideas but limited, so far at least, when it comes to implementation capabilities. Federal lands, while incredibly important in their own right, are not a major focus here—except insofar as they are part of many private-public collaborative projects.

About a dozen regional planning cases are included in chapter 4. They range from large watershed, mountain, and wetland regions to metropolitan areas. Management approaches vary greatly from one place to another, with some having little in the way of a formal management scheme and others more akin to a quiet revolution project. Successes and shortcomings of each are covered, with a view to the quieter revolution's potential—and challenges—in dealing with substantial geographic regions.

Chapter 5 is mostly about managing growth and protecting valued environments. We begin by looking at urban sprawl's emergence on the public policy agenda, then consider quieter revolution approaches to its management. The main focus is on federal and state programs to preserve farmland, manage growth, and enhance local places by protecting lands and waterways for their ecological and recreational values. While many more regional- and local-level efforts conceivably might be included under this umbrella, they are instead reserved for chapter 6.

Federal initiatives aimed at comprehensively supporting local programs—among them the Livable Communities and Better American Bonds programs, as well as the Community Character Act—all have faltered or died. But state planning and smart growth programs continue their expansion, even in times of severe fiscal constraint. Among the leaders are Maryland, New Jersey, Oregon, and Pennsylvania. And many other states also are putting significant programs in place. NGOs and localities are active as well. The Congress for the New Urbanism, which promotes compact, sustainable development, and the National Association of Home Builders both are key players.

The contributions of various smart growth players are reviewed. Of particular interest are environmental justice implications of these varied programs that seek to guide suburban development, promote urban redevelopment, and reclaim brownfield sites. While affordable housing is featured in the smart growth and "new urbanist" agendas, it is not always front and center when it comes to their implementation.

Chapter 6 is about local land use initiatives: land trusts, local watershed associations, ballot measures, and greenways. Land trusts acquire lands and hold easements that restrict the uses of privately held lands. Although the land trust movement maintains a significant national presence through the front offices of the Land Trust Alliance, Trust for Public Land, and the Nature Conservancy, its real strength is in the many organizations active at the local and regional levels. The dramatic recent growth in numbers and reach of these organizations is reviewed and illustrated. The case is then made that their influence often extends beyond what the acreage numbers might suggest.

Local watershed associations also have surged in numbers and coverage, providing new opportunities for civic engagement and redefining environmental management's spatial character. Numbers, activities, potential influence, and civic roles of watershed associations are covered in chapter 6. Many greenways—usually linear parks that follow terrestrial, river, canal, lake, or coastal features—also have been put on the map in recent years. This phenomenon is briefly characterized, and the greenway's place within the quieter revolution suite of land management activities is addressed. Finally, ballot measures have become important tools and means for environmental protection. Why is this the case and how does ballot box planning work? Questions of voter interest and social justice associated with the growth of the ballot measure as an enabler, of sorts, of a more comprehensive approach to land use management are examined.

Chapter 7 is about resistance to the quieter revolution. While organized opposition to land use planning has long been with us, the property rights and wise use movements were energized in the mid-1990s by the ascension of the Gingrich Congress and its "Contract with America." The movements' origins, growth, strategies, and effectiveness are described. Supreme Court decisions that have reframed the private property "takings question" and associated issues of compensation for property owners whose options are restricted by environmental regulations also are briefly reviewed. Voter approval of Oregon's Measure 37 is instructive in this regard: it requires governments to compensate landowners whose property value is reduced by environmental regulations. The Supreme Court's 2005 Kelo decision, which supported a controversial municipal use of eminent domain power, has breathed new life into the wise use/property rights movements—and has probably broadened their popular appeal. By conflating takings and eminent domain issues, property rights advocates have been able to press for new federal and state legislation and gain support for procompensation ballot measures, mainly in western states.

From the environmental left comes another line of attack not necessarily directed toward quieter revolution programs but with important implications for them. This critique comes in the form of direct action. Among the more extreme actions are the burning of a ski lodge in Vail, Colorado; destruction of suburban housing developments in environmentally sensitive areas; and vandalizing of SUVs. From this critical perspective, quieter revolution programs are seen as grossly insufficient, if not entirely irrelevant or even counterproductive.

Chapter 7 considers the ways and extent to which these and other countervailing forces are shaping—and perhaps even dramatically transforming—the quieter revolution. Quieter revolution counterstrategies also are examined.

Chapter 8 concerns itself with evaluating programs and policies described in earlier chapters. A matrix-style evaluation chart is not provided; instead, broad evaluatory dimensions are discussed. While a checklist of sorts is offered, it is not one that will work as a cookbook evaluation scheme. Instead, it is meant to be provocative and relevant to those who do develop detailed evaluation protocols. Among its dimensions are ecosystem health, residential and commercial development patterns, cost-effectiveness, environmental justice, capacity building, civic engagement, environmental footprints, and vulnerability reduction. Several cautionary notes about conducting evaluations are included at chapter's end.

Chapter 9 sums up and looks ahead. In light of what we have learned from preceding chapters, the quiet and quieter revolutions are again contrasted and the question of whether or not the quieter revolution is a movement is taken up. Then we consider the quieter revolution's broad accomplishments and failures in controlling sprawl and development patterns, protecting ecosystems and ecological services, developing civic culture, working in cost-effective ways, and advancing environmental justice. Finally, the quieter revolution's prospects are addressed. Its greatest potential, it seems, is as a laboratory for innovation and in developing infrastructure that can be called into service to help meet carbon emission targets and confront issues of petroleum dependence.

CHAPTER TWO

LEAD-UP TO THE REVOLUTION

C ontrary, perhaps, to much popular thinking, environmental and land use concerns did not simply spring forth sometime during the past few years—or even the last several decades. Indeed, America's relationship with its natural environment is a lengthy, complex, and conflicted affair, in which the quiet and quieter revolutions are but two of the latest installments. For most historical narratives written before 1990, the main story line is one of unrestrained exploitation from early European settlement through the mid-1800s, followed by a century of impassioned struggles over nature protection and resource conservation. Pollution issues come forward in the 1950s and 1960s, and the modern environmental movement comes into full bloom around 1970 (Nash 1982; Dowie 1996; Opie 1998; Andrews 2006b; Rothman 2000; Shabecoff 2003).

The mid- to late 1800s are a starting point for many of these environmental histories—though some historians go back much further, examining precolonial and colonial environmental conditions and human influences (Cronon 1983; Opie 1998; Isenberg 2000; Merchant 2002; Steinberg 2002). Early environmentalism, by many mainstream accounts, grew from the Romantic-era embrace of wilderness, with artistic and literary works leading the way toward political action. Preservationist thinking, embodied in the writings and actions of Sierra Club founder John Muir, represented one response to Frederick Jackson Turner's popular notion of the post-1890 "closing of the American frontier" (Turner 1920).

But these preservationist impulses ran counter not only to "frontier think-ing" that has persisted to the present day but in many ways also to the more tempered conservationist view that resources are there to be used, al-beit wisely. Gifford Pinchot, confidant of President Theodore Roosevelt and first head of the U.S. Bureau of Forestry (later the U.S. Forest Ser-vice), is widely regarded as the conservation movement's "father" (Miller 2001).

The early national park and forest systems are crowning achievements of the late 1800s and early 1900s, lauded then as well as now. But the con-troversial Hetch Hetchy Dam, which flooded a valley adjacent to cele-brated Yosemite Valley, became a flashpoint issue that drew a sharp line between conservationist and preservationist thinking. Preservationists—along with many allies coming from widely diverging places and political perspectives—lined up in opposition. Conservationists, arguing that re-sponsible attention to human needs (drinking water in this case) must come first, were for the project. By 1923, the dam was completed and the valley was then flooded. But a new and popular form of environmentalism had been ushered in, and it was in sharp contrast to the more elite-based environmentalism of the latter 1800s.

Planning histories, while sharing much with broader environmental histories, do give fuller due to urban planning projects of the mid-1800s to early 1900s. The garden city, ideal communities, and city beautiful movements, as well as the advent and spread of zoning and building reg-ulations, figure prominently in these narratives (Krueckeberg 1983; Wil-son 1989; Sies and Silver 1996; Hall 2002; Cullingworth and Caves 2003; Platt 2004; Talen 2005). So, too, does urban park planning—especially the many city parks of the mid- to late 1800s that are Frederick Law Olm-sted's legacy. These developments were immensely important to urban set-tlement and quality of life, and thus influenced larger regional settlement patterns and landscapes. But city planning developments will not be viewed here as direct historical antecedents for the quiet and quieter rev-olutions; instead, their significance is seen as rather more indirect and contextual. More immediately relevant are the watershed management schemes for large cities, such as New York and Boston, that involved land acquisition and imposition of regulations over large regions (Platt 2004). These are important forerunners for many of today's watershed manage-ment projects, large as well as small.

Federal land and soil management programs, launched in the New Deal years, represent a second major era in American environmentalism. Conservation and social equity values are deeply embedded in the missions and activities of the Soil Conservation Service, Tennessee Valley Authority (TVA), Civilian Conservation Corps, and Works Progress Administration. The TVA's wide-ranging approach, in particular, embraced watershed management, land use, housing, recreation, and health care at the regional scale (Platt 2004). At least, that was the TVA's early vision. But in rather short order, the agency seemed to lose sight of those grand goals, turning its attentions mainly to power and fertilizer sales (Friedmann and Weaver 1979; Selznick 1953; Sussman 1976). The 1930s also witnessed the ascendance of the National Resources Planning Board (Clawson 1981; Platt 2004), and—under the direction of Rexford Tugwell's Resettlement Administration—creation of several carefully planned greenbelt towns (Platt 2004). These endeavors tended to be top down and paternalistic, affirming the centrality of government in directing environmental policy. While redistributive justice was central to many of these projects, neither the impetus for nor direction of social and environmental change tended to be grassroots based.

The third major era in American environmentalism got fully under way around 1970, the year Earth Day was first celebrated. But it was preceded by major conferences addressing physical and economic resource concerns (President's Materials Policy Commission 1952; Resources for the Future 1954; Thomas 1956), increasing state- and national-level policy debate in the 1950s about pollution (Solecki and Shelley 1996), publication of Rachel Carson's *Silent Spring* (1962), and beautification and land protection programs initiated in the 1960s. The 1969 Santa Barbara oil spill drew wide public attention, and during that same year the National Environmental Policy Act was passed. A year later, the Environmental Protection Agency (EPA) was born. Landmark air and water quality legislation followed in the early 1970s, and the Endangered Species Act was signed into law in 1973. This period of intense excitement and accomplishment was followed by something of a strategic retreat during the energy crisis years of the 1970s. Even though energy-efficiency improvements brought major environmental benefits of their own, these gains were offset, at least in part, by relaxation of environmental regulations in support of accelerated energy development. Further regulatory stagnation marked much of the 1980s and 1990s. But it was punctuated by some exceptionally lively bursts of activity, especially in the years around 1990, when attention focused on climate change, the *Valdez* oil spill, and the 1992 Conference on Environment and Development in Rio de Janeiro. And it seems that once again we are entering a period of rekindled concern, with climate change (Gore 2006) and resource scarcity finding prominent placement on local, state, and national policy agendas.

Collectively, these last four decades seem to fit the pattern of Anthony Downs's (1972) "issue-attention" model: a period of "alarmed discovery and euphoric enthusiasm" is eventually followed by a decline in public interest. But through all the ups and downs, the issues remain firmly woven within the sociopolitical fabric, since basic institutions, policies, and programs are firmly anchored. Over the long term, a background level of public concern is sustained and may be punctuated by occasional bursts of much stronger interest.

Several recent accounts of American environmentalism—most of them post-1990—give much greater attention than their predecessors to public health issues, urban sanitation and waste management, environmental hazards in the workplace, and inequities in the social distribution of environmental burdens (Hays 1987, 2000; Gottlieb 2005; Merchant 2002). It is not that these issues were bypassed in earlier histories—they were even the main theme of some works (Hays 1959; Melosi 1981; Tarr 1996)—but they usually were not given a lead role in the fuller historical narrative. Robert Gottlieb's (2005) widely read *Forcing the Spring* is highly critical of historical approaches that focus almost exclusively on resource conservation struggles. Gottlieb gives much attention to public health and labor reforms of the Progressive Era, as well as the democratic, progressive ideals of wilderness advocate Robert Marshall.

Shellenberger and Nordhaus (2004) go so far as to proclaim the "death of environmentalism"—at least the 1970s brand of environmentalism. They argue that environmental proposals must be framed in terms that resonate with core American values such as economic efficiency, small government, and religious faith. The environmental movement, they maintain, has been so repelled by America's post-1970s rightward shift that many of its efforts have become disconnected and even counterproductive.

But all in this crop of recent writers are asking critical and hopeful questions about the future—the impending "fourth wave" of the American environmental movement. The case for transformation is urgently made—a transformation to a less elitist, more locally based environmentalism that reaches ordinary Americans (Gottlieb 2001, 2005; Dowie 1996; Shabecoff 2003; Shellenberger and Nordhaus 2004). These authors raise critical environmental and social questions that speak directly to place-based environmental thinking. Only during the past decade or so have those issues begun to work their way, haltingly at that, onto the mainstream national environmental agenda. And while room for these concerns can be found in the broad "smart growth/livable communities" agendas introduced below, so far—at least—the environmental justice perspective favored by many fourth wavers has not been perched very high on the smart growth agenda.

American environmentalism thus finds itself at a very interesting and hopeful place. Highly regulatory, command-and-control approaches to environmental management may never again find the favor they did in the 1970s. At the same time, there is ample opportunity to expand our environmentalism across orders of spatial scales, from global to local. Our globalized economy brings us sprawling Wal-Marts filled with Chinese products and in turn transports electronic and other wastes not only across state borders but all the way to Africa and China. This is but one example linking global processes to local pollution and land use issues. A new environmentalism might well focus locally but also give national, global, and regional processes their due. Just how the twenty-first-century version of "think globally, act locally" might play out policywise is yet to be seen. But in the land use arena, at least, we shall consider how quieter revolution trends toward devolved, place-based planning speak to global, as well as local and regional, concerns. We begin, though, by describing the quieter revolution from its quiet revolution antecedents to the present.

Lead-up to the Quiet Revolution in Land Use Control

The quiet revolution emerged from the environmental movement of the late 1960s and early 1970s (Bosselman and Callies 1971). But its roots run deeper (Mason 1992a); Hawaii had already enacted its state land use plan in 1961 (Myers 1976). And efforts to centralize control over private land use go back much further. Beginning in the late 1700s, the federal government passed a series of laws—among them the Homestead Acts, Land Grant Acts, Timber Culture Act, Desert Act, and Timber and Stone Act—seeking to transfer vast portions of the public estate into private hands. In its promotion and oversight capacity, the government encouraged use and development of those lands—thus ensuring for itself a major role in managing private as well as public lands. For the public estate, it was only after the late 1800s that environmental preservation began to compete as a policy priority with development (Clawson 1983; Wright 1993; Nelson 1995; Platt 2004). But while federal land management is complementary to and often deeply intertwined with the current crop of place-based planning endeavors, it is not a defining dimension of the quieter revolution. Nor was it the central focus of the quiet revolution.

Comprehensive regional land use planning found favor following World War I, when large farmland surpluses and a weakening agricultural economy led to calls for agricultural "readjustment." Among other things, this involved land classification and rural zoning, aimed at eliminating submarginal farms (Guttenberg 1973). At about the same time, a report contained in the *1923 Yearbook of Agriculture* sounded the alarm about impending land scarcity in America. It called for a joint federal-state land use program to classify lands and guide the expansion of agriculture, forestry, and other land uses (Gray et al. 1924). This forward-looking report emphasized the habitat and recreation values of protected lands.

Though no federal action was forthcoming, some states acted during the 1920s. Wisconsin, Michigan, and New York put into place land classification programs, and Wisconsin—seeking to promote reforestation of cutover lands through its 1927 Forest Crop Law and 1929 amendments—went so far as to restrict specific land use designations, as well as location of public and private facilities (Guttenberg 1973). The 1920s also marked the ascendancy of American regionalism (Talen 2005), which was championed by the Regional Planning Association of America (RPAA) and drew on the work of such visionaries as Paul Vidal de la Blache (Buttimer 1978) and Patrick Geddes (Glikson 1971; Stalley 1972). In an approach similar to that favored by today's advocates of watershed and bioregional planning, planning regions were meant to conform to natural boundaries. Regionalists of the 1920s envisioned decentralized yet interconnected regions comprised of city, countryside, natural resources, and wilderness (Dickinson 1964; Friedmann and Weaver 1979; Luccarelli 1997; Talen 2005). RPAA members called for a "fourth migration" to accommodate urban expansion, with garden cities, scenic highways, affordable housing, and rural electrification (Sussman 1976). One RPAA project that came to fruition, linked to the organization through forester/planner Benton MacKaye, is the 2,100-mile Appalachian Trail. The Maine–Georgia mountain corridor is designed to link farms and working forests and provide recreation for the urban population of the East (Foresta 1987; Anderson 2002). Though critics of the regional planning movement (Friedmann and Weaver 1979; Weaver 1984; Talen 2005) argue that rural development was given short shrift, promotion of indigenous folk culture was little more than elitist fancy, and dense urban settlement patterns were rejected, these planning visions did represent a comprehensive new approach to thinking about the American land.

A high-water mark for regional planning came in the New Deal era. In 1933, the National Planning Board was created, later to become the National Resources Commission before being eliminated in 1943. Though it was geared mainly toward provision of public works, the board/commission did advocate watershed and state-level planning (Reagan 2000). Also, as noted earlier, the Tennessee Valley Authority Act was passed in 1933, launching a grand experiment in comprehensive river basin development. Others were to follow—including the New England Regional Commission, the Colorado River Basin Compact, and the Pacific Northwest Regional Planning Commission (Friedmann and Weaver 1979)—but from the beginning, these efforts were far more circumscribed in scope and ambition than the TVA.

By the late 1930s, as America was becoming consumed with war, regional planning efforts retreated. Of course, we could look to that period's shared sense of sacrifice—accompanied by victory gardens, gasoline rationing, and widespread recycling—as models for today's sustainability efforts. But in the war's immediate and celebratory aftermath, that collective conservation ethic was all but abandoned. What emerged in the late 1940s and 1950s was a booming economy and dramatic expansion of the private housing market. William Levitt, father of the Levittown model of mass-produced tract housing, exhorted his wartime comrades to "build, build, build" when they returned home. Government policies, some of them dating to prewar days, helped fuel the postwar suburbanization boom. Low-cost, limited-term mortgages underwritten by the Federal Housing Authority and Veterans Administration, redlining practices that steered loans away from many urban neighborhoods, tax deductibility of mortgage interest and property tax payments, and the 1956 Interstate Highway Act, which authorized creation of the national system of limited-access highways, have had enormous, if indirect, influence over the settlement and land use patterns that characterize contemporary America (Jackson 1985; Rome 2001; Squires 2002; Hayduk 2003).

Although there was considerable academic interest in comprehensive regional planning in the immediate postwar era, widespread legislative activity would not reemerge until the 1960s (House 1983; Platt 2004). Major federal laws of the mid-1960s with important implications for regional planning include the following (adapted from Platt [2004]):

- Outdoor Recreation Coordination Act (1963)

- Wilderness Act (1964)

- Urban Mass Transportation Act (1964)

- Appalachian Regional Development Act (1965)

- Land and Water Conservation Fund Act (1965)

- Highway Beautification Act (1965)

- Water Resources Planning Act (1965)

- Metropolitan Development Act (1966)

- Historic Preservation Act (1966)

- New Communities Act (1968)

- National Flood Insurance Act (1968)

- Wild and Scenic Rivers Act (1968)

- National Trails System Act (1968)

Watershed planning—though of a rather more structural variety than that advocated today by most watershed associations and even government agencies—got under way in earnest. Though most of the New Deal–era initiatives had been disbanded or reformulated, the 1960s and 1970s brought a raft of new interstate river basin planning programs (Friedmann and Weaver 1979). In addition to compacts establishing the Delaware River Basin Commission, Interstate Commission on the Potomac River Basin, and Susquehanna River Basin Commission, seven commissions were created under Title II of the 1965 Water Resources Planning Act, replacing earlier informal bodies that were largely ineffective. Those seven commissions are: Pacific Northwest Rivers, Great Lakes, New England Rivers, Ohio River, Souris-Red-Rainy Rivers, Upper Mississippi River, and Missouri River Basin. Federal financial assistance was made available, but the commissions were limited to coordinating roles, since they lacked regulatory power (Featherstone 1996). Formally disbanded by executive order in the early 1980s, the commissions continue to function in various ways without federal participation (Kenney 1997).

The Quiet Revolution in Brief

The big burst of state-sponsored activity came in the early to mid-1970s. Was it in fact a revolution? Or do we accept that it is so simply because Bosselman and Callies (1971) said so and we like their moniker? Perhaps, some accounts would have it, the phenomenon was overblown. But the activities chronicled in *The Quiet Revolution* did amount to something new and important, unmatched before or since in their dramatic break with land use planning convention. Though some earlier regional planning visions may have greatly exceeded the quiet revolution in idealism, reach, and sense of possibility, none can compare when it comes to concrete legislative and regulatory achievements in just a few short years.

Hawaii's state land use plan, adopted by the legislature in 1961, is an early outlier. Basically a state zoning plan, it was supported by large agricultural producers intent on protecting their investments in the face of rapid urbanization and the onset of mass tourism at the dawn of the jet age (Myers 1976; Bosselman 1986; Callies 1984).

The early 1970s gave birth to a stream of new programs, some statewide in scope, others covering specific ecoregions or geomorphic provinces, and yet others applying to specific landscape features, such as wetlands. Bosselman and Callies's (1971) case studies included Hawaii's

25

plan, as well as Vermont's statewide development review and planning program, the New England River Basin Commission, Massachusetts' wetlands protection program, Wisconsin's shoreland protection program, Maine's site location law, the San Francisco Bay Conservation and Development Commission, Minnesota's Twin Cities Metropolitan Council, and Massachusetts' zoning appeals law (in effect, an affordable-housing program). Mention also was made of critical areas legislation: the Tahoe Regional Planning Agency, New Jersey's Hackensack Meadowlands Development Commission, New York's Adirondack Park Agency, and Delaware's Coastal Zone Act. Several state wetland and shoreland protection programs also were noted, and reference was made to other, more comprehensive land use programs—still at the study commission stage—in Colorado, Washington, and Alaska. While a strong regulatory component was not common to all efforts discussed by Bosselman and Callies (1971), increased and more centralized regulation clearly was a trend they wished to spotlight.

And there were more quiet revolution programs than those just mentioned. Complementing the lot of them was a detailed and considerable literature—going well beyond Bosselman and Callies's (1971) pathbreaking work—that described the programs and tracked their progress (see Reilly 1973; Linowes and Allensworth 1975; Mandelker 1976; Popper 1981; DeGrove 1984). What most of these schemes had in common was the notion that states should "take back" at least some of the planning power they had ceded to localities. In the face of urban expansion, increasing demands for second homes and recreation, and conversions of critical ecological areas, it was widely felt that local governments alone were not up to the task of comprehensive regional land use management (Babcock 1966; Babcock and Siemon 1985).

Oregon, Florida, and Vermont were leaders in adopting statewide growth management programs. In 1969, Oregon required local governments to adopt land use plans, and its 1973 Land Use Planning Act (Senate Bill 100) established statewide planning goals. Oregon's scheme is widely recognized and acclaimed for its creation of urban growth boundaries (Abbot, Howe, and Adler 1994; Weitz and Moore 1998; Weitz 1999; DeGrove 2005). Florida's Environmental Land and Water Management Act of 1972, based broadly on the American Law Institute's Model Land Development Code, regulated areas of critical concern and developments of regional impact. The 1975 Local Government Comprehensive Planning Act mandated local planning statewide (Carter 1974; Pelham 1979; DeGrove and Juergensmeyer 1986). Vermont's Act 250 was passed in 1970, just as increased interstate highway access and rapidly rising participation in outdoor leisure activities conspired to bring major second-home and recreational development to a state accustomed to slow growth and change. Vermont's regulatory program relies principally on regional-level review of developments of major impact, administered through nine district commissions (Heeter 1976; Dean 1996; Sanford and Stroud 1997; Sanford and Lapping 2003).

In 1972, California voters approved creation of a state coastal commission and six regional commissions, as well as giving the go-ahead for a California Coastal Plan. Initially, at least, much of the planning and development review responsibility was vested at the regional level, but the regional commissions were later phased out and local governments brought more directly back into the regulatory process (Mogulof 1975; Healy 1978; Sabatier and Mazmanian 1979; Fischer 1985). North Carolina adopted its Coastal Area Management Act in 1975; this program—more quiet than quiet revolution in style—favored persuasion and accommodation of local concerns over regulation and mandates (Owens 1985).

Though New York's state-owned Adirondack and Catskill Forest Preserves had been subject to considerable government control since their creation in 1885, the quiet revolution brought with it a stringent new regulatory program for the 60 percent of the Adirondack Park in private ownership. The Adirondack Private Land Use and Development Plan was the product of a dominant state political culture that consistently supports protection of the state's valued natural environments. By the early 1970s, the six-million-acre Adirondack Park faced threats from huge second-home developments, which would have meant thousands of new dwellings in sensitive forest areas. What was enacted in 1973 is essentially a regional zoning plan; it encourages development in and near existing settlements and hamlets, and it places stringent conditions on growth in other areas (Graham 1978; Liroff and Davis 1981; Knott 1998; Terrie 1999; Mc-Martin 2002).

New York State also created the Tug Hill Commission in 1972. In contrast to the neighboring Adirondacks program, this is very much a bottom-up effort, with meaningful local government involvement and

well-established lines of communication between planning agency and local residents. The commission is directed by local residents and employs
"circuit riders" who travel to town meetings and other local events (Dyballa, Raymond, and Hahn 1981; Marsh 1981). The Tug Hill Commission has not generated the kind of local controversy associated with most
regional planning agencies; in fact, recent surveys indicate support among
local leaders as high as 90 percent (Tug Hill Commission 2007). But neither does the Tug Hill Commission have the regulatory powers of an
Adirondack Park Agency or Pinelands Commission. Still, in demonstrating what can be accomplished through devolved communication and persuasion, it is a fine exemplar for the current crop of quieter revolution
initiatives.

Planning for the Lake Tahoe basin commenced as early as the 1950s,
but it was during the quiet revolution years, as development was booming,
that more substantive efforts got under way. In 1969, President Nixon
signed legislation ratifying the California-Nevada Interstate Compact.
Subsequently, the bistate Tahoe Regional Planning Authority was created
and given sweeping regulatory powers—though in practice the exercise of
those powers has been quite limited by restraints built into the enabling
legislation (Constantini and Hanf 1973; Strong 1984; Twiss 2004).

Other states, such as Washington, established state planning commissions but were unable to follow through, initially at least, with substantive
new planning requirements for localities (Bosselman and Callies 1971;
Weitz 1999). Yet other states attempted but failed to pass new planning legislation in the early 1970s. Georgia, for example, attempted but did not succeed in regulating critical areas in 1973 and 1974 (Weitz 1999). Likewise,
the federal government tried—and did almost succeed—in passing national
land use legislation in the early 1970s. The National Land Use Policy Act
had the support of a broad coalition of interests and included some large
developers as well as environmentalists. Unlike small home builders, who
were comfortable dealing with—and in many cases dominating—local
planning and zoning boards, the big national players had an interest in
working within a framework of consistent rules. For them, properly crafted
national legislation could be a means of leveling the playing field and neutralizing local antigrowth movements.

But the national law was not to be (Lyday 1976; Plotkin 1980). Although the Senate did pass bills in 1973, so much negotiation took place

that they became "little more than a request by the national government that the states voluntarily review local land use decisions having a regional impact" (Plotkin 1980, 433). And the proposed legislation met with even more resistance when it went to the House. With strong opposition from the National Association of Home Builders, whose principal constituents are small and medium-size developers; the Nixon administration, consumed by the Watergate scandal and trying to curry favor with holdout conservative supporters (who overwhelmingly opposed the legislation); an economic downturn in 1973–1974, which ensured a less favorable climate for land use regulation; and Mayor Daley encouraging Chicago's congressional delegation to vote against the legislation because he feared it would give the upper hand to Illinois' Republican governor in a dispute over expressway construction in Chicago (Mandelker 1989), the legislation was doomed (but just barely—the bill was defeated in 1974 by a vote of only 211–204). Watered down as the bill may have been, the United States came remarkably close to having a national land use policy. Ironically, such a bill might have provided a systematic means to confront the 1970s oil crises by encouraging less energy-consumptive land use patterns. But by 1975, when Representative Morris Udall attempted to reintroduce the bill, the momentum was gone.

Walker and Heiman (1981) make the case that the quiet revolution had substantial support from major corporate interests and builders— although not from most local and state-level builders. Support from big corporations was not vocal but more behind the scenes, aimed at securing the most favorable regulatory regime possible. Megadevelopers felt that if there must be new regulation, then consistent, predictable land use regulations would be preferable to a labyrinth of local rules. And these big corporations could lobby and in other ways exert influence most effectively at the national level. As I discuss in later chapters, there are parallels here with the quieter revolution. Indeed, corporate collaboration and sponsorship now are out of the closet, clearly on display in the recent "smart growth" movement. Because it emphasizes planning partnerships rather than centralized regulation, the smart growth movement can be much more up front about seeking corporate funding and boasting about corporate support than its quiet revolution predecessors might ever have dreamed possible. Moreover, the development community now deploys social justice arguments to cast its members as good guys, championing affordable housing in the face of exclusionary no-growth and low-growth sentiment in many suburban locales.

But before looking too closely at current conditions, let us first explore what happened after the quiet revolution peaked.

After the Quiet Revolution

The failure to enact national legislation seemed to mark the start of a long retreat for land use planning. New state initiatives were few, and when Ronald Reagan was elected president in 1980, prospects for federal action dimmed even further. But in fact, the retreat was not total (Popper 1988).

To begin with, the strongest quiet revolution regulatory programs—such as those in Oregon, Florida, Vermont, and the Adirondack Park—were firmly enmeshed within the sociopolitical fabric. A certain measure of acceptance, or at least resignation, had set in among detractors. Opponents remained vocal and continued to extract concessions, as they still do today, especially when state leadership is sympathetic to their viewpoint. But none of the major quiet revolution programs is likely to be repealed or fatally weakened, even under hostile state leadership. While it may be difficult to expand or strengthen many of the early initiatives, it is equally difficult to do away with them. As discussed below, most programs manage to adapt to political and economic circumstances. A special exception involves Oregon's 2004 passage of planning-unfriendly Measure 37, discussed in chapter 7.

In some cases, at least, regulation actually increased in the decade or so following the quiet revolution. Coastal zone management bears mention. From a land use regulatory perspective, coastal areas may comprise America's most critical geomorphic province. Given recent coastal population growth, along with more frequent and intense hazards that climate changes threaten to bring, planning becomes all the more imperative. The federal Coastal Zone Management Act (CZMA), passed in 1972 and thus more a product of the quiet revolution than part of its aftermath, is structured similarly to what was envisioned for the failed national land use legislation. Indeed, the CZMA may be the closest thing we have to a federal land use policy. It seeks to balance environmental protection and economic development, but not by imposing regulatory controls. The CZMA model is one of federal guidance and financial grants, state administration, and local implementation. In addition to promoting systematic coastal zone planning, the CZMA authorized the National Estuarine Research Reserve System, which promotes stewardship of these premier ecological and economic resource areas (Beatly, Brower, and Schwabb 2002). The 1982 Coastal Barrier Resources Act (CBRA), enacted at a time of low ebb for new planning initiatives, is less regulatory than CZMA; it simply eliminates federal subsidies for development of barrier islands (Gordon 1984; Platt 1994). What is important here is that federal planning legislation was enacted at all in 1982.

Popper (1988) claims that land use regulation became more centralized in the quiet revolution's aftermath. Citing not only the CZMA but also the 1980 Alaska National Interest Lands Conservation Act, 1976 Federal Land Policy and Management Act, 1976 National Forest Act (both 1976 acts apply to federal lands), and 1977 Surface Mine Control and Reclamation Act, as well as the earlier Safe Drinking Water Act (1974), Flood Disaster Protection Act (1973), Clean Water Act (1972), and Clean Air Act (1970), he argues that land use regulation "has probably changed more since 1970 than in any comparable period in the nation's history" (Popper 1988, 291). Wetlands and endangered species protections also were strengthened considerably during the 1970s, with major implications for land use planning and management (Platt 2004). And the Chesapeake Bay Program—a cooperative effort involving six states, the District of Columbia, and several federal agencies—came into place in 1983. Though chronically afflicted with funding shortfalls, limited regulatory and monitoring capabilities, and strategic differences among key participants, the program does represent a serious commitment to improving water quality and marine life in a major and complex watershed area (chapter 4).

While the 1985 Farm Bill did little to limit bloated agriculture subsidies, it did shift at least some payments toward conservation. The Conservation Reserve Program provides compensation to farmers who take highly erodible lands out of production, the "swampbuster" program discourages conversion of wetlands by withholding agricultural subsidies to those who farm wetlands, and the "sodbuster" program restricts what can be planted on highly erodible land. When the Farm Bill was reauthorized in 1990, a Wetland Reserve Program was added. The act was reauthorized, revamped, and considerably expanded in 1996 and 2002. Source protection for water supplies, under the Safe Drinking Water Act of 1996, is yet another federal program that compels regional planning (Featherstone 1996).

But state governments (Rabe 2006), not the federal government, were the focal point for the quiet revolution—and through the 1970s, 1980s, and 1990s many state governments continued to lead on land use issues. Leadership is exercised not only via explicitly labeled land use initiatives, as Popper (1988) and Diamond and Noonan (1996) observe, but also through multitudes of environmental impact assessment, transportation, housing, land acquisition, and other facilities-oriented laws, regulations, and programs at the state and local, as well as federal, levels.

Quiet revolution programs themselves have adapted to changing political circumstances: some, such as Florida's, Vermont's, and Oregon's, were strengthened. Florida, in particular, striving in the 1980s for a more efficient and equitable planning system, created a more centralized one. A comprehensive plan was adopted, review of local plans was strengthened, coastal planning became more rigorous, and the Development of Regional Impact Program became more stringent (DeGrove and Juergensmeyer 1986; Popper 1988; Weitz 1999). Other initiatives—such as Colorado's Land Use Commission—were weakened (DeGrove 1984, 1989). Generally, early programs were retooled for enhanced administrative efficiency and greater local-level public involvement (Popper 1981, 1988; DeGrove 1984); additionally, more economic assistance in various forms was disbursed to localities (Mason 1992). Weitz (1999) characterizes these "second and third wave" growth management programs as moving away from coercive regulatory approaches and toward strategies that empower localities and encourage them to comply with regional goals and policies.

Some existing statewide planning programs were greatly expanded in the 1980s and at least one entirely new one—New Jersey's state plan— came on line during that decade. Gale (1992) reviews and compares eight plans and programs, most of them from the 1980s. Based on plan requirements, plan review procedures, requirements for consistency and compatibility within plans and among various levels of government, role of state government, imposition of sanctions on nonparticipants and noncompliers, and other criteria, he characterizes Oregon, Maine, Florida, and Rhode Island as "state-dominant," Vermont and Georgia as "regional-local cooperative," New Jersey as "state-local negotiated," and Washington as a "fusion" model that combines elements of the other approaches. Washington's case is interesting; long inspired by neighboring Oregon, it has strived for similar outcomes with a less top-down model. Its early 1990s Growth Management Act and subsequent amendments are more devolved in their implementation than Oregon's and more reliant on state fiscal sanctions in cases of noncompliance with urban growth boundary and other planning requirements (Weitz 1999). Although Gale speculates generally that future programs may tend more toward the flexible, negotiated model than the coercive, he also sees potential for a second quiet revolution.

Not all post–quiet revolution programs have rejected strong regulatory approaches. Comprehensive planning for New Jersey's Pinelands National Reserve commenced in 1980, with adoption of a regional management plan resembling the regulatory one adopted in the Adirondacks nearly a decade earlier. Pinelands planning, though, includes a formal federal role and also has allowed for greater local involvement from the outset (Berger and Sinton 1985; Collins and Russell 1988; Mason 1992, 2004). That the Pinelands program is a quiet revolution outlier seems in keeping with New Jersey's land use planning exceptionalism (Gale 1992; Mason 1992; Solecki, Mason, and Martin 2004). Some of New Jersey's success in sustaining the quiet revolution can be credited to adaptiveness. During its first decade, Pinelands planning expedited its permitting functions and provided substantial financial assistance to localities (Mason 1992, 2004).

But while New Jersey found success with centralized planning in a rather inhospitable era, the limits of second-wave centralized regulation were perhaps nowhere more starkly apparent than in the Adirondacks. When Governor Mario Cuomo's Commission on the Adirondacks in the Twenty-First Century (1990) released its report in 1990, it ignited a firestorm. Though tempered by the inclusion of proposed economic, housing, health care, and education subsidies, the report's calls for more stringent regulation and an expansion of park boundaries met with such local hostility—culminating in motorcades, marches, and a fistfight over road access to a wilderness area—that virtually none of its recommendations were enacted (Mason 1995a; Knott 1998; McMartin 2002). But Adirondacks planning was not weakened, either; planning opponents were unable to roll back what was already in place, even though they had gained the upper hand in discouraging the governor and legislature from dealing seriously with the commission's recommendations.

The Adirondack and Pinelands schemes are cited as premier examples of "greenline parks." The greenline concept, popular chiefly during the 1970s and 1980s, favors intergovernmental partnerships for managing working landscapes, usually close to urban areas and containing a mix of public and private lands (Corbett 1983; Hirner 1985; Hirner and Mertes, Mason 1994; Hamin 2001). Though national greenline legislation faltered in 1977, and thus no formal system for recognizing greenline parks was put into place, various state and federal parks, recreation areas, and heritage areas came to be regarded in varying degrees as greenline models (Little 1990; Mason 1994). Though the term "greenline" is rarely heard these days, its themes are embraced in many of today's quieter revolution/smart growth programs.

Does all this mean that the only new programs likely to come on line are small-bore efforts relying almost entirely on goodwill, collaborative spirit, and mild incentives and penalties? Yes and no. While full-blown quiet revolution programs could be extraordinarily difficult to put into place today, some of the most recent programs are far, indeed very far, from inconsequential. Among others, Everglades restoration (chapter 4), growth management in Pennsylvania and New Jersey (New Jersey State Planning Commission 2001), smart growth in Maryland, and scores of farmland and open-space protection programs are of considerable scale and consequence (chapter 5). The vision behind them may, arguably, be narrower than many 1970s visions. But the inspiration, or more aptly the "trigger factor," may not differ all that much. Some of the strongest of the quiet revolution initiatives were triggered by fears about imminent mega second-home developments and loss of amenity and production landscapes. Similarly, quieter revolution programs are set off by concerns about traffic congestion, first-home developments, and loss of amenity and recreational values. It is in the responses to the threats that we find some major differences.

But if this latest planning wave is truly a revolution, it must move beyond responding to discrete threats and provide a more comprehensive vision of land use and landscape. If this is to happen—and it has not happened yet, at least not widely—the quieter revolution's brightest prospects may lie in strategic integration with a larger, more broadly based environmentalism. Are we, perhaps, at the cusp of just such a fourth environmental era? And, if so, how big a part does the quieter revolution play?

A Fourth Era for American Environmentalism?

At first blush, it might seem that place-based planning is one of the latest installments in the nature protection narrative described earlier. But let us first further examine some major environmental developments of the past quarter century that can help better situate the quieter revolution.

American environmentalism was undergoing a shift during this era, away from its pre–Earth Day emphasis on nature and ecology and toward toxic chemical and human health concerns (Russell 1997). Clearly, the nature and health threads are deeply interwoven and each is critical, even if—as noted earlier—their relative historical importance has become a matter of contestation. But the dramatic events of the late 1970s at the Three Mile Island nuclear reactor in Pennsylvania and Love Canal hazardous waste site in New York State did put toxics and public health issues center stage. In 1980, the federal Superfund law (Comprehensive Environmental Response Compensation and Liability Act) was passed, providing funds to clean up abandoned hazardous waste sites and respond rapidly to chemical accidents. Technological hazards concerns were further attenuated by international events of the mid-1980s: the 1984 Bhopal tragedy, involving release of a toxic gas at a pesticide plant in India, and the 1986 Chernobyl nuclear disaster. In 1986, Superfund was amended; SARA (Superfund Amendments and Reauthorization Act) put in place emergency planning requirements and a comprehensive reporting system for emitters of toxic chemicals, ushering in a new era of "regulation by information." Strengthening the public's right to know offered an approach distinctly different from, if not entirely incompatible with, the prevailing command-and-control pollution regulatory system (Press and Mazmanian 2003).

Environmental justice also emerged as a prominent issue in the 1980s and especially 1990s, with much of the movement's attention focused on toxics issues (Dowie 1996; Ringquist 2003). Initially, variations in environmental burdens by race and economic class were identified, particularly by the EPA, as environmental equity issues. But the prevailing terminology quickly shifted to the more evocative "environmental justice" and more targeted "environmental racism." Environmental justice concerns are very much intertwined with land use decisions, particularly facility-siting decisions. But only very recently have environmental injustices associated with smart growth policies begun to gain serious recognition. These linkages are addressed in chapters 5 and 7.

At the same time—and partly in response to passions aroused by toxics and environmental justice issues—the federal government responded with calls for "risk-based" environmental policy strategies. The George H. W. Bush–era EPA, under the direction of William K. Reilly, vigorously promoted this perspective (Reilly 1990; United States Environmental Protection Agency 1987, 1990). Risk would become the basis for federal agencies' resource allocation decisions, and perhaps this would be the case as well for some state environmental agencies. Research showing that the general public was "overly" concerned with local toxics issues and under-appreciative of global threats was used to bolster the case for this new, risk-based approach (United States Environmental Protection Agency 1987, 1990). Rational as that approach might be, as a broad policy development principle, it gained only limited traction in the 1990s. Political realities still trump systematic policy approaches, and while risk-based approaches continue to be promoted today (Andrews 2006a), they are not commanding the attention they did fifteen to twenty years ago.

If indeed a case can be made for a fourth major environmental era, then that era may have begun to take shape in the late 1980s. In no small part, it seems that it was driven by a conspiracy of discrete events: in 1988, an unusually dry and warm summer through much of the United States directed attention to ozone pollution and global climate change; George H. W. Bush exploited Boston Harbor pollution as a 1988 presidential campaign issue; and the 1989 *Exxon Valdez* oil spill brought oil and wilderness issues to the fore, derailing Bush's drive for oil exploration in the Arctic National Wildlife Refuge (Mason and Mattson 1990). Earth Day 1990, the twentieth-anniversary celebration of the first Earth Day, brought much fanfare, along with generous corporate support. While this mini-movement did not bring a clamor for federal legislation comparable to that of the late 1960s/early 1970s, it did yield at least some important laws. There was the Oil Pollution Act of 1990, a direct response to the *Exxon Valdez* spill. And after more than a dozen years of legislative stalemate, the Clean Air Act was finally renewed in 1990, with provisions for a 50 percent reduction in sulfur-dioxide emissions. In 1991, Congress also passed the Intermodal Surface Transportation Efficiency Act (ISTEA), requiring state and local governments to develop comprehensive plans for federally funded transportation projects and providing funding for mass transportation, bikeways, and many other programs aimed at reducing traffic congestion and improving environmental quality. ISTEA and its progeny (chapter 5) represent a dramatic shift, redirecting Highway Trust Fund monies that for decades had been spent almost entirely on building road capacity. At a broader scale, the 1992 United Nations Conference on Environment and Development kept global environmental issues front and center—though by this time President Bush was beating a strategic retreat from his self-anointment as the "environmental president," in late 1992 referring to vice presidential candidate Al Gore as "ozone man."

Public support for broad environmental goals has held fairly steady over the past thirty to forty years (Dunlap 1992; Bosso and Guber 2006; Guber 2003), with 83 percent of respondents to a 2000 Gallup poll agreeing with the environmental movement's broad goals (Guber 2003). Yet the depth of that support may not even begin to approach its breadth. Only 16 percent of respondents to the 2000 Gallup survey regard themselves as active participants in the environmental movement; knowledge about specific issues is quite limited; and environmental issues ranked behind drugs, crime, health care, and hunger/homelessness (Guber 2003). Does this mean, then, that apparently high public environmental consciousness is nothing more than a shallow consensus that could easily weaken in unfavorable circumstances (Guber 2003; Rothman 2000)? If national voting behavior is any indication, it would seem that environmental concerns only rarely are important enough to determine election outcomes for national offices, though they often do have at least some influence (Bosso and Guber 2006). It would seem safe to assume that prevailing public sentiment about environmental protection does present some political opportunities and constraints but that its reach is fairly limited. Only when specific problems flare up at the local and regional level—as is sometimes the case with traffic, growth management, and facility-siting issues—are these concerns likely to play a lead role in reshaping the political landscape.

But, as already noted, we may be at a tipping point. Climate concerns and higher oil prices are conspiring to resituate environmental issues on the American political agenda. They are already high and getting higher on the international agenda. And with Al Gore's (2006) recent book and associated film—both titled *An Inconvenient Truth*—summer 2007 mega climate concert event, and Nobel Peace Prize nomination, the tide may be turning in America. It is about much more than just Gore, of course. As a candidate in 2000, George Bush had advocated mandatory carbon emission caps. While he is unlikely to revisit that pledge, expectations are that the next president—Democrat or Republican—will advocate strongly for greenhouse gas action and associated environmental initiatives. Much is already happening at the state and local levels (Rabe 2006). A renewed environmentalism, of course, will also redefine the quieter revolution's relevance and role.

The Quieter Revolution in Full Bloom?

Increasingly, Americans concerned about the impacts of sprawl favor smart growth solutions. But just as with environmental concerns generally, those sentiments may be more wide than they are deep. And they are uneven. Respondents to a 2000 Pew Center for Civic Journalism (2004) survey identified "development/sprawl/traffic/roads," along with "crime/violence," as top local problems. The 2004 American Communities Survey (Belden, Russonello & Stewart 2004) reveals that Americans favor compact, walkable communities; provision of affordable housing; and protection of open space. A recent survey of New Jersey residents (New Jersey Future 2000) indicates strong support for growth management, perhaps not a surprising finding given New Jersey's status as the country's most densely populated state. Yet even in New Jersey—with its state plan; regional plans for the Highlands, Pinelands, and Hackensack Meadowlands; and activist Supreme Court decisions requiring communities to provide affordable housing—citizens are ambivalent about government regulation of land use. Concerns about private property rights are very much on citizens' minds, with respondents indicating—albeit by a very slim margin—that they would not support coordinated planning if it meant loss of some local authority over growth management (New Jersey Future 2000).

While concern and even revulsion at prevailing land use patterns seem to be widespread, it is not at all clear that an auto-dependent America is quite ready to take drastic steps—such as enacting a substantial gasoline tax, requiring significant reductions in carbon emissions, or adopting stringent development controls—aimed at dramatically altering the current state of affairs. Though the 2006 election may mark the start of major change, neither Congress nor the White House has vigorously advocated national energy independence—a theme deeply intertwined with land use management—since the 1970s. Indeed, Congress has been unwilling even to strengthen the CAFE (Corporate Average Fuel Economy) standards, which have not been amended since 1985. In the aftermath of the September 11 attacks, a few forceful calls were made for a "Declaration of Energy Independence," renewable energy "Manhattan Project," new "moon shot," and the like. The Apollo Alliance, a recently formed environmental/labor/political/church-based coalition, is promoting renewable technologies, along with efficiency improvements in the automotive, manufacturing, construction, and consumer sectors; new public transportation options; and smart growth approaches to urban and regional planning (Apollo Alliance 2004). Energy independence was featured in the Kerry presidential campaign (Johnkerry.com 2004) and is becoming a common refrain for many in the Congress elected in 2006. If the connections between growth management and energy consumption, alternative fuels production, and hazard resilience receive the attention they merit—and this is still a mighty big "if"—then the quieter revolution may be greatly bolstered or otherwise radically transformed.

But it is not clear that there is much appetite for significant new regulatory programs aimed at protecting lands outside the sprawling suburbs and exurbs. A revival of the quiet revolution fervor for ecoregional planning simply is not in the cards for the immediate future. Still, positive public sentiment toward the general notion of land protection may be sufficient to allow space and latitude for environmental NGOs and local governments—with higher-level governmental and corporate support—to successfully continue to promote softer, gentler quieter revolution options for place-based planning. And those efforts only stand to be bolstered by increased concerns about climate change and resource availability.

The roots of this accelerating momentum shift might be found in the events of the past decade and a half. While the "think globally, act locally" admonition that surfaced in the early 1990s may not have played out entirely as environmentalists had hoped it would, it did help advance the notion of a spatial-scale-spanning-planning framework. Against the backdrop of broad public support for environmental protection cited earlier, local interest in land use and growth-related issues has flourished in recent times. One take on this rising localism is that it is an expression of elitist, exclusionary sentiment; it pits established suburban residents against low- and middle-income seekers of new homes outside the urban core, socially conscious higher-income types against shoppers grateful to have Wal-Marts in their communities, and distant environmental advocates against local residents whose livelihoods are tied to natural resource extraction. And there is much to support this view. Still, it seems that some fraction of this localized concern has been successfully harnessed toward systematic, comprehensive growth management rather than simply advancement of selfish ends. And increased environmental justice activism reframes at least some local actions, linking them to larger social, economic, and political processes and advancing redistributive political change.

Yet all the ambivalence about appropriate responsibilities for government has served to limit at least the federal government's role in managing growth. The Clinton years and beyond—the main focus for the rest of this book—might be viewed as the era of small-bore federal environmental initiatives. Still, at least some of these programs are very much about land use and smart growth—and many are ambitious in vision if not necessarily implementation. At the same time, we have entered into an era of vigorous state and local environmental activity (Rabe 2006). Though the "fourth environmental movement" did not fully ramp up in the 1990s, a new and quieter growth management movement was already in the ascension. States, localities, and NGOs were becoming the test labs for innovative responses to complex issues. And they would do so at spatial scales that fit the problems. They would be supported, perhaps, by the federal government—but not directed or even strongly influenced by it.

This is the essence of the quieter revolution, and it brings with it much less prospect for strong regulatory schemes than did its predecessor revolution. Even the threat of greater central regulation—as an inducement to "force" more effective land use planning and growth management at the local level—is at best a rather hollow threat in many places. If the quieter revolution is to produce results, it must rely on collaborative, capacity-expanding approaches. Public-private collaboration is not just a feel-good concept; it is a necessity, given the paucity of politically practical alternatives.

With its emphasis on livable communities, sustainability, and public-private collaboration, the quieter revolution is a rather upbeat affair. The anger manifest in earlier environmental movements is not front and center this time. This is not to say that the quieter revolution is all about front porches, engaged citizens, and watershed stewardship. There is protest, anger, elitism, and exclusion. Angry residents in rapidly growing communities seek to stop growth, to "shut the door." Renewable energy advocates have used images of terrorism to depict America's obsession with SUVs. And, inevitably, some of the residuals of production and leisure—everything from public recreation corridors and wind-turbine farms to waste-disposal facilities, highways, and prisons—must go somewhere. And housing is needed for those who are not wealthy or even middle class. Where and how are these needs to be accommodated? These locational issues bring us back to the critical questions of scale, social and political inequity, and race and class.

But the clear targets of earlier environmental advocacy have become fuzzier, if not having receded entirely into the background. Pollution, health, and workplace safety issues can and do coexist with the quieter revolution focus on collaborative land use management. But to the extent that all these concerns come under the broad umbrella of "environmentalism," we may have witnessed a significant shift in the relative public interest and emphasis accorded them. While confrontation and adversarialism are unlikely to lose their critical place in American environmentalism, particularly with conservative Republicans occupying many powerful positions in the federal government, they may very well continue on a course of broad retreat. And this may be especially so at the state, regional, and local levels, where quieter revolution approaches are making their marks.

The quieter revolution does indeed constitute something of a fourth wave—or third wave, depending on how one counts—in American environmentalism and land use management. But thus far it is more a series of cumulative undulations than an event of tsunamic proportion. Quieter revolution activities may in the future come to be viewed collectively as a phase—perhaps a Downs-style (1972) cyclical phenomenon that bursts forth and then recedes into the institutional landscape. Or maybe it will not even realize this degree of historical heft. It may even be vanquished by ascendant wise use/property rights movements. But it is highly unlikely that the quieter revolution will be defeated or simply fade into obscurity; if there is enough collective activity to characterize it as at least a quasi movement, then there should be enough diversity among its many components to ensure that it persists. After all, adaptive management is central to the quieter revolution. And, as already noted, the quieter revolution stands to be a major beneficiary if national energy independence ever is truly embraced and/or climate concerns become a policy priority. This would put it in alliance with a revived environmentalism, sowing the seeds for a stronger supermovement that could synergistically link economic, ecological, and equity dimensions of sustainability.

What comes next is a critical look at the quieter revolution's "politics in place" underpinnings, followed by examination of its multiple elements and their interconnectedness—or, as the case may be, lack of interconnectedness. And, at book's end, a framework for understanding and evaluating quieter revolution activities, separately as well as collectively, is outlined.

CHAPTER THREE
THE POLITICS OF PLACE

One of the most exciting things about the quieter revolution is its potential for stimulating local civic engagement in environmental affairs. Deeply rooted communities, thoughtfully and deliberately shaping their environmental futures, are what placed-based planning advocates will justifiably boast about. In the most idealized scenarios, diverse interests—"stakeholders"—work toward mutually beneficial solutions to problems that historically have divided them. Government agencies and professional planners do not plan *for* people; they work *with* them. That is the ideal: democratic, inclusive, informed, mutually respectful. In reality, the idealized narrative can be quite elusive, hindered by selfishness, ignorance, greed, exclusionary impulses, apathy, and simple lack of time.

Though much of this chapter is about collaborative, place-based planning, there is more to the quieter revolution than collaboration and "civic environmentalism" (John 1994; Porter and Salvesen 1995; Bernard and Young 1997; Knopman, Susman, and Landy 1999; Landy, Susman, and Knopman 1999; Grant 2003). Too often, civic collaboration is regarded as a defining characteristic, if not *the* defining characteristic, of contemporary environmentalism (John 1994; Sirianni and Friedland 2001). But devolved, collaborative approaches are not the quieter revolution's be-all and end-all. First of all, conventional regulatory approaches have important parts to play. While regulation is much less in favor today than three decades ago, it still looms very large. Not only the older quiet revolution programs, but also the occasional newer one—like New Jersey's Highlands

Conservation Act (chapter 4)—work side by side with and sometimes as integral parts of the more devolved quieter revolution initiatives. Most advocates of collaborative approaches see them as a complement to, rather than replacement for, federal- and state-level regulations (John 1994). Moreover, comparatively rigid laws and regulations often serve as examples of what can happen when the softer, gentler approaches fail but political will remains strong. In other words, they act as an effective threat that can help keep quieter revolution efforts on track.

Second, cooperation should not necessarily be equated with a soup-to-nuts collaborative process, at least as place-based planning advocates typically define that process. Cooperation is sometimes a matter of simple expediency in getting a parcel of land purchased or a management agreement in place as quickly as possible. That was what happened in the late 1980s in northern New York and New England, after large parcels of land had been acquired by companies with no interest in sustaining the region's traditional forest-based economy (chapter 4). In this case and others, stakeholders with common or widely diverging interests may find that it makes sense to cooperate but not engage in a complex, lengthy collaborative process. There may not be time; the collective will and energy may be lacking; the process may be too cumbersome, even among allies; or there may be the general feeling that the expedient outcome would differ little from the one brought about by a more deliberative process. This is not to say that deliberative collaboration never plays a role in such cases; indeed, collaborative relationships already in place—what Duane (1998, 57) terms the "fertile soil" of "pre-existing social capital"—may allow for a sort of fast-tracking of certain actions. If there is a climate of trust and goodwill—or, alternatively, a well-founded fear of the messy consequences of bringing all the stakeholders into a structured process—then previous collaborative experience may be the enabler for expeditious, minimally deliberative action.

Even if a model collaborative process unfolds in response to a fast-breaking situation, it still may dissipate after the job is done. The social capital that would be the basis for further place-based collaboration may not be built up or may not prove adaptive over the longer term. Indeed, as Wondolleck and Yaffee (2000) observe, some collaborative projects yield a signature achievement or two and then turn sour.

Third, we know rather little about those potential collaborative ventures that for various reasons never get off the ground. There are some analyses of failed collaborative projects (Moote, McClaran, and Chickering 1997; Napier 1998; Singleton 2002; Thomas 2003). But what about unrealized potential? Why do some projects almost materialize, but in the end not make it? Why is a collaborative approach not even considered in other cases, where the appropriate preconditions seemingly are in place? Perhaps there is a vast field of potential collaborations laying in wait, ready to bloom when the right conditions and support structure present themselves. Indeed, many proponents of collaboration would assume so. But even if they are correct in this assumption, it is not at all clear that policy approaches aimed at incubating new collaborative ventures will be the most ecologically, economically, and otherwise productive ones.

Fourth, not only the collaborative process but also the concept of place may in many instances yield to opportunity. As already noted, land use crises produce opportunities; so, too, does the course of ordinary events. When the window of opportunity opens, often it is a window for very quick action rather than the somewhat broader policy window typically described in the literature (Kingdon 2002). If, for example, a parcel of land unexpectedly comes on the market, and funds are available to add it to the inventory of local open space, not all that much thought will necessarily be given to how the addition fits with conceptions of "place-making" or "place-enhancement" (Brandenburg and Carroll 1995). Sufficient time for careful deliberation simply may not be available. In many instances, such situations are handled via rapid-response plans, with key government and nongovernment actors having already established priorities, spending limits, and fund-raising strategies. But even the best of plans cannot anticipate every contingency.

Fifth, decisions about allocating money and resources that give birth to and foster collaborative projects may themselves be made without any serious collaboration or civic engagement (Bierle 1999, 87). Resources may be allocated through ballot measures and legislative programs for open-space and farmland protection, in the form of political earmarks or "pork," or through various superstructural state- or national-level programs (chapter 5). The resources that subsequently flow may support collaborative planning; indeed, collaboration may be a precondition for receiving resources. But the political actions behind these programs need not necessarily be the result of careful, deliberative, collaborative processes.

This last point reaffirms the importance of geographic scale to place-based planning. Typically, the notion of place involves relatively local, knowable environments (Hiss 1990; Kemmis 1990; Beatley and Manning 1997; Box 1998; Tuan 2001; Cheng and Daniels 2003; Manzo and Perkins 2006). Cheng and Daniels (2003, 844), reviewing the literature on place and scale, posit the following:

- Stakeholders involved in place-based planning processes at small geographic scales articulate ways of knowing the place that reference specific place features.

- Working relationships among stakeholders in place-based planning processes at relatively small geographic scales are likely to generate shared ways of knowing.

Indeed, local places are where familiarity with land use issues runs deep and where solutions to local problems often are best crafted. Yet for all the condescension sometimes directed at "distant," "disengaged" state and federal bureaucrats remote from the real issues, local problems are in no small part the product of extralocal processes. Localities need to respond and adapt, but when it comes to solutions it often turns out that they are victims of a spatial mismatch. They may be in no position to take actions needed to get at the root of the problem. Community-level consequences of reduced salmon runs in the Pacific Northwest as well as Chesapeake Bay pollution traveling from upstream Pennsylvania farms and distant Ohio Valley power plants are but two examples.

Beyond this, local empowerment has its dark side. Singleton (2002) cites as an example the history of racial segregation in America, while Putnam (2000) points to the conformity and social division associated with high levels of social capital in small-town America of the 1950s. A similar characterization might apply to some of today's local antigrowth sentiments, which can be more a product of exclusionary and even racist thinking than profound convictions about environmental protection. And environmental concerns themselves can be distorted in the service of narrow self-interest. Fiorina (1999) offers an example of what she sees as local civic activism run amok in Concord, Massachusetts, where the elite private Middlesex School sought approval for a modest expansion plan in the 1990s. The school had already pledged fifty acres to a local ecological reserve project, the core of which would be 670 acres owned by Harvard University. But the recently formed Thoreau Country Conservation Alliance, which had been active in efforts to preserve Walden Woods, vigorously opposed the plan. They saw the school's proposed expansion as a simple matter of destruction versus preservation. After much controversy, expense, and legal wrangling, the local authorities approved a version of the plan only slightly scaled down from the original, with conservation easements placed on parts of the school's lands. The school, strapped for funds, withdrew its offer of fifty acres for the local reserve. The original plan, argues Fiorina, posed no serious ecological threat, yet a small minority of the town's residents managed to hijack the political process to an unreasonable end.

Similarly, Robert Tucker—who sees most environmental impulses as tools of the privileged classes—comments on a New Jersey-based herpetologist:

> Working out of his home, Zappalorti was soon making consulting fees of $10,000 for two to three weeks scouring proposed construction sites to help suburban communities locate endangered species that could block unwanted projects. . . . All this, of course, only represents upper-middle-class people using their professional and legal skills to twist and turn environmental concerns to their own purposes. (Tucker 1982, 184)

Resurging localism should not be seen as a purely bottom-up phenomenon. Increasingly, the value of local places is finding generic recognition. Regional, countywide, state, and even national and international programs are establishing criteria and putting resources into place to protect valued places across wide geographic areas. The World Heritage program, for example, does so at the global level (United Nations Educational, Scientific, and Cultural Organization [UNESCO] 2007). The National Trust for Historic Preservation (Stokes, Watson, and Mastran 1997) and the Center for American Places (2007) take a national approach to protection and sustenance of local places. State- and county-level farmland, open space, and heritage area programs (chapter 5) provide resources and expertise for preservation of places within their jurisdictions.

At the local and regional levels, at least, place-based stakeholder networks almost invariably coalesce around, or become intricately intertwined with, land use concerns (Cheng and Daniels 2003). Given the face-to-face contacts and shared experiences of participants, it is not surprising that new "communities of place" are created around emerging issues, in specific physical locations (Calthorpe and Fulton 2001; Michaels, Mason, and Solecki 2001; Schneider et al. 2003). Indeed, these communities may be fostered by government programs, such as the National Estuary Program (see Schneider et al. 2003). In contrast with most national policy networks, many place-based networks are inclined to span a wide ideological spectrum. Unlike communities of interest or identity, communities of place are defined by shared physical space (Duane 1997, 1998). For most proponents of collaborative, place-based planning, communities of place are where issues should be hashed out and critical decisions taken. But those sentiments are not universally subscribed to; some interest group representatives, as noted below, are vehemently opposed to any such devolution of power.

In the ideal narrative, the power of place triumphs over social, economic, political, and cultural differences. But unlike bowling or charity projects, land use and environmental issues can be contentious in the extreme. As a result, we often witness multiple local networks, representing divergent political and ideological perspectives and working at cross-purposes. Conflict does not go unrecognized by place-based planning's proponents, but frequently it is underrecognized.

This chapter is mainly about broadened citizen involvement, individual as well as institutional, in American land use management. When Alexis de Tocqueville toured America in 1831, he was particularly struck by the strength and effectiveness of the political associations he witnessed. Contemporary observers, among them Galston and Levine (1998), Putnam (2000), and Skocpol (2003), have closely examined the dramatic changes in the character of American civic culture and social capital occurring over the past several decades. The marked drop-off in local, face-to-face interaction seems to be the result of a combination of factors, including generational change, distracting influences of television and other electronic media, increasingly pressured lives, and sprawled suburban development patterns (Putnam 2000). Labor unions, bowling leagues, "animal clubs," and other fraternal organizations all have seen marked declines in membership. In contrast, according to Putnam (2000), grassroots environmentalism—and this includes groups with tax-exempt status along with those operating below the IRS radar—is alleged to have grown substantially since 1970. Some, such as Perlman (1978), Skocpol (2003), and Gottlieb (2005), see local environmental justice and other groups reaching sufficient critical mass to become an enduring, national social movement. Putnam (2000), on the other hand, contends that while this may be true for toxics and land conservation groups, the evidence for environmentalism more generally is too sketchy and contradictory to draw any firm conclusions.

National environmental organizations did experience a dramatic growth spurt in the 1980s. The national movement also has become increasingly organized and professionalized, with only small numbers of group members engaged beyond the level of basic membership and dues paying (see McCarthy and Zald 1973; Bosso 2005). This fits with Theda Skocpol's (2003, 174) conception of a "new civic America" that has

> taken shape since the 1960s, as professionally managed advocacy groups and institutions have moved to the fore, while representatively governed, nation-spanning voluntary membership federations—especially those with popular or cross-class memberships—have lost clout in national public affairs and faded from the everyday lives of most Americans.

Environmental groups have long tended toward the elitist but the rise of professional, corporate-style management structures is a more recent phenomenon. In addition to the traditional base of membership support, foundations have become an essential source of funds for major environmental organizations, as well as some of the grassroots groups. While foundations benefit from tax-exempt status, they largely evade democratic accountability (Skocpol 2003). In contrast with most environmental NGOs, foundations are not accountable to a mass membership.

Skocpol (2003) points out that some local environmental groups are very much tied into national issues; local chapters of the Sierra Club and other national organizations—if indeed they can be regarded as truly "local" groups—often are mobilized in support of national campaigns. The quieter revolution is at the nexus between national, professionalized environmentalism and the local politics of place. National-level initiatives and organizations support quieter revolution activities and lobby for federal funding, but most projects are actually local-, regional-, or state-level in scope.

What does all this mean with regard to the quieter revolution's civic character? Unfortunately, no simple answers emerge. The nature and extent of citizen engagement in land use matters are tricky to characterize and difficult to assess, in part because they can be defined in so many diverse ways. But regardless of definition, some observers see civic engagement as an end in and of itself. Although greater civic engagement may enable more informed, enduring, and ecologically sound land use management, this should not be presumed universally to be the case. Nor should we accept uncritically the proposition that a strong civic infrastructure—something larger and more enduring than single-issue public involvement— is prerequisite to better, more sustainable environmental conditions (McGinnis, Woolley, and Gamman 1999). Neither proposition, each with its own definitional and measurement imponderables, is being rigorously tested here. Rather, civic engagement is viewed as one dimension of land use management—one that is generally desirable, one that in at least some cases facilitates solutions to problems that otherwise would remain intractable, and one that also faces many questions about fairness, equity, and efficiency. While civic engagement should not be regarded as an end in and of itself, it does serve as an important criterion in the general evaluation scheme outlined in chapter 8.

What Is Civic Engagement/ Public Participation/Public Involvement?

Public participation in environmental affairs takes many forms, perhaps the most basic of which is voting. Environmental concerns often feature prominently in political campaigns, with the League of Conservation Voters (2006) and other organizations doing their best to showcase candidates' environmental records. But even though pro-environment sentiments frequently resonate with a majority of voters, this does not mean they determine election outcomes, at least at the national level. In the end, environmental concerns often give way to matters of higher salience. At most, environmental issues may be a small factor in a presidential race and occasionally influential in a congressional contest (Bosso and Guber 2006).

But state and especially local elections can be a different matter entirely. The closer the vote is to home, the more likely—or at least feasible—it is that environmental concerns will play prominently in voters' choices. New England town meetings excepted, citizens do not usually have the opportunity to vote directly on all matters of concern, whether they involve environmental choices or others. But environmental and land use issues often do tend to be more on voters' minds at the state and local levels. Moreover, voters often *can* vote on specific environmental questions, put to them in the form of local and state referenda (chapter 6).

Beyond the voting booth, citizens become engaged through participation in environmental NGOs. Most typically, this consists of contributions to environmental organizations, though in some instances it will extend to volunteering for political and nonpolitical environmental activities. In the marketplace, citizens may choose to purchase environmentally appropriate products and services, boycott inappropriate ones, and invest in stocks and mutual funds that meet certain environmental criteria. Public meetings, hearing testimony, letters and e-mails to political representatives, petitions, letters to the editor, service on environmental commissions and advisory committees, and educational activities are among the many additional ways citizens become involved in environmental affairs (National Research Council Commission on Behavioral and Social Sciences and Education 1996; Cunningham 1972; Rowe and Frewer 2000; Creighton 2005). Increasingly, citizens are becoming engaged as "citizen scientists," directly monitoring water quality and other environmental variables (Sirianni and Friedland 2001). And while many descriptions of citizen participation exclude them, lawsuits, arbitration, rallies, civil disobedience, and even violent confrontation also are options.

Such deliberate and structured activities as study circles, round tables, focus groups, citizen juries, simulation games, design charrettes, and visioning exercises are used to gauge public opinion and/or bring members of the public directly into the planning process (Moore 1995). While these efforts generally are instigated and overseen by planners and policymakers, in some cases they come in response to public pressures for greater involvement in the planning process. But with the exception of particularly salient local issues, these varied forms of participation tend to involve only a very small portion of the general public. Those with time, interest, and ability tend to come forward to participate, though—as discussed below—deliberate efforts often are made to ensure that participants are demographically representative of the larger population.

Those who stand to benefit from "concentrated" incentives are especially motivated and energetic in comparison with the broad pool of potential participants. Concentrated-incentive parties include traditional ranching, timber, mining, and other commodity extraction interests; land speculators and developers; and—in ever-increasing numbers—recreation service providers. Interest in long-term environmental protection—watershed and habitat protection, for example—usually is spread over a rather widely dispersed constituency. Overdest (2000) contends that it is difficult to mobilize these diffuse-interest stakeholders as effectively as those who see more immediate benefits. This may help explain why property rights and other "anti-environmental" interests have been so effective in recent years—but it is only part of the explanation (chapter 7).

The wider "public interest" is perhaps best assessed through opinion surveys and focus groups that seek to sample public opinion broadly, with scientific credibility. Still, issue salience is not easily gauged from most of the available data. As already noted in chapter 2, public support for environmental issues has been consistently quite strong over the past several decades—yet since the early 1970s, environmental and land use concerns have only rarely taken center stage, or anything close to center stage, at the national policy level. At the local and regional levels—this book's main focus—it can be an entirely different story.

Public Participation in Context

Public participation in civic and governmental affairs is widely regarded as fundamental to a healthy democratic society (Almond and Verba 1963; Pateman 1970; Sewell and O'Riordan 1976; Dahl 1989; Fagence 1977; Checkoway and Till 1978; Renn, Webler, and Wiedemann 1995; Poisner 1996; Box 1998; Putnam 2000; Skocpol 2003). The implicit or explicit assumption in much of the literature is that direct citizen participation is integral to healthy democratic governance. The presumption is that if citizens are directly involved in civic matters, above and beyond the act of voting, both process and outcome are likely to be better and more democratic. Direct citizen participation is seen as offering benefits for government, citizens, and the environment. While low voter turnout itself can be regarded as symptomatic of a dysfunctional system, this democratic deficit is offset, at least in part, by the ease with which America's citizens can become directly engaged in the policy process.

Why is participation viewed so favorably? The participatory process lends legitimacy to government actions, while providing external oversight of formal decision making (Rosenbaum 1976; Irvin and Stansbury 2004). Participation can expand government agency capacity to carry out existing missions; it may also enable agency missions to be expanded (Van de Ven and Ferry 1980; Breckenridge 1999; Michaels, Mason, and Solecki 1999). In some instances, it acts to break policy gridlock (National Research Council Commission on Behavioral and Social Sciences and Education 1996; Innes and Booher 1999b), though in others it may defuse pressure for serious policy reform (Irvin and Stansbury 2004). Participants can bring new knowledge, insights, and methods to the planning process (Beierle 2002), thus helping improve the substantive quality of decisions (Beierle 1999). Burby (2003), in his study of planning in Florida and Washington State, finds that broadened stakeholder involvement produces stronger plans and higher rates of implementation. Though Burby's findings about stakeholders are typical of most participation studies—among them Beatley, Brower, and Lucy (1994) and McCool and Guthrie (2001)—Brody's (2003) results differ. His study of ecosystem planning in Florida reveals that broad stakeholder representation does not significantly affect plan quality. But the presence of certain individual stakeholders, such as those representing resource commodity interests, does have a significant positive effect.

Of course, the democratic process can be time-consuming, cumbersome, and unpredictable. Some public participation programs fall flat due to lack of sustained citizen interest (Irvin and Stansbury 2004). Conversely, active civic engagement may obstruct projects and plans. Environmental, antigrowth, and NIMBY (not in my backyard) organizations often employ public participation mechanisms to precisely those ends. While such outcomes will be regarded favorably by these groups—as well, perhaps, as those who see NIMBYism leading toward a more socially and environmentally just society (Heiman 1990)—this is obviously not the view held by project proponents. Along with the proponents are planners and policy analysts (Wolpert 1976; Connor 2001) who see these obstructionist outcomes as part of civic engagement's "dark side," described earlier.

Civic engagement in environmental affairs can be of a formal, structured nature or more informal and ad hoc in character. Much local-level activity falls somewhere in between. To set the context here, let us begin with the larger national context for formal, directed public participation in environmental decision making.

In contrast with many of its industrialized peers, the United States has placed a premium on allowing for—indeed encouraging—direct public involvement in environmental decision making and enforcement of environmental laws (Cunningham 1972; Kauffman and Shorett 1979; Sirianni and Friedland 2001). Federal procedures for citizen participation were written into the 1946 Administrative Procedures Act (APA), which expanded and standardized requirements for public hearings in advance of administrative rule making. As Ethridge (1987) points out, though, judicial review of agency actions actually was established procedure long before the APA was enacted. Major environmental laws—such as the National Environmental Policy Act (NEPA), Clean Air Act, Clean Water Act, and Superfund laws—include specific requirements for citizen participation, with the public's right-to-know about toxic chemical emissions being one of the defining elements of the Superfund Amendments and Reauthorization Act of 1986 (Langton 1978a; Sirianni and Friedland 2001). NEPA and its state-level progeny are public participation pioneers (Poisner 1996). Though NEPA alone cannot compel project proponents to stop or alter projects, it does provide public access to the planning process. Public notification and comment periods are central elements of NEPA, which has served as a model for much of the world. Granted, the Bush administration has vigorously sought to limit public access to information and involvement in environmental decision making. Even so, the legal and administrative foundations for transparency and access—though they are being shaken—remain firmly in place. And state- and local-level decision making, too, has become much more open over the past thirty to forty years.

Much of the public participation literature from the 1960s and 1970s, and even well into the 1980s, views the participatory enterprise as government initiated and programmatic (Strange 1972; Fagence 1977; Sewell and Coppock 1977; Langton 1978b; Sewell and Phillips 1979; Grima and Mason 1983; Verba and Nie 1987). Citizens would react to existing plans and programs by testifying at hearings; responding to invitations to serve in advisory capacities on committees, boards, or panels; and participating in structured exercises. Activities outside this field—such as citizen-initiated ballot initiatives and policy projects, protests, and lawsuits—were recognized but not generally regarded as mainstream participation. Langton (1978b), for example, makes a sharp distinction between the citizen action movement and government-initiated citizen involvement. The ascension of collaborative, place-based planning has not made Langton's differentiation irrelevant, but it has blurred his citizen–government boundary. Still, those whose sole purpose is to undermine the process, whether for environmental or anti-environmental reasons, usually are regarded as outliers and outcasts. As we shall see below, though, it would be a mistake to give short shrift to their role in shaping the quieter revolution.

Participatory Process and Products

Before delving too far into the participatory enterprise, we should direct our attention toward some very basic questions. First of all, who participates (Verba et al. 1993; Sirianni and Friedland 2001)? Is demographically based participation more just than interest-based participation? Or vice versa? Here you may recall the reason that James Watt, President Reagan's controversial secretary of the interior, was relieved of duty. It was not his utterances about the Lord's second coming or conciliatory posture toward strip mining but instead his 1983 remark about the typical policy advisory committee: "I have a black, I have a woman, two Jews and a cripple" (Shabecoff 1983). Watt was framing his ill-considered observation, it would be fair to say, as a representational issue: certain demographic groups and interests are guaranteed representation, whatever their relative numbers. Is this an appropriate way to conceive of the broader public interest? Clearly, there is no easily defined "public interest" but rather a set of interests. Some of those interests are defined mainly by ethnicity or other demographic characteristics, others principally by their economic, cultural, political, or other positions or concerns. Multiple spatial scales also are involved, ranging from the very local to the national and even international.

How, then, should the public interest—or interests—be represented (Day 1997)? Is demographic representation critical, even when key demographic groups may have little interest in or engagement with the issue at hand? Should different interests be weighted differently—for example, by giving compensatory weighting to traditionally underrepresented interests and demographic groups? Perhaps such efforts are doomed to failure, if in the end political processes overwhelm attempts at balanced representation, instead imposing their own distributive outcome, awarded on the basis of relative power, finances, and political skills. Just how much, then, should we agonize over issues of definition and representation of the public interest?

These are elusive, complex questions. And they are very relevant to the quieter revolution. Different programs will approach them in different ways, with some neglecting them entirely. No prescriptions are offered here, but it does seem reasonable to conclude that policy outcomes *are* affected by structured—and unstructured—participatory processes. Those with interests in the issues, who determine that it is worth their while to become involved, must then decide how best to allocate time and resources. Perhaps, in some instances at least, they will want to participate in hearings and advisory groups at the same time as they run political campaigns or mount protests that speak to the issues at hand. It can be very difficult, indeed, to sort out the relative value of mainstream participatory efforts, alternative political and civic activities, and even such external factors as economic trends, which sometimes have a way of overshadowing the most deliberative efforts. If, for the time being, we limit consideration to formal participation programs—setting aside larger issues about whether they are the best way to represent public interests— then some narrowly defined questions can be taken up.

Research results are decidedly mixed, making it difficult to generalize beyond specific case-study results. Gundry and Heberlein (1984), studying public meeting attendance for three separate environmental projects in Wisconsin, found that relevant publics are broadly represented, demographically and in terms of interest, when meetings are well publicized and readily accessible to all and when participants are consulted about their opinions. McComas and Scherer's (1998) study of landfill siting in central New York State yielded similar findings. Yet Beierle and Konisky (2001), in a study of environmental planning in the Great Lakes region, found that advisory committees often fail to engage wider publics in decision making, are demographically unrepresentative, and do not include the full range of relevant public interests. Verba et al.'s (1993) broad study of citizen activism reveals that activists and nonactivists hold rather similar views but differ demographically. The disparity is greatest when it comes to contributions to political candidates, which come overwhelmingly from the economically advantaged.

In many participatory programs, something of a self-sorting occurs, where those most interested in the issues are the ones who participate most fully. Yet there are other factors, besides issue salience, that come into play. Time, resources, and political skills are needed for effective participation. Stakeholders who lack any or all of these may be restricted to participating, if they participate at all, in more limited ways than they would like. This should not necessarily be construed as lack of interest. Moreover, as some of the above-referenced research indicates, their interests may be well represented by those who do attend the meetings. Still, limited time, resources, skills, and motivation may mean limited awareness of just what one's own interests are. This is where civic culture plays a lead role; the stronger the civic culture, the more informed and politically effective the general citizenry is likely to be on specific issues. Of course, the civic sphere is populated with diverse viewpoints—but a well-developed civic culture tends to ensure that multiple perspectives are represented, even when individual citizens lack the wherewithal to act directly on each and every issue of concern and when their views do not happen to coincide with those of well-financed commercial and lobbying interests.

Beyond representation, participatory process and outcomes are central to our understanding of environmental civic culture. Participatory process receives much attention; typically, process-oriented evaluations consider such questions as timing and representativeness of public involvement, responsiveness to public concerns, transparency, and fairness and equity (Sewell and Phillips 1979; Renn, Webler, and Wiedemann 1995; Beierle 1999; Innes and Booher 1999a; Tuler and Webler 1999; Webler and Tuler 1999; Beierle and Konisky 2000; Rowe and Frewer 2000; McCool and Guthrie 2001; Smith and McDonough 2001; Brody 2003; Santos and Chess 2003; Irvin and Stansbury 2004). Process evaluations generally are based on achievement of stated goals and often rely heavily on participant perceptions. Frequently, this framework is inherently biased toward the interests and needs of the sponsoring or lead government agency; this was especially so in earlier decades (Sewell and Coppock 1977; Sewell and Phillips 1979; Grima and Mason 1983).

Product-oriented evaluations look at outcomes—often, though not necessarily, with respect to stakeholder goals and interests. Depending on the particular participatory project, product measures might examine any of several outcomes: whether or not a plan was produced, and, if so, the plan's "quality," the degree to which it has been implemented, and the degree to which it is accepted by its constituents (McCool and Guthrie 2001). Though it is difficult, usually, to disentangle process from product, important distinctions can be made. A fair and equitable process, for example, provides us with no guarantee of a fair and equitable outcome. Nor does it ensure improved environmental quality. As already noted, Brody (2003)—in a study of comprehensive plans in Florida—found that broad representation of stakeholders does not necessarily produce better plans. More generally, those who denounce collaboration (discussed below) tend to believe that whatever merits the process possesses, the outcomes are likely to be detrimental to their interests. If one is dissatisfied with the outcome, then he or she may be inclined to view the entire venture as a wasteful and inappropriate allocation of resources. This is not always the case, though; the "losers" do sometimes respect the process at the end of the day (Connor 2001).

Some evaluators focus on a "good government" approach, one that is very much tied to an agency-based, public administration perspective (Beierle 1999, 2002; Beierle and Konisky 2000; Beierle and Cayford 2002). Beierle (1999) lists five "social goals" for evaluation:

- Educating and informing the public

- Incorporating public values into decision making

- Improving the substantive quality of decisions

- Increasing trust in institutions

- Reducing conflict

Separately, Beierle (1999) identifies cost-effectiveness as a goal. These criteria range over, and in his thinking beyond, product and process. Though environmental quality is not listed, appropriate evaluation measures could be included if it is regarded as a yardstick for gauging decision quality. For some, of course, environmental conditions are the *sole* measure of success. More broadly, evaluations may consider physical, social, behavioral, and

Table 3.1. Evaluation Criteria for Collaborative Natural Resource Management Programs

Typical Evaluation Criteria	
Process criteria	Broadly shared vision
	Clear, feasible goals
	Diverse, inclusive participation
	Participation by local governments
	Linkages to individuals and groups beyond primary participants
	Open, accessible, and transparent process
	Clear, written plan
	Consensus-based decision making
	Decisions regarded as just
	Consistent with existing laws and policies
Environmental outcome criteria	Improved habitat
	Land protected from development
	Improved water quality
	Changed land management practices
	Biological diversity preserved
	Soil and water resources conservation
Socioeconomic outcome criteria	Relationships built or strengthened
	Increased trust
	Participants gained knowledge and understanding
	Increased employment
	Improved capacity for dispute resolution
	Changes in existing institutions or creation of new institutions

Source: Conley and Moote (2003), 376.

economic outcomes; participant perceptions; and the participatory process itself. Table 3.1 lists typical evaluation criteria. Daunting as the project may seem, all of these criteria can be bundled together (Conley and Moote 2003). Indeed, chapter 8 suggests that multiple evaluatory perspectives be brought under one umbrella.

A sensible, predictable, transparent process that does not impose excessive time or financial burdens on participants generally produces a sustainable participatory process (Irvin and Stansbury 2004). Smith and McDonough (2001) suggest fairness as a central theme around which public participation be assessed. Their case study of a Michigan ecosystem project finds that participants value the following elements of fairness: diversity and broadness of participants, voice and participation in decisions, serious consideration of their ideas and concerns, a logical decision process, and outcomes that are to the participant's personal benefit, congruent with their values, or in accord with their sense of present or future equity. While the process's perceived fairness may shape participants' thinking about its outcomes, the diversity of ways in which participants judged outcomes in the Michigan study casts some doubt on the prospects for easily achieving the win-win outcomes so often promoted by collaborative planning proponents.

From Participation to Collaboration

Sherry Arnstein's (1969) "ladder of citizen participation" (figure 3.1) has been cited often in the nearly four decades since it first appeared. Simply, but elegantly, it covers the ground from citizens as simple recipients of information to full citizen empowerment. While there was considerable interest in raising the people's power to the ladder's higher rungs, through the federal Model Cities Program of the 1960s and at least some environmental programs of the 1970s, in the end rather few programs managed to make it even into the middle rungs.

In contrast with Arnstein's ladder, Wengert's (1976) five-part classification of public participation programs mainly reflects the sponsoring agency's perspective:

- Participation as policy

- Participation as strategy

- Participation as communication

- Participation as conflict resolution

- Participation as therapy

Burke (1968) describes five "strategies" for citizen participation, with each strategy serving different institutional and individual interests. Those strategies are:

- Education-therapy

- Behavioral change

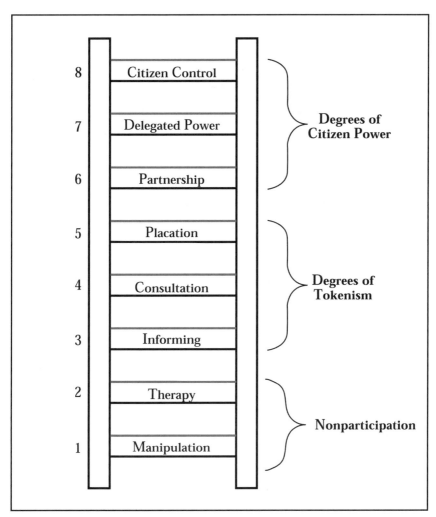

Figure 3.1. A Ladder of Citizen Participation
Source: Arnstein (1969), 217.

- Staff supplement

- Co-optation

- Community power

Again, most environmental programs of the 1960s and 1970s provided for limited or no power sharing; public participation, while often viewed as important and meritorious, was undertaken on government agency terms. For a time in the 1980s and 1990s, it seemed that conflict resolution/environmental mediation/consensus building might form the guiding narrative for environmental civic engagement, or at least for a large segment of it (Bingham 1986; Amy 1987; Crowfoot and Wondolleck 1990; Forester 1999; O'Leary and Bingham 2003; Innes and Booher 1999a; Susskind, Levy, and Thomas-Larmer 1999; Susskind, McKearnan, and Thomas-Larmer 1999; Susskind, Van der Wansem, and Ciccarelli 2000). But while it remains a central land use management theme, conflict resolution no longer dominates the discourse. Rather, it has become quite accepted, professionalized, and institutionalized; consulting firms, facilitators, government agencies, and courts all are involved in recommending, offering, or requiring environmental mediation. Ongoing conflict management, in contrast with resolution of discrete conflicts, often is regarded as a key element in collaborative approaches to land use planning (Daniels and Walker 2001). So, too, is consensus building.

While the 1980s, 1990s, and 2000s have witnessed a shift in terminology away from public/citizen participation and toward civic engagement, collaboration, partnership, and comanagement (Gray 1989; Gunderson, Holling, and Light 1995; Long and Arnold 1995; Selin and Chavez 1995; McNeely 1995; Randolph and Bauer 1999; Kenney et al. 2000; Weber 2000a, 2000b; Wondolleck and Yaffee 2000; Mullner, Hubert, and Wesche 2001; Koontz et al. 2004; Plummer and FitzGibbon 2004; Randolph 2004; Innes and Booher 2004; Healey 2006), 1960s and 1970s public participation models—where government directs the process—are still very much with us. Advisory groups continue to be deeply involved in the policy process, as required under numerous environmental laws. Not only environmental advocates but also industry representatives and even those who reject most environmental regulation (chapter 7) serve in advisory capacities. The controversy over Vice President Cheney's energy task force, which advised the administration in 2001, shows this only too well. Legal challenges aimed at revealing the identity of the task force's members have failed. Though details about its workings obviously are sketchy, enough is known to suggest that this will become a textbook case of how the participatory process can be misused. And it can be co-opted not only by industry but also by environmental interests, growth control proponents, and many others. Of course, these participants will claim that they *are* acting in the public interest and that the outcome justifies the participatory means.

Though government-sponsored participation has hardly faded away, collaborative approaches are occupying an expanding niche. As new planning landscapes emerge, at spatial scales ranging from very local places to vast regions, government management becomes less feasible and broad nongovernment stakeholder involvement becomes more necessary. Stakeholders have place-based knowledge and capabilities essential for sound planning, and their concerns span traditional political boundaries (Mullner, Hubert, and Wesche 2001). At the same time, as many agency budgets have shrunk and the political climate has turned more conservative, government has become a diminished force in land use policymaking. Indeed, in some instances, a government "seal of approval" or agency staffing for a local collaborative project may be tantamount to a kiss of death (Chess, Hance, and Gibson 2000).

Stakeholders representing both environmental and private property interests are likely to be wary of too large a government role. NGOs have become more numerous and, in most instances, larger, better funded, better connected, more influential, and savvier than they were three or four decades ago. They are players now—and in at least some cases, they set the collaborative terms. The proliferation of land trusts, watershed conservancies, ballot issues, and the like (described in later chapters) is at the heart of this expansion of participatory land use democracy. National- and state-level policy apparatuses have not necessarily become all that much more enamored of citizen engagement than they ever were—but fiscal and political circumstances, combined with a profusion of new collaborative projects and programs—have compelled them to become seriously involved.

Collaborative innovation, according to Wondolleck and Yaffee (2000), takes place because the costs of impasse are unacceptable, mistrust of government is pervasive, no other options are available, and policy entrepreneurs emerge to step into the breach. Collaborative projects often are built from the ground up; stakeholders come together to solve problems rather than being brought together through more traditional, top-down public participation enterprises. Collaboration is flexible and adaptable (Holling 1978; Lee 1993; Gunderson, Holling, and Light 1995), a mutual learning experience among stakeholders. This, at least, is the ideal view—but this bottom-up scenario may be overrepresented in the literature. As noted earlier, the conditions that give rise to and nurture collaborative projects often are set at the state and national levels. When capacity, ability, or political will to support traditional government regulatory action is lacking, resources and guidance may be directed toward local stakeholders. And local participants, in turn, may be inspired to act in response to real or perceived threats of additional government regulation (Kagan 1997).

The notion that government actors can adjust readily to new collaborative approaches, acting as a partner among equals, may also be overrated. In many instances, it seems, inertia-driven bureaucratic actors lack the flexibility and administrative latitude to act as equal-share stakeholders (Wondolleck and Yaffee 2000). Moreover, government as well as nongovernment actors compete for attention and credit; even those deeply committed to the same basic goals may find themselves downplaying or even subverting the contributions of their partners. After all, because successes sustain organizations and bring them funds, it is in their long-term interest to demonstrate their capability to bring results.

In recent years, the ecosystem management model also has found increased favor (Cortner and Moote 1994, 1998; Grumbine 1994, 1997; Haeuber 1996; Yaffee et al. 1996; Vogt et al. 1997; Slocombe 1998; Szaro, Sexton, and Malone 1998; Weber 2000a, 2000b; Gray, Enzer, and Kusel 2001; Mullner, Hubert, and Wesche 2001; Meffe et al. 2002). Though ecosystem approaches have been with us at least since the 1930s (Leopold 1949; Caldwell 1970; Scheiber 1997), they began to move conspicuously from the purely experimental and academic domains into the applied realm in the late 1980s and 1990s. In no small part, this was because the ecosystem approach offered a holistic, practical alternative to the single-species approach that brought so much animosity and spawned so many lawsuits under the federal Endangered Species Act (chapter 4). During the 1990s, with the Clinton administration promoting ecosystem management, upwards of twenty federal agencies adopted it in some form. And agencies at all levels of government have been developing interagency agreements that address ecosystem issues across bureaucratic and geographic boundaries (Stein and Gelburd 1998; Bengston, Xu, and Fan 2001; Thomas 2003).

But what is "ecosystem management"? Those who grapple with this question commonly opt for rather wide-ranging, often amorphous, characterizations—but most do feature collaborative stakeholder involvement. While some ecosystem proponents take a very biocentric view, relegating human populations to a less-than-leading role in the larger ecological scheme of things (O'Riordan 1981; Devall and Sessions 1985; Naess 1989; Klyza 2001; Haeuber 1996; Soulé and Terborgh 1999; Foreman 2004), the most widely circulated definitions are not so ecologically deterministic. Typically, humans are viewed as "embedded" in nature (Grumbine 1994b) and collaborative ecosystem management strategies are likely to include diverse, multiple layers of government as well as nongovernment stakeholders (Grumbine 1994b, 1997; Haeuber 1996; Yaffee et al. 1996; Cortner and Moote 1998; Slocombe 1998; Szaro, Sexton, and Malone 1998; Weber 2000a, b; Mullner, Hubert, and Wesche 2001; Meffe et al. 2002). In this regard, it seems, many ecosystem management proponents engage in their own personal adaptive behavior; biocentric ideals may be in their hearts, but their heads are cognizant of political and economic realities. Most have realized that wide acceptance of ecosystem management is only likely if humans are regarded as a central, even privileged, part of the ecosystem. It may make for messier, more contested, less idealized ecosystem management than they would want, but it does make for more ecosystem management.

Ecosystem approaches typically define management areas using ecological boundaries, focusing on patterns and processes, biodiversity, species populations, adaptive strategies, and a long-term, evolutionary view (Grumbine 1994b; Haeuber 1996). Often, watershed boundaries define ecosystem management areas. Ecosystem management's holistic emphasis is widely viewed as a practical alternative to trying to provide for the habitat needs of a multitude of individual species (chapter 4). Bengston, Xu, and Fan (2001, 473), adapting and expanding upon More's (1996) summary, list the following elements of ecosystem management:

1. Maintain ecosystem health (e.g., maintain and protect ecosystem integrity and functions, restore damaged ecosystems).

2. Protect and restore biodiversity (protect native genes, species, populations, ecosystems).

3. Ensure sustainability (e.g., incorporate long time horizons, consider the needs of future generations, include both ecological and economic sustainability).

4. Engage a systems perspective (e.g., have a broad, holistic approach to management; manage at multiple spatial scales and consider the connections between different scales; coordinate across administrative, political, and other boundaries to define and manage ecosystems at appropriate scales).

5. Have human dimensions (e.g., incorporate social values and accommodate human uses within ecological constraints; view humans as embedded in nature).

6. Incorporate adaptive management, in which management is conducted as a "continuous experiment where incorporating the results of previous actions allows managers to remain flexible and adapt to uncertainty" (Grumbine 1994b, 31).

7. Involve collaboration, in which planning and management are joint decision-making processes that involve sharing power with key stakeholders.

Contrast today's emphasis on collaboration, trust, and power sharing with ecologist Garret Hardin's admonitions of the late 1960s and early 1970s (Cortner et al. 2001), when the environmental movement was in a different and more adversarial phase. In his widely debated essay, "Tragedy of the Commons," Hardin (1968) emphasized the need for mutual coercion. His example of a cattle pasture at carrying capacity, with individual herders inclined to act in their self-interest by adding just one head of cattle, is instructive. That one additional animal would have only a marginal impact spread over the one hundred herders in Hardin's mythical pasture—but then herder after herder would be tempted to improve their own welfare at seemingly minimal cost to the collective. And the result would be environmental disaster. Hardin's logic is still applied to fisheries and other common pool resources, but we hear little of it from the pro-collaboration, ecosystem management community. One wonders if stakeholder communities have matured sufficiently in recent decades that mutual trust can replace mutual coercion. As we see below, some environmentalists, such as the Sierra Club's Michael McCloskey, seem to think not.

Some Leading Collaborative Cases

Yaffee et al.'s (1996) national ecosystem management inventory identified 519 projects and analyzed 105 of them. A more recent, similarly comprehensive compilation is not available—and any attempt to produce one is complicated by questions of project definition and scale. But undoubtedly many hundreds of efforts are or have been under way over the past decade. Weber (2000b) estimates that two hundred communities are involved in "grass roots ecosystem management," but his criteria are perhaps a bit narrow and the sources he draws upon are mostly from the mid-1990s. In any case, several projects stand out because they are so often featured as models—generally as models of success, but also, at times, as examples of what can go wrong with collaborative environmental management. Many of these examples are Western examples, illustrative of emerging trends in the "New West." That New West vision is briefly discussed below.

Quincy Library Group

California's Quincy Library Group is one of the more famous of these leading cases (Duane 1997; Weber 2000a, 2000b; Wondolleck and Yaffee 2000; Brick, Snow, and Van de Wetering 2001), recognized by President Clinton and other high-profile politicians. It was showcased as the kind of win-win planning that Clinton officials hoped to advance with the Northwest Forest Plan in the Pacific Northwest (DellaSala and Williams 2006) and habitat conservation planning for endangered species elsewhere (chapter 4). To the consternation of some participants, federal legislation was passed in support of the Quincy project. What had started as a local collaborative effort, to their thinking, should have remained that way.

Quincy is a small town in the Sierra Nevada, close to Lake Tahoe, traditionally dependent on forestry for much of its livelihood. But during the 1980s, local loggers and environmentalists found themselves in deep disagreement about the community's future and they interacted with one another mainly as adversaries. One of the adversaries, attorney Michael Jackson, managed to bring local logging virtually to a halt. In the early 1990s, county supervisor Bill Coates and timber industry lobbyist Tom Nelson responded to the standoff by initiating a series of meetings at the Quincy Library. What eventually emerged was near unanimous agreement on a forest management plan covering 2.5 million acres. Nearly a million acres were to be protected as reserves, and additional restrictions were imposed on riparian zones. Logging was allowed on about 1.6 million acres, but small, selective cuts were favored over the clear-cutting that had been common practice in the area. Negotiations were arduous and contentious but were propelled forward by the confluence of power held by environmentalists, economic needs of local residents, and a widely shared interest in moving beyond stalemate. But not everyone supports the collaborative effort; national environmental groups fear that this form of local planning privileges commodity interests over national, legally established interests in environmental protection. The Wilderness Society and Sierra Club oppose the Quincy plan (Blumbert and Knuffke 1998; Weber 2000a), and Coggins (1999) sees it as an example of federal resource agencies passing the management buck.

Applegate Partnership

The Applegate Partnership's (KenCairn 1996; Yaffee et al. 1996; Nickelsburg 1998; Johnson and Campbell 1999; Weber 2000a, 2000b; Wondolleck and Yaffee 2000; Brick, Snow, and Van de Wetering 2001; Koontz et al. 2004) goals are similar to Quincy's: keep local jobs and protect the local environment. The Applegate Watershed is a large and diverse half-million-acre area in southwestern Oregon's Siskiyou Mountains, with a population of about twelve thousand. Around 70 percent of the land is in federal ownership, 10 percent in the hands of large timber companies, and 20 percent in smaller private ownership. Massive clear-cutting had taken place in the 1980s, and environmentalists responded with protests and tree-spikings. Pressures for rural residential development also threatened agricultural lands and wildlife habitat in the watershed. But by the early 1990s, federal court injunctions had shut down most logging on federal lands, in order to protect spotted owl habitat.

In 1992, local environmentalist Jack Shipley brought together a diverse coalition of local interests, seeking to identify common ground and work toward a watershed plan. Like the Quincy Library Project, the Applegate Partnership attracted the Clinton administration's attention, becoming a poster child "adaptive management area" under the president's Northwest Forest Plan (DellaSala and Williams 2006). Starting with very limited resources, the project got under way in earnest. But the process proved contentious; the organization Headwaters, one of the main environmental participants, withdrew from the partnership in 1994. Yet the Headwaters representative opted to remain in the partnership, wearing the hat of a local watershed group he chaired. Matters were further complicated when the timber industry invoked an obscure provision of the Federal Advisory Committee Act (FACA) that bars federal agency officials from meeting regularly with nongovernment groups to proffer information or advice about agency actions. This legal provision, enacted at the height of early 1970s adversarialism, was not well suited to an emerging world of place-based collaborative planning. While individual agency representatives wanted to maintain the working relationships they had developed with other partnership participants, they were hampered in doing so. Eventually, the White House was able to somewhat ease up on FACA's interpretation, and the collaboration carried on.

After recovering from these "near-death" experiences, the Applegate project went on to achieve agreement on timber sales and management practices, and it spawned several successful projects for improving watershed health and fish habitat. It also brought greater trust, understanding, and accountability within the community. Interestingly, a big factor in holding the partnership together has been general animosity toward the U.S. Forest Service, viewed by local environmentalists and loggers alike as an incompetent forest manager. Given the powerful position in which federal endangered species laws have placed environmental interests, it is not surprising that in the Applegate case, once again, national environmental groups harbor deep reservations about the local collaborative approach. Coggins (1999), too, sees the Applegate case as yet another abdication of federal management responsibility.

Willapa Alliance

Southwest Washington's Willapa Bay is an exceptionally clean estuary that supports oyster farming, cranberry production, and salmon fishing. It also is a prized tourist destination. But by the late 1980s, the local resource-based economy was suffering, in large part because of dramatic declines in salmon, steelhead, and cutthroat trout runs. One of the main contributing factors was increased sediment loads, caused by accelerated erosion associated with Willapa watershed forestry practices.

Begun in a rather ad hoc fashion in 1992 by two environmental NGOs—The Nature Conservancy (TNC) and the locally based Ecotrust, a major part of whose mission is protection of salmon habitat—the Willapa Alliance is addressing these issues (Johnson and Campbell 1999; Kenney et al. 2000). The alliance and the associated Willapa Watershed Restoration Partnership Program have developed hatchery programs, restored watershed lands, and worked to eradicate spartina, an invasive cordgrass that poses a major threat to the bay's shellfish industry. Wide public participation characterizes the alliance's efforts, accompanied by a rigorous program for monitoring and evaluating its work. The Weyerhaeuser Corporation, which owns most watershed lands, has contributed substantial funds and other resources toward the watershed restoration work. The Willapa project is of a more local character than the Quincy Library and Applegate projects, since it does not involve the major federal land management agencies. Nor is it exemplary of post–resource extraction, New West economic trends; instead, it is an adaptive experiment in balancing marine and terrestrial resource harvests (Manning 1997).

Big and Little Darby Creeks

The Big and Little Darby Creeks watershed area, designated by The Nature Conservancy in 1991 as a "last great place," covers 560 square miles west of Columbus, Ohio. TNC initiated the Darby Partnership, whose goal is to maintain and enhance mussel and fish populations, as well as protect stream and watershed biodiversity more generally. Main participants are NGOs and federal and state government officials; local officials are inconsistent participants. Rather than the major land and easement acquisition approach typically favored by TNC, the Darby project focuses more on education, information sharing, and improved land use planning and regulation. TNC covers the partnership's overhead and administrative costs, while government agencies make indirect contributions.

The Darby Creek Partnership has been a rather low-key affair, generally meeting only four times per year and remaining quite flexible in its approaches to local issues. While it supports numerous watershed projects, just how much more has been accomplished than would have been achieved without the partnership's efforts is difficult to determine. Koontz et al. (2004) point to the Darby Creek Partnership's value in raising local environmental awareness and fostering watershed consciousness, enhancing communication, bringing forth new information, and establishing itself as a legitimate neutral presence. Yet Napier and Johnson (1998) found that partnership programs generally had not succeeded in motivating farmers to adopt conservation practices and were even bringing net negative results in some instances. In the late 1990s, perceptions of the partnership's neutrality were somewhat shaken, when TNC—but not the partnership itself—expressed support for creating a Little Darby Wildlife Refuge. Facing considerable local opposition, the U.S. Fish and Wildlife Service withdrew the refuge proposal in 2002.

But the watershed continues to face intense development pressures, and quieter approaches are being deployed to confront them. The City of Columbus and the Ohio (EPA) imposed moratoriums on sewer line extensions into parts of the watershed. Ohio EPA is basing its "adaptive watershed management" program on TMDLs (total maximum daily loads—see chapter 6), Section 208 areawide water quality planning under the federal Clean Water Act, and local environmental assessments (Ohio Environmental Protection Agency Division of Surface Water 2004, 2006). Key to this approach is comprehensive land use planning. The Big Darby Accord, a multimunicipal plan published in 2006, seeks to reduce nutrient and sediment inputs into the Big Darby and its tributaries, protect streamside habitat, and concentrate development in areas best suited, environmentally, to accommodate it (EDAW Inc. 2006). The approaches embraced by the Big Darby Accord are on the proactive end of the quieter revolution spectrum; as a consequence, they are evoking considerable local opposition. Detractors are concerned primarily about loss of property values (including speculative value) and proposed high-density development in parts of the watershed. But momentum seems to be with the accord, with six of ten participating towns having approved the master plan (EDAW Inc. 2006) as of early 2007.

Many more examples of local, place-based collaboration might be examined; some are included in subsequent chapters. Some of these efforts, such as the National Estuary Program (Gregory 2000; Schneider et al. 2003; U.S. EPA 2005) and habitat conservation planning (chapter 4) under

71

the federal Endangered Species Act, are mainly government inspired. Others are entirely local ventures; many of these are short lived and may slip under the radar of national and state inventories of place-based initiatives. Most fall somewhere in between; they are largely locally inspired but sustained by funds and recognition from above.

Collaborative Management's Future

Haeuber (1996) argues that ecosystem management (EM) missed its policy window of the mid-1990s because there were too many competing policy proposals, none of them sufficiently developed; unresolved technical and definitional concerns; issues about ecological appropriateness of management scales; and a shortage of widely recognized success stories. Yet he is quite hopeful when sketching scenarios in which the concept reemerges in a "decisive" way. And even though this has yet to happen, ecosystem management hardly has faded away; indeed, it surfaces repeatedly at various scales: watersheds, large vegetational ecoregions, and even urban regions—as discussed in chapter 5. Bengston, Xu, and Fan's (2001) analysis suggests that ecosystem management does not receive the attention it once did because it is now fairly conventional wisdom, on the downside of Anthony Downs's (1972) "issue-attention" cycle. Downs did point to the likelihood of "spasmodic recurrences" of interest in topics that travel through the cycle, and this may well be the case for ecosystem management. Another issue here is that of scale. Though Haeuber (1996) is concerned about confusion of ecosystem management scales, the diversity of overlapping geographic scales may yet turn out to be an asset, with mutual reinforcement bolstering the overall strength and resilience of the ecosystem management concept.

Weber's (2000b) outlook differs dramatically from Haeuber's; he sees grassroots ecosystem management (GREM)—with its devolved governance arrangements, broad civic engagement, results-oriented approach, and holistic perspective—diffusing across the American landscape. To be more precise, the collaborative ecosystem management phenomenon he describes seems to be overspreading America's western lands. Weber draws his case studies exclusively from the West, and most others who write about collaborative, place-based planning likewise use mainly western examples. Indeed, several recent works are exclusively about the West

(Wright 1993; Kenney 1997, 1999; Kenney et al. 2000; Brick, Snow, and Van de Wetering 2001; Baron 2002; Knight, Gilgert, and Marston 2002; Brunner et al. 2005; McKinney and Harmon 2004; Jackson and Kuhlken 2006; Pritchett, Knight, and Lee 2007). Is this because the collaborative approach is taking root mostly in western settings? In part, the explanation has to do with recent interest in collaboration by western public land managers and users. While eastern collaborations involve rather different sets of private and public stakeholders, it is not clear that the collaborative spirit is any less vigorous east than west. Indeed, Yaffee et al.'s (1996) earlier compilation of ecosystem management projects had them clustered in the Northeast and parts of the West, with approximately equal numbers overall in the East and the West. And Koontz et al.'s (2004) more recent book, *Collaborative Environmental Management*, draws heavily on cases from Ohio and North Carolina, while Wondolleck and Yaffee (2000) include several examples from Michigan.

But in contrast with the old, postindustrial East and traditional Dixie, the idea of a New West provides the nurturing backdrop for fresh, collaborative approaches to protecting places and constructively resolving deep-rooted conflicts. Though the ascension of a New West may be much overstated by those who envision a landscape of amenities, recreation, high-tech service centers, well-planned residential growth, and citizens acting in their enlightened self-interest, important demographic and development shifts are taking place, at least in parts of this vast region stretching from the Great Plains almost to the Pacific coast (Riebsame 1997). In some areas, growth is out of control and new concentrations of wealth are crowding out the middle and lower classes. New West proponents see collaborative ecosystem management as a way to deal with growth and resource issues—and ecosystem management has become a central element in the New West narrative (Abbott, Adler, and Abbott 1997; Riebsame 1997; Duane 1998; Jackson and Kuhlken 2006).

Indeed, ecosystem management very well could become the narrative thread that binds together many of the quieter revolution's disparate elements. But not all the elements described above are readily applicable to all quieter revolution programs. Instead of ecosystem management, the rather more inclusive notion of collaborative, place-based planning might be put forward as the narrative line that best fits current conditions. But for reasons given at this chapter's outset—basically, that many place-based efforts work without "deep collaboration"—collaboration is an imperfect fit. "Place-based" is perhaps too vague, given the multitude of scales involved, ranging from the very local to the international. Still, even if they stop short of providing us the ideal all-encompassing narrative, collaborative, place-based planning (Beatley and Manning 1997; Box 1998) and ecosystem management are defining elements for today's land use management systems.

Is the quieter revolution really improving civic engagement? and environmental quality? While preceding waves of environmentalism and land use planning innovation brought with them legal requirements for public involvement, the quieter revolution holds forth the prospect of building a more enduring civic participation infrastructure (Webler and Tuler 1999). To be sure, it is developing unevenly and haltingly, but the overall trend would seem to be toward more—and more robust—local, place-based collaborative projects. This emerging infrastructure, to a greater extent than was the case for many earlier advances, is built around local problems and issues.

Though these local and regional collaborations may have strong local roots, it should not be presumed that they simply spring from the fertile earth of the watershed or bioregion. Indeed, most are incubated with state or federal funds and other incentives. And the government role is not limited entirely to one of financial and logistical support. In their analysis of Ohio farmland preservation programs, Koontz et al. (2004) found that governments did more than set broad goals and provide financial resources. In this case, they framed the issue as one of farmland protection, exclusive of associated concerns about open-space management. Especially the state government's imprint—but local governments' as well—was upon all aspects of process and outcome. Koontz et al.'s (2004) analysis led to the conclusion that money can buy and significantly shape collaboration.

Place-based infrastructural capacity that can be tapped to address specific local and regional issues—"civic engagement on demand"—can very effectively support environmental planning and land use management. While this approach can yield positive, widely accepted ecological and economic results, this is far from a given (Moote, McClaran, and Chickering 1997; Napier 1998; Singleton 2002; Thomas 2003). Indeed, this place-based infrastructural framework is built from the notion that diverse stakeholders should work together in identifying and responding to local issues. But, as noted earlier, the collaborative approach is not universally embraced by environmentalists and other key stakeholders. Former Sierra Club executive director and chairman Michael McCloskey (1999) goes so far as to call collaboration a betrayal of democracy, a de facto substitution of minority rule for majority rule that threatens to undo a century of environmental gains (Marston 2000). As Singleton (2002, 72) sees it:

> A fundamental dilemma for collaborative, "place-based" processes in natural resource management is that while the process is local, many of the sources of the problems it seeks to address and the constituencies it must respond to are not.

Coggins (1999) characterizes collaboration as nothing more than a fad, and a dangerous one at that, because it is based on an abdication of federal responsibility. As Coggins (1999, 603) puts it:

> The underlying theory is that a self-selected group of local people who promise to be civil with one another can do a better job of allocating federal resources than the duly constituted federal authorities.

Power, he argues, is being devolved to local populations that harbor disproportionate numbers of extremists, demagogues, and crooks. Kenney (2000), himself an advocate of the collaborative approach, raises similar points about representation. But he goes on to refute many of them.

Looked at from another perspective, agency managers may see collaboration as a threat to their power and influence (Selin, Schuett, and Carr 2000). Then there are the more extreme property rights advocates, unwilling to collaborate because they see ecosystem management leading toward a federal takeover of all land management, on private as well as public lands (Fitzsimmons 1998).

Many critiques of collaboration come from the western states. In the northeastern context, Sayen (1994, 144) rather dismissively describes the Maine Forest Biodiversity Project as

> a collection of "stakeholders" in Maine that struggled in vain from 1994 to 1998 to develop consensus over some modest biodiversity protection strategies on state-owned lands, which cover about 4 percent of the state.

Much of the criticism is based on perceived abrogation of national or state responsibility for management of public lands. Though public lands are not the main focus of this book, they are very much bound up with the themes addressed here, since so much quieter revolution activity involves areas in mixed public-private ownership (Fairfax et al. 1999). This is especially the case for the collaborative efforts of which McCloskey is so critical. Those efforts may actually expand conservation options on private lands, though possibly at the expense of curtailing them on public lands. The bottom line is that net ecological gains—or losses—can be incredibly difficult to assess. Not only are there the inherent measurement difficulties, as well as the long time frames usually needed for adequate assessment, but also the imponderables: what might have happened in the absence of collaboration? Might federal agencies have been delinquent in their environmental duties had there been no collaborative oversight or admonishment? Conceivably, more might have been accomplished via an imperfect collaborative approach than a more rigorous conventional planning approach.

McCloskey's indictment is so all-encompassing as to leave little room for cases where collaboration satisfies interests at multiple scales, without in the process sacrificing those interests' integrity. In some instances, local environmental groups are quite willing to be part of a collaborative process, while their national counterparts reject collaboration in favor of confrontation. And there are also property rights and wise use groups with divergent national and local postures (Marston 2000). One of the dilemmas confronting collaborative planning proponents is how to regard participation by those fundamentally opposed to the environmental project with which they now find themselves involved. On the one hand, these representatives might be seen as dangerous and threatening to the collaborative process, with the best strategy being to marginalize them. But their involvement can be viewed in an entirely different way: if they are invested in the process, these stakeholders will come to support it. While such participants may not experience a life conversion, enormous potential exists for their becoming meaningfully engaged, relaxing their intransigence, and working constructively with environmentalists and other counterparts.

And for all the collaborative success stories cited, there are all those instances where projects never get off the ground. We may have no good way of inventorying all those cases, or of assessing what proportion of "needy places" actually do develop collaborative responses—but it is a question to be put critically to those who showcase the success stories as new wave environmental management icons.

Quieter revolution programs are putting in place a rather extensive, if highly uneven, infrastructure for place-based planning, in the form of a network of "distributaries" that can allocate resources. This network's connectedness and potential are greatly enhanced by the power of the Internet (Levitt 2002), as well as the user-friendliness of geographic information system (GIS)–based mapping and analytic capabilities (Randolph 2004; Berke et al. 2006). Should governments find it increasingly in their interests to support quieter revolution activities, then they can greatly amplify their effectiveness by funneling money and other resources into existing distributaries. While this may mean greater central control over local projects, as well as some dampening down of innovation and co-optation of grassroots interests, it will also mean greatly expanded local capacity. It is a third way, between highly centralized regulatory planning and genuine grassroots activity. And should the salience of climate change, hazard vulnerability, oil dependence, and other major national environmental issues be elevated sufficiently, then such increased government support—bolstered by foundation funding and perhaps corporate support—may make the third way very attractive, to a very broad constituency.

CHAPTER FOUR
PROTECTING REGIONAL LANDSCAPES

As the quiet revolution was coming into bloom in the early 1970s, regional and statewide planning were front and center, seemingly the wave of America's land use future. In characterizing the phenomenon, Bosselman and Callies (1971) featured a selection of state, substate, and metropolitan programs (these are highlighted in chapter 2). And they predicted that more such programs would be forthcoming. Indeed, some new programs did emerge, but their numbers and regulatory scope were limited and they did not reach the potential that once seemed their destiny. This is especially so for the large regional endeavors. Yet regional environmental planning did not just fade away; instead, it has resurfaced in new and, perhaps, less-effective-than-once-hoped-for forms: habitat conservation plans; watershed management projects; large-scale environmental restoration, as with the Buffalo Commons; "greater" ecoregions built around core protected areas, as with the greater Yellowstone and Sierra ecoregions; and working landscapes, such as the Northern Forest of New York and New England.

As this list implies, environmental regions are defined in a multitude of overlapping, often conflicting, ways. While federal agencies are working toward a common, hierarchical ecoregion classification framework, they are still far from reaching consensus (Omernik 2004). And such a consensus is unlikely to greatly influence planning designations in any case. Further confusion may arise from terminology used to describe environmental regions; they are variously characterized as bioregions, ecoregions, biophysical regions, and more. This is not a matter for much concern here; regardless of specific terminology, the focus is on regions defined principally by natural, rather than political, features. A word is in order, however, about bioregionalism, an ecopolitical philosophy that embraces a rather "deep" form of local sustainability (Parsons 1985; Sale 1985; Mason, Solecki, and Lotstein 1987; McGinnis 1999). While ecoregional definition is central to the bioregional vision, bioregionalism is far more than a mapping and regional planning exercise.

The Quiet Revolution Adapts

The quiet revolution was largely about zoning and regulation. To be fair, Bosselman and Callies (1971) included a broad range of management options—but at the end of the day, their revolution was driven by the belief that at least some local planning powers should be taken back or reconfigured by state governments. Many quieter revolution programs, by contrast, actually begin with local initiative and fully embrace it. At the same time, established quiet revolution programs are very much part of the current scene. Most have adapted and retooled, moving toward the quieter revolution model of incentives, collaboration, and place-based planning. The Adirondack Private Land Use and Development Plan, perhaps the most stringent of them all, tacked in the mid-1970s in directions more conciliatory to local interests. Among other things, the development review process was simplified and speeded up, restrictions were eased, and civil penalties replaced criminal penalties for violations of Adirondack Park Agency (APA) orders (Liroff and Davis 1981; Popper 1981; Mason 1992a; McMartin 2002). Most other quiet revolution programs also made concessions (Popper 1981; DeGrove 1984, 1989; Mason 1992a). The Comprehensive Management Plan for the Pinelands, already something of a quiet revolution temporal outlier, made adjustments similar to those in the Adirondacks (Mason 1992a, 2004). Indeed, Pinelands regional planning, having learned from the APA's early trials and tribulations, began with significantly greater local representation than was the case in the Adirondacks. The Pinelands Commission, responsible for implementing the Pinelands Comprehensive Management Plan, consists of seven gubernatorial appointees, seven county-level appointees, and one federal representative. Though five of the APA's eleven members must be park residents, they are appointed by the governor. The Pinelands program has had a developments rights program from the outset. During the plan's early implementation, additional concessions were made to localities, including streamlining the development application process, payments in lieu of taxes on publicly owned lands, funding for local infrastructure, and other incentives and financial assistance (Mason 1992a, 2004).

Some of these changes—in the Pinelands and elsewhere—seriously compromise ecological protection goals. At the same time, regional planning capacity in many protected areas has been expanded by the recent proliferation of land trusts, watershed organizations, local ballot measures, and other quieter revolution features.

Not surprisingly, the boundary between quiet and quieter does not stand in bold relief. Upstate New York's 1970s-era Tug Hill Program, for example, is a quieter approach, while New Jersey's Pinelands National Reserve—created about a decade after the height of the quiet revolution— is very much a regulatory-style quiet revolution program. So, too, is the much more recent New Jersey Highlands program, described below. Many initiatives, like the spatially expansive Chesapeake Bay Program discussed below, combine quiet and quieter elements.

Quieter Revolution Regional Initiatives

This chapter's focus is mainly on regional initiatives of the past two decades or so. Those initiatives face tremendous challenges in deploying place-based, collaborative approaches over large geographic areas. In small counties, towns, and watersheds, a sense of identification, shared ownership, and meaning—that is, a sense of place—may be deeply rooted or at least have the potential to develop. But the larger regions, though they may be much appreciated and valued, usually do not foster the same sort of shared identity (Cheng and Daniels 2003). Local residents really know and care most about their more immediate surroundings—their towns, lakes, rivers, and woods—rather than the full reach of the larger environmental region of which they are a part. Government agencies and NGOs, on the other hand, often will be inclined toward the big picture. This only exacerbates tensions between insiders and outsiders, full-time and part-time residents, newcomers and old-timers—making it all the more challenging to reconcile local sense of place with a larger regional perspective.

This can become all too evident when a locality is asked to sacrifice economic development—or, alternatively accept high-density growth—in the interests of the larger region.

Besides the matter of regional consciousness, there is the question of physical definition. Take, for example, the Northern Forest of New York and New England. The Adirondacks are part of the Laurentide ecoregion, while the rest of the Northern Forest belongs to the Appalachian ecoregion. This is not to argue that the Adirondacks, Green Mountains of Vermont, White Mountains of New Hampshire, and Maine's vast forests should not be considered together for planning purposes but simply to point out that they also have other biophysical allegiances. New Jersey's Highlands region, as noted earlier, is part of a larger New York/New Jersey/Pennsylvania/Connecticut Highlands region, which is part of the Appalachians. Indeed, small physiographic regions usually are nested within larger regions. Watersheds, in particular, are hierarchical (Singleton 2002)—even though, as the saying goes, we all live downstream. Pennsylvania and Delaware's Brandywine Valley, for example, is part of the Delaware River watershed. The Columbia River Gorge National Scenic Area, though not itself a subwatershed, is situated within the huge Columbia River basin. Yellowstone National Park, another administratively defined terrestrial region, is part of the Greater Yellowstone Ecoregion, which in turn is part of the Rocky Mountain Cordillera and is claimed by the recently minted Yukon to Yellowstone project.

At the megascales—national, continental, global—various approaches to regional representation of protected areas are taken. One strategy is to have no overarching plan; each region stands on its own. But, in fact, guiding principles of biodiversity and ecosystem representation are considered in global biosphere and world heritage area designation, as well as designation of U.S. national parks. These principles, of course, must accommodate themselves to political, economic, and cultural circumstances (Porter and Wallis 2002). In North America, one of the consequences has been an emphasis on alpine protected areas, what Foreman (2004) calls "rocks and ice."

Over the past decade or two, conservation biologists and other ecological planning proponents have proposed continental ecosystem management approaches (Noss and Cooperrider 1994; Soulé and Terborgh 1999; Foreman 2004). Dave Foreman, founder of the eco-activist organization Earth First! and current chairman and executive director of the Rewilding Institute (2007), is promoting a vision for "rewilding" North America (Foreman 2004) (figures 4.1, 4.2). While he lauds the many small landscape restoration projects proliferating across the nation, he quotes Daniel Simberloff and coauthors in describing them as "museum pieces." What we need, Foreman argues, is a continental strategy, with big, connected ecoreserves. He calls for native species and habitat protection, ecosystem restoration, exotic species control, prevention of additional land fragmentation, and adaptive management that takes climate change into account. The Alaska National Interest Lands Conservation Act of 1980 (Layzer 2006), which conferred protected status on more than one hundred million acres of public lands, is cited as a good, if imperfect, model. This is a far more ambitious scale than those at which most collaborative ecosystem planning practitioners work. Yet Foreman's vision represents a less strident view, actually, than the one originally taken by the Wildlands Project, which he cofounded in 1991. Early wildlands proponents were quite frank about removing human inhabitants from at least some areas of extraordinary ecological value. Today, however, Foreman argues that passive recreation can be quite compatible with wilderness protection and that livestock grazing, where it cannot be eliminated, should be reformed to be more environmentally compatible. The Sky Islands Wildlands Network, in southern Arizona and New Mexico, is illustrative of this approach. It includes low- and moderate-use areas, along with core protected areas and wildlife linkages (figure 4.2).

Other continental-scale programs, if less grand in reach than the Wildlands Project, are putting significant nongovernment resources into lobbying and land and easement acquisition. Major environmental organizations often use ecoregional templates to guide selection of places they seek to protect. The Natural Resources Defense Council's (NRDC) Biogems program (Natural Resources Defense Council 2006), the Sierra Club's Critical Ecoregions Program (Sierra Club 2007a), and The Nature Conservancy's (TNC) Last Great Places program are leading national initiatives. NRDC prompts its supporters to send electronic messages to politicians, administrators, and other key actors, urging them to enact various measures to protect the biogems. The Sierra Club identifies twenty-one "critical ecoregions." Like NRDC, the Sierra Club calls for political actions to address critical threats within each ecoregion. Unlike NRDC's

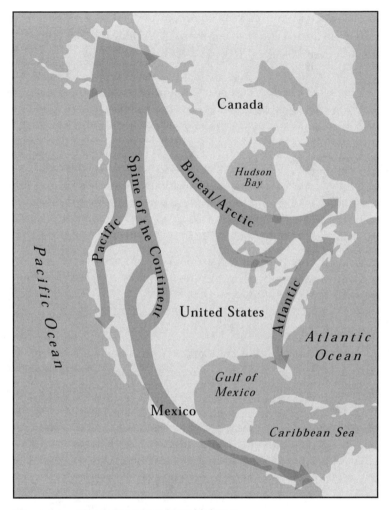

Figure 4.1. North American MegaLinkages
Source: Wildlands Network

initiative, the Sierra Club identifies large ecoregions rather than smaller places (figure 4.3). TNC's program recognizes large and small places; in contrast with the other programs, TNC acquires land and easements, often increasing their reach by working in conjunction with government agencies and NGOs.

Overall, quieter revolution regional initiatives are developing unevenly. Some have fallen far short of initial hopes. Others have stumbled

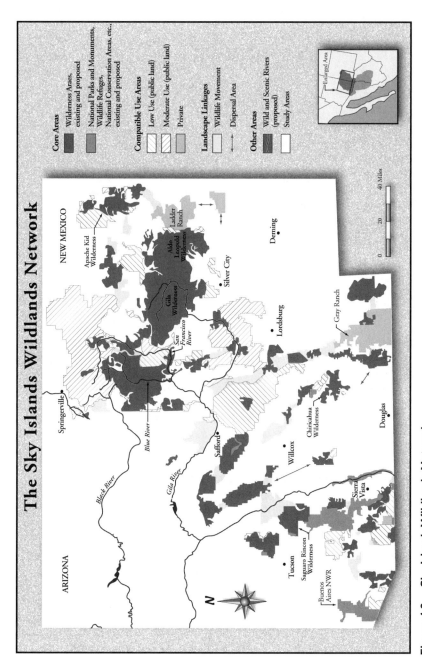

Figure 4.2. Sky Islands Wildlands Network
Source: Wildlands Network

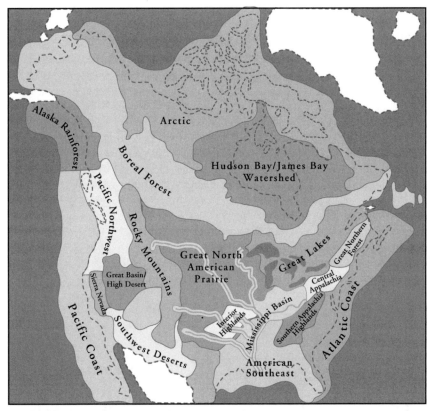

Figure 4.3. The Sierra Club's Critical Ecoregions
Source: Reproduced from sierraclub.org with permission of the Sierra Club, © 2007 Sierra Club. All Rights Reserved.

but persisted. And some have managed to bring tangible—if limited—environmental, civic, and social results across the larger landscape. Below we look at several regional initiatives. Most are large, defined by major watersheds, mountain ranges, and wetlands: Chesapeake watershed, Everglades, Catskills watershed, Sierra Nevada ecoregion, New York/New Jersey/Pennsylvania/Connecticut Highlands, and Louisiana Gulf Coast wetlands. Some are delineated, mainly, as historic or extant habitat regions: Southern California's habitat areas, the Buffalo Commons, and the Greater Yellowstone Ecoregion. Land ownership patterns and historic/aesthetic factors define the Columbia River Gorge National Scenic Area and Northern Forest region. The final section is about several political regions: greater Baltimore, Cleveland, Pittsburgh, Chicago, Portland (OR), and Seattle. None of these places, as we shall see, is exclusively defined by a single factor.

As already discussed, regional consciousness and environmental management strategies vary enormously from case to case. Common to many, but not all of them, is a quintessential quieter revolution element: purchase lands and acquire easements to protect critical subareas within the larger regions and provide incentives designed to concentrate growth. In some places—though usually more in an ad hoc than consistent manner through large regions—conservation design principles are adopted. These are meant, among other things, to reduce the environmental footprints of residential development and maintain distinct boundaries between developed and natural areas (Yaro et al. 1988; McHarg 1995; Arendt 1996; Thompson and Steiner 1997; Trombulak 2003).

Taken together, these regions and other areas like them cover enough of the lower 48's land base to make us take notice. But their purposes, resources, and accomplishments are simply too varied to regard them collectively as a national ad hoc ecoregional land management project.

Chesapeake Bay

The Chesapeake Bay is exceptional for many reasons. A very shallow bay with a long, convoluted shoreline and extensive system of tributaries, its ratio of shoreline to aqueous surface area is unmatched by any other bay on the planet. As a result, the Chesapeake has been remarkably productive—and also extraordinarily vulnerable to human impacts. The bay is—or at least has been—an unusually rich source of oysters, clams, crabs, shad, and striped bass. Its easily navigable river system fostered early settlement, and the bay quickly became the main receptacle for a growing population's effluvia (Davidson et al. 1997). By the late 1800s, industrial activities were bringing enormous pollution loads to the Chesapeake. Several decades of conferences, studies, and efforts to reduce pollution loads—begun in the 1920s—failed to stem the deterioration of the bay's ecological health (Ernst 2003). By midcentury the situation was critical. During the 1960s, in synch with national environmental trends, Chesapeake Bay pollution and larger ecosystem issues began to move from the confines of elite scientific and policy communities into wider public view. In 1967, the nonprofit Chesapeake Bay Foundation was established under the "Save the Bay" banner, and the new organization dedicated itself to education, research, and policy advisory and watchdog work (Chesapeake Bay Foundation 2006). Although new pollution controls, federal funding for wastewater treatment plants, and new wetlands protection laws came into place in the early 1970s, the bay's ecological conditions generally continued to worsen, in considerable part due to rapid increases in regional population. Finally, in 1980, the groundwork for a major restoration effort was laid with creation of the Chesapeake Bay Commission. Advisory only, the commission started with members from Maryland and Virginia; Pennsylvania joined in 1985. In 1983, the first Chesapeake Bay Agreement was signed by the governors of the three states, as well as the District of Columbia mayor, EPA administrator, and Chesapeake Bay Commission chair. Soon after, this would become the administrative foundation for the Chesapeake Bay Program, a collaborative effort supported mainly by the U.S. Environmental Protection Agency (Ernst 2003).

While widely lauded by supporters from its three-state (plus the District of Columbia) region and beyond, the Chesapeake Bay Program is also a frequent target of withering critiques, especially from the environmental community (Horton 2003). The program—with its ambitious goal of restoring the ecological health of America's largest estuary—was launched during a difficult time for environmentalism and charged with a complex, wide-ranging mission that spans a multitude of political constituencies. With the participation (but not representation on the Chesapeake Bay Commission) of New York State, Delaware, and West Virginia via a Memoranda of Understanding first signed in 2000, the program reaches out to government and nongovernment stakeholders over an area of sixty-four thousand square miles (figure 4.4). The Chesapeake Bay Program is an ideal example of "big watershed" planning, quieter revolution style. While it is not the only example, it is the river basin where cooperative pollution management has been taken furthest and most seriously. The Great Lakes Basin, focus of an international ecosystem management initiative encompassing the five lakes' enormous watershed area, might be the most relevant case for comparison.

Hierarchical goal setting is the basic structural framework for the Chesapeake Bay model. The overarching commitment, which is the foundation for the original agreement as well as subsequent agreements signed in 1987 and 2000, is "to nurture and sustain a Chesapeake Bay Watershed

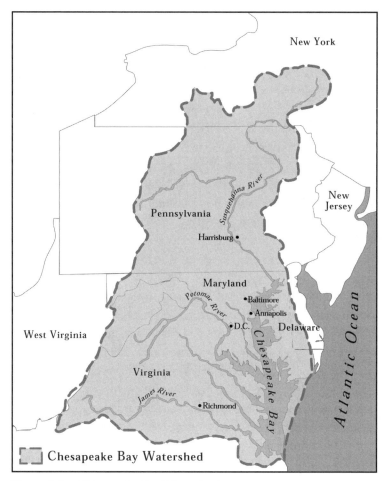

Figure 4.4. Chesapeake Bay Watershed
Source: Chesapeake Bay Program

Partnership" (Maryland Department of Natural Resources 2007). Broad goals follow for protection and restoration of aquatic life, habitat, and water quality. These are followed by subgoals for habitat protection and restoration, as well as for "sound land use" and "stewardship and community engagement." Subordinate goals are more specific—far more so in more recent agreements than the initial one—though most still are cast in rather general language. But the agreement does contain some numerical targets, including the 40 percent nutrient reduction first agreed to in 1987, as well as a tenfold increase in oysters over a 1994 baseline level. In addition, the agreement includes targets for restoration of fish passages, submerged aquatic vegetation, wetlands, and brownfield sites; protection of lands from development; and provision of public access points, water trails, and pump-out facilities (Maryland Department of Natural Resources 2007).

Success in achieving goals and meeting targets rests mainly with the states. And in this regard, the Chesapeake Bay Program exhibits quiet and quieter revolution elements. The federal commitment largely involves coordination, research, technical assistance, and funding—but little in the way of forcing mechanisms. Strong regulatory components are evident in Maryland's Critical Areas Act (CAA) and Virginia's Chesapeake Bay Preservation Act (CBPA), as well in the states' regulation of blue crab harvests. Virginia's 1988 Chesapeake Bay Preservation Act requires a one-hundred-foot vegetative buffer along the coast. But implementation and enforcement have been highly uneven; Horton (2003) characterizes it all as a failure.

Consistent with its national leadership role in advancing the "smart growth" approach to growth management (chapter 5), Maryland has done more (Barker 1990; Davidson et al. 1997). Its 1984 CAA establishes a thousand-foot setback for nearshore development and also mandates low-density development (one home per twenty acres) and protection of vegetation in a one-hundred-foot zone adjacent to the bay. Despite various loopholes, the law has succeeded in restricting development along the bay's shores—no small feat, given the incredible value of and demand for bayshore real estate. With regard to blue crab harvests, Maryland again has pursued more aggressive regulation than Virginia (Horton 2003). In July 2006, Virginia followed Maryland's lead of a year earlier, adopting a cap on the take of menhaden (Shear 2006). Menhaden, a small, oily fish used in diet supplements, is vital to the bay's ecology; it is a key link in the food chain and an efficient filter of pollutants.

Adoption of "best management practices" on agricultural lands throughout the basin holds great promise for reducing nutrient loading into the bay. But these programs are largely voluntary and their success has been limited. Even though Pennsylvania, in the early 1990s, and Maryland, in the late 1990s, enacted enforceable farmland management regulations, control over farm practices is notoriously difficult to implement and enforce. Indeed, the programs are widely viewed as insufficient in overall scope, as well as levels of compliance. Chesapeake watershed states do subsidize voluntary compliance, but as with all such basin programs, available resources cannot meet potential demand (Davidson et al. 1997; Ernst 2003; Horton 2003).

The Chesapeake Bay Program has brought a wide diversity of stakeholders, over a vast region, into the planning process. A framework for continuing collaboration is securely in place, and great strides have been made in developing indicators for measuring progress (Chesapeake Bay Commission 2005). Progress itself, though, has been halting and uneven, constrained by practical limits to the federal government's reach, emphasis on good intentions over concrete actions, differing state- and local-level political cultures, funding insufficient to meet program goals, and simply the enormity of the tasks at hand.

Just as with pollution control more generally, where we have found it much simpler to build sewage plants than deal with nonpoint source pollution, some of the Chesapeake's greatest recent successes have come from structural measures. Fish spawning has improved with installation of passageways and clearing of blockages. But diffuse-source problems, such as nutrients from farmlands and atmospheric deposition, are much harder to remediate. The Chesapeake Bay Commission (2005), while remaining hopeful about the future, minces no words in characterizing the current situation as a crisis. The year 2005 was not encouraging, with its widespread dead zone and low dissolved oxygen levels. Much blame is placed on continuing suburban sprawl and expansion of impervious surfaces—this despite concerted efforts to control sprawl, especially in Maryland.

Ernst (2003) and Horton (2003) are among the critical analysts favoring a more forceful approach to regional environmental protection. Still, they see considerable unrealized potential in the Chesapeake's quieter approach, potential that may come closer to realization if a robust federal total maximum daily load (TMDL) approach to water quality management (chapter 6) can act as a sort of regulatory "safety net" (Ernst 2003; Horton 2003). More financing, of course, is crucial if the program is to ultimately succeed in meeting its goals. In addition to base federal funding for Chesapeake programs, there is the federal Farm Bill (chapter 5). State governors and the Chesapeake Bay Commission are requesting substantial increases in funds in the 2007 bill, mainly for payments and other assistance to farmers in the watershed (Chesapeake Bay Commission 2005). Another way to secure increased funds—particularly when legislative bodies are unwilling to allocate them—is through ballot measures for land acquisition and other environmental programs. Pennsylvania voters passed a statewide measure in 2005 (Mason 2005), but Virginia and Maryland's constitutions do not allow for such statewide measures (Ernst 2003); thus, local ballot questions become all the more important for those two states.

Given the size and diversity of the Chesapeake watershed, many equity issues present themselves: is it appropriate for Pennsylvania and its farmers to bear the costs of improved farming methods, local environmental benefits notwithstanding, given Pennsylvania's distance from the bay? Federal stewardship incentive programs are designed to address this concern, at least in part, by spreading those costs more broadly. Environmental protection programs themselves may exacerbate social and economic inequities. To what degree, for example, has state land use legislation increased bayshore land values and contributed to gentrification (Davidson et al. 1997)? Wider imposition of real estate transfer and other taxes directed at capturing some of the increased amenity value—and directing the proceeds toward environmental programs—might be more seriously considered. What costs, long-term and short-term, fall upon the watermen, who have long depended on the bay's bounty? Though they benefit from improved ecological conditions, some of them face high short-term costs because of restrictions on fish and crab harvests. Finding ways to sustain this population, without "museumizing" what is left of it, is a particularly vexing challenge for regional governments and planners.

New York City's Catskills Watershed

Now we turn to a much smaller watershed, entirely contained within southeastern New York State and sharing a hydrologic boundary with the Chesapeake Basin's uppermost reaches. New York State's two forest preserves—one in the northeast, in the Adirondack Mountains, and the other in the Catskills, in the southeast—were created in 1885. Preserve lands are to be forever protected as wild forest. The original intent was to limit destructive logging practices; this, it was thought, would be sufficient to protect downstream water, especially in the Hudson River as it reached New York City. Each preserve is situated within a larger state park, consisting of mixed private and public landholdings. In the six-million-acre

Adirondack Park, New York State owns about half the land. The remaining private lands, as chapter 2 reveals, are governed by a quiet revolution plan: the Adirondack Private Land Use and Development Plan.

No such plan is in place for the more than 60 percent of Catskill Park lands in private ownership. In the 1970s, the Temporary State Commission to Study the Catskills proposed a regional planning scheme for an expanded Catskill Park. But when the state legislature failed to renew the commission in 1977, regional planning for the Catskills was all but dead. Dyballa (1979) attributes this failure to conflicting definitions of the region and regional issues, a general backlash against Adirondack Park planning, disagreements among interests represented on the commission, and the commission's unresponsiveness to local concerns. But little more than two decades later, the debate over regional planning would reemerge in the portion of the Catskill region that supplies water to New York City.

New York City has long enjoyed excellent drinking water, of such high quality that when *Consumer Reports* rated it favorably in comparison with several bottled waters in the mid-1980s, cunning retailers started stocking their shelves with bottled city tap water. New York first drew surface water in the 1840s from the Croton system of reservoirs in Westchester County, north of the city and east of the Hudson River (figure 4.5). Starting in 1915, the portion of the Catskills that drains into the Mohawk/Hudson system came on line to supply New York's rapidly growing population. Then, in the 1950s and 1960s, storage capacity was again greatly expanded through the creation of several reservoirs in the Upper Delaware River watershed (Weidner 1974; National Research Council Committee to Review the New York City Watershed Management Strategy 2000). Following a major drought in the early to mid-1960s, the Delaware River Basin Agreement was signed. Under that agreement, New York must ensure that sufficient water reaches the Delaware to support minimum flow levels for navigation, oyster production, and keeping the estuarine salt front from advancing too far upstream. During the major 1960s drought, the salt front nearly reached the city of Philadelphia's Delaware River water intake. Ironically, a recent series of floods has prompted downstream interests to pressure the multistate Delaware River Basin Commission to study the feasibility of holding more water in the reservoirs, conceivably to allow for greater control over flood events.

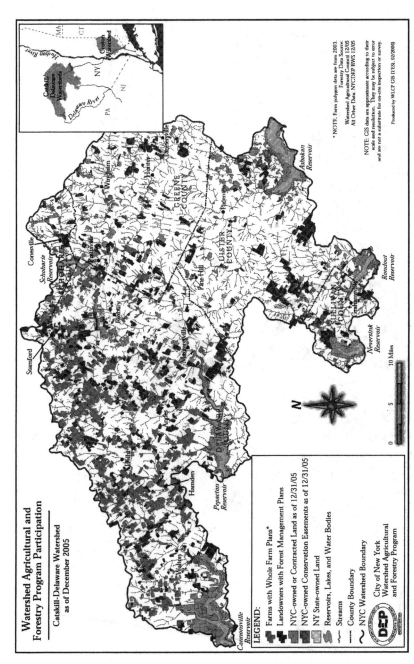

Figure 4.5. New York City Catskill/Delaware Watershed
Source: Reproduced with permission of the New York City Department of Environmental Protection.

As figure 4.5 shows, most of the Catskill Park serves as watershed for New York City. Relations between the city and local residents have long been rather contentious (Weidner 1974; National Research Council Committee to Review the New York City Watershed Management Strategy 2000); such tensions are the norm when a distant urban government manages rural watershed lands. Boston's "hydrologic colonization" of Quabbin and Wachusetts Reservoir watershed lands in central Massachusetts has engendered similar issues. Boston, however, owns more of its watershed land than does New York (Steinberg and Clark 1999; National Research Council Committee to Review the New York City Watershed Management Strategy 2000; Platt, Barten, and Pfeffer 2000). The New York City Board of Water Supply, authorized by state enabling legislation passed in 1905, has the power to acquire land beyond city limits using eminent domain. And in the early days of Catskill/Delaware watershed development, the city exercised its power with relative abandon, running roughshod over local landowners in the interests of the "greatest good for the greatest number of people for the longest time," to borrow conservationist Gifford Pinchot's words (Miller 2001). Although Pinchot might have described these actions as necessary to ensure "wise use" of resources, today's wise use advocates (chapter 7) are not at all on board when it comes to broad invocation of eminent domain powers.

By the 1970s, the Catskills situation had settled into one of simmering resentment not only over New York City's displacement of towns and villages to make way for reservoirs but also its acquisition of adjacent watershed lands. New York owns about 6 percent of the total Catskill/Delaware watershed lands, with 42 percent of that total consisting of submerged reservoir lands. Remaining lands are about three-quarters in private ownership and 20 percent in New York State ownership (Pires 2004) (figure 4.5). Tensions between local residents and the New York city and state governments moved toward the boiling point in the 1970s, as Catskill regional land use planning was studied and proposed. But as regionwide planning schemes were played down and finally abandoned, concerns subsided.

What stirred things up again in the 1990s has its origins in federal legislation: the 1986 Safe Drinking Water Act Amendments. In 1989, the U.S. Environmental Protection Agency issued a rule requiring most major purveyors of surface water to use filtration. If alternatives to filtration could be demonstrated to meet water quality objectives to the EPA's satisfaction, a filtration avoidance determination (FAD) could be issued. In New York City's case, a filtration system would be enormously expensive—about $6 billion to install, with annual maintenance costs on the order of $300 million. Obviously, this was something New York wanted to avoid—and the city was able to negotiate with the EPA for an alternative, in this instance watershed management. Though some critics question the premises on which the EPA's filtration requirements and alternatives are based— arguing that no empirical evidence supports the notion that restoring watershed lands to a more natural state will reduce pathogenic organism counts in surface water (Sagoff 2002)—New York City felt it had little choice but to work within the EPA framework. Several other major cities, including Seattle, Boston, San Francisco, and the Portlands (Oregon and Maine) also have been granted FADs and must meet EPA conditions (Pires 2004).

New York's initial approach was to act as a quiet revolution planning body, overseeing the development of local comprehensive plans that would include watershed and water quality protection measures. Upon each plan's approval, New York would provide funds for infrastructure development and ease mandatory land use restrictions. This "whole community planning" process would feature extensive public participation and consensus building. Given that a majority of towns lacked comprehensive planning, this would be a major step toward an Adirondacks-style planning system, for at least a part of the Catskill Park. Although several towns did participate in the program, many balked.

Whole community planning came to an end in 1993, when New York reverted to conventional, tried-and-true methods: the city would acquire ten thousand acres of critical watershed lands, using its power of eminent domain as needed. The city had already given up on an earlier plan to acquire in fee simple or via easement a total of 240,000 watershed acres. Had New York taken more land back in midcentury, when it perhaps could have done so in the sweeping Robert Moses style (Caro 1974), it might not have found itself in the fix it was in. But the 1990s political climate and power dynamic differed dramatically from those of decades past. New York's acquisition plans faced a firestorm of local hostility, with local property owners successfully framing the issue in social equity and victimhood terms. The economic costs of keeping New York's water clean, it was argued, would be imposed upon local Catskills residents. The Coalition of Watershed Towns brought suit against New York City, and the watershed planning process reached a stalemate. New York was forced to rethink its approach.

A new round of negotiations ensued, and what emerged was a complex memorandum of agreement (MOA), brokered by New York State governor George Pataki and signed in 1997 by New York City, New York State, the EPA, seventy-three municipalities, eight counties, and five environmental NGOs. The MOA provides for land acquisition on a willing-seller basis, with towns and villages having the ability to designate areas as exempt from eligibility for acquisition. City-owned lands allow for recreational use—mostly passive, nonmotorized activities—and taxes are paid to local governments. The Catskill Fund for the Future disburses grant funds to localities for "environmentally sustainable" economic development projects.

An agricultural easement purchase program also is in place, with the easements held in perpetuity by the New York State Department of Environmental Conservation. The program is jointly implemented by New York City and the local Watershed Agricultural Council (figure 4.5). The MOA also calls for legislation regulating polluting activities within the watershed, as well as a phosphorous offset program, allowing for pollution credit trading among point and nonpoint dischargers. Quieter revolution incentives are an important part of the MOA; funding is available for wastewater treatment plants, septic system repair and replacement, stream bank stabilization, sand and salt storage facility upgrades, stormwater management, forestry and agricultural programs (figure 4.5), and public education and outreach. Riparian buffers are paid for through the Conservation Reserve Enhancement Program (CREP), modeled in part after the federal Conservation Reserve Program (chapter 5). Under CREP, farmers and foresters are compensated for temporary retirement of buffer lands, as well as adoption of best management practices. The MOA, to which the Trust for Public Land is a signatory, calls for creation of a regional land trust. Though several local land trusts are active in the region and the Trust for Public Land is a signatory to the MOA, a watershed-wide trust has not yet emerged (Land Trust Alliance 2006). The watershed initiative entails much more than this (Pfeffer and Wagenet 1999; National Research Council Committee to Review the New York City

Watershed Management Strategy 2000; Platt, Barten, and Pfeffer 2000; Pires 2004), but these programs and projects are the essence of it.

New York City's Catskills watershed program is more a quieter revolution than a quiet revolution program. But it has some big advantages over quieter programs elsewhere. For one, ample funding is available. New York City is expected to spend "only" $1.5 billion over ten years on the watershed program, compared with the $6 billion cost, plus annual maintenance costs of $300 million, for a filtration system (National Research Council Committee to Review the New York City Watershed Management Strategy 2000, 26–27). Of course, that $1.5 billion is a lavish sum in the world of regional watershed management; such an amount would never be allocated were it not for the prospect of a much larger outlay as the alternative. And then there is the threat of eminent domain. In today's hostile climate, the exercise of this power is fraught with political peril (chapter 7). Widespread use of eminent domain power by the city of New York might well prompt legislation curtailing the city's ability to use it. But because we are not at that point, land condemnation still looms as a threat. Even if it is a somewhat neutered threat, it still has its role in making quieter programs all the more feasible, even attractive, in many instances. Watershed planning also is bolstered by economic development subsidies that flow to localities. The resultant benefits help the watershed program gain grudging local acceptance. Doubtless, many residents are not enamored of government economic development programs—but those taking place in the Catskills probably are more acceptable than the state prisons and other unwanted land uses embraced by many Adirondack, as well as at least some Catskill, communities. Given the depressed state in which the Catskills' resource and resort economies find themselves, combined with regional potential for new recreation and amenity-based enterprises, subsidized watershed management may make just enough economic sense to allow it to gradually win over a reluctant, skeptical local populace. In order to succeed, watershed projects have to do enough to placate some of the more vocal local critics. This is New York's target audience, because in all likelihood, a majority of regional residents probably are only mildly offended—if they are offended at all—by New York's actions. After all, a large and growing share of the area's population consists of recent part-time and full-time migrants from New York City and its suburbs.

Florida Everglades Restoration

Before significant European settlement, South Florida was essentially one large wetland, over which sheets of water gently flowed from north to south. In the not-too-distant future, if predictions of global warming and rising sea levels come to pass, the region may be inundated. In the interim, much of the area has been drained, channelized, farmed, and covered with residential and commercial development (McCally 1999). Water that does flow through the Everglades is polluted by urban and agricultural runoff that contains high levels of pesticides, metals, and nutrients such as phosphorous and nitrogen.

The region's unique ecology has long captured the national imagination, even if conservation efforts have failed, dismally, to keep pace with land use transformations. Everglades National Park was created in 1947 and subsequently recognized in 1976 as an International Biosphere Reserve, in 1979 as a World Heritage site, and in 1987 as a Wetland of International Importance. Big Cypress National Preserve was designated in 1974, after the Big Cypress Swamp had nearly been turned into a giant jetport complex. In 1982, Governor Bob Graham broke with Florida tradition and—with the support of the Everglades Coalition—shepherded into place the Save Our Everglades project. Main project elements included Kissimmee River restoration, adoption of best management practices on dairy farms north of Lake Okeechobee, dechannelization of drainage canals, and state acquisition of critical lands. All this had to be done without significant federal support, which the Reagan administration was unwilling to provide.

Save Our Everglades, as big a project as it was, was designed to fix links in the ecological chain rather than repair the whole system (Grunwald 2006). It would be almost two decades, following rounds of political wrangling and litigation, before the next megaproject would commence. The plan that emerged—the Comprehensive Everglades Restoration Plan (CERP)—followed exhaustive meetings and multiple compromises in the U.S. Congress and Florida legislature. It is a science-based ecosystem management plan, incorporating principles developed by the U.S. Man and the Biosphere program (Harwell et al. 1999). Yet it is also very much a negotiated political settlement. In order to get a plan, "big sugar" and other major resource interests were brought on board. Secretary of the Interior Bruce Babbitt had negotiated an earlier deal—enshrined in

Florida's 1994 Everglades Forever Act—under which federal phosphorous pollution lawsuits would be dropped and forty thousand acres of filter marshes would be built by the state of Florida. Sugar growers would have to pay only a part of the marsh construction costs, spread over a period of twenty years. Sugar growers also escaped a "penny-a-pound" tax, after Florida voters narrowly rejected it, and instead became beneficiaries of federal buyout funds for retiring fifty thousand cropland acres. Though troubling equity questions about these cost-sharing arrangements persist, the phosphorous reduction program is, to date, an Everglades success story. Phosphorous discharges have been reduced more than 50 percent through a combination of agricultural management practices and marsh filtration. CERP provides for additional federally funded filter marshes (Grunwald 2006).

Though many environmentalists were deeply dismayed with final CERP compromises, enough were willing to support it to avert a last-minute train wreck. There was no real alternative in the wings; the CERP plan appeared to be the "last best chance" for the Everglades. The signing ceremony took place at the White House in December 2000, just as the U.S. Supreme Court was hearing final arguments in the Bush versus Gore case. Led by the U.S. Army Corps of Engineers and South Florida Water Management District, CERP carries a price tag of $7.8 billion, to be shared equally by the federal government and a combination of state, tribal, and local entities. Given its sixty-eight separate projects, spread over thirty-eight years, many expect that figure to go much higher (Grunwald 2006).

CERP relies heavily on Corps of Engineers–style structural approaches (figure 4.6), but it is not a conventional structural engineering project. Instead, it entails a combination of construction and deconstruction. Water would be held during the dry season, in huge above- and below-ground reservoirs, to be released during the wet season (Vos 2004; U.S. Department of the Interior and U.S. Army Corps of Engineers 2005; Grunwald 2006). Water needs for agriculture, mining, and community uses would be met, and water would also be directed toward restoring natural flow patterns. But human uses come first; South Florida's population is allowed to double under CERP—and water is made available to support that growth. Indeed, in CERP's first incarnation, the Everglades were almost ignored. Then, under intense pressure from the environmental

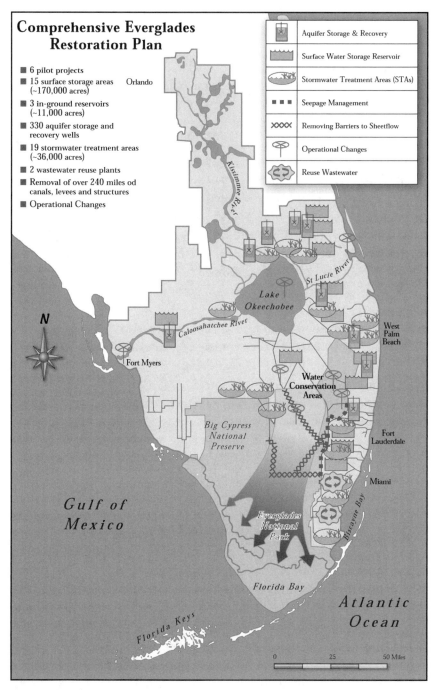

Comprehensive Everglades Restoration Plan

- 6 pilot projects
- 15 surface storage areas (~170,000 acres)
- 3 in-ground reservoirs (~11,000 acres)
- 330 aquifer storage and recovery wells
- 19 stormwater treatment areas (~36,000 acres)
- 2 wastewater reuse plants
- Removal of over 240 miles od canals, levees and structures
- Operational Changes

Aquifer Storage & Recovery	
Surface Water Storage Reservoir	
Stormwater Treatment Areas (STAs)	
Seepage Management	
Removing Barriers to Sheetflow	
Operational Changes	
Reuse Wastewater	

Figure 4.6.   Comprehensive Everglades Restoration Plan
Source: South Florida Water Management District

community and its political and financial allies, a "watered-down" environmental restoration commitment became part of the plan. Ecosystem management is the plan's celebrated rationale—but the loopholes are in the details (Grunwald 2006).

CERP's objective is to restore something resembling traditional flow patterns to an Everglades region that is effectively half the size of the original Everglades. It is a mammoth regional plumbing experiment, the Army Corps version of adaptive management. CERP's many uncertainties mean that the plan will be adapted and adjusted in many ways during its implementation. Not only political adjustments but also technical to habitat conservation planningadjustments can be expected. Questions persist, for example, about whether or not the huge quarries that store water will actually be leakproof, as planned.

Project critics argue that the level of government coordination required by the scheme may be impossible to achieve, that water supply needs are favored over ecological restoration, that pilot projects are not being completed on schedule (none have yet been completed), and that various technological and cost uncertainties may mean generally flawed implementation (Vos 2004; Grunwald 2006; Sheikh and Carter 2006). Though CERP is billed as adaptive ecosystem management, quiet revolution regulatory approaches have been shunned in many instances. As the region is replumbed, residential and commercial growth will continue almost unabated outside the parks and preserves. Though Florida was a quiet revolution pioneer, its sprawl management efforts in the Everglades' vicinity lack the teeth to significantly slow the spread of golf courses, gated communities, and office complexes that are mushrooming outside the protected Everglades areas. Nor are effective quieter approaches coming in to fill the gap.

In the end, CERP is not so much about collaborative local planning as it is about compromise among major players. It is a structural strategy first and a behavioral and land use approach a distant second. Everglades proponents—as well as those who profit exorbitantly from South Florida's resource base—invoke sense of place and the memory of Marjory Stoneman Douglas, the celebrated author and Everglades activist, at every opportunity. But CERP is really big planning—big structural planning—for the twenty-first century. Land and easement acquisitions do play a large part, with as many as two hundred thousand acres yet to be protected. But this is not the brand of place-based, collaborative planning so central to most quieter revolution initiatives. It is, however, cited as a model for other major environmental management projects, such as restoring Iraq's marshes, which were destroyed by Saddam Hussein. In the United States, some see it as an exemplar for the Chesapeake Bay watershed and Great Lakes cleanups, as well as restoration of Louisiana's coastal marshes, described below (Grunwald 2006).

Habitat Conservation Planning in Southern California

One of the most contentious pieces of federal environmental legislation is the Endangered Species Act (ESA). This one law can stop logging, prevent dam construction, and bring major residential development projects grinding to a halt—all in the service of a single listed species. That is because the ESA prohibits the "take"—that is, killing or harming—of a listed species or its habitat on public or private land. The ESA is perhaps enemy number one for the wise use and property rights movements (chapter 7), but for environmentalists it is a savior. Those seeking a third way, like former president Clinton, began promoting a multispecies approach to habitat conservation planning in the 1990s.

Habitat conservation planning, as this approach is also known, is famously exemplified in the Northwest Forest Plan, which seeks to balance local economic needs with habitat protection for the northern spotted owl and other species (DellaSala and Williams 2006). Bruce Babbitt, as Clinton's secretary of the interior and subsequently as private citizen, has promoted this approach widely (Babbitt 2005).

Though the ESA prohibits the "take" of listed species, the secretary of the interior can allow a take in certain circumstances—and this regulatory flexibility is central to habitat conservation plans (HCPs). HCPs are built around agreement among an applicant, the U.S. Fish and Wildlife Service (FWS), and additional stakeholders. Once this is negotiated and formally approved, FWS issues an "incidental take permit," which relieves the applicant of liability if an endangered species or critical habitat is harmed during project implementation. The applicant must have in place mitigation strategies; these may include anything from translocation of species to payment of a development fee. Typically, the regional plan will specify areas of habitat protection, where development is strictly regulated or prohibited, and other places where development can be allowed, subject to various rules. All of this is negotiated and decentralized in its implementation (Beatley 1994; Duerksen et al. 1997; Noss, O'Connell, and Murphy 1997).

The first HCP was developed in 1983, and by 1992 only fourteen more permits had been issued for HCPs. But in the early 1990s and beyond, HCP activity took off. Secretary Babbitt, a powerful HCP advocate, streamlined the HCP process, emphasized social and economic cost-effectiveness, and instituted the "no-surprises" policy, which protects landowners from any imposition of new restrictions beyond the original HCP terms. Other "second-generation" (Bean 2006) ESA enhancements include Safe Harbor Agreements, which encourage private landowners to agree to habitat protection steps beyond those required by law; Candidate Conservation Agreements, which may ensure sufficient protection to keep a candidate species from being listed; and funding programs directed toward private landowners.

As of mid-April 2007, FWS had approved 505 HCPs (U.S. Fish and Wildlife Service 2007). While there are a great many small HCPs, ranging all the way down to those that apply to small residential lots, several regional plans range over millions of acres. The largest of the HCPs are in the western states and Alaska.

Regional-scale HCPs can be the basis for comprehensive regional planning—but do any live up to this potential? Most regional HCPs rely on large-scale reserves as their main mitigation measures because this is the cleanest, simplest way to offset impacts of incidental takes of protected species. Fees assessed upon developers, who build in permitted parts of a region, are used to purchase and maintain habitat lands in other parts of the region. Most protected areas are managed by local governments and land trusts (Thompson 2006).

Areas not designated as reserves might be subject to habitat-related conditions governing forestry, agriculture, construction, and other practices. But landowners are resistant to such government intrusion; indeed, farmers and ranchers often choose not to participate in HCPs when they fear that farming practices will be regulated. Agencies, too, are reluctant, because of the difficulty of defining loophole-free conditions, as well as the extensive and costly monitoring required (Thompson 2006). In a few instances, though, working-lands management is fully integrated with

HCP planning. Thompson (2006) cites the Natomas Basin Habitat Conservation Plan, which covers an area north of Sacramento. Here, a local land trust acquires lands and then leases them to rice farmers. The trust, recognizing the value of rice lands as habitat, requires farmers to adopt "best practicable" management practices. Under the Wisconsin Karner Blue Butterfly Habitat Conservation Plan, logging and utility companies have agreed to promote habitat on their own lands and to encourage private landowners to adopt habitat-friendly practices.

But administrative expedience often triumphs over elaborate integrated planning. A study conducted by the University of Michigan School of Natural Resources (Anderson and Yaffee 1998) finds that the multistakeholder HCP process often is inadequately managed by FWS. The agency's priorities are more with streamlining the process, maintaining congressional support for the ESA, and ensuring that landowners are satisfied. Other stakeholders, in most of the HCP cases studies, were not fully brought into the process. Doremus (2006), too, takes issue with HCP, finding the process imposes too many built-in barriers to public participation.

Long before there was an ESA, states had primary responsibility for wildlife management. And they continue to play lead roles today (Niles and Korth 2006). Some states have developed exemplary habitat conservation programs, and California is exemplary among the exemplary. Its Natural Community Conservation Planning (NCCP) program, begun in 1991, is similar to the federal HCP program but is adapted to California's ecoregions (figure 4.7). While NCCP plans involving federally listed species ultimately are subject to FWS approval, NCCP's general approach seeks to be broader, more flexible, and more predictable than the federal one (Randolph 2004).

NCCP areas have been designated throughout the state, but they overlay the Southern California coastal landscape in a dense patchwork fashion (figure 4.7). This region is extraordinarily rich in biological diversity but also faces tremendous growth pressure, traffic congestion, and water supply problems. More than 80 percent of the area's original coastal sage scrub habitat has been replaced with other forms of land cover. During the 1980s, habitat protection for the kangaroo rat in Riverside County and the tiny California gnatcatcher, in Orange County, became flashpoint issues. These controversies played a large part in bringing NCCP into being in 1991. Yet habitat conservation is but one dimension in a regional

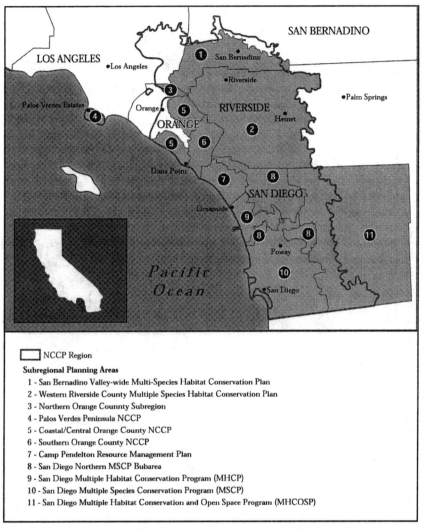

Figure 4.7. Southern California Coastal Sage Scrub NCCP Region
Source: Natural Community Conservation Planning (NCCP) Program

planning matrix that includes land conservation, housing development, and transportation planning.

As figure 4.7 suggests, habitat conservation planning, Southern California–style, is a complex quiltwork. Physical conditions, demographic characteristics, population densities, and political cultures vary tremendously across the subregions. Traditionally, water and development interests have dominated land use decision making in Southern California. But the growth coalition (Logan and Molotch 1987; Jonas and Wilson 1999) that includes bankers, chambers of commerce, builders, and other leading economic interests has broadened in recent years, to accommodate environmental and other NGO representatives, freelance individual activists, homeowners, and others (Pincetl 2004). This diversity of interests, in combination with the legal landscape that has evolved since the 1970s, means a less unitary focus on economic development and much greater attention to growth management and habitat protection.

Pincetl (2004) examines NCCP programs county by county. Orange County was an early NCCP adopter, driven by fears in the early 1990s of federal listing of the California gnatcatcher. Though there is much variation within Orange County, generally the county is proactive in working to protect habitat in advance of the march of development. In Riverside County, strategic efforts to acquire land and easements are under way in the rapidly developing western part of the county, whereas in the eastern part of the county, where development pressure is less intense, greater effort can go into creating large reserves in anticipation of future development patterns. But rather little planning coordination takes place between the eastern and western parts of Riverside County. San Bernardino and Los Angeles counties presently have the least habitat preservation activity. Ventura County is particularly concerned with protecting agricultural lands and has consistently deployed a variety of growth management techniques.

From all this, Pincetl (2004) sees a new urban growth regime emerging. It involves government actors at multiple levels, private landowners, and NGO representatives. The Nature Conservancy and the Trust for Public Land are especially active in several Southern California counties, purchasing land and easements and becoming involved in multistakeholder negotiations. In a larger context, Wolch, Pastor, and Dreier (2004) also are hopeful about Southern California's future. For one thing, despite the extravagant huge-lot sprawl in some places, most of the region's new development is at much more modest densities. Indeed, infill development and development adjacent to existing settlement is quite the norm. But beyond this, the hope is that "equity-based regional planning" will prevail. This entails new coalitions—in place of the traditional growth coalitions—advancing equity-based regionalism, sustainability, and a smart-growth agenda that meaningfully addresses the full range of regional concerns. Wolch, Pastor, and Dreier (2004) believe that Southern California may just be starting to "get it," with emerging coalitions working on issues of affordable housing, transportation needs of poorer residents, and habitat for endangered species. Perhaps California will once again show the nation the way.

Sierra Nevada Ecoregion

The "Range of Light"—America's longest continuous mountain chain outside Alaska—is variously associated with the California gold rush, Sierra Club founder John Muir, crown-jewel national parks, logging communities, spotted owl and old-growth forest controversies, hippies and communes, residential and commercial sprawl, gambling casinos, ski resorts, and "New West" sensibilities about place. The Sierra Club (2007a) has its home region as part of the Pacific Coast ecoregion (figure 4.3), while Foreman's (2004) Wildlands Project places it in the Pacific Mega-Linkage (figure 4.1). At a finer resolution, this fast-changing region might best be regarded as a set of diverse subregions. The simplest subdivision is one of northern and southern ecoregions, but Duane (1998) goes further, dividing the Sierra Nevada into six subregions: Gold Country, Lake Tahoe, Northern Sierra, Mother Lode, Eastern Sierra, and Southern Sierra (figure 4.8).

Approximately 60 percent of the Sierra Nevada ecoregion is in federal ownership. Eldorado, Inyo, Lassen, Plumas, Sequoia, Sierra, Stanislaus, Tahoe, and Toiyabe national forests account for over 80 percent of these lands, with Kings Canyon, Sequoia, and Yosemite national parks totaling about 10 percent; remaining federal lands are under Bureau of Land Management administration. Nearly one-third of the public lands are designated as wilderness (Duane 1998).

Though no overarching Sierra Nevada planning program is in place, various projects, organizations, and programs are or have been active. One

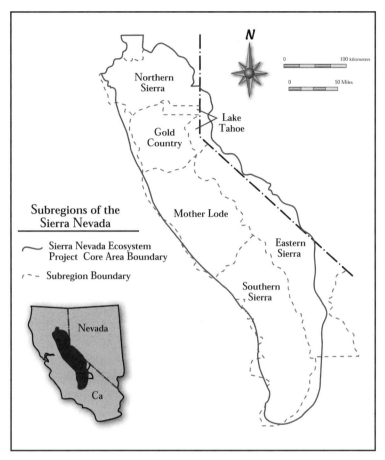

Figure 4.8. Sierra Nevada Subregions
Source: Duane (1998), 82.

of the original quiet revolution programs is the bistate Tahoe Regional Planning Agency, included in the Bosselman and Callies (1971) quiet revolution monograph and briefly discussed earlier in this book (chapter 2). Following the *Sacramento Bee*'s 1991 publication of a Pulitzer Prize–winning five-part series of critical articles titled "Majesty and Tragedy: The Sierra in Peril," concerns about the region's future were stirred. It was in this climate that the Sierra Summit was convened in November 1991, followed by a series of contentious regional workshops in 1992 (Duane 1998). In 1993, Congress authorized the Sierra Nevada Ecosystem Project (SNEP), a detailed regional ecological assessment. Completed in

1996, the SNEP study is a comprehensive three-volume state-of-the-region scientific appraisal (Sierra Nevada Ecosystem Project 1996). While it is optimistic about prospects for collaborative, adaptive ecosystem management, at the same time it is vague on how to achieve it, especially how to fund it.

The Sierra Nevada Alliance, comparable to the Greater Yellowstone Coalition and Northern Forest Alliance described below, was founded in 1993. Its wide-ranging list of members includes land trusts, watershed associations, chapters of major national environmental organizations, and smart growth and recreation associations. The alliance seeks to provide a unified voice for Sierra activists; deliver technical, legal, and organizational support to partner organizations; build coalitions and foster collaboration; and engage in public education and outreach activities. Program activities include watershed restoration, encouraging adoption of concentrated development and open-space protection provisions in county plans, making habitat enhancement and restoration part of the development process, and ensuring economic as well as environmental sustainability (Sierra Nevada Alliance 2007). Like its Rocky Mountain and northeastern counterparts, the alliance's strengths are in research, technical assistance, outreach, and fostering collaborative relationships. Besides the alliance, the Sierra Business Council (2007) produces a wealth of information on regional, economic, social, and physical conditions; the state of regional agriculture; and community land use planning and economic development strategies. As Innes and Rongerude (2006) put it, the council is a civic entrepreneur, helping to fill the governance gap by raising awareness and building a sense of region.

As demographic, economic, and social forces continue to transform the Sierra Nevada ecoregion, local responses to environmental threats are emerging, quite unevenly, through the area (Duane 1998; Dardick 1999). Though the traditional, mainly resource-based economy is giving way, especially in the Gold County, Tahoe, eastern, and southern regions (figure 4.8), this does not mean that a fully formed, New West environmental ethic is taking root. While new migrants may support environmental protection more than old-timers, at least as measured by public attitude survey questions, they do not necessarily walk the walk of environmentally sustainable lifestyles and smaller ecological footprints. For one thing, the sheer number of new residents—all requiring roads, services, and amenities—imposes enormous environmental burdens. Many new arrivals live in gated communities and drive huge SUVs. Granted, the gas guzzlers' impacts may be more global than local, but lifestyle choices do speak to environmentalism as practiced. One of the greatest threats to regional ecological integrity is posed by large-lot housing development, which fragments habitat and increases fire-related risks (Duane 1998). While new residents usually are more supportive of regional planning than old-timers, their interest often is driven by exclusionary impulses. But perhaps all this is irrelevant to ecosystem management advocates, who must recruit allies where they can be found, however conflicted their environmental or social ethics. Indeed, ecosystem management is inclusive by definition, and all stakeholders are welcomed into the planning process.

California has a fairly aggressive agricultural land protection program (chapter 6). And the Golden State is the land of the ballot question, local as well as statewide. In the Sierra region, Placer County voters are liberal in their approval of open-space acquisition funding (Trust for Public Land 2007b). Several local and statewide land trusts are active in the region (Land Trust Alliance 2006). And the "moderate growth" coalitions popping up in the northern Sierras—in Nevada, Sierra, Placer, and El Dorado counties—are succeeding in drafting forest management plans and stymieing some individual resort and big-box development projects. While a regional collaborative infrastructure is emerging (Innes and Rongerude 2006), the optimism with which Dardick (1999) greets these collective developments may be a bit premature. In his view, the more moderate constituencies have turned the tide, prevailing over the old "development at any cost" local regimes.

In Duane's estimation, no single quieter-style approach is sufficient to stem the tide of agricultural and open-space conversion over the larger region. While some subregions may be more effective at addressing sprawl's impacts than others, the most effective strategy overall, he argues, is a combination of techniques (Duane 1998, 309):

- Strict regulation in sensitive areas (e.g., existing use zoning)

- Clear identification of targeted development areas (e.g., within an urban growth boundary)

- Full infrastructure cost recovery (e.g., pricing policies that encourage more compact infill where infrastructure already exists)

- Property tax incentives for preservation (e.g., Williamson Act and TPZ designations)

- Conservation easements (e.g., through landowner donations as part of the development approval process or purchase by open-space districts)

- Fee-title acquisition (e.g., by the city, county, or an open-space district)

Duane particularly favors conservation subdivision design, which reduces the environmental footprint of new residential subdivisions. Creative design techniques are employed to increase residential density, maximizing public open space while minimizing the amount of private space needed to maintain a sense of household privacy (Arendt 1996; Randolph 2004).

Advocates of collaborative, place-based planning (Duane 1998; Dardick 1999; Sierra Business Council 2007) vest their hopes in a sort of "thousand points of light" strategy, involving face-to-face contact, social networks, and town meetings in communities across the region. The resultant social capital, their thinking goes, will build community capacity needed to cope with the threat and impacts of rapid development. But until some of Duane's favored strategies, listed above, are embraced at the multimunicipal and regional levels, we are likely to continue to have highly uneven environmental management patterns across the Sierra Nevada. Less-planned development will, naturally, occur in places with less planning.

Columbia River Gorge Scenic Area

Is the Columbia River Gorge National Scenic Area (CRGNSA) (figure 4.9) another example of a linear greenway (chapter 6)? a public-private greenline park (chapter 2)? a stretch of scenic river with major dams that preclude a federal scenic river designation? Yes to all three, but it also is something more. It is the country's first national scenic area, and it includes considerable acreages on both the Washington and Oregon sides of

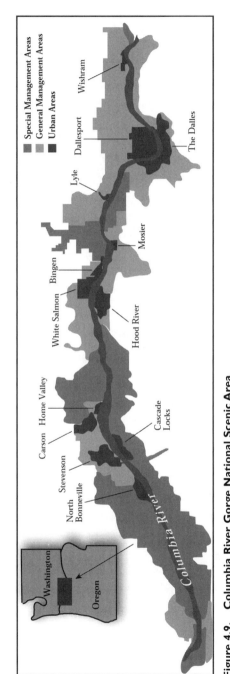

Figure 4.9. Columbia River Gorge National Scenic Area
Source: Columbia River Gorge Commission

the river. What it is not, principally, is an ecosystem management project, even though it is part of the much larger Columbia River Basin, where vital timber and salmon resources make for highly contentious environmental planning issues (Lee 1989; Blumm 1997; Weaver 1997).

Abbott, Adler, and Abbott (1997) see the CRGNSA as an icon of the New West, that land of majestic natural amenities, thriving urban centers, high-tech exurban oases, and growing service sectors and creative classes (Riebsame 1997; Duane 1998; Jackson and Kuhlken 2006). Its inhabitants, in Abbott, Adler, and Abbott's (1997, 6) words, "tend to look out their windows and see scenery, not resources, thus modifying the meanings of place." The scenic area was created in 1986, through congressional legislation calling for protection and enhancement of the area's scenic, cultural, natural, and recreational resources, as well as economic development consistent with those goals and population growth directed toward existing urban centers. A bistate compact, authorized by the legislation, places most management responsibility with the states of Oregon and Washington. The CRGNSA is an example of a greenline park, which seeks to sustain a "working landscape," balancing local economic sustainability with environmental sustainability (Mason 1994; Abbott, Adler, and Abbott 1997; Hamin 2001; see also chapter 2).

Concerns about urban sprawl and second-home development drove the interest in a regional plan. Environmentalists led the charge, mobilized through a "friends group"—Friends of the Columbia River Gorge. At the same time, property rights interests vigorously opposed the project. The plan is not as regulatory as its quiet revolution greenline-park predecessors, such as New York's Adirondack Park and New Jersey's Pinelands National Reserve (chapter 2). Nor is it as enforceable as Oregon's land use program, though CRGNSA's Oregon lands do come under the state's regulatory overlay. While the federal government is not directly engaged in local planning, the U.S. Forest Service's administrative role is a red flag and rallying cry for the regional scheme's opponents. The CRGNSA plan, administered by the Columbia River Gorge Commission, is organized around broad themes of protecting and enhancing scenic, cultural, natural, and recreational resources (Columbia River Gorge National Scenic Area 2007). As with most regional plans, CRGNSA's reflects multiple compromises among various interests. Though federal management of the area had been proposed—as one of several options—that option came off the table as the legislative process moved forward. Both Oregon and Washington called for a stronger role for state and local governments; this was especially so with Washington, where Governor Dixie Lee Ray was a leading national critic of much mainstream environmental thinking. In the end, mandatory land acquisition provisions were eliminated from the plan, a proposed development moratorium was dropped, and economic concessions were made to the timber industry. Funds were made available for local economic development projects and payments in lieu of taxes to localities. And the U.S. Forest Service, with its multiple-purpose, resource-based mission—rather than the more protection-oriented National Park Service—reluctantly became the lead federal agency (Abbott, Adler, and Abbott 1997).

Total scenic area acreage is 292,630 acres, with about 70 percent of it in private ownership. Total population in 1987 was approximately fifty-two thousand (Abbott, Adler, and Abbott 1997, 8). Figure 4.9 shows the three CRGNSA management areas. The regional plan is a general zoning scheme that provides broad guidance but lacks the regulatory force characteristic of many quiet revolution predecessor plans. Yet there is a quiet element to gorge planning, in that the Columbia River Gorge Commission must approve county plans; in the absence of an approved plan, the commission is empowered to become the local planning authority for general management area (GMA) lands. This is more than a mere threat; it has been done in some instances (Abbott, Adler, and Abbott 1997).

The special management area (SMA) covers 115,100 acres, mostly national forest lands. The Forest Service is charged with creating and implementing a management plan for these lands. Under the plan, little new development is to occur on private lands within the SMA. The general management area (GMA) consists of 149,004 acres, mostly privately owned. These are "working lands," with a mix of resource uses and some housing. Urban areas, 28,511 acres in total, are exempt from the general management plan, but governments can receive economic development and other federal grants if they cooperate with plan implementation. The general objective is to concentrate new development in existing urban areas. Although the plan has quite specific land use prescriptions, implementation is largely left to county and local governments. In contrast with New York's Adirondacks and New Jersey's Pinelands, the gorge commission does not have the power to override local decisions.

Abbott, Adler, and Abbott (1997) see the CRGNSA as a triumph of the New West over the old. Though many concessions had to be made, the Friends of the Columbia River Gorge and the largely metropolitan-based interests it represents triumphed over the local resource-based stakeholders and national representatives of the property rights movement who joined in the battle. And this broad victory may hasten the transition toward a different kind of place, not only through the general planning prescriptions themselves but also through approval of such commercial activities as "bed-and-breakfast inns, cottage industries, and home occupations" in designated growth areas (Abbott, Sy, and Abbott 1997, 137). Though federal funding for land acquisition is very limited, the national Trust for Public Land (TPL) and local Columbia Trust have stepped in, quieter revolution style. TPL works with the Forest Service, acquiring lands and transferring them into public ownership. In 1991, TPL purchased the small, rundown historic settlement of Bridal Veil, situated within the GMA at the western end of the gorge. In a controversial move, TPL evicted the residents and destroyed the homes, arguing that they had been too altered to retain historic value (Abbott, Sy, and Abbott 1997). This action brings into sharp relief differing versions of place, one that values local places, rustic blemishes and all, versus another that emphasizes ecological integrity and public access. These dueling visions continue to play out in quieter revolution programs across the country.

Greater Yellowstone Ecoregion

The Greater Yellowstone initiative principally involves public lands. And while federal lands management is not one of this book's themes, the Greater Yellowstone Ecoregion is sufficiently large, complex, contentious, and exemplary to warrant some attention here. Moreover, as is typically the case with such projects, substantial acreages of private lands *are* included. Private landowners are concerned not only about the Greater Yellowstone plan's consequences for their lands but also the impacts of a whole host of public, private, and NGO actions in the region. One prominent example is the Church Universal and Triumphant's plans for the twelve-thousand-acre Royal Teton Ranch, adjacent to Yellowstone National Park, which it had purchased from Malcolm Forbes in 1981. The church, anticipating the nuclear holocaust predicted by leader Elizabeth Clare Prophet, began building underground fallout shelters in the mid-

1980s. This galvanized concern from many quarters because the church planned to tap into the geothermal groundwaters that are Yellowstone's defining feature. Though the Carter administration had sought to purchase the land in 1980, the Reagan administration dropped the deal. President Clinton's Interior Department, using Land and Water Conservation Fund monies, spent $13 million in 1999 to acquire nine thousand acres plus rights, via easement, to the groundwater (Wald 1999). The church episode has been and continues to be (the church still owns land, and there are still cattle grazing issues) high on the Greater Yellowstone Coalition's agenda.

Yellowstone's name recognition makes it an ideal focal point for a major environmental campaign. Yellowstone National Park, designated in 1872, is generally regarded as the world's first national park. Formal international recognition came in 1972 with designation as a United Nations Biosphere Reserve and again in 1978, with ascension to the World Heritage list. Despite its iconic status, Yellowstone's management history always has been contentious, pitting issues of resource use against scenic and ecological preservation. Congress approved the park's initial designation only after being convinced that Yellowstone was too rugged and inaccessible to be of value for resource extraction yet still capable of attracting lucrative tourist traffic. In recent decades, intense battles have erupted over wolf reintroduction, government responses to the 1988 fires that overspread nearly half the park's lands, proposed removal of grizzly bears from the endangered species list, and snowmobile use in the park, recently approved by the Bush administration (Chase 1986; Mason and Mattson 1990; Keiter and Boyce 1991; Runte 1997; Wilson 1997). The Greater Yellowstone initiative only adds more fuel to these long-raging fires.

The Greater Yellowstone Ecosystem (GYE) (figure 4.10) covers fifteen million acres and is overseen by more than two dozen government entities, federal to local. Within the region are Yellowstone and Glacier national parks, and Beaver, Bridger-Teton, Caribou, Custer, Gallatin, Targhee, and Shoshone national forests. Though most GYE lands are federal lands, the National Park Service and U.S. Forest Service—as we have already observed—have quite different missions. Parks are to be preserved for future generations, while forests are to be sustainably managed—per conservationist Gifford Pinchot's maxim about the greatest good for the greatest number over the longest time—for multiple uses. Among those

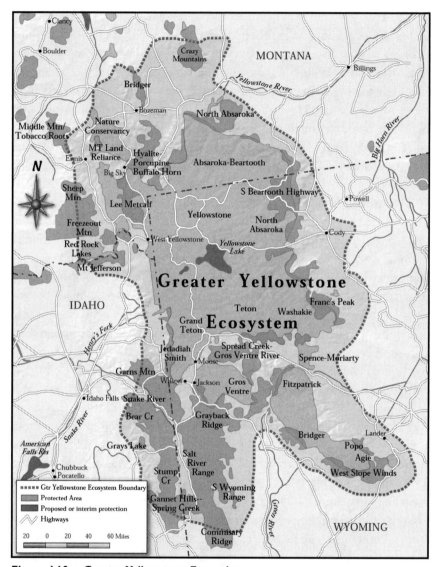

Figure 4.10.   Greater Yellowstone Ecoregion
Source: Yellowstone to Yukon Conservation Initiative

uses are timber cutting, mining, ranching, flood control, irrigation, and recreation. Proponents of a GYE framework call for a broad regional approach that embraces unity of purpose, interagency coordination, and science-based management (Clark and Harvey 1990). What they propose is a cooperative, integrative ecosystem management model, inclusive of humans but guided by overarching ecological principles.

Following several years of study, the National Park Service and U.S. Forest Service produced a draft "vision" document, outlining a framework for coordinated GYE management (U.S. Department of Agriculture, Forest Service, and U.S. Department of the Interior, National Park Service 1990). The report describes fourteen goals and many subgoals, but the essential points are three: "(1) conserve the sense of naturalness and maintain ecosystem integrity; (2) encourage opportunities that are biologically and economically sustainable; and (3) improve coordination" (Freemuth and Cawley 1998, 213). The report met with intense criticism, especially from the wise use/property rights community (chapter 7). A second draft was released in 1991, affirming the separate missions of the Park Service and Forest Service. While the revised document still stressed coordinated ecosystem management, it had been purged of any hint of a commitment to implementing ecoregional planning (Freemuth and Cawley 1998).

Although no new regulation was proposed, most local, resource-dependent interests vigorously oppose the Greater Yellowstone project. Those directly dependent on tourism might be expected to support the initiative, but even they are rather reluctant to fully embrace ecosystem management, results of a late 1980s survey show (Reading and Clark 1994). Deeper opposition comes from loggers, miners, and ranchers, who are still simmering about wolf reintroduction and grizzly protection policies. They see "ecosystem management" as code for a vision that excludes them (Freemuth and Cawley 1998). Even though the region's economic fortunes have long depended heavily on federal investment and subsidies, the GYE initiative is viewed as a menacing, meddlesome expansion of government control.

Not only did the GYE vision invoke the wrath of an energized local opposition, it also failed to draw much support from major national environmental organizations (Freemuth and Cawley 1998). The megavision has to be regarded largely—though not totally, as we see below—as a quieter revolution failure. Though Lichtman and Clark (1994) argue that the process would have fared better had there been improved education, more meaningful communication, more clearly stated goals, and sounder technical analyses, they recognize the limits of such approaches. Still, they do not regard the GYE experience as a complete failure—and indeed, there is more to the story than the initiative's painful rejection. First of all, some ecosystem management objectives have been achieved: wolves were reintroduced, grizzly bear policies generally support healthy bear populations, and the Yellowstone snowmobile policy, while allowing the machine into the garden, does so with many restrictions. Second, tourism and recreation now outpace extractive industries in economic value (Power 1991). This trend is likely to be sustained, perhaps gradually bringing with it public opinions more accommodating toward ecosystem management. Finally, there is a place for quieter revolution action without the larger vision framework. Small, place-based collaborative projects are materializing in parts of the region. Easement purchases are taking place on private lands; recently The Nature Conservancy, Trust for Public Land, the Conservation Fund, Gallatin Valley Land Trust, Teton Regional Land Trust, Gallatin County, and other entities have been acquiring farm and ranchland conservation easements in the region. Major support comes from the Doris Duke Foundation, which identifies the GYE as a national biodiversity "hotspot."

And the Greater Yellowstone vision lives on in other ways. The Northern Rockies Ecosystem Protection Act has been introduced in Congress every year since 1993—in its latest incarnation as the Rockies Prosperity Act. The act would create new wilderness areas, 4.2 million acres of them in the GYE; study the creation of a Flathead National Park and Preserve; add river segments to the National Wild and Scenic River System; establish ecological restoration projects; and create biological corridors to connect core ecosystems. Two ecoregional organizations, Alliance for the Wild Rockies (2007) and Wild Rockies Action Fund (2007), are relentlessly promoting the legislation and the larger vision. The Yellowstone to Yukon (Y2Y) initiative promotes conservation over seventeen Rocky Mountain subregions reaching from the Yukon Territory in the north to the Greater Yellowstone Ecosystem in the south. Supported by foundation and other NGO funding, Y2Y focuses on research, outreach, and creation of wildlife corridors across highways, towns, and resort areas (Clark and Gaillard 2001; Schulz 2005; Yellowstone to Yukon Conservation Initiative 2005; Dean 2006). At an even grander scale, Foreman (2004) identifies the "Spine of the Continent MegaLinkage," reaching from Alaska to South America (figure 4.1); the GYE is one of the jewels in the continent's crown.

New York/New Jersey/Pennsylvania/Connecticut Highlands

Here we focus on one small part of the Appalachian region: the New York/New Jersey/Pennsylvania/Connecticut Highlands subregion. As figure 4.11 shows, this band of land is near to, but physically separate from, the Catskill Mountain region from which New York City draws water. Though its highest elevations are only around two thousand feet, the rocky, windy, exposed ridge tops very much resemble those of the higher Appalachian peaks to which they are physiographically linked. But why separate out this subregion? The case for doing so is more political, economic, demographic, and administrative than it is geomorphic. This region is very close to—and portions of it are included within—the New York metropolitan area. Despite constraints imposed by steep slopes, thin soils, fragile ecosystems, and limited public transportation options, much of the region is very attractive not only to New York area commuters building first and second homes but also to light industry, shopping malls, ski resorts, and other recreation facilities. Regional population growth averaged 11.5 percent between 1990 and 2000. Recent development patterns threaten the region's biological integrity, mainly through habitat fragmentation and alteration. But open space and ecosystems are being at least partially protected, with approximately 20 percent of the Highlands area currently in some sort of protected status; more than half of that protected land is under state management. Yet half the land area not currently protected is described as "critical" in a 2002 U.S. Forest Service report (Phelps and Hoppe 2002).

Suburban and exurban sprawl is a huge Highlands issue. Counties in nearby northeastern Pennsylvania—dominated by the Pocono plateau but separate from the New York/New Jersey effort described below—experienced exceptionally rapid growth between 1990 and 2000: Pike at 65.2 percent, Monroe at 44.9 percent, and Wayne at 19.5 percent. Counties in New York, New Jersey, and Connecticut had much lower growth rates, but they are more populated (higher base populations) and more built out to begin with. Even so, several New York/New Jersey counties

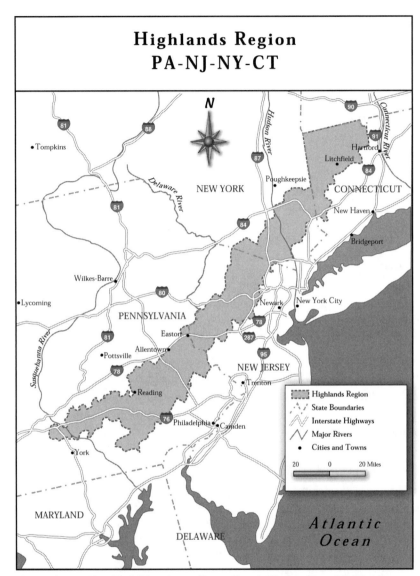

Figure 4.11. New York/New Jersey/Pennsylvania/Connecticut Highlands Subregion
Source: U.S. Department of Agriculture Forest Service, Northeastern Area

situated partially within the Highlands had double-digit population increases between 1990 and 2000.

First studied in the early 1990s in New Jersey by the New Jersey Conservation Foundation (Mitchell 1992) and in New York and New Jersey by the Forest Service (Michaels et al. 1992), the New York/New Jersey Highlands region is the focus of a comprehensive report authorized under the 1990 Farm Bill and released in 2002 (Phelps and Hoppe 2002). The Highlands Stewardship Act, passed by Congress in 2004, extends the regional definition to include portions of northwestern Connecticut and eastern Pennsylvania. The latest Forest Service study covers the expanded area (USDA Forest Service, Northeastern Area 2007). As already noted, the new study does not include Pennsylvania's Poconos counties; it is limited physiographically to the Reading Prong. Situated to the Poconos' south, this geomorphic feature is a continuation of the New Jersey area included in the New York/New Jersey Highlands designation. The Poconos region, though identified by The Nature Conservancy as a last great place, does not receive the same level of federal and state attention as the Highlands. In part, this may be because Pennsylvania has not placed the same priority on regional environmental protection as have New York and New Jersey. More telling may be that the federal resources targeted to those two states reflect the power and persistence of their House and Senate members.

The Highlands is aptly described as a land of overlapping regions and subregions, whose political boundaries have immense consequences for environmental management. Though the New York/New Jersey border may be invisible physiographically, it separates two environmental policy systems. And the Highlands region is further fractured by many municipal boundaries. At another level, there are the synthetic regions. The "Skylands" is a tourism region, designated mainly for marketing reasons, that covers much of northern New Jersey. New York State's corresponding designation—the Hudson Valley region—includes within it New York's Highlands. Two more recently designated areas—the Hudson River Valley National Heritage Area and Hudson River Valley Greenway—slice through New York's share of the Highlands region. And in 2004, New Jersey created a new planning area, almost entirely coincident with its share of the Highlands shown in figure 4.11, where it is implementing a quiet revolution–type regulatory program.

CHAPTER FOUR

The 2002 New York/New Jersey Highlands Regional Study (Phelps and Hoppe 2002), covering an area just over 1.4 million acres in size, is guided by an ambitious suite of goals first set forth in the 1992 Forest Service study:

1. Manage future growth;

2. Maintain an adequate supply of quality water;

3. Conserve contiguous forests;

4. Provide appropriate recreational opportunities; and

5. Promote economic prosperity that is compatible with goals 1–4. (Michaels 1992, reprinted in Phelps and Hoppe 2002, 2)

Within this framework, the 2002 study reassesses regional conditions, identifies areas for protection, and sets out strategies for the region.

Can these ambitious if rather vaguely elucidated goals be achieved using quieter revolution tools and strategies? Probably not sufficiently to satisfy most local environmentalists, regional planners, growth-control advocates, and ecosystem management proponents. Yet the past fifteen years have brought a surprisingly solid string of achievements, with some parts of the Highlands—aside from New Jersey's highly regulated subregion post-2004—having put in place more regional planning practices than might be expected of a nonintrusive quieter revolution endeavor.

Substantial federal, state, local, and private funds are directed to the region for land and easement acquisition. The quieter revolution poster project is in Sterling Forest, along the New York/New Jersey border (Botshon, Botshon, and Botshon 2007). This twenty-thousand-acre tract in the rolling hills northwest of New York City, once owned by the Harriman family, came under major development threat in the 1990s when the Sterling Forest Corporation (SFC) started drawing up plans for mixed-use, integrated development with an eventual population of thirty-five thousand to forty thousand. The prospect of such a thorough regional transformation prompted a major land acquisition effort, accelerating a process begun by the state of New Jersey in 1988, when it purchased 2,074 acres from the SFC. A decade later, with wide bipartisan support and leadership from the Trust for Public Land and the New York–based Open

Space Institute, a deal was put together to buy 15,280 acres from the Swiss investment company that then held title to the land. The $55 million needed to purchase the land was cobbled together with $17.5 million from the federal Forest Legacy program (chapter 5), $16 million from New York State, and $10 million from the state of New Jersey; additional contributions came from foundations, institutes, and other organizations. In short order, management of the newly acquired land became the responsibility of the New York/New Jersey Palisades Interstate Park Commission. In 2000, more lands were acquired, followed by additional small purchases in subsequent years.

Sterling Forest is important watershed land for northern New Jersey, as well as a significant regional recreation resource. Though most of the land is in New York State, New Jersey contributed generously to the Sterling purchase because of its boundary-crossing watershed value. With respect to recreational access, the extent to which this newly public land is actually accessible to the public and used by a diversity of socioeconomic groups is something that bears watching. When Fire Island, to New York City's southeast, became a national recreation area in the 1970s, policies were put in place that limited access to parts of it, protecting it for well-to-do residents (Foresta 1984). Sterling Forest appears to be an entirely different situation, without the local administrative barriers that have limited public access to Fire Island, as well as to New Jersey's nearby beaches. Still, potential Sterling Forest recreationists have to be able to get there—and options for doing so, other than by private car, are very limited. Given recreation's role in justifying massive public investment in this area, it is appropriate that not only ecosystem and watershed integrity but also recreational use patterns be carefully monitored.

But there is much more to the New York/New Jersey Highlands than the Sterling Forest crown jewel. Though no formal federal regional designation is in place, various federal and state programs support regional land protection. The Forest Legacy program has provided funds not only for the showpiece Sterling Forest purchase but also for land and easement acquisitions throughout the New York and New Jersey Highlands. Technical and planning support, as well as limited financial assistance, is available to private landowners through the Forest Service's Economic Action Program, Stewardship Program, Forest Land Enhancement Program, and Urban and Community Forestry Program. Under the Conservation

Reserve Program, farmers are eligible to receive rental payments in exchange for taking environmentally sensitive land out of production; in most cases, the land is converted to forest cover. The Wetlands Reserve Program provides assistance for taking marginal farmlands out of production and restoring them to wetlands. Payments for instituting farm conservation practices come via the Environmental Quality Incentives Program, while U.S. Fish and Wildlife Service programs make funds available for habitat protection and restoration. Planning and technical assistance also come from the National Park Service's River Trails and Conservation Assistance Program, as well as through Wild and Scenic River designation. The partially completed Highlands Trail, one of fifty national "millennium legacy trails," will link the Delaware River in New Jersey with the Hudson River at Storm King Park in New York State. The Lower Delaware River, in the eastern reaches of the Highlands, is designated a Scenic and Recreational River, making localities eligible for technical and financial assistance. Moreover, the legislation authorizing the Hudson River Valley Greenway calls for cooperative regional planning, though community participation is voluntary (Hudson River Valley Greenway Communities Council Greenway Conservancy for the Hudson River Valley, Inc. 1997). Because of their impacts on estuarine water quality, parts of the Highlands are involved with the New York/New Jersey Harbor Estuary Program, which to date remains largely a study program (Phelps and Hoppe 2002).

Mainly through their farmland and open-space protection programs, and to a lesser extent their forest management initiatives, New York and New Jersey have put substantial sums into land and easement acquisition. New Jersey, in allocating funds from its 1998 open-space bond referendum, gives priority to the Highlands. And its State Development and Redevelopment Plan (New Jersey State Planning Commission 2001) gives "special resource area" status to the Highlands. New York, too, has targeted the region, adding acreage to several state parks and acquiring other critical lands in the Hudson Highlands region (separate from the Highlands study region), east of the Hudson River. More than sixteen thousand farmland acres came under protection in the New York/New Jersey study region between 1992 and 2002. Over the same period, New Jersey acquired conservation easements on more than 15,500 acres in the Pequannock Watershed, which is owned by and supplies water to the city of

Newark. As part of its watershed Land Acquisition and Stewardship Program (described above for the Catskill Mountains), New York City protects over 4,500 acres in the Croton Reservoir watershed, east of the Hudson River (figure 4.5). Stewardship is promoted through training programs that encourage forestry practices aimed at minimizing nonpoint source pollution.

Counties and localities, too, have active farmland and open-space programs (Phelps and Hoppe 2002). And local land trusts and watershed organizations are an important part of the collaborative mix. In addition to the general land protection and technical assistance programs noted above, the U.S. Forest Service has supported—on a fifty-fifty match basis—several local collaborative efforts. Among these are an update of the Comprehensive Plan and Zoning Ordinance of Philipstown, New York; a regional greenway plan for southeastern Sussex County, New Jersey; a conservation initiative—which includes land acquisition and planning programs—for watershed lands surrounding New Jersey's Spruce Run Reservoir; and assistance to Morris County, New Jersey, in setting water quality standards (Phelps and Hoppe 2002).

As already noted, the 2004 Highlands Conservation Act adds portions of Connecticut and New Jersey to the federally defined Highlands Region. Citing the Sterling Forest project as a collaborative model, the act authorizes $10 million in federal funding over ten years, to be used for technical assistance to states and localities, and for matching grants for land and conservation easement purchases on a willing-seller basis. The act significantly extends the quieter revolution model for the Highlands, spatially as well as financially. Another key regional player is the Highlands Coalition (2007). Established in 1988, it is a relative old-timer on the local scene. This expansive association, most of whose members are conservation NGOs, lobbies the federal and state governments for Highlands funding and program support. Many of its members are very active in defining and implementing local projects funded under the Highlands Conservation Act and other programs.

In 2004, with passage of the Highlands Water Protection and Planning Act, New Jersey went well beyond quieter revolution incentive and payment programs. The act ushered a quiet revolution regulatory program into a policy landscape dominated by quieter approaches. Preceding the act was a study, commissioned in 2003 by New Jersey governor James

McGreevey and completed in less than a year, that sounded alarms about the rapid pace of land conversion in New Jersey's Highlands. The study's call for regional planning led to adoption of the 2004 legislation.

The Highlands plan is modeled after southern New Jersey's Pinelands plan, whose implementation got under way a quarter century earlier (Mason 1992a). The eight-hundred-thousand-acre Highlands planning area is divided into a 398,000-acre core preservation area, where little new development is permitted. Surrounding it is the planning area, where development is permitted but strictly regulated. The fifteen-person Highlands Planning and Protection Council, whose membership consists of state and local officials and citizens, is charged with developing a regional master plan. Municipal master plans and zoning ordinances for towns with land in the preservation area must conform with the regional plan. For the planning area, compliance is voluntary—but it brings eligibility for a variety of government benefits. As of early 2007, the plan is being implemented by the New Jersey Department of Environmental Protection and other state agencies. When the final plan is adopted, the planning council will take over implementation and exercise review authority over major development proposals in the preservation area. That review becomes optional once a municipality's plan and ordinance are certified as being in compliance with the regional plan (New Jersey Department of Environmental Protection [NJDEP] 2007a; New Jersey Highlands Council 2007).

The Highlands effort has met with intense opposition from home builders, farmers, and many local governments and individual citizens (chapter 7). But it has taken some lessons from the earlier Pinelands planning effort, seeking to address issues of tax stabilization and accommodation of regional growth early on. Unlike the Pinelands, where designated growth areas must serve as receiving areas for transferable development rights (TDRs) and thus accommodate higher-density development, the Highlands plan does not create mandatory growth areas. Instead, it calls for voluntary establishment of TDR receiving areas. In addition to planning grants to localities, tax stabilization payments are to be made to governments experiencing revenue losses associated with increased open-space acreages (NJDEP 2007a; New Jersey Highlands Council 2007). This is something that did not happen in the Pinelands until several years after plan implementation began.

The Highlands program began as a rather modest effort and then expanded very appreciably, geographically as well as in terms of regional planning, over the past fifteen years. As we have seen, management tools and strategies are quite uneven across the four states involved. Because of this, the Highlands program demands careful appraisal. Especially worthwhile would be controlled comparisons of New Jersey and New York's relative successes in restraining sprawl, as well as investigation of the very contentious questions regarding planning's impacts on regional housing supply and affordability. Other dimensions for evaluation, across the entire region, include recreational access, tax impacts, and ecosystem integrity (chapter 8).

The Northern Forest: From Quiet to Quieter Revolution

New England and New York's northern forests were so heavily exploited in the 1700s and 1800s that today's landscape actually is a much more wooded one than that of a century ago. And as those forests regenerated, deciduous trees were favored, making for more of the colorful displays that bring hordes of tourists to the region each autumn (Dobbs and Ober 1996). Forestry, while not so dominant as it once was, continues to be a very large part of regional life. Tourism, recreation, home building (first and second homes), and exurban migrants' demands for goods and services now vie for economic primacy with the traditional resource-based economy. And the resultant changes to the region's ecological, social, and political character have set the stage for a major rethinking of the forest's future. In turn, various regional and subregional land use initiatives have been introduced.

Like the Highlands region, the Northern Forest is a political creation, its northern and eastern reach defined by the Canadian border and its southern limit stopping short of Vermont's southern Green Mountains, Massachusetts' Berkshires, and New York's Catskills (figure 4.12). The Adirondacks are part of the Laurentide physiographic region, while the rest of the Northern Forest belongs to the Appalachian Mountains. Northern Maine is largely in the hands of timber companies, which own vast acreages. In the other states, smaller private holdings are more typical, with large public landholdings in the Green Mountain National Forest (Vermont), White Mountain National Forest (New Hampshire), and New York's Adirondack Park. All told, though, only about 15 percent of the region's twenty-six

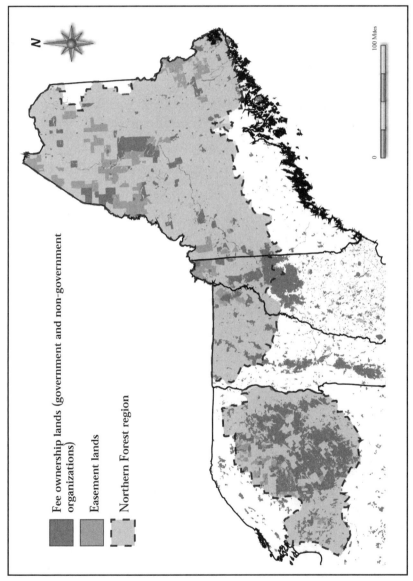

Figure 4.12. Northern Forest Protected Lands
Source: Appalachian Mountain Club

million acres is in public ownership (Northern Forest Lands Council 1994, 23). And, as local residents are quick to point out, states and localities are strongly differentiated by political cultures. But there are also commonalities through the vast region that Congress and the states have defined as the Northern Forest: great expanses of woodland, thousands of lakes, countless wetlands, economically important natural resources, widespread poverty and tremendous growth in extent, economic value, and environmental impacts of tourism and recreation in recent decades.

Northern Forest planning contrasts sharply with the Highlands program: while the latter has become more ambitious over time, the former has been scaled back over the course of two decades. During the hostile-takeover era of 1980s, a policy window opened in the Northern Forest region when British-French corporate raider Sir James Goldsmith acquired the Diamond International Corporation. With the takeover came 976,000 forested acres in northern New York and New England, which had been consolidated over the previous four decades from smaller private holdings. Public concern grew steadily, reaching a crescendo in 1987, when Goldsmith sold the land to the European communications company Cie General Electricite (CGE). Not at all interested in forest management, CGE moved quickly to sell off its newly acquired assets. Lands that had long supplied timber to north-country mills came under speculative threat, as real estate companies moved in, vulture-like, to acquire the so-called Diamond lands. The Nature Conservancy made bids on some parcels that CGE had put up for sale, but its bids were rejected. In New York, ninety-six thousand acres were bought by Lassiter Properties of Georgia; New York State later acquired fifteen thousand of those acres in fee-simple and secured easements on forty thousand more. Then, in 1988, Rancourt Associates agreed to purchase ninety thousand acres in New Hampshire and Vermont. A proportionate government response—perhaps in the form of a new National Forest area—would have been too complicated and time-consuming. Instead, a collaborative effort involving The Nature Conservancy, Society for Protection of New Hampshire Forests, and the U.S. Forest Service, through negotiations with Rancourt, yielded a deal for purchase of 46,700 acres. Ultimately, the Forest Service would acquire easements on critical lands from the state of New Hampshire. The entire episode, while testament to the potential of spirited collaboration, was very costly, with public and private entities having to pay more than market price to troubled real estate firms at a time when the land market had started a downturn (Reidel 1994).

The Diamond crisis brought a determined political response, with the powerful regional congressional delegation securing a $250,000 appropriation for the Forest Service, in conjunction with a four-state Governor's Task Force, to conduct a Northern Forest Lands Study (Tuler and Webler 1999). The Forest Service's charge was to identify and assess the following:

1. Forest resources, including timber, fish and wildlife, lakes and rivers, and recreation

2. Historical landownership patterns and projected future landownership, management, and use

3. The likely impacts of changes in land and resource ownership, management, and use patterns

4. Alternative strategies to protect the long-term integrity and traditional uses of land. (Harper, Falk, and Rankin 1990, v)

The report describes the rapid changes overtaking the region and lays out several alternative strategies for the future. Though such options as new national parks and expansion of the Green and White Mountain national forests were considered, the final report did not take a strong policy stand. The Governors' Task Force on Northern Forest Lands (1990) called for creation of a Northern Forest Lands Council and favored tax incentives and land and easement acquisition. Federal funding of $25 million per year, from the Land and Water Conservation Fund, was requested for a four-year period. The entire study process, including the release of a draft report, was highly controversial. Some environmental organizations supported major land acquisition programs; others favored creation of a regional "green line," within which quieter revolution strategies would be deployed; and the Wilderness Society (Sayen 2001) proposed the "Maine Woods Reserve"—a greenline-type park surrounding Baxter State Park. Restore (Restore: The North Woods 2007), founded in 1992, continues to make the case for a 3.2-million-acre "Maine National Park." In the early 1990s, Preserve Appalachian Wilderness called for a large preserve, extending into Canada, with multiple wilderness core areas surrounded by buffer zones, all interconnected by ecological corridors (Sayen 1994).

Property rights groups vehemently opposed even an advisory federal role in regional land use management, never mind creation of new national parks and wilderness preserves. And their influence was felt in Congress and the state houses. In the Adirondacks, at the same time as the Northern Forest controversies were raging, the recommendations of the Commission on the Adirondacks in the Twenty-First Century (1990) were released. The response to the commission's report was so hostile that Governor Mario Cuomo backed away from many of its recommendations (chapter 2). In November 1990, New York voters rejected an $800 million environmental bond issue, which would have directed half its funds toward land acquisition (Klyza 1994; Mason 1995a; Dobbs and Ober 1996).

The Northern Forest Lands Council (NFLC), authorized in the 1990 Farm Bill, almost failed to materialize. But it did manage to sustain itself, as heir to the Governor's Task Force, even if its mission was reduced largely to one of seeking to reinforce, rather than significantly alter, existing land ownership patterns (Reidel 1994). The 1990 Farm Bill also created a model quieter revolution program: the Forest Legacy program. Initially, it supported pilot programs for Northern Forest conservation easement purchases; subsequently, it was expanded into a national program (chapter 5).

The NFLC (Northern Forest Lands Council 1994) released its report—*Finding Common Ground*—in 1994, and then disbanded, leaving no overarching government presence in the Northern Forest region. *Finding Common Ground*, a detailed follow-on to the 1990 Forest Service study (Harper, Falk, and Rankin 1990), is guided by the principle that traditional land ownership and use patterns should be reinforced. This is to be achieved by the following:

- Enhancing the quality of life for local residents through the promotion of economic stability for the people and communities of the area and through the maintenance of large forest areas

- Encouraging the production of a sustainable yield of forest products

- Protecting recreational, wildlife, scenic, and wild land resources
  (Northern Forest Lands Council 1994, iv)

Though the council shied away from proposing large land acquisitions, purportedly because of the influence exercised by the timber industry (Klyza 2001), it did make thirty-seven recommendations for fostering private-lands stewardship, protecting exceptional resources, strengthening rural economies, and promoting more informed policy decisions (Northern Forest Lands Council 1994). A progress report on implementation of those recommendations, released in 2000 by the North East State Foresters Association (Malmsheimer, Bentley, and Floyd 2000), found much unevenness, with the federal government lagging well behind the four states in implementing the 1990 agenda. The Forest Legacy program has significantly supported land and easement acquisitions, but declining federal funding left it well short of NFLC goals. Nor have adequate funds been authorized under the Land and Water Conservation Fund (chapter 5). State land acquisition programs, by contrast, have enjoyed stronger support, through bond issues and trust funds. Though the federal Stewardship Incentive Program faltered, sustainable forestry certification programs have grown and states have expanded current use taxation programs for resource lands. Various other federal and state landowner-incentive programs also were enhanced between 1994 and 2000. The bottom line is that most of the land protection action has been at the state, not the federal, level. NGOs also play key roles, but the contributions of The Nature Conservancy and Trust for Public Land are only briefly noted in the North East State Foresters Association progress report (Malmsheimer, Bentley, and Floyd 2000).

On *Finding Common Ground*'s tenth anniversary, the North East State Foresters Association (2005) embarked on a review and reanalysis of its findings. Funded by the U.S. Forest Service and other parties, the report is a mere shadow of its 1994 predecessor. Prepared with rather little representation from environmental interests, it stresses economic and community development, support for private landowners, and collaborative approaches to regional management. In contrast with earlier studies, major public land and easement acquisitions are not emphasized.

Meanwhile, there is a lingering regional institutional presence, in the form of a nongovernmental coalition, the Northern Forest Alliance (2007).

Its members range from the relatively conservative National Wildlife Federation to—at one time at least—the ecocentric Restore. The alliance supports a suite of initiatives that range from wildlands restoration proposals to sustainable, small-scale private forestry projects. An even smaller regional organization, based in Concord, New Hampshire, is the Northern Forest Center (2007); it is all about heritage, culture, human capital, and place-based collaboration. But these two groups seem to lack the cohesion and purposefulness that enable some of their property-rights counterparts to be so effective (Dobbs and Ober 1996). It is one of those classic cases, referred to in chapter 3, where concentrated-interest stakeholders (resource-based interests) are more readily mobilized than diffuse-interest stakeholders (environmental interests) (Overdest 2000).

What we have today, with the land sale threats of the 1980s and 1990s seemingly at bay and the political climate more conservative, is a whisper of a regional program (Breckenridge 1995). Most land use projects and controversies are defined and acted out on the state and local, rather than regional, scales. The narrowly defeated 1997 "Compact for Maine's Forests" ballot question, which would have regulated but not banned clear-cutting, is just one example of this. Maine's voters decided they did not want to shift the locus of forestry decision making. Barring any major economic or political upheaval, we can probably anticipate a relatively steady, devolved state of affairs through much of the Northern Forest region, at least for the near term.

Great Plains/The Buffalo Commons

Books, film, poetry, music, journals, photographs, scholarly treatises—and now websites and blogs—all tell us stories of the Great Plains (Popper and Popper 1998). Some stories are hopeful, some are about bitter defeat—but an ecological restoration story line? This is the narrative that Frank and Deborah Popper developed in a short 1987 article—"The Great Plains: Dust to Dust"—about the future of this complex, conflicted region (Popper and Popper 1987). Neither a full-blown wildlands approach (Locke 2000) nor a Nine Nations pop-region piece (Garreau 1981), the "Buffalo Commons" is a planner and geographer's cojoined vision of a sustainable, if scaled-down, regional future.

That 1987 piece told a story of decline and despair—not everywhere in the Great Plains but through great swaths of the region. The Poppers characterized the settlement of the plains as "the largest, longest-running agricultural and environmental miscalculation in American history" (Popper and Popper 1987, 12) and forecast an almost total depopulation within a generation. Continued depletion of the Ogallala Aquifer, soil degradation, and potentially harmful climate trends all pointed toward a bleak agricultural future, in the Poppers' estimation. What the Poppers first proposed was a policy that would allow places doing well to continue to thrive, while transforming the rest of the plains into a "Buffalo Commons" (figure 4.13 shows an early and rough—but still very relevant—approximation of the Buffalo Commons lands). This massive project would be undertaken by the federal government, perhaps through a Tennessee Valley Authority–type agency. The details were to be worked out, but major buyouts and land retirements would be central to the scheme.

Needless to say, hostility toward government and suspicion of New Jersey–based academics made for an initially rough reception for the Buffalo Commons idea. Plains towns did not want to have their obituaries presented to them. Nor was the dominant cattle culture about to yield easily, arguing that cattle ranching is efficient and profitable and that buffalo could spread brucellosis, a disease that can induce abortions in cattle.

Not surprisingly, no major federal Buffalo Commons initiative emerged in the years following publication of "The Great Plains: Dust to Dust." But various federal, state, and provincial projects, mostly quieter revolution-type efforts, are being implemented. The Conservation Reserve Program, Grassland Reserve Program, and related federal initiatives (chapter 5) are removing critical habitat lands from production. The U.S. Fish and Wildlife Service keeps adding new incentive programs for habitat protection and restoration on private lands. But most of the action, so far, has not been government inspired, at least not directly. A gradual, uneven transformation toward the Buffalo Commons is being achieved largely by ranchers, Native American organizations, land conservancies, and tourism promoters. Buffalo ranching is growing, with luminaries like Ted Turner acquiring enormous acreages and markets becoming increasingly receptive to this low-calorie, low-fat, low-cholesterol, environmentally correct addition to the meat-based layer of the food pyramid. And buffalo tourism also has grown in popularity, with tourists coming from across America as well as Europe, Japan, and other parts of the globe. Ranching and tourism alone do not make for regional

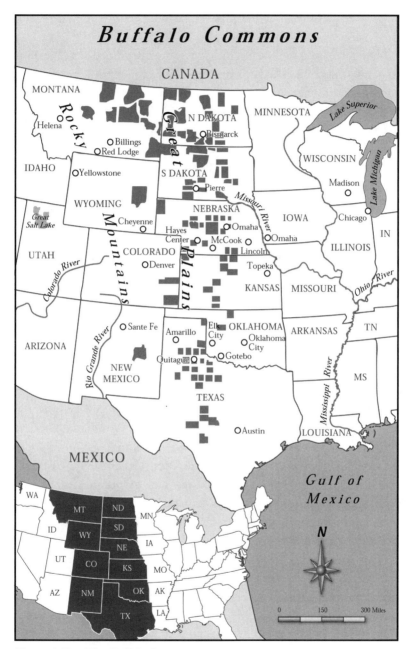

Figure 4.13. The Buffalo Commons
Source: Popper and Popper (1994), 89–100; Matthews (1992), x; Matthews (2002), viii.

ecological restoration, but they are very much part of the larger sustainability vision.

Though there is no overarching government-guided restoration program, environmental NGOs have stepped into the breach in a major way, organizing regional and subregional ecological protection efforts (Matthews 2002; Popper and Popper 2006). The Nature Conservancy is buying lands and acquiring easements throughout the region, while Ducks Unlimited's waterfowl habitat programs have protected and restored millions of wetlands acres. The Great Plains Restoration Council's (GPRC) Million Acres Project seeks to stitch together public and private lands into a contiguous prairie ecosystem. The GPRC's sustainability vision is expansive; the organization engages not only in habitat protection but also urban community development and city parks projects (Great Plains Restoration Council 2007). The American Prairie Foundation and World Wildlife Fund, in collaboration with other government and nongovernment partners, are acquiring private lands in order to create a prairie ecosystem reserve in northeastern Montana (American Prairie Foundation 2007). And many smaller organizations are engaged in more modest restoration projects across the plains.

The naysayers are coming around, the Poppers feel vindicated, and the notion of a Buffalo Commons is now widely understood, if still not fully embraced, within the regional and national popular cultures (Williams 2001). Ernest Callenbach, who wrote of a fictional West Coast *Ecotopia* in the mid-1970s, more recently produced a nonfiction work about populating the plains with buffalo and wind turbines (Callenbach 1996). Daniel Licht (1997), writing from a conservation biology perspective, calls for a system of ecological reserves, large and small. Though supportive of the federal Conservation Reserve Program (chapter 5), he feels its effectiveness is very limited because the tracts taken out of production are simply too small and are not managed for ecological restoration. Licht's rewilding approach would cleanse the landscape of all material remnants of human settlement, including "buildings, rock piles, old machinery, wells, shelterbelts" (Licht 1997, 143). This puts him at odds with potential quieter revolution collaborators who value cultural and historical, as well as physical, landscapes (Stokes, Watson, and Mastran 1997; Alanen and Melnick 2000). Indeed, this is a point of land management contestation that is more about aesthetic and philosophical convictions than integrity of the basic resource; in New York's Adirondacks, controversies have raged between rewilders, eager to remove all fire towers from protected peaks, and many local (and nonlocal) people who want these vestiges of regional history to remain in place.

The plains will not, it seems, become the huge federal reserve once envisioned by the Poppers, or by geographer Bret Wallach (1985), who twenty years ago proposed that the U.S. Forest Service administer a sweeping retirement of marginal agricultural lands. Instead, the region is becoming a quiltwork of large and small protected areas, returned and restored Native American lands, buffalo ranches, and tourist destinations.

A complicating factor for the Buffalo Commons future—at least on the region's eastern margins—is the current ethanol and biodiesel boom. If cellulosic ethanol—produced from grasses, among other varieties of biomass—becomes more economically and technologically feasible, then the Buffalo Commons might be directly affected. If so, the ecologically hopeful scenario could look something like this: ethanol-driven demand for cellulosic feedstocks is linked with native grassland and habitat restoration. But if corn, soybeans, and other crops remain the main ethanol feedstocks, then the ecological consequences—as well as net energy implications—may not be so bright (Hill et al. 2006). In that scenario, the Buffalo Commons would not necessarily sustain major ecological losses, since greatest impacts would be to their east. In the end, federal policies, global fuel demands, and market dynamics will determine which, if either, scenario prevails.

Louisiana Gulf Coast

Gulf Coast restoration was featured in this chapter's early outlines, well before Hurricane Katrina hit New Orleans. In disaster's wake, typically, we witness renewed clamor for structural responses to hazard: dams, diversions, levees, floodwalls, flood- and earthquake-resistant housing, and so on. Recent decades, though, have brought more attention to nonstructural approaches to hazard management. Land use planning, ecological buffers, warning systems, evacuation plans, and education programs are some of the options gaining growing acceptance. We have yet to fully realize the full implications for nonstructural approaches of such recent disasters as the Delaware River's three one-hundred-year floods in a one-and-a-half-year period, western wildfires and earthquakes, the Asian tsunami, and, of course, hurricanes.

Clearly, nonstructural responses have an important place in the national debate, especially as global warming threats loom large. Many of these responses will be in the quieter revolution mold. But a strong case also may be made for regulation, especially when the situation is widely perceived as being at or near crisis level. Still, the American tendency is toward softer approaches. The National Flood Insurance Program (NFIP), despite its very mixed implementation record, is in many ways a quieter revolution approach. It does regulate, but local participation is optional—and incentivized. The incentive for meeting the program's land use management and building conditions is access to federally subsidized flood insurance (Platt 2004). Unfortunately, as NFIP's critics are quick to point out, it has repeatedly subsidized those who choose to live in harm's way. But NFIP's flaws are more in its details and implementation than its underlying policy approach to coping with hazard.

In the Gulf Coast case, it is far from assured that restored ecological buffers alone could protect the shoreline from the fury of a Category 5 hurricane. New Orleans, situated as it is mostly below sea level, is highly dependent on exquisitely engineered water management systems. It is not a city "designed with nature"—and it is unrealistic to expect that healthy ecosystems can transform it into one. But surely environmental buffers can and should play a part in reducing storm impact—and providing other essential ecological services as well. Before Katrina, at least, those rationales were not enough to secure adequate funding for a major Louisiana coastal restoration program. But with crisis comes opportunity: New Orleans's rebuilding provides a rare opportunity to build a newly ecological city, with renewed commitment to restoring coastal ecosystems.

In addition to the storm surge buffering services they provide to coastal environments and populations, the Gulf Coast wetlands between Texas and Mississippi support fishing, oyster harvests, oil and gas production, wildlife habitat, ecotourism, and Cajun and Creole culture. Yet the massive reengineering of the Mississippi Delta—involving Mississippi River channelization, as well as a criss-crossing network of navigational channels and oil and gas pipelines—has deprived coastal wetlands of the regular flow of fresh water and silt that sustained them before the twentieth century. Combined with geologic subsidence, this has caused wetlands to sink into the sea at an alarming rate over the past several decades. Annual loss rates averaged thirty-nine square miles per year between 1956 and 1978, with that rate declining somewhat in more recent years (National Research Council Committee on the Restoration and Protection of Coastal Louisiana 2006, 2).

If there is a viable solution, what is it? Several wetlands protection and restoration initiatives were in place prior to Katrina (Streever 2001; National Research Council Committee on the Restoration and Protection of Coastal Louisiana 2006). Research results characterizing the extent of the ecosystem damages were published in the early 1970s, and momentum toward a government response was building in the 1990s. In 1989, the Louisiana legislature passed Act 6, creating a coastal restoration authority. The authority's funding comes through an oil and gas revenues trust fund, which was established via a voter-approved constitutional amendment. In 1990, the federal Coastal Wetlands Planning, Protection, and Restoration Act (CWPPRA) was passed; it provides the bulk of the funding for an array of restoration projects.

In 1998, *Coast 2050* was released (Louisiana Coast Wetlands Conservation and Restoration Task Force and the Wetlands Conservation and Restoration Authority 1998). This plan, involving multiple levels of government and endorsed by a wide-ranging group of stakeholders, calls for restoring ecological functions, rebuilding barrier islands, and generating limited, controlled flooding. Shell Oil, with its huge investments in offshore drilling platforms, came on board by funding a public relations campaign focusing on "America's Wetland" (America's Wetland 2007). *Coast 2050* laid the foundation for the Louisiana Coastal Area (LCA) Program, a massive undertaking proposed by the Army Corps of Engineers meant to mimic natural flows of fresh water into the deteriorating coastal marshes. In this respect, it resembles the Everglades replumbing efforts, described earlier, that are meant to restore ecological functions in South Florida.

The Gulf Coast project comes with a price tag estimated at more than $14 billion, and the Bush administration, initially at least, was unwilling to consider anything in this ballpark. Prospects for funding of that order were further dimmed by the departures from Congress of influential Representative Livingston, in 1999, and Representative Tauzin and Senator Breaux, both in 2005. Nor have those prospects been helped by Senator David Vitter's support for clear-cutting coastal cypress forests, to benefit timber companies who will turn the cypress into mulch, at the same time he professes support for ecological restoration (Grunwald and Glasser 2005). The LCA proposal was subsequently trimmed to a series of near-term projects, at a total cost of $1.9 billion (U.S. Army Corps of Engineers New Orleans District and State of Louisiana 2004).

Hurricanes Katrina and Rita, of course, have brought renewed attention and urgency to Gulf Coast restoration. A National Research Council (National Research Council Committee on the Restoration and Protection of Coastal Louisiana 2006) review of the LCA, begun several years earlier but released after the hurricane, finds that most LCA elements should move forward but that the goal of "no net loss" would not be realized given the actions proposed. A more expansive, comprehensive approach is recommended. Over the short term—the next ten years—some LCA projects would be abandoned and others completed. Adoption of a long-term, much costlier, thirty-year planning horizon also is suggested.

Comprehensive planning—currently in place in half the coastal parishes studied—should be adopted by all, urges the NRC. The report hits the appropriate collaborative, place-based notes, recommending broad stakeholder involvement and an adaptive management strategy. Moreover, it recognizes not only the regional value but also the national importance of protecting unique coastal ecosystems. At the same time, it is careful to acknowledge the uncertainties involved with specifically assessing their economic benefits. And the value that healthy ecosystems provide in reducing storm risks, while regarded as a top priority, likewise is difficult to forecast. Clearly, though, wetland restoration has its place as part of a larger risk reduction strategy for coastal Louisiana.

But the current focus on New Orleans reconstruction and levee rebuilding in effect limits the attention and funding directed toward restoration. Although President Bush did sign legislation directing $650 million of offshore oil and gas revenues toward coastal restoration, most of that funding will not become available until after 2017. Critics claim that if coastal wetlands are to be salvaged, then much more urgent attention is critical. If a viable program does get under way in the near future, it could serve as a model for damaged coastal wetlands along the East Coast, San Francisco Bay, Columbia River estuary, and other places. If a major infusion of federal funding is not soon forthcoming for Gulf Coast restoration, then prospects for doing so elsewhere in the country—where no recent major tragedy has focused attention—are all the dimmer.

Urban Ecosystems and Sustainability

Though core urban areas are not a main focus for this book, their fate is very much linked with quieter revolution fortunes. If city life becomes more attractive—for economic, cultural, social, or other reasons—the implications for reining in sprawl, reducing carbon emissions, and downsizing environmental footprints are potentially enormous. But urban areas themselves are critical environments, with fully functioning ecosystems, watersheds, and microclimatic systems nested within regional and larger systems (Platt 2006). In recent years, several cities have made extraordinary efforts to understand urban ecologies and improve environmental stewardship. Among the leaders are Chicago, Pittsburgh, Cleveland, Portland, and Seattle. Ecological and sustainable cities are the focus of academic programs at the University of Massachusetts and University of Southern California, among other institutions.

The Baltimore Ecosystem Study (2006) is a major interdisciplinary research effort, supported through the National Science Foundation's Long-Term Ecological Research program, that seeks to better understand the Baltimore region's ecological dynamics. Biological, physical, and social dimensions at the metropolitan ecosystem scale are the project's focus. Not only are energy fluxes and spatial dynamics at the heart of this work; so, too, are issues of ecological literacy and the relationships between metropolitan ecology and citizens' everyday lives.

Other urban projects are directed more toward immediate action. Founded in 1992, Ecocity Cleveland (2006) has had success with "branding"; it has a catchy name and produces first-rate publications and maps that help advance the debate about city and regional futures. Though it networks extensively with planners and municipal officials, has it actually moved sustainability initiatives forward? One sign of success may be that the city of Cleveland, at the urging of Ecocity Cleveland and other NGOs, recently hired a sustainability programs manager. His charge is to consider the environmental, economic, and equity impacts of city programs with an eye to supporting collaboration and promoting environmentally sustainable practices that save money. Ecocity Cleveland also has developed Cleveland Ecovillage, a transit-oriented urban redevelopment project committed to green building design, ethnic diversity, and affordable housing. Ecocity Cleveland is creating something of an environmentally themed "intentional

143

community," by organizing new residential development projects and maintaining Ecovillage real estate listings, which are handled by a firm named Progressive Urban Real Estate.

Central to Sustainable Pittsburgh's efforts is its regional indicators report for Southwestern Pennsylvania (Sustainable Pittsburgh 2004); included in the report are environmental, economic, social, and well-being indicators. Although using only a two-year interval for comparison, Sustainable Pittsburgh concludes that the region is headed mostly in the wrong direction. Despite some successes with employment stability, cost of living, and water quality, the Pittsburgh region is experiencing rising poverty and inequality, increased fossil fuel consumption, and declining recycling rates. Still, the organization remains hopeful, as it carries out its mission of collaboratively promoting smart growth, transportation reform, sustainable business practices, and public education. Indeed, future reports will be brightened by inclusion of several central Pittsburgh infill development projects, now in their early stages, that are providing at least some mixed-income housing (Deitrick and Ellis 2004)

In other cities, municipal government is setting the sustainability agenda. Mayor Richard M. Daley is deeply committed to making Chicago a model American green city, and to that end the city is adopting and encouraging practices already common in many European cities. Chicago is planting hundreds of thousands of trees, restoring scores of brownfields, promoting green buildings and green roofs, expanding parks, restoring wetlands, innovatively managing urban runoff, and developing renewable energy sources. Landmark accomplishments include the green roof on Chicago City Hall and the 24.5-acre Millennium Park in the city's core (Schneider 2006). Chicago is going well beyond demonstration projects, seeking to do enough to make a meaningful difference across the city. The goal for energy, for example, is to have clean and renewable energy meet 20 percent of the city's needs within the near future; already, by some estimates, the city is at 10 percent. Green roofs are promoted through a small-grants program to businesses and individual homeowners.

Portland, Oregon's efforts benefit from the State of Oregon's leadership in growth management—particularly its designation of urban growth boundaries (chapter 5). But a great deal has been done locally, as well, to promote sustainability (Ozawa 2004). Although the city already had a Sustainable Development Commission (Portland, Oregon, 2007), in 2000 it created a new Office of Sustainable Development, incorporating within it solid waste, recycling, energy, and green building functions. In 1993, Portland became the first American city to adopt a strategy for reducing carbon emissions—and it has already realized a 12.5 percent reduction. Energy conservation, green architecture, and promotion of local food production all are on the agenda. The city leads by example and is a national model for sustainable practices.

Sustainable Seattle (2007) produced several sustainable indicators reports in the 1990s and is currently preparing an updated report. Not only is this research being pursued at the regional level but also at the neighborhood level. Sustainable Seattle is examining the local impacts—particularly sustainability benefits—of local spending, especially within the local food economy. Also on the organization's agenda are various education, outreach, and other collaborative programs.

Most American cities have some sort of sustainability effort in place. While the physical spaces occupied by cities—or for that matter metropolitan regions—at best match up imperfectly with biophysical boundaries, urban areas nevertheless function as ecosystems, with inputs, outputs, and movement of energy and materials through the urban system. And established urban and regional institutions have the capacity to at least begin to address sustainability questions at appropriate spatial scales. Though many metropolitan regions are willing to embrace energy efficiency, carbon emissions reductions, green building practices, sustainable local food systems, and intraregional equity, the commitments needed for substantial progress are difficult, economically and politically, to put into place. At least they are often perceived as such. While research programs and indicators assessments are important steps, often attractive because they are more politically palatable than action plans, how do cities move further? The political, social, and economic challenges in doing so make urban sustainability programs prime candidates for collaborative, incentive-based, quieter revolution approaches. And, as at least some cities are demonstrating, those approaches can always be made more robust by bolstering the incentives and putting in place serious disincentives when their efforts are not producing desired results.

Summary

What has been presented here is a sampling of quieter revolution programs that cover relatively large regions. The grandest of them—the Sierra Club and Wild Earth schemes that carve the North American continent into great ecoregions—are conceptual only. Their applied value is in showing us the big picture and guiding activities, projects, and plans at the local and subregional scales. Agencies and NGOs that take a national view can use these schemes to prioritize, select, and direct their programs across the nation. Wild Earth is seeking to do just that, by investing substantial institutional capital in ecoregional planning in New Mexico (figure 4.2).

The real work is being done in the small to medium-size regions. Even here, regional approaches are quite devolved, with planning actions mostly taking place at local levels. Although a regional perspective may be encouraged and incentivized, these projects differ from quiet revolution programs that imposed regional zoning schemes. Emphasis today is on land and easement acquisition, incentives for farmers and foresters, and financial and technical assistance to localities. Big, region-spanning projects do materialize, but usually in response to crisis, as was the case in the Northern Forest lands of New York and New England, the Everglades, and the Highlands region of New York, where the Sterling Forest purchase was the culmination of a colossal collaborative effort.

These region-scale endeavors work as well as they do because they are integrated with local initiatives—including those undertaken by local land trusts, watershed conservancies, and local governments. Without the integrated local action network, regional efforts would be all the less effective. Though there are some notable exceptions, such as the threat of species listings under the Endangered Species Act in Southern California and New York City's prospect of having to filter its Catskills water, the levers available to move the process forward usually are limited to incentives and subsidies.

These regional efforts also receive support from federal and state programs, some of them discussed in chapter 5. The more local efforts—land trusts, watershed conservancies, ballot questions, greenways designation—are the focus of chapter 6. These local programs not only are the supporting cast for many regional initiatives, they also are of great consequence—perhaps greatest consequence—in what they achieve locally.

A great many more ecoregional, bioregional, sustainable community, watershed, and other initiatives are emerging over a wide range of spatial scales; some of them—such as those carried out by land conservation and watershed organizations—are included in other chapters. If we could look at each and every one of these projects, we would see a very uneven pattern, with some appearing as shining beacons of enlightened environmental management and others barely able to get out of the starting gate. Nationally, capacity for such programs seems to be expanding; whether or not this increase is sufficient to produce significant, landscape-altering cumulative change is taken up in chapters 8 and 9.

CHAPTER FIVE
SLOWING SPRAWL, SAVING SPACES

Has the battle to rein in sprawl already been lost? In some ways, it has—given that sprawl, like climate change, is on a trajectory that limits the effectiveness of our responses. Even if we were able to put into place draconian planning regulations to stop low-density, land consumptive development, what would we do about historically sprawled lands (see, for example, figure 6.3)? Indeed, in many places sprawl is already well beyond containment. Once-tidy landscapes, with clear rural-urban boundaries, have been transformed by an explosion of new housing, commercial development, and traffic congestion. Released from many of the economic, political, and social constraints that once constricted urban form, our cities, suburbs, and exurbs have spread ever further into the former countryside. Even more sprawl is a foregone conclusion, facilitated by infrastructural and other investments, as well as planning approvals, already in the pipeline. Removal of all this existing development to make way for large-scale environmental reclamation simply is not going to happen, though at least one free-choice critic of environmental regulation argues that the market would impose this solution if the need is sufficiently pressing. In Julian Simon's (1998) view, we can always remove houses and malls if we must. But short of such drastic land reclamation efforts, we can adapt, densify, and reconfigure at least some of our existing sprawl, thus reducing its environmental impacts. We can also do much more than we have been willing to do in the past to manage and control future growth and development. These are the approaches now pursued by ever growing legions of state and local governments.

Still, while sprawl is being seriously confronted in some places, in many others we are doing little more than tweaking and tinkering. Even some of the most forward-looking approaches rely on tools quite ill suited to the enormity of the problem. While there may be widespread dissatisfaction with the consequences of sprawl, efforts to seriously constrain it can be politically unpopular, costly, inequitable, and economically inefficient, sometimes bringing major environmental impacts of their own.

There is no undoing the political and institutional history—including the interstate highway system, tax deductions for home mortgages, and other subsidies (chapter 2)—that has fostered sprawled patterns of development. Nor, as mentioned, is there much political will to impose strong legal controls, beyond the more or less accepted zoning and subdivision regulations, that could simply stop sprawl. But we are adopting policies that can slow sprawl. Increasingly, federal and state policies and subsidies are being reconfigured to promote more concentrated, environmentally less damaging development. Localities, too, are reacting to growth—sometimes in knee-jerk fashion, in other instances in more measured, comprehensive ways. What is emerging is a highly uneven national pattern of mostly incentive-based, quieter revolution programs, plus stronger regulatory and planning programs in some states and communities. Governments are the major actors here, but, increasingly, environmental NGOs are disbursing funds and expertise, in synch with local and regional land management priorities. Further discussion of their activities is included in chapter 6.

Quieter approaches to sprawl management seek to direct future growth in ways that make environmental sense, by limiting the footprints of suburban and exurban growth, reducing traffic congestion, and reclaiming urban core areas and brownfield sites. How is this being achieved? Some local governments—not necessarily with the purest of environmental motives—are making extraordinary efforts to limit growth, restore ecosystems, protect agricultural lands and open space, and manage stormwater sustainably. But many governments lack the political will and wherewithal to seriously confront growth and its impacts. And most are constrained by limited resources. Moreover, these problems do not respect local political boundaries—yet resistance to intermunicipal cooperation can be intense (Mason 2005).

Calthorpe and Fulton (2001) offer up the optimistic view that we are trending toward more mature local and regional planning, with sprawl coming to an end and the regionalism of the 1920s reinventing itself for the twenty-first century. Their "new urbanist" notion of the "regional city" is built on renewed cites, maturing suburbs, and emerging regions. Some exceptional metropolitan areas—Portland, Seattle, and Salt Lake City—are cited in support of their thinking. And they foresee ecological, as well as economic and social, regions emerging across the national map. Pastor et al. (2000), too, believe that we can build new regions and direct our energies toward greater intraregional equity. Katz (2000) and Barnett (2000)—along with their co-contributors—also take hopeful, though more qualified, stands on the new regionalism's potential. A rather contrary view holds that the new regionalism is unlikely to take root widely unless there are superstructural political, economic, and social transformations (Talen 2005). Indeed, Talen's (2005) characterization of such iconic new communities as Riverside, Illinois; Mariemont, Ohio; and Radburn, New Jersey may be an apt metaphor for future conditions. She sees these places as exceptionally well-planned communities, anchored in a sea of sprawl.

Quieter revolution approaches—with their reliance on incentives, inducements, collaboration, and good intentions—may bring us more such landscapes. Most are supported by regional, state, or national programs that provide funds, expertise, and other resources (Koontz et al. 2004). Their specific design and implementation are shaped by a host of local variations in physical environments, political influence, administrative competence, and fiscal capacity.

This chapter is mostly about centralized government programs that impose conditions and distribute funds, technical expertise, tax exemptions, and other inducements meant to guide growth, enhance recreational opportunities, and protect local places from the adverse effects of urban sprawl. These programs are in contrast to the more local efforts described in chapter 6. But many of those local initiatives would never have materialized had there not been support from the kinds of programs described below. It would be an overreach, in most cases, to draw too sharp a distinction between the bottom-up accomplishments described in chapter 6 and the top-down potential of those described here. They are mutually supportive, synergistic endeavors. This chapter begins with an overview of the sprawl problem, then examines federal programs that target funds and resources to land use programs and projects, and finally hones in on state and substate activities.

Sprawl on the Agenda

In the early 1970s, urban sprawl's negative economic consequences were documented in the Real Estate Research Corporation's (1974) comprehensive report, *The Costs of Sprawl*. These concerns, frequently cited by planners, local citizens, and environmental organizations, were influential in the quiet revolution's development.

But quiet revolution responses to sprawl, it seems, were hardly proportional to the enormity and reach of the late-century sprawl phenomenon. First, though, how do we define sprawl? Ewing (1997) reviews several characterizations, while Soule (2006a, 3) offers the following succinct definition:

> Sprawl is low density, auto-dependent land development taking place on the edges of urban centers, often "leapfrogging" away from current denser development nodes, to transform open, undeveloped land, into single-family residential subdivisions and campus-style commercial office parks and diffuse retail uses.

In most metropolitan regions, urbanized land acreage is increasing much faster than population numbers; in other words, development patterns are highly land consumptive. And many traditional high-density metro areas are "de-densifying" at remarkably rapid rates (Fulton et al. 2001).

Though successes in reining in sprawl in the 1970s were limited and relatively local, the issue did make it onto the national radar screen. As "edge cities" grew at the metropolitan fringes (Garreau 1991), big-box retailing firmly took hold, and per-capita vehicle miles continued to rise dramatically (Benfield, Raimi, and Chen 1999), sprawl's impacts were greatly amplified over the succeeding three decades. While sprawl did not exactly drop off the agenda after the mid-1970s, concerns about its effects did seem to subside for a time. It was not until the mid-1990s and beyond that it would reemerge as a top environmental concern (Bank of America 1995; Young 1995; Burchell et al. 1998; Leo et al. 1998; Benfield, Raimi, and Chen 1999; Sierra Club 1999). The current discourse is dominated by a repackaging of growth-control strategies under the smart growth "brand name," which is examined below.

Responding to Sprawl and Protecting Places

Let us now turn to federal and state responses to land conversion and sprawl-related issues. We begin with farmland preservation, then consider government responses more generally, and finally attempt to place all of it in broader context.

Farmland Protection

Federal programs to retire farmland have been with us for decades. But only over the past thirty years or so have ecological concerns become a defining element in shaping federal agricultural policy. While the United States is not about to run out of farmland, the consequences of massive land conversions have taken on increased urgency (Mason and Mattson 1990). Part of the concern is about historic ecological transformations, such as loss of wetlands in the Mississippi Valley and conversion of most native grasslands in the Great Plains. In the Northeast, Middle Atlantic, West Coast, and other areas with large metropolitan populations, agricultural runoff and loss of prime farmland to residential and commercial development are major issues. Metropolitan concerns are partly driven by worries about the aesthetic character of the peri-urban countryside but also by fears of a future in which sustainability options are restricted. If we grow more food closer to where it is consumed, carbon emissions and other environmental impacts are lowered. At the same time, food quality generally improves. Farmland protection programs preserve these options.

The alarm was sounded in earnest a quarter century ago, with release of the National Agricultural Lands Study (Gray et al. 1981). While federal, state, and local concerns clearly were in evidence before 1980, with numerous farmland protection programs already having been put in place (Furuseth and Pierce 1982; Lehman 1995), the study lent new urgency to the issue. Though its findings did not resonate with the incoming Reagan administration, the Farmland Protection Policy Act of 1981 nevertheless did become law, requiring federal agencies to take steps to ensure their actions do not contribute to irreversible farmland conversion.

153

A powerful new federal policy on farmland conservation emerged in mid-decade, with the 1985 passage of the Food Security Act, or Farm Bill (Zinn 1995). The act, along with its successors, embraces quieter revolution approaches to land use policy, relying on incentives to influence farmers' behavior. A signature environmental policy achievement was to tie eligibility for long-standing federal agricultural subsidies to "conservation compliance" by farmers; if farmers fail to meet certain conditions in managing their highly erodible lands, they lose eligibility for various federal payments for *all* their cultivated lands. Of course, federal payments to farmers are at the pleasure of the government; depending on one's viewpoint, the Farm Bill provisions may be interpreted as punitive or as putting to productive use a federal subsidy program that perhaps should not exist in the first place.

The Conservation Reserve Program (CRP) provides payments, under ten-year contracts, for farmers to remove highly erodible croplands from cultivation. As of early 2005, at an annual cost of nearly $2 billion, thirty-five million acres were enrolled. To put the acreage figure in perspective, highly erodible lands nationwide total about one hundred million acres, and total cropland area is over four hundred million acres (Claassen 2004). Most CRP enrollments are in the dry plains states, with Texas, Montana, and North Dakota leading (Zinn and Cowan 2005, 5). The national enrollment figure represents a slight decline from mid-1990s levels, when several of the early Farm Bill programs seemed to have peaked and congressional pressure to rein them in mounted (Zinn 1995). A major concern about the CRP's effectiveness is the fate of the land after the contract period ends; there is at least some evidence indicating that a majority of farmers are interested in returning the land to cultivation, if market conditions are favorable (Zinn 1995). Most of those farmers would be subject to conservation compliance provisions, and they also might be eligible for Farm Bill conservation programs—several of them noted below—created by Farm Bill reauthorizations subsequent to their initial entry into the CRP. As for new land coming into production, the Farm Bill's "sodbuster" provisions deny federal benefits to farmers who bring highly erodible lands into production without an approved conservation plan, while its "swampbuster" provisions apply similar conditions to farmers bringing wetlands under cultivation.

The 1990 Farm Bill added the Wetlands Reserve Program, which provides payments to farmers for wetlands protection easements and wetlands restoration. Through 2004, 1.63 million acres had been enrolled, with easements on 1.17 million acres (Zinn and Cowan 2005, 16). The Environmental Quality Incentive Program (EQIP) and Wildlife Habitat Incentive Program (WHIP), first authorized in 1996, provide for various incentive and cost-sharing payments for environmental improvements and habitat protection on working farms. Through fiscal year 2004, over 2.8 million acres had been enrolled in WHIP (Zinn and Cowan 2005, 17). The Farm and Ranch Lands Protection Program provides funds to states, localities, and NGOs for purchasing development rights on farmlands. This modest, but growing, program is exemplary of a quieter revolution infrastructure that distributes resources from central pools to local places. As of 2004, 870 easements had been acquired, accounting for almost 180,000 farm and ranch acres, with nearly 1,000 more easements pending on over 200,000 acres. Lead states, by acres, are Vermont, Pennsylvania, and Maryland (Zinn and Cowan 2005, 12). Also added in 1996 was the Conservation Reserve Enhancement Program (CREP), a subprogram of the CRP that targets assistance within designated substate areas, such as watersheds. As of early 2005, CREP had enrolled 130,000 acres in twenty-six states, with more in the pipeline. Pennsylvania, Illinois, and Minnesota are the acreage leaders (Zinn and Cowan 2005, 6). Money also is allocated for watershed protection projects. In 2002, the Conservation Security Program and the Grassland Reserve Program, which focus on native-grass grazing lands, were added to the reauthorized legislation, which took on the post–September 11 appellation "Farm Security and Rural Investment Act." Several demonstration programs and other modest initiatives also were included (U.S. Department of Agriculture [USDA], Natural Resources Conservation Service 2002; Claassen 2003). The bill is up for renewal in 2007, and new forestry provisions are likely to be part of this next version.

The turn of the century presaged a new Farm Bill emphasis, shifting away from compliance conditions and land retirement toward increasing farm acres and numbers of farmers covered by conservation programs. Restoration, as opposed to mere retirement of wetlands, receives much higher funding priority than in earlier years. And there has been a shift away from competitive bidding practices and reliance on environmental indices in program decisions (Cattaneo et al. 2006; Claassen 2003). The latter may have significant effects on the environmental results and cost-effectiveness of conservation programs.

The Farm Bill has expanded environmental protection activities during a political period not generally welcoming to expanded environment and land use programs. It has done so, in part, by marrying environmental protection with federal farm subsidies. This policy shift may make it all the more difficult to seriously reduce or do away with those subsidies, as it has given environmental advocates reasons to join forces with the pro-subsidy coalition. Beyond restructuring farm payments, though, the Farm Bill has expanded its programs that support local farmland preservation and watershed protection efforts. These efforts, which provide assistance to land trusts and encourage local collaborative efforts, are very much in the quieter revolution mold. But these programs are constrained by their costs; in contrast with the initial strategy of attaching conservation conditions to funds already being spent, they require new cash outlays.

Much farmland protection activity is in the form of state and local initiatives, especially in places imminently threatened by urban sprawl (Sorensen, Greene, and Russ 1997; Stokes, Watson, and Mastran 1997; Sokolow and Zurbrugg 2003) (figure 5.1). All states have some form of "preferential assessment," so that farmlands are not taxed at their "highest

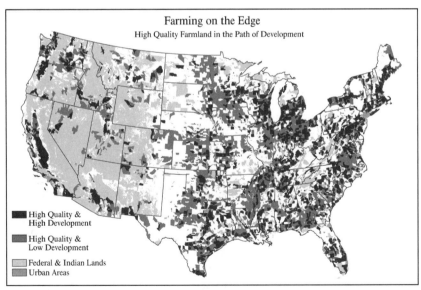

Figure 5.1. Farming on the Edge: High Quality Farmland in the Path of Development
Source: American Farmland Trust

use" value (i.e., for residential or commercial development). Many states include restrictions that prevent wealthy hobby farmers and speculative developers from reaping these tax benefits or that force them to pay penalties if they do (Daniels and Bowers 1997). Various additional state tax credits favor agriculture, with some states imposing special taxes on farmland sales. All states also enable localities to have right-to-farm laws, providing farmers with liability protection against lawsuits over such nuisance issues as odors, noise, and pesticide drift. These legal and economic measures are relatively straightforward and noncontroversial.

As of June 2005, according to the American Farmland Trust, Farmland Information Center (2005), forty-eight states had legislation enabling conservation easements, and twenty-seven had programs for acquiring conservation easements on agricultural lands. This is not the universe of state-level farmland easement programs, since easements can be acquired under other state programs, whose primary stated purpose may not be agricultural land preservation. Still, the data provide a reasonable representation of the scope of state efforts. A total of 1.362 million acres have come under easement protection, at a cost of $1.85 billion to the state programs. An additional $886 million came from various other sources, including local governments, land trusts, foundations, and federal transportation enhancement funds (described below). The most active states, acreage-wise, are Pennsylvania, Maryland, Colorado, New Jersey, and Vermont. It is not surprising that these programs are particularly active in the smaller, highly urbanized eastern and mid-Atlantic states.

The American Farmland Trust, Farmland Information Center (2005) counts fifty local purchase-of-agricultural-easement programs as of June 2005. A total of 241,181 "independent acres" have been protected, at an "independent cost" of $762 million. The "independent" qualification excludes projects jointly undertaken with other government agencies. The states where easement acquisitions are taking place are California, Colorado, Georgia, Illinois, Kentucky, Maryland, Michigan, Montana, New Jersey, New York, North Carolina, Pennsylvania, Virginia, Washington, and Wisconsin. The municipalities and counties that are most active trend toward the relatively wealthy. As with the state programs, these data do not represent all activity involving agricultural easements.

A transferable development rights (TDR) program requires more of governments than does easement acquisition. A sending area—usually, but not necessarily, consisting of agricultural land—is designated, as is a receiving area—an area determined to be suitable for higher-density development. If the program is to be effective, sending and receiving areas must be appropriately defined and zoned, and market forces must be robust enough to ensure a sustainable flow of development rights between the two. In some cases, government agencies purchase and bank the easements, but more typically the agency sets the land use parameters and then lets the market alone drive the process.

As of 2000, the American Farmland Trust, Farmland Information Center (2001) identified fifty active TDR ordinances, most of them adopted by counties and municipalities. Out of a total of 88,575 protected acres, 67,707 agricultural acres were being protected. Montgomery County, Maryland (Banach and Canavan 1987)—which boasts the premier TDR program in the nation—was responsible for a whopping 60 percent of protected farm acres nationwide, while twenty-two of the programs had protected no acres. While most TDR programs are enacted by local governments, New Jersey's state/federal Pinelands National Reserve also has a substantial TDR program (Mason 1992a, 2004), as does the state's Highlands region. Given the complexity of setting up TDR programs, their immediate potential is likely to remain limited to a relatively small number of places.

The American Farmland Trust, Farmland Information Center (2002) defines agricultural district programs, in most cases, as projects authorized by states and implemented by localities. As of 2002, sixteen states had laws enabling agricultural districts. The districts they authorize are meant to maintain a supportive environment for agriculture by offering incentives to participating farmers, who may be required to agree to keep their land in agriculture for a specified number of years (Stokes, Watson, and Mastran 1997; Daniels and Bowers 1997; Daniels 1999). Ideally, government actions, such as water and sewer infrastructure provision, attempt to steer development away from these areas. More restrictive agricultural protection zoning is generally established locally. Provisions vary from place to place, but the main objective is to limit or exclude land uses that conflict with agriculture (Stokes, Watson, and Mastran 1997; American Farmland Trust, Farmland Information Center 2002).

This review has touched upon some of the more consequential state, federal, and local farmland programs. Much more detailed appraisals can be found in Daniels (1999); Daniels and Bowers (1997); Sokolow and Zurbrugg (2003); Randolph (2004); and Zinn and Cowan (2005).

Other National Programs

As with the farmland programs, most initiatives described below provide support to states, localities, and individuals. But the federal government's indirect influence over land use dwarfs most of these efforts. Since the 1950s, for example, the interstate highway system has enormously influenced settlement patterns, while today's federal support for ethanol is influencing agricultural land use. These examples are major initiatives; the cumulative impacts of a myriad of more modest programs and policies also are very consequential. So, too, are the substantial—if often unintended— effects of air, water, and other environmental laws and regulations; funded and unfunded government mandates of all sorts; and general tax policies.

But the focus here is mainly on federal programs that are directed, purposeful land use management programs. Again, federal lands management is not one of this book's themes, but it is frequently touched upon because public lands planning is very much linked with private lands issues. We now review several major programs.

Land and Water Conservation Fund

Created in 1965, the Land and Water Conservation Fund (LWCF) is the premier federal program for supporting land acquisition by the federal, state, and local governments. LWCF is funded mainly through royalties paid for offshore oil and gas leases. But Congress must appropriate the funds each year, and appropriations have been highly variable, yo-yoed by shifting congressional and presidential priorities. In only a few years have appropriations approached the authorized level of $900 million (figure 5.2). Various congressional efforts to make LWCF act as a true trust fund, with guaranteed annual funding levels, have not succeeded, and the drive to do so seemed to be running out of steam in the immediate post–September 11 era (Zinn 2005). But long-term prospects for revived federal interest in LWCF appear more favorable.

LWCF provides funds for most land acquisitions by the four main public lands agencies: the U.S. Forest Service, National Park Service, Fish and Wildlife Service, and Bureau of Reclamation. Though agency policies

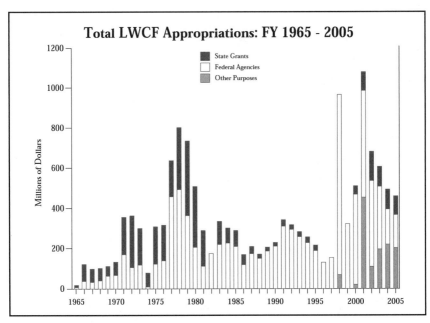

Figure 5.2. Land and Water Conservation Fund Appropriations
Source: Zinn (2005), 3.

are in place for prioritizing land acquisitions, and agencies make requests to Congress, most of the actual purchases are specified through congressional earmarks. Funds frequently are provided to expand public holdings in greenline parks, defined typically as complex, lived-in landscapes with mixed ownership patterns (Mason 1994). Among the fund recipients are Cape Cod National Seashore (Massachusetts), Pictured Rocks National Lakeshore (Michigan), Sleeping Bear Dunes National Lakeshore (Michigan), Cuyahoga Valley National Recreation Area (Ohio), Pinelands National Reserve (New Jersey), Delaware National Scenic River (New Jersey/New York/Pennsylvania), and Santa Monica Mountains National Recreation Area (California) (U.S. Department of the Interior, National Park Service 2007b). In recent years, more funds have been directed toward acquisition of conservation easements and cooperative, multistakeholder programs aimed at protecting larger landscapes. Though total LWCF funding is very limited, and far below its potential, it increasingly is funneled into collaborative, place-based planning projects.

One such initiative funded by LWCF is the U.S. Forest Service's Forest Legacy Program (FLP), established by the 1990 Farm Bill as a response to the Northern Forest Lands study (chapter 4). Initially, the program was limited to northern New England, where it remains very active. FLP is very much a quieter revolution program; it directs funds to states—which in turn may support specific local projects—for fee-simple land acquisition and purchase of easements on privately owned forest lands (USDA Forest Service 2005). The main objective is to protect working forests, especially those facing threats of subdivision and conversion to resort and housing developments. Landowner participation is voluntary, and FLP is meant to complement local and state forest protection efforts. FLP's policy is to authorize payments in lieu of taxes for fee-simple land acquisitions, but not in the case of easement acquisitions (USDA Forest Service 2003).

States make recommendations, which are then subject to Forest Service review and consolidation at the national level. Approved projects may be included in the president's budget request to Congress, thus politicizing the process. Meritorious projects indeed are approved, but merit, as defined by Forest Service guidelines, is not the only consideration. Land trusts become involved in the process in several ways: as intermediaries in acquiring land and easements that are later passed on to the Forest Service, as purchasers of proposed lands or easements not approved by the Forest Service, as easement monitors, and as participants at various levels in the project development and approval processes (USDA Forest Service 2003). As of early 2007, the FLP was credited with protecting 1,475,310 acres in thirty-four states and Puerto Rico, with requests for funds coming from several additional states. More than 900,000 of those acres are in the "Northern Forest" states of Maine, New Hampshire, Vermont, and New York (USDA Forest Service 2007).

LWCF also makes grants directly to states, though funding amounts have become much smaller as a proportion of total monies allocated than was the case in the 1970s and early 1980s. Administered through the National Park Service, the grant funds are meant for land acquisition and development of outdoor recreation facilities. The funds generally are not congressionally earmarked but instead allocated to the fifty states via formula; states then make grants for specific projects, subject to final National Park Service approval on a fifty-fifty match basis. Typical LWCF state-initiated projects include municipal and county park development, hiking and bike trails, river corridor and lakeshore acquisition, and purchases of ecologically valued land parcels (U.S. Department of the Interior, National Park Service 2007b).

To provide just one recent example, the LWCF takes great pride in the 2004 acquisition of most of 677-acre North Bass Island in Lake Erie's southwestern reaches. LWCF's $6 million grant is the largest ever provided for a single-site, state-initiated project. Funds also came from the Ohio Department of Natural Resources, with the entire deal being facilitated and brokered through the nonprofit Conservation Foundation, which provided additional support from its Great Lakes Revolving Fund. Each party takes more than its share of credit for the outcome, but it likely would not have happened without the efforts of all three. During LWCF's earlier years, when more federal funds were available, most projects were intergovernmental efforts. More recently, as the Bass Island case illustrates, LWCF's much decreased funding capacity is being compensated for, at least in part, by increased flexibility and immediate access to funds made possible through collaboration with NGOs.

TEA

Another major source of federal funds is the rather clumsily titled, if cutely acronymed, Intermodal Surface Transportation Efficiency Act (ISTEA) and its progeny. The TEA acts represent a major redirection of highway trust funds, away from road projects and toward other transportation options. It started as ISTEA in 1991, then was amended in 1998 to become the Transportation Equity Act for the 21st Century (TEA-21), and finally reauthorized in 2005 as the Safe, Accountable, Flexible, Efficient Transportation Equity Act (SAFETEA). These various brews all provide federal Department of Transportation funds covering up to 80 percent of total costs for bicycle and pedestrian paths, acquisition of scenic easements, and preservation of historic sites, among other things (National Transportation Enhancements Clearinghouse 2002, 2007a). Between fiscal years 1992 and 2005, $8 billion was made available to the states for these "transportation enhancements," though for various reasons not all that money was actually spent. Approximately twenty-one thousand projects were funded, with about half the federal funds going to bicycle and pedestrian facilities, 16 percent to landscaping and scenic beautification, 8 percent to rails-to-trails, but only 3 percent to acquisition of scenic and historic easements (National Transportation Enhancements Clearinghouse 2007b).

Though TEA funding does not contribute much to systematic planning or management of large landscapes (Giuliano 2004), it does support a great many smaller projects, especially those involving protection of and access to land and water corridors. Local recreation opportunities, along with history and heritage, figure prominently into TEA-supported projects. Protection for ecologically critical land areas often is directly supported with TEA funds; moreover, the many small projects that promote bicycling and walking, as well as those meant to enhance urban amenities and protect rural viewscapes, can have significant landscape and ecological implications.

Transportation enhancement activities often involve collaboration that reaches beyond the state and federal governments. Anza-Borrego Desert State Park, in Southern California, provides an example. In 1993, when the 884-acre Senetec Canyon and Cienega property went on the market, park officials and the Anza-Borrego Foundation sprang into action. The parcel, containing riparian and wetland habitat, was seen as a critical—yet very costly—addition to the park. Acquisition was made possible through a $1 million transportation enhancement grant, matched by $120,000 raised locally. The area's proximity to major transportation routes, combined with its attractiveness as a destination for passive recreation, made it a winning candidate for the federal grant.

One concern with TEA is that its flexibility hastens devolution of fiscal and planning authority to the local level. While it does make sense to address local problems locally, transportation issues rarely are confined within local boundaries. Moreover, it turns out that local governments are not always acting in their own best interests; some adapt their planning priorities simply to meet TEA funding conditions. And competition for limited funds often pits municipalities within a region against one another, counter to the intraregional cooperation theme advanced by smart growth proponents (Giuliano 2004).

Heritage Areas

Heritage areas usually are defined on the basis of both physical and cultural attributes; typical heritage area features are land and water transportation corridors; forges, furnaces, and mills; historic settlements; and key battlefield landscapes. Heritage area attributes usually include some combination of educational, ecological, and economic features. While some areas may be little more than tourism promotion gimmicks, others are venues for enjoying and reflecting about landscape, history, and culture (Eugster 2003).

A national heritage area (NHA) is defined by the National Park Service (U.S. Department of the Interior, National Park Service 2007a), as

> a place designated by the United States Congress where natural, cultural, historic and recreational resources combine to form a cohesive, nationally distinctive landscape arising from patterns of human activity shaped by geography.

The NHA website promotes partnerships, collaboration, local control, celebration, and solutions to challenges and threats posed by imminent, inappropriate development. Some NHAs cover rather expansive regions, on a par with several of the regional planning efforts described in chapter 4. But generally, heritage areas are smaller in scale, and the planning goals and strategies are more circumscribed. Congressional proposals to create a formal national heritage areas system, with standards for designation and management, faltered in the mid-1990s and again in 2005 and 2006 (Vincent and Whiteman 2006). As of early 2007, Congress had designated new heritage study areas, but prospects for a renewed drive to establish a formal heritage areas system were not bright.

The National Park Service (NPS) is the lead heritage actor at the federal level. And any federal involvement with local planning, no matter how minimal, is filled with minefields. In part because of draconian land acquisition practices of years past, the NPS is greeted with extreme hostility in some areas. As a consequence, the agency now goes to elaborate lengths to stress that it is acting only as a partner (albeit with pockets), not proposing land acquisition, and fully respecting local land use control (Pontier 1987; Hamin 2001). Heritage areas are meant to be not only locally managed but also locally inspired. Yet because Congress makes the designation, the role of senators and representatives—keen to bring recognition and resources to their districts—is not to be underestimated. As figure 5.3 shows, the NHA program has a very strong eastern bias, which means that mostly private lands are involved.

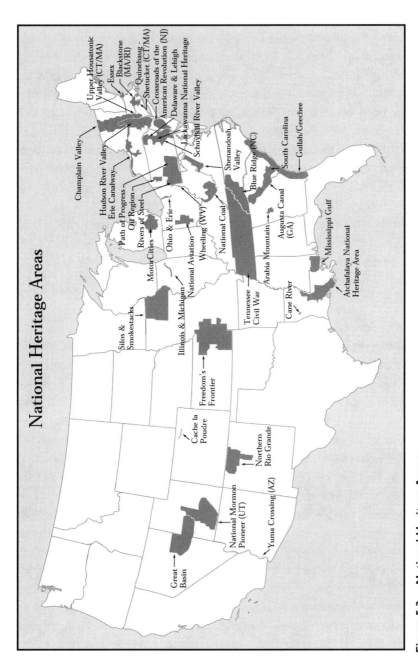

Figure 5.3.   National Heritage Areas
Source: U.S. Department of the Interior, National Park Service (2007a)

NPS designation means national recognition, as well as planning and interpretation expertise and seed money. A management plan is required and must be approved by the Department of the Interior, but it is a locally developed plan. NPS's role in implementation is strictly advisory. Though NPS grants are made available, funding usually is modest. Of course, national designation increases the potential for leveraging funding with resources from other federal agencies, as well as state and local agencies, environmental NGOs, foundations, and private sector interests. NPS data show that as of January 2004, $122 million in NPS funding had been leveraged eightfold. One slice of the funding pie, nearly equal in size to total NPS base funding, represents Transportation Efficiency Grants (U.S. Department of the Interior, National Park Service 2004).

Several states have their own heritage area initiatives. Maryland, Pennsylvania, New York, Louisiana, and Utah have programs, while Texas and Indiana have elements that replicate the national model (U.S. Department of the Interior, National Park Service 2007a).

Wild and Scenic Rivers

The National Wild and Scenic Rivers System (Palmer 1993), initially authorized in 1968, is overseen by the four major federal agencies involved with land management: the National Park Service, U.S. Forest Service, Bureau of Land Management, and U.S. Fish and Wildlife Service. State agencies manage some river segments, and many river designations are partly or wholly coincident with heritage area, park, and greenway designations. Rivers are congressionally designated, but—as just noted with respect to heritage areas—agencies go to great lengths to ensure that the federal government is not a land use planner and that land and easement acquisition is very limited and only used as a last resort (Interagency Wild and Scenic Rivers Coordinating Council 2004). This comes in response to the tremendous hostility triggered in some rural locales by even the hint of a federal presence. Experience along the seventy-three-mile riverine New York/Pennsylvania border is illustrative (Pontier 1987). The Upper Delaware attained scenic and recreational river status in 1978, but only after years of controversy—controversy that would continue flaring up for years to come. In the early 1990s, one could see signs advising NPS to "get out of town" and, during the first Gulf war, urging NPS personnel to relocate to Iraq. Intense, lingering ill will from earlier NPS condemnation of downstream lands for the Tocks Island Dam and associated reservoir, which were stopped by environmental opposition in the 1970s, helps explain the local sentiments.

Emphasis today is on a collaborative approach for protecting "river values." The federal role is mainly one of coordination, technical assistance, and financial responsibility for public information and recreation provision. Depending on their condition and uses, river segments are designated as either "wild," "scenic," or "recreational." Actions requiring federal approval, such as dams or diversions, are prohibited or strictly limited to protect free-flowing river character. Across the country, 11,338 river miles are designated, with the Pacific Northwest amply represented. Wild rivers account for 5,353 miles, scenic rivers for 2,481 miles, and recreational rivers for 3,503 miles (Interagency Wild and Scenic Rivers Coordinating Council 2004).

National Trails System

Federal land management agencies also administer the National Trails System, established by legislation in 1968. Twenty-four national scenic trails and national historic trails, totaling 40,723 miles in length and including such well-known, country-spanning trails as the Appalachian, Pacific Crest, North Country, and Lewis and Clark, have been designated by Congress. An additional nine hundred recreation trails are recognized by the secretaries of agriculture and the interior. Federal agencies maintain trails, develop interpretive programs and facilities, organize cooperative and interagency agreements, and provide financial assistance to partner organizations (U.S. Department of the Interior 2007c). The Rails-to-Trails Conservancy, which organizes an army of volunteer laborers, is one of those organizations. Most states also have their own trail systems, and there are a great many county and municipal systems as well (chapter 6).

Brownfields

In a mainly urban context, we have brownfields redevelopment. By Environmental Protection Agency (EPA) estimates, there are more than 450,000 sites whose "expansion, redevelopment, or reuse . . . may be complicated by the presence or potential presence of a hazardous substance, pollutant, or contaminant" (U.S. Environmental Protection Agency [EPA] 2007d). Though the acreages directly involved often are fairly small, associated urban redevelopment has the potential to influence larger urban and regional land use patterns, limiting sprawl by helping attract residential and commercial development to core urban areas (National Governors Association 2000). That relationship between redevelopment and curtailment of sprawl is yet to be satisfactorily documented, but in any case additional environmental and equity benefits associated with urban revitalization and economic development argue in support of brownfields reclamation. Brownfields remediation is a winning political issue, enjoying wide bipartisan support at the national and state levels and appearing as a plank in most smart growth and sustainable development platforms.

The federal brownfields program began in 1993, with funding coming through Superfund appropriations. Total funding in fiscal year 2002 reached nearly $100 million (Reisch 2002, 9). While EPA may be the eight-hundred-pound federal brownfields gorilla, many other federal agencies and offices also administer brownfields programs (SRA International Inc. 2005). As of mid-2006, EPA had awarded $225 million in grants for site assessment, $187 million in revolving loan fund grants for site cleanup, and $42.7 million in direct cleanup grants (U.S. EPA 2007d). In addition to the grant activity, federal legislation limits liability of small businesses associated with brownfields reclamation and provides tax incentives to those involved with redevelopment. Most states have their own brownfields initiatives (Bartsch and Dorfman 2002), many of them part of a smart growth bundle of programs. Brownfield projects typically involve considerable leveraging of funds from multiple government and private sources.

The National Governors Association (2000), in touting brownfields' potential, points to data showing that nearly half of brownfields redevelopment projects include mixed-use (residential/commercial) projects; other uses include industry, offices, sports facilities, and public schools. Among the projects showcased are Atlanta's Atlantic Steel Project, site of a transit-oriented mixed-use development; River's Edge Project in Traverse City, Michigan, a "new urbanist" development occupying a long-vacant foundry site; Lily Tulip Plant Redevelopment Project in Holmdel, New Jersey; and Pittsburgh's Washington Landing, which occupies an island—linked to downtown by a pedestrian bridge—and includes housing, trails, and other recreation facilities. Denver's former Stapleton Airport is being transformed into a huge model new urbanist, mixed-use development (Berke, Godschalk, and Kaiser 2006).

Despite the many smart growth benefits, brownfields reclamation is hardly issue free. Not all neighborhoods welcome brownfields redevelopment with open arms; indeed, in some instances it is rejected. Along with economic benefits come health questions related to the toxic residuals left in place (Litt, Tran, and Burke 2002). And there also may be issues about the types of economic opportunities created and their beneficiaries.

The Larger Federal Picture

The initiatives just described are some of the largest federal programs that distribute funds and resources for land use related purposes. There are many more (Randolph 2004). The National Park Service has a Rivers, Trails, and Conservation Assistance Program (U.S. Department of the Interior, National Park Service 2007d); the Environmental Protection Agency has its watershed programs (see chapter 6) and a host of other programs; the Fish and Wildlife Service has Habitat Conservation Planning grants, Cooperative Conservation grants, North American Wetlands Conservation Act grants, and Private Stewardship grants; the U.S. Department of Agriculture has numerous programs beyond those already noted; and the departments of Housing and Urban Development, Defense, and Energy—among others—also administer various programs (General Services Administration 2007). The National Natural Landmarks (NNL) program, administered by the National Park Service, recognizes—but has little funding to support—protection of mostly small, privately owned parcels of land of exceptional natural value. Approximately six hundred NNLs have been designated (Shafer 2004). Much larger regions are recognized through the National Estuary Program (NEP), administered by the U.S. EPA (2005). The program supports collaborative, science-based planning in twenty-eight estuarine areas nationwide. Chesapeake Bay, since it has its own legislatively authorized program, is not part of the NEP. And then there are the many state (The Nature Conservancy 2004), county, and municipal programs, some of which are addressed in other parts of this book. An overarching feature is the emphasis on partnerships, collaboration, and—real or apparent—a bottom-up approach to planning. The bottom line, though, is that total federal funding remains relatively modest, especially if the benchmark is the founding intent of the LWCF.

Though comprehensive federal land use legislation like that introduced during the quiet revolution (chapter 2) is unlikely to resurface anytime soon, attempts have been made at bundling together land use, environment, and quality-of-life initiatives at the national level. Indeed, the Clinton-Gore Livability Initiative seemed to be the embodiment of the quieter revolution—all about community, place, partnering and neighboring, and choices and incentives. Unveiled by Vice President Gore in 1999, the initiative embraced the smart growth agenda, just as the smart growth concept was gaining serious national momentum. Local initiative is at the heart of it all, according to the Clinton-Gore manifesto, and a lengthy list of successful local collaborative ventures is cited in support of the Livability Initiative. Urban revitalization, controlled suburban and rural development, and a renewal of civic spirit are all part of this lofty vision, which has these elements (Livable Communities 2000, 25):

- Revitalizing existing communities

- Improving the environment, public health, and quality of life

- Providing more transportation choices

- Improving schools and making them centers of communities

- Expanding economic opportunity

- Increasing public safety and crime prevention

- Protecting farmland and open space

- Becoming disaster resistant

How would all this be achieved? "Better America Bonds," inspired by the many local ballot questions across the country (chapter 6), would enable state and local governments to issue $10.75 billion worth of bonds to support parks, open space acquisition, agricultural lands preservation, wetlands protection, brownfields redevelopment, and water quality improvements. Collaboration is encouraged, but project decisions are to be entirely local (Fisher 2000–2001). Beyond the bonds, $600 million would be made available through the Lands Legacy Initiative as grants to state and local governments, land trusts, and other nonprofits for land acquisition generally, as well as for establishment of urban parks and forests, and protection of farmlands, wetlands, forests, wildlife habitat, and coastal areas. Conservation easements would be eligible for matching grants. And the initiative would provide money for public transportation, traffic congestion mitigation, land use planning grants to localities, Transportation Enhancements Program (described above) expansion, and an array of smaller transportation-related projects. More federal money would also become available for brownfields cleanup, incentives for affordable housing, and data collection for crime fighting. Energy efficiency, renewable energy, metropolitan air quality, and disaster resistance also are addressed. The latter would be achieved not only through disaster-resistant building strategies but also by enhancing community civic capacity, thus enabling improved disaster response. EPA funding for watershed and airshed improvements, as well as local planning generally, would be boosted. These are just the main points; many more, mostly small-bore, items are on the "livability" list.

This ambitious agenda, had it advanced into the implementation phases, probably would have been grossly underfunded and might well have been cut up into smaller, perhaps disconnected, pieces. Though those pieces might have thrived without the broader agenda's supportive framework, most of them dropped off the Bush administration's radar. Still, even in the Bush era, something resembling the livability agenda would be resuscitated—albeit in a more modest, "livability-lite" guise. Smart growth advocates Earl Blumenauer, a Democratic congressman from Oregon, and Rhode Island Republican senator Lincoln Chaffee introduced the Community Character Act in spring 2001. Though the legislation was twice voted out of committee in the Senate, it has not come before the full Senate. The bill had the support of some Republicans, many state and local governments, the National Association of Realtors, and the American Planning Association, among others. But strong opposition was mounted by the National Association of Home Builders, President Bush, many Republicans in Congress, and various property rights groups and right-wing think tanks. The legislation was cast as a federal bribe, land grab, stepping stone to communism.

Though there are differences in the two versions of the bill, the essence of the legislation was authorization of federal funds—in its 2002 versions, between $50 million and $125 million over a five-year period— to be disbursed as grants to states and communities. Funds would be used for developing plans and planning legislation, promoting coordination across state and local boundaries, and acquiring related technical expertise and resources. Local participation, livability, and smart growth were strongly emphasized by the Community Character Act's proponents (American Planning Association 2001, 2002; Salkin 2002a).

The basis for the Community Character Act is a 1,400-page volume produced by the American Planning Association and funded by a consortium of federal agencies and foundations led by the Department of Housing and Urban Development (Meck 2002). This legislative guidebook is a compilation of model planning statutes and ancillary information for all levels of government, meant to adapt for the twenty-first century the Standard City Planning and Zoning and Enabling Acts of the 1920s and the American Law Institute's Model Land Development Code of the 1970s. At the least, this tome will serve as a comprehensive reference and guide; beyond this, it has the potential—some believe—to revolutionize planning from the bottom up.

All these federal schemes, including the stillborn livability initiatives, are no match for the power of past and current government policies that foster sprawl. First, those policies and associated programs have been in place for decades; there is no undoing the Interstate Highway System or the effects of subsidized home mortgages and discriminatory lending practices. Some of the "damage" is being repaired in some places, as with the major redevelopment of Denver's old Stapleton Airport. As part of a larger regional growth strategy, it is being transformed into a new, walkable community that combines jobs, housing, and commercial activities (Berke, Godschalk, and Kaiser 2006). Transit-oriented development is now promoted in many parts of the country, reclaiming some of the vast parking lots that surround existing transit hubs and turning them into mixed-use developments. And many more urban infill projects in cities and older suburbs, and reincarnations of ghost malls, whose corpses litter many an urban fringe area, also are helping to reclaim metropolitan landscapes. But the debt is so huge that these actions, laudable as they may be, are only working around the edges, thus far. As a rule, metropolitan regions continue to "de-densify." But while we may not be able to pay down the debt, to use the federal budget metaphor, turning the annual environmental "deficit" associated with new development into a "surplus" may be within reach. But if the goal is to rein in sprawl, then we must acknowledge that the resources, political will, and behavioral adaptations needed to make this happen are well beyond the federal commitments we are presently willing to make. This is where state and local governments come in, in new and hopeful ways.

More than ever, states and localities are becoming the main stages for innovation in land use management. Indeed, these are the scales at which the most purposeful, directed actions are taken. While federal policies and programs are enormously consequential, most were not designed to account for land use consequences, at least not before the advent of the National Environmental Policy Act (NEPA) and other major environmental legislation of the 1970s. And even in the post-NEPA era, most of us—property rights and wise use advocates excepted—are slow to reconceptualize our view of central government, to understand its importance as a driver of land use and landscape outcomes. State- and local-level planning programs, rather than federal actions, are widely viewed as deliberative, accessible, and influential. And these are the spatial scales at which quieter revolution activity is now most in evidence. This is not to deny the need—indeed, imperative need—for federal action. But that is not where we, as a nation, are right now.

State and Local Quieter Revolution Programs

While this section is mainly about state and local land use programs, references also are made to federal efforts with which they are linked; most of those federal programs already have been described. Some may object to the "smart growth" brand name, ever so popular nowadays with growth management advocates. Granted, not all that much is new under the smart growth sun, but this is how growth management is now being packaged and presented in many places, often with much success. There is no denying that the smart growth phenomenon has taken on a life of its own, playing an important part in shaping land use and growth management debates and bringing new resources—if not necessarily new planning techniques—into play.

What Is Smart Growth?

Given that various versions of smart growth are endorsed by organizations ranging from the National Association of Home Builders to the Sierra Club, it should come as little surprise that no single definition suffices. As with notions of "sustainability" and "sustainable development," the term is adapted to different interests and ends. This definitional limberness allows the smart growth tent to accommodate diverse, sometimes discordant stakeholders. And to some collaborative planning advocates, this is its singular achievement—regardless of what does or does not emerge in the way of legislation, funding, plan implementation, and plan outcomes.

Many organizations, agencies, and individuals have assembled lists of smart growth principles. Do they labor over each word and sentence to try to find language agreeable to as broad a constituency as possible? There is no way to be sure, but judging by the contents of the lists and the similarities among them, it would seem that considerable care goes into producing a streamlined, consensus-friendly product. Common to most lists is an emphasis on compact urban and suburban form, open space and farmland protection, reduced automobile dependence, and housing affordability. These concerns are framed as matters of choice, fairness, equity, diversity, cooperation, and attractiveness. The following list is from the Smart Growth America (2007) website:

- Mix Land Uses
- Take Advantage of Compact Building Design
- Create Range of Housing Opportunities and Choices
- Create Walkable Neighborhoods
- Foster Distinctive, Attractive Communities with a Strong Sense of Place
- Preserve Open Space, Farmland, Natural Beauty and Critical Environmental Areas
- Strengthen and Direct Development Toward Existing Communities
- Provide a Variety of Transportation Choices

- Make Development Decisions Predictable, Fair and Cost Effective

- Encourage Community and Stakeholder Collaboration

The list reaffirms the notion, introduced above, that smart growth is essentially a repackaging of a set of basic comprehensive planning principles. But branding is important, and it has helped growth management advocates enlist the support of a wide range of government, nongovernment, and business sector actors. Though this may make for some seemingly strange bedfellows, upon closer consideration, some of these alliances make quite a lot of sense.

The housing industry, for instance, while not entirely on board with every element of the smart growth agenda, does have a keen interest in opening up housing markets in places where antigrowth sentiment is powerful. Organizations like the National Association of Home Builders can present themselves as champions of social justice by supporting affordable housing for all communities. From an environmental justice perspective, we might ask why urban dwellers who have reached the point where they can afford to move out of the city should be induced to stay, for the sake of environmental protection, sustainability, or sensible planning. If others before them could avail themselves of a desirable suburban lifestyle, why should they be denied? This question is especially compelling when applied to those whose mobility was constrained in the past by systemic inequities or overt exclusion on the basis of race or class. Indeed, Kahn's (2001) analysis finds that sprawled development increases homeownership options for blacks. This is not to take away from the pressing issues of urban disinvestment and neglect, only to place residential choice in a broader equity framework. Exacerbating smart growth's conflicted relationship with environmental justice is its handling of housing affordability. While affordable housing usually is included as part of the smart growth package, it often encounters opposition—sometimes from growth management activists themselves, who prefer it be built somewhere else, not in their communities. And there always seem to be good environmental rationales favoring those alternative locations.

It may be relatively painless to embrace a broad smart growth agenda, but implementing its individual elements is a different story, involving serious political, social, and economic commitments and consequences. Anthony Downs (2001), recognizing the degree to which varied constituencies differentially embrace the smart growth agenda, uses a fourteen-item checklist to analyze views of three major advocacy groups. The results are reproduced here as table 5.1. Though the summary descriptions attached to each group's views necessarily oversimplify the nature of their smart growth support, they nonetheless offer a reasonable overview of the state of smart growth advocacy today.

Given this diversity of constituencies, smart growth is aptly characterized as the art of the possible, politically and economically (Soule 2006b). While there is a huge toolbox full of techniques and strategies upon which to draw (Daniels 1999; Kayden 2002; Porter, Dunphy, and Salvesen 2002; Randolph 2004; Berke, Godschalk, and Kaiser 2006) and prior experiences from which to learn, the realistic range of options almost always is far more limited than growth management advocates would like it to be. Kayden (2002, 160–61) provides a good summary of the planning instruments most commonly deployed:

- Traditional zoning tweaked to encourage high-density development near public transportation nodes

- Mixed-use zoning encouraging combinations of retail, residential, and small office uses in the same structure

- Inclusionary zoning securing affordable housing as part of a new private market-rate housing development

- Cluster zoning authorizing tighter layouts of housing units than traditional single-family zoning would otherwise permit, securing open space throughout the rest of a land parcel

- Agricultural zoning, floodplain, wetlands, and habitat protection controls, and other land use/environmental laws protecting sensitive land from inappropriate development, thereby preserving open space

- Historic preservation ordinances protecting landmark structures and historic districts in existing built-up areas, downtowns, and main streets

Table 5.1. Potential Elements of Smart Growth

ASPECTS OF FOURTEEN POTENTIAL ELEMENTS OF "SMART GROWTH"

Potential "Smart Growth" Element	Views of Advocate Groups Toward Each Element				Prevalence in U.S. Metro Areas	U.S. Metro Areas Where This Element Exists
	Anti-Growth	Pro-Growth	Inner-City			
1. Limiting outward extension of growth	Strongly favor	Strongly oppose	Favor		Rather rare	Portland, Lexington, Boulder
2. Financing added infrastructures by loading costs onto new developments	Strongly favor	Strongly oppose	Favor		Widespread Practice	Many cities in California
3. Reducing transport auto dependence by increasing emphasis on transit	Strongly favor	Oppose	Strongly favor		Widespread Attempts	Portland, San Diego, Atlanta
4. Promoting compact, mixed-use development	Strongly favor	Oppose	Strongly favor		Moderately frequent	Portland, Seattle, State of Maryland
5. Creating financial incentives for local governments to designate growth areas	Favor	Oppose	Neutral		Rare	State of Maryland
6. Adopting fiscal resource sharing	Favor	Oppose	Favor		Very Rare	Twin Cities
7. Choosing some form of regional governance or planning coordination	Oppose	Strongly oppose	Oppose		Rare	Portland, Twin Cities, Atlanta
8. Adopting faster and more certain development permission processes	Oppose	Strongly favor	Neutral		Rare	Portland
9. Creating widespread affordable housing	Oppose	Favor	Favor		Rare	Montgomery Co., Maryland
10. Developing consensus-building process	Favor	Oppose	Favor		Rare	Seattle
11. Preserving open space and environment	Strongly favor	Favor	Favor		Widespread	Boulder, Lexington
12. Redeveloping inner-core areas and encouraging development on in-fill sites	Strongly favor	Favor	Strongly favor		Widespread Attempts	Denver, Seattle, Portland
13. Encouraging new forms of urban design	Strongly favor	Strongly favor	Favor		Widespread	Seaside
14. Creating a stronger sense of community	Strongly favor	Favor	Strongly favor		Rare	Portland

Source: Anthony Downs, senior fellow, Brookings Institution

- Planned unit development (PUD) and traditional neighborhood development (TND) ordinances seeking mixtures of land uses over large land areas

- Urban growth boundaries promoting development within and limiting development outside built-up areas

- Exactions and impact fees conditioning land use regulatory approval on the developer's agreement to provide or pay for roads, water and sewer facilities, schools, open space, and other physical and social infrastructure needed by the proposed development

- Adequate public facilities and concurrency rules prohibiting development until it can be demonstrated that public infrastructure and services are sufficient to meet the needs of the proposed development

- Infrastructure turndowns, such as no curb cuts on this road or no hook-up onto the water and sewer system, effectively controlling if and when development occurs

- Growth caps restricting the amount of development permits in a given year or time period

- Moratoria temporarily halting land development while government prepares land use or capital infrastructure plans or otherwise works to ensure the availability of adequate infrastructure to service anticipated growth

Adopting the smart growth package means adopting many of these elements. But in the years following the quiet revolution, many communities have embraced various parts of this agenda, with or without state or federal government urging and support. Local planning has become far more sophisticated and environmentally conscious than it was thirty-five years ago. Steep slopes, stormwater runoff, aquifer recharge, farmlands, and critical habitat are addressed in many more plans and ordinances now than then. But the local planning landscape remains highly uneven; for the most part it is poorly coordinated across regions, with some places simply having become far smarter about being exclusionary than they were years ago. Berke, Godschalk, and Kaiser (2006) conclude that despite recent environmental progress, most localities remain very progrowth.

Smart Growth Comes of Age

The 1990s and the dawn of the new millennium have brought us something of a smart growth boomlet. A mini-industry, replete with symposia, conferences, assessments, how-to publications, model laws, and more, is in full bloom. The smart growth phenomenon is unfolding mainly at the state and local levels, supported in some measure by the constellation of federal programs described earlier. Geographically, the burst of activity is quite uneven, favoring the old quiet revolution states but with many new places introducing substantial planning reforms.

The federal government's role in promoting smart growth already has been described. But, in fact, states and localities are the prime movers. Between 1999 and 2001, over two thousand planning bills were introduced in state legislatures, and about one-fifth of those were enacted. Executive orders were issued in seventeen states (Johnson 2002). Increasingly, this activity is occurring in states other than the coastal states (figure 5.4).

Figure 5.4 is from the American Planning Association's (APA) 2002 evaluation of state smart growth programs (Johnson 2002). Indicators used in this analysis include planning legislation enacted, executive orders issued, task force reports released, and ballot questions passed. Perhaps not surprisingly, states having progressed furthest with program implementation include quiet revolution leaders: those who years ago put into place, or at least attempted to put into place, state or substate programs. They are Florida, California, Vermont, Georgia, Rhode Island, Oregon, and Washington. Interestingly, Hawaii does not make the cut. Some new states also are in the top tier, along with several that are at least at the early stages of planning reform. Though most Sun Belt states are rather conservative in political temperament and averse to government regulation, they face the greatest growth pressures. Figure 5.4 reveals that many of them are responding with new smart growth initiatives. Several Great Plains states, along with a few states in the South and Midwest, stand out as laggards in APA's assessment. Population growth rates in those states have been relatively low, negative in the past few years in North Dakota.

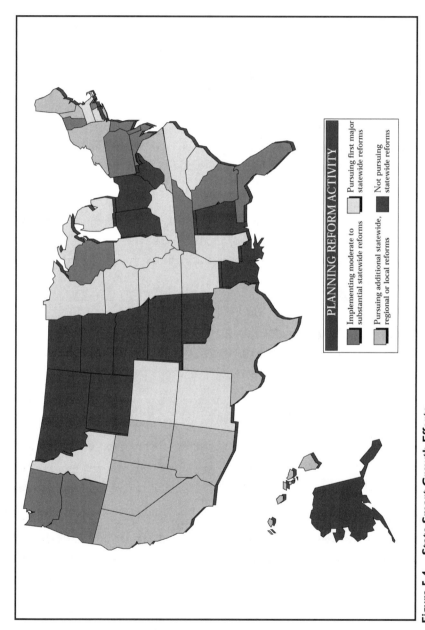

Figure 5.4. State Smart Growth Efforts

Source: Reprinted with permission from *Planning for Smart Growth: 2002 State of the States,* published by the American Planning Association.

Next we present some specific cases, from three leading smart growth states.

The Oregon Precedent

Oregon's dramatic coastline, soaring peaks, powerful Columbia River, fertile Willamette Valley, and eastern desert all contribute to its popular image as a natural paradise. Overlay this tableau with an historically resource-based economy and vibrant, rapidly growing urban centers, and the result is a very complex landscape upon which to superimpose environmental policies. Yet Oregon has emerged as an environmental and growth management leader (Judd and Beach 2003). Despite recent passage of a ballot measure requiring that landowners be compensated for property value reductions due to government regulations (chapter 7), Oregon remains a smart growth poster child. Central to Oregon's program is a hard regulatory approach, dating back to the quiet revolution. Faced with rapid growth and fears of "Californication" in parts of the state, legislation requiring local land use and growth management plans was passed in 1969. That law, however, was not judged to be very effective (DeGrove 1984, 2005).

In 1973, the more broad-ranging Land Use Planning Act (S.B. 100) was passed, creating statewide planning goals and requiring cities to establish urban growth boundaries (UGBs). Central to the act are nineteen goals, five of them added in 1976, in the areas of citizen involvement; land use planning; agricultural lands; forest lands; open spaces, scenic and historic areas, and natural resources; air, water, and land resources quality; areas subject to natural disasters and hazards; recreational needs; economic development; housing; public facilities and services; transportation; energy conservation; urbanization; Willamette River Greenway; estuarine resources; coastal shorelands; beaches and dunes; and ocean resources (Oregon Department of Land Conservation and Development 2007). The considerable attention to coastal and urban areas is quite striking, given that Oregon's push toward comprehensive planning was, at the outset, directed principally toward farmland protection. Initially, the act was to have created regional councils, but this provision was scratched and the compromise solution was to vest greater authority for comprehensive planning with county governments. A provision that would have identified critical planning areas was dropped entirely. In the end, the legislation was not nearly as top-down as many environmentalists might have wanted, but it provides far more state oversight than planning legislation passed by most other states (DeGrove 2005; Judd and Beach 2003).

Early on, the emphasis was more on what was happening outside the urban growth boundaries than inside them. Nelson's (1999) analysis of farmland preservation, for example, reveals that Oregon was largely succeeding in protecting prime farmland but not in limiting the spread of hobby farms. But as smart growth proponents well know, the processes unfolding in the two critical spatial domains—inside the boundary and outside the boundary—are deeply linked. Nelson and Moore's (1996) detailed study gives Oregon rather mixed grades; larger cities, they find, are more successfully containing new development within UGBs than are smaller municipalities.

Inside UGBs generally, Weitz and Moore (1998) demonstrate, most new development has not been dispersed; rather, it is contiguous to existing development. In other words, sprawl is effectively being managed, even within the growth areas. As concerns about urban form came to the fore in 1995, designated municipalities were required to provide for a twenty-year supply of developable land within their UGBs. For Portland, this meant densification within the UGB, as well as expansion of the boundary in keeping with the twenty-year requirement. Those expansions are contested by growth management advocates, who contend that prime farmland is being sacrificed in violation of state law (Weitz 1999).

Oregon continues to promote sustainability and smart growth. Representative Earl Blumenauer is an outspoken smart growth proponent, adept at amplifying the Oregon experience on the national stage. In 2000, Governor John Kitzhaber issued an executive order directing state government to become sustainable by 2025. This was followed up by additional decrees in 2003 and 2006. The multiple sustainability initiatives support not only in-house practices involving procurement, energy efficiency, and carbon emissions but also state actions affecting an array of projects related to land use, agriculture, ecosystem management, brownfields restoration, and watershed management (SustainableOregon.net 2007). Among those projects are the Applegate Partnership, a watershed management project that brings together interests in timber harvesting and environmental protection; the Applegate experience often is held up as a premier example of collaborative, place-based planning (chapter 3). All these recent initiatives are more quieter revolution than quiet revolution in character.

Oregon's land use program has been contested almost continuously. A series of ballot questions, aimed at undoing it in whole or in part, all have failed—except Measure 7, which was passed in 2000, requiring that landowners be compensated for losses in property value due to regulation. Although Measure 7 was declared unconstitutional, it was reborn as Measure 37, and voters passed it in 2002 (chapter 7). In part, Oregon's success in facing down challenges can be attributed to strong gubernatorial support for state land use planning, especially early support from Governor Tom McCall, who was instrumental in the act's passage in 1973. Oregon is not the only state where a former governor leaves an outsized legacy. In Maryland, Governor Parris Glendening was a tireless smart growth advocate in the 1990s, while in New Jersey, Governor Brendan Byrne's vigorous 1970s and early 1980s advocacy led to creation of the Pinelands National Reserve (Mason 1992a).

Upon leaving office in 1975, Governor McCall cofounded the NGO named 1000 Friends of Oregon. This organization inspired sibling groups in several other states, with Pennsylvania ratcheting the nomenclature up a notch to 10,000 Friends of Pennsylvania (see below). Although 1000 Friends of Oregon claims five thousand members, much of its work is through formal partnerships with local NGOs across the state. Over the decades, the organization has moved from legal advocate toward coalition builder, adapting from its quiet revolution beginnings to a quieter revolution political climate. It has cultivated relationships with several resource-based organizations, and in 1994 it led the effort to found the Coalition for a Livable Future (1000 Friends of Oregon 2007). The coalition's broad mission includes environmental justice, housing affordability, and transportation planning (Coalition for a Livable Future 2007).

Oregon is an innovator in downtown planning; Portland's thriving city center, with its mixed commercial and residential land use, light-rail transit network, and waterfront park, is a national urban model (Ozawa 2004). Portland's favorable economic conditions, relatively limited occurrences of concentrated poverty, and long-range planning vision all have contributed to its success. Obviously, no American state or city—including Oregon and its municipalities—is free of economic, political, social, and environmental challenges. But it seems that Oregon's very deliberate and comprehensive city planning efforts have played an important part in meeting these challenges and shaping its urban character (Ozawa 2004).

To portray the Oregon experience entirely as a top-down, state regulatory approach would be to mischaracterize it. Though it is defined by its quiet revolution origins, it is adapting to a quieter revolution political climate. If Oregon is to continue to be a leader, it will have to either overturn Measure 37 or find ways to make its land use policies work in a post–Measure 37 world. This will be a supreme test of Oregon's adaptive management capabilities.

Like Oregon, neighboring Washington State is a state planning leader, but its system is more devolved, less stringently imposed than Oregon's. But UGBs are part of Washington's state planning infrastructure. Boulder, Colorado, and Concord, New Hampshire, also have created UGBs (Gillham 2002), and other urban areas may eventually follow suit. But without a strong state or regional commitment, it may not be possible to effectively contain growth within the boundary. New growth will simply leapfrog to areas where regulatory oversight is less demanding.

Maryland's Smart Growth Initiatives

Maryland is another smart growth poster child, whose efforts might best be characterized as robust quieter revolution approaches. All but the state's western extremity is within the Chesapeake Bay watershed (chapter 4)—and it is in the Chesapeake experience that Maryland's current smart growth programs are rooted. The 1984 Critical Areas Act sought to regulate development within a thousand feet of the bay's shoreline, but its effectiveness was limited by a number of statutory loopholes. Acting on recommendations of the Year 2020 Panel—a commission assembled by the Chesapeake Bay state governors—the Maryland General Assembly passed and Republican governor William Donald Schaefer signed into law the Economic, Growth, Resource Protection, and Planning Act of 1992. Unlike the Critical Areas Act, which covers only about 10 percent of Maryland's land base, this law applies to the entire state. While it emphasizes the primacy of local planning, encourages economic growth, and streamlines the regulatory process, the act also places obligations on local and state governments, in accord with a set of "visions" adapted from the

2020 report. Those visions seek to concentrate development, protect sensitive areas, direct rural development to population centers, protect the Chesapeake Bay, conserve resources, and provide the needed funding to realize these goals. Local plans must comply with the act's prescriptions, and the Economic Growth, Resource Protection, and Planning Commission was created to provide oversight. But many of the act's requirements, the result of legislative compromise, are too vaguely defined to allow for meaningful enforcement (DeGrove 2005).

A rare Democratic gubernatorial victor in the Republican revolution of 1994, Parris Glendening was a staunch supporter of the 1992 act and the growth commission. But Glendening took things up a level with his signature Smart Growth and Neighborhood Conservation Initiative. In bringing his proposals to the General Assembly, he was careful to emphasize economic growth and the primacy of local planning. But a strong, if nonregulatory, role for state government is central to Maryland's smart growth program. Local governments retain full planning and zoning authority, but they lose state funding if they fail to comply with the law's provisions. Interestingly, some of the strongest opposition to Glendening's initiatives came from the Maryland Association of Counties, whose members were fearful of losing control over planning decisions (Gurwitt 1999).

Glendening's Smart Growth and Neighborhood Conservation Initiative consists of a series of laws passed in 1997. Priority funding areas (PFAs) are established, some by the state and others by authority vested in counties. Growth is encouraged in these areas through state investments in roads, housing, schools, and other infrastructural elements. Rural legacy areas are the preservation counterpart to PFAs; state funding for farmland and open space protection is targeted to these areas. The Brownfields Voluntary Cleanup and Revitalization Program is a particularly popular part of the initiative; it addresses cleanup standards and provides liability protection for those involved with site redevelopment. The Job Creation Tax Credit is targeted to PFAs, and the Live Near Your Work Program provides cash grants to homeowners living in eligible areas (DeGrove 2005).

In early 1998, Governor Glendening issued an executive order aimed at bringing state agencies fully in line with provisions of the 1992 growth act. More legislation was passed in 2000, promoting "smart codes" and tax relief for building rehabilitation, creating model codes and guidelines for infill development, and providing incentives for establishing transferable development rights programs in rural legacy areas. The 2001 legislative session brought new funding for parks and playgrounds, a system of connected ecological reserves, revitalization of distressed areas, public transportation, and new and upgraded schools located to minimize sprawl. In creating the Commission on Environmental Justice and Sustainable Communities, Glendening acknowledged the relationship between environmental justice and smart growth, calling for environmental justice implications of state initiatives to be taken into account. Also in 2001, the Office of Smart Growth was established, to serve as an information clearinghouse and provide general oversight for implementing smart growth programs. In 2001, Glendening also exercised the state's authority to intercede in local government proceedings, supporting decisions favoring transit-oriented and infill developments and opposing a Wal-Mart proposal. The year 2002 brought legislation establishing the Community Legacy Program, with $10 million in funding directed toward community revitalization, and a $500 million program for mass-transit improvements (American Planning Association 2002; DeGrove 2005; Maryland Department of Planning 2007).

Parris Glendening succeeded in institutionalizing smart growth planning in Maryland. In the 2002 gubernatorial contest between Democrat Kathleen Kennedy-Townsend and Republican Robert L. Ehrlich Jr., it was a critical issue, with both candidates voicing strong support for Glendening's programs. When Ehrlich took office, he was not about to undo Maryland's smart growth planning infrastructure. This parallels New Jersey's situation in the early 1980s, when Republican governor Tom Kean, to the chagrin of some of his supporters, basically stayed the course with the brand-new Pinelands preservation program that had been shepherded into place by his predecessor, Brendan Byrne (Mason 1992a). Of course, the Ehrlich administration did reshuffle some of Maryland's growth management priorities; for example, more attention was directed toward the urban part of the smart growth agenda, with less emphasis on the expensive—and in some places more politically contentious—open space acquisition and farmland protection programs (DeGrove 2005). With the 2006 election of Democrat Martin O'Malley, state government can be expected to do more than just sustain the smart growth agenda; it will again be placed front and center.

Maryland's smart growth efforts seem to be succeeding in keeping public offices and schools within developed areas, redesigning roads, and encouraging new urbanist and transit-oriented development (Johnson 2002; "Maryland Smart Growth Laws Having an Impact" 2002). Local governments, however, have been slow to embrace the state's smart growth prescriptions. Though Maryland's is one of the country's most vigorous and far-reaching smart growth efforts, its effectiveness still seems to be highly uneven. It is likely to yield the greatest results in those places most willing and able to take advantage of state incentives and assistance. A critical question for Maryland involves the distribution of those benefits: to what extent are they being fairly distributed across the social, economic, and political landscapes?

Growing Greener in Pennsylvania

Pennsylvania provides an example of a gentle growth management strategy, even by quieter revolution standards. Pennsylvania's 1990–2000 population growth rate was the third smallest in the country, and its major cities and many of its rural areas are experiencing population stagnation or decline. At the same time, suburban locales—and especially some outer suburban and exurban areas—are witnessing dramatic increases in population. Although Pennsylvania's total population grew by only 2.5 percent between 1982 and 1997, consumption of farmland and open space per additional resident was second in the nation only to Wyoming (Brookings Institution Center on Urban and Metropolitan Policy 2003, 9). Some regions, until recently rural in character, are becoming part of the expanded commuter sheds for out-of-state metropolitan areas. Monroe, Wayne, and Pike counties in the Poconos region of northeastern Pennsylvania are home to thousands of recent settlers who make one-way commutes of up to two hours or more to New York City and northern New Jersey. Pike County, whose population grew 65 percent between 1990 and 2000, is now classified for census purposes as part of the New York Metropolitan Statistical Area. The south-central part of the commonwealth houses many who work in the Baltimore and Washington metropolitan areas. Adams, Lancaster, and York counties are experiencing growth rates well above the state average (Brookings Institution Center on Urban and Metropolitan Policy 2003, 21). Lancaster County, blessed with extraordinarily rich soils and home to large Amish and Mennonite populations, has had to contend with intense residential growth pressures in recent years (Brookings Institution Center on Urban and Metropolitan Policy 2003).

Though 84 percent of its citizens reside in metropolitan regions, Pennsylvania is a state of small towns, with 2,566 municipalities in total. Rural Pennsylvania still enjoys considerable political clout, disproportionate to its population. Across the state, economic conditions are highly variable, ranging from depressed coal regions to successful high-tech minicorridors. Political cultures, too, are widely divergent. The result is a complex sociopolitical landscape, made simple by Democratic political consultant James Carville's characterization: Philadelphia and Pittsburgh, with Alabama in between.

Pennsylvania's environmental management programs are in part inspired by and in some instances developed in cooperation with neighboring environmental policy leaders Maryland, New Jersey, and New York. Signing onto the Chesapeake Bay Agreement, joining the Delaware River Basin Commission, setting mercury standards more stringent than the federal government's, and—along with other northeastern and northwestern states—adopting California's strict auto emission standards are examples. At the same time as they are taking these environmentally progressive steps, Pennsylvania's lawmakers must balance a complicated, stressful transition to a postindustrial economy with deep-rooted cultural and economic imperatives to realize maximum yields from the commonwealth's resource base—especially its coal.

Only about half of Pennsylvania's municipalities have comprehensive plans; approximately the same proportion have zoning. But most towns in major urbanized regions have planning and zoning ordinances; about 90 percent of the commonwealth's residents live in places that do have zoning (Pennsylvania Department of Community and Economic Development 2001, 2003, 2007).

Given these complex, highly uneven conditions, how has Pennsylvania responded to land use and growth-related issues? It appears that something of a tipping point was reached in the 1990s, and political action followed. A series of amendments to the Municipalities Planning Code was enacted, providing localities with an arsenal of new planning tools. Among the items added to the planning tool kit were transferable development rights, impact fees, and the ability for curative amendment challenges—often brought by developers alleging that municipalities are skirting "fair share" housing requirements—to be dealt with on a multi-municipal, regional basis rather than only by one township at a time.

Toward the end of the decade, Republican governor Tom Ridge responded forcefully to growing national, regional, and local concerns about sprawl and its impacts. Polling data from the period indicate that sprawl and related traffic issues indeed had achieved high salience in the region (New Jersey Future 2000; Millersville University Center for Opinion Research 2001; Belden, Russonello & Stewart 2004; Pew Center for Civic Journalism 2007a, 2007b). Not coincidentally, Ridge's efforts were bolstered by the political presence, research findings (Clarion Associates 2000), and outreach efforts of Pennsylvania's "friends" group—10,000 Friends of Pennsylvania—which was founded in 1998. During that same year, a milestone report—the *Report of the Pennsylvania 21st Century Environment Commission*—was released by the governor's office. That report ranges over many environmental and energy issues but calls particular attention to the negative impacts of sprawl. It proposes voluntary, locally based solutions; embraces a progrowth philosophy; and recommends additional changes to the commonwealth's Municipalities Planning Code (MPC), planning assistance to localities, and reform of state policies and practices. This is very much a quieter revolution document, proposing state incentives, assistance, and leadership by example to cope with the residuals of Pennsylvania's history of resource extraction and industrial production, while ensuring that future development patterns are sustainable (Pennsylvania 21st Century Environment Commission 1998).

In short order, Governor Ridge rolled out his Growing Greener initiative. In January 1999 he issued an executive order that guides agency decisions, requiring land use impacts to be taken into account. In December of that year, he signed into law the Environmental Stewardship and Watershed Protection Act; it was reauthorized in 2002. The act authorizes a total of $1.3 billion through 2012, distributed as grants and loans, for purchases of easements on agricultural lands, brownfields restoration, watershed management, and other environmental programs. Growing Greener was followed in 2000 by Growing Smarter legislation: Acts 67 and 68. Enabling and encouraging multimunicipal planning, and ensuring greater consistency between plans and zoning ordinances, are among these acts' main aims. The legislation also allows for designation of growth and rural resource areas and authorizes transferable development rights, tax revenue sharing, and impact fee assessment under "intergovernmental co-operative agreements" (American Planning Association 2002; Denworth 2002; Mason 2005).

Pennsylvania's entirely voluntary provisions—with their accompanying incentives considerably scaled back in the legislative process—lack the force of Oregon's or even Maryland's laws. An amendment to the Municipalities Planning Code that would allow designation of growth boundaries was considered but dropped. Critics also point to the continuing concessions to mining, timber, corporate farming, and home building interests. For example, forestry must be a permitted use in every zoning district in every municipality in Pennsylvania. Central Philadelphia and Pittsburgh, even, must make allowances for forestry (Lioz 2001). Nonetheless, Growing Greener supporters claim some success; for instance, over a quarter of the commonwealth's municipalities are participating in some fashion in multimunicipal planning (10,000 Friends of Pennsylvania 2007).

Democratic governor Edward Rendell was elected in 2002. His initiative, Growing Greener 2, had as its centerpiece a ballot question authorizing an $800 million environmental bond issue. The House passed the bill at that funding level, but the Senate version put the funding at $625 million, the amount in the bill's final incarnation. Voters approved the ballot question, approximately 60 percent to 40 percent, on primary day in May 2005. Growing Greener 2 funds, distributed through several state agencies, go toward farmland, gameland, and open space protection; state park and forest improvements; urban revitalization projects; brownfields redevelopment; energy projects; and cleanup of acid mine pollution, among other things. County governments, traditionally not very powerful actors in the Pennsylvania planning process, are eligible to receive up to $90 million through an Environmental Block Grant Program. But Growing Greener 2 goes well beyond distribution of resources among various levels of government; substantial funding also is going to land trusts and watershed conservancies (PA 2007; Pennsylvania Department of Conservation and Natural Resources 2006).

Oregon, Maryland, and Pennsylvania are smart growth leaders. As figure 5.4 shows, many more states have programs in various stages of development. And numerous counties and municipalities, with and without strong state support, are engaging in very determined efforts of their own.

All these programs enjoy the support and encouragement of a national network of organizations that act as information clearinghouses, sounding boards, and smart growth promoters.

Smart Growth's Support Network

Smart growth, by most definitions, is very much about collaborative networks. And indeed, such networks are active at the local and state levels, as described in the cases above. Had the Clinton-Gore Livability Agenda been launched, or the Community Character Act passed, a substantial national smart growth infrastructure might now be in place. But even in the absence of a comprehensive superstructure, we have several elements of a national smart growth support system.

Federal departments and agencies whose portfolios include environment, land use, housing, and even health are giving attention—albeit usually rather limited attention—to smart growth. Of course, federal programs can and do invoke parts of the smart growth agenda, without necessarily adopting the terminology. Still, many federal smart growth activities have been downsized or eliminated since 2000. The EPA remains the federal leader; its smart growth efforts are the most visible, with a website, publications, modest grant programs, technical assistance, and an annual smart growth awards competition (U.S. EPA 2007f). Under EPA's smart growth umbrella are its brownfields programs (described above) and the collaborative Smart Growth Network (SGN).

In 1996, various NGOs and government organizations joined with the EPA to create the SGN. As might be expected, several environmental and land protection organizations are members. But so too are organizations concerned with housing issues, among them the National Association of Realtors, National Multi-Housing Council, and National Neighborhood Coalition. The SGN describes itself as a forum, seeking to develop and disseminate information, raise public awareness, and promote practices and strategies that advance smart growth (Smart Growth Network 2007).

SGN is not the only national smart growth umbrella organization. Smart Growth America (SGA), which came into being in 2000, focuses on coalition building, communications, federal-level policy development, and research. Smart growth is defined broadly to include traffic issues, open space and farmland protection, air and water quality, social equity, and affordable housing. SGA members include environmental protection and environmental justice groups, community development associations, and various land use and smart growth organizations. SGA acts as an information clearinghouse and is a prolific producer of smart growth publications in its own right (Smart Growth America 2007). It also was instrumental in developing the Smart Growth Leadership Institute and National Smart Growth Council, which seek to train leaders, influence officials, and remove barriers to adopting smart growth planning strategies. Former Maryland governor Parris Glendening and former New Jersey governor and EPA administrator Christine Todd Whitman are cochairs of the leadership institute.

The Smart Communities Network is a project of the National Center for Appropriate Technology (NCAT), an organization supported in the 1970s by the former Community Services Administration. NCAT is a story in survival. It had as its original mission development and dissemination of simple, affordable energy conservation and other small-scale technologies. NCAT came through a near-death experience in the Reagan years, transforming itself from grantee to much scaled-down government contractor. The organization continued carving out niches for itself and securing more federal monies. NCAT's current focus is mainly on its smart communities and sustainable development information portal, which is funded by nongovernment sources. Its website is a guide to case studies, financial and technical resources, and model codes and ordinances for localities (Smart Communities Network 2007). Another smart growth information portal is the Sustainable Communities Network (2007).

Major national environmental organizations are members of the national coalitions but also have their own smart growth programs and projects. A leading case in point is the Sierra Club. The club's 1999 report, *Solving Sprawl: The Sierra Club Rates the States* (Sierra Club 1999), garnered considerable attention, as such rating exercises so often do. And the club's user-friendly website includes a set of calculators for comparing impacts of sprawled development with smart growth development patterns, as well as a series of local, place-based images illustrating how attractive added density and mixed uses can be in contemporary suburban settings (Sierra Club 2007b). The Natural Resources Defense Council's website has a similar section, with informative fact sheets and Q&A discussions. NRDC also produces widely distributed reports on sprawl (Benfield,

Raimi, and Chen 1999) and smart growth (Benfield, Terris, and Vorsanger 2001). Through its chapter organizations, the National Audubon Society promotes smart growth; Environmental Defense, similarly, is directing efforts toward the regional level. Among other national organizations promoting smart growth strategies are the leading land conservation organizations: The Nature Conservancy, Trust for Public Land, and Land Trust Alliance.

Professional societies and think tanks also are on board, promoting the smart growth agenda in whole or in part. The American Planning Association (APA), of course, was involved with growth management issues long before smart growth nomenclature became fashionable. More recently, APA has been adapting at least some of its many programs to fit with the new emphasis on smart growth; this is perhaps most evident in its publication of the mammoth *Growing Smart Legislative Guidebook* (American Planning Association 2002; Godschalk 2003). In its advocacy of compact, pedestrian-friendly, mixed-use neighborhoods, the Congress for the New Urbanism (CNU) supports one of the most elemental dimensions of smart growth: concentrated development. To this end, CNU works with architects, planners, and developers to promote its vision of sustainable urban form (Calthorpe 1993; Calthorpe and Fulton 2001). Another coalition deeply involved with smart growth is the Surface Transportation Policy Project, which seeks to improve transportation options while promoting economic development, environmental protection, and improved public health. Other professional organizations directly involved with smart growth include the American Institute of Architects, Urban Land Institute, International City/County Management Association, Local Government Commission, Local Initiatives Support Corporation, and National Association of Counties. Several think tanks, including the Brookings Institution, University of Maryland's National Center for Smart Growth Research and Education, and Northeast-Midwest Institute, also work on smart growth issues. So, too, does the Heritage Foundation and other conservative think tanks—but from a rather different political and planning perspective than the more "liberal" think tanks. Private foundations large and small fund programs that support various parts of the smart growth agenda, from open space protection to urban development. The Funders' Network for Smart Growth and Livable Communities (2007), founded in 1999, serves as a resource and guide for funders and fund recipients.

One NGO that has a distinct take on the issues is the National Association of Home Builders (NAHB). Not only is the NAHB mother ship very much involved with smart growth issues—so, too, are most of its state-level affiliates. In its 1999 report (NAHB 2002), NAHB makes it abundantly clear that smart growth is to be equated with local economic growth and satisfying demand for housing. By looking only at the national supply of farmland, and setting aside local concerns about retaining agricultural lands, the report dismisses the need for farmland preservation programs. The organization favors an orderly, predictable planning process and believes that local comprehensive planning should be encouraged—but not mandated—by governments. NAHB supports high-density residential development, including cluster development and transit-oriented development—where market forces and/or government policy facilitate it.

City versus Suburb

Urban areas pose some of the most intractable smart growth challenges. While brownfields remediation programs—with their promises of housing, commerce, jobs, and economic relief for land developers—are widely accepted, other urban programs are not. Metropolitan governance or tax base sharing, for instance, may make sense from a regional equity perspective, but few municipalities are willing to seriously consider such schemes (Gillham 2002).

Much of the fervent antigrowth sentiment in suburban and exurban locales is not accompanied by comparable support for restoring economic and ecological health to core urban and inner suburban areas. Each locality tends to see itself as a fiefdom, part of a region in name only. Conceivably, local pressures to halt growth—combined in some states with plans that seek to redirect it—may be forcing growth into more urbanized areas, in the form of infill and denser development (Lindstrom and Bartling 2003). But there is no consistent evidence to support this contention, at least in states that rely on entirely voluntary approaches to growth management. In states with strong growth management programs, such as Oregon and Florida, it seems that sprawl rates have been reduced (Nelson 1999)—but it is not clear how much of the reduction is explained by growth-control measures (Kline 2000). And for those states with less vigorous, less enforceable growth management plans, the explanatory power of the state plan is further diminished. New Jersey planners are hopeful that their state plan, driven by incentives rather than regulation, is having some effect in redirecting growth. What seem to be more significant causal factors, however, are the actions of individual localities in accepting or rejecting growth. The state plan may bring some influence to bear on those municipal decisions, but the state's leverage is limited. When Merrill Lynch was encouraged in the late 1990s to locate a major new facility on available land in the city of Trenton, rather than in cornfields north of the city, the investment firm balked. They threatened to locate in nearby Pennsylvania, and New Jersey backed off. Office buildings sprouted in the cornfields. But as the development community is well aware, this cannot continue for much longer. Given its limited total area, and increasing proportion of lands in protected status, New Jersey will be forced to either "densify" or grow more slowly, regardless of what the state plan prescribes.

To the extent that urban centers become more vibrant, attractive, and affordable—through some combination of policy actions, economic trends, and renewed desirability of urban life for young professionals and aging baby boomers—more residential decision makers will opt for urban over suburban living. But urban residential choices are not shaped entirely by culture, restaurants, creativity (Florida 2005), and shortened commutes. Other decision factors include housing affordability, access to recreational space, aesthetic character of the built environment, and ease with which basic activities, such as grocery shopping, can be done.

Thus, even when urban quality of life clearly is superior—as defined by education, safety, consumer convenience, and cultural and recreational features—an urban renaissance is not necessarily assured. Although sprawl has been facilitated by a multitude of government policies, combined with fears and concerns about urban life, none of this obviates the cultural imperative and associated consumer desires driving Americans to live in quasi-rural settings (Gordon and Richardson 1997; Simpson 1999; Dimond 2000; Talen 2005; Willmer 2006). Those desires, common to so many Americans, can be offset in part—but probably only in limited part—by improved quality of urban life and government policies that encourage—or at least do not discourage—higher-density development.

The case for revitalizing urban areas, smart growth style, is not always a simple open-and-shut one. Issues associated with gentrification and resultant displacement of populations are well documented. But there are other issues, too. Infill development is not necessarily embraced in urban neighborhoods, especially when it brings higher-density development, with larger or taller buildings, into those areas (Berke, Godschalk, and Kaiser 2006). Indeed, some detractors call it "vertical sprawl" (Confessore 2006). Likewise, transit-oriented development, for all its benefits, can be a hard sell to those living adjacent to proposed projects. Brownfields redevelopment brings economic and employment benefits but also concerns about toxics in soils and groundwater. Questions often are raised about "how clean is clean enough?"—but clean enough for whom, where?

Nor does urban revitalization necessarily ensure a reduced environmental footprint. Indeed, demands may mount for an urban *and* rural life, the best of both worlds. Wealthy Americans have enjoyed both for more than a century, and those of lesser means have done so mainly in the post–World War II era. If "best of both worlds" demands increase, then so may carbon impacts and ecological threats. Travel miles may rise, and shorelines, alpine areas, and forest regions may face new threats. Concern about an explosion of second-home development, as noted in chapter 2, was one of the main factors leading the way toward regional land use planning in places like New York State's Adirondack Park and the Lake Tahoe region in California and Nevada.

What about "smarter" suburban development, then? Smart growth efforts are sometimes helped, but often hindered, by the antigrowth—and especially anti-high-density growth—sentiment that runs so deep in many suburban locales. Affordable housing and transit-oriented development projects can encounter enormous resistance. Even modest changes to subdivision plans—things like narrower streets, elimination of cul-de-sacs, porous paving, and biologically diverse stormwater detention basins—are hampered by both the inertial tendencies of local planning and approval processes and residents' fears of such things as mosquito breeding in marshy areas (Willmer 2006).

The new urbanism offers hope for reducing new developments' environmental footprints, as well as promoting infill development in underpopulated urban and older suburban locales (Arendt 1996; Duany, Plater-Zyberk, and Speck 2000; Talen 2005). Rather than the traditional cookie-cutter subdivisions, we restore and build new neotraditional neighborhoods, replete with front porches in some places. But most of these projects are tilted toward the well-to-do; they are intentional communities for those who want and can afford the lifestyle offered them by a new urbanist residential choice. Moreover, these projects occupy greenfields much more often than infill areas or places adjacent to built-up areas; surprisingly, perhaps, their ecological footprints can be quite large (Beatley and Manning 1997; Pollard 2001). But to be fair to new urbanists, their design principles are increasingly being deployed to create mixed-income communities and reclaim abandoned and underused suburban spaces. Some suburban locales are fashioning town centers in places that never grew up around a central business district. The aesthetic result may be rather peculiar in some instances, but the resultant concentration of commercial and administrative functions can help shrink the local environmental footprint.

A critical bottom-line question about smart growth programs has to do with their effects on housing affordability. Conceivably, growth management may increase demand and thus decrease housing affordability in urban and/or suburban areas. Nelson et al.'s (2002) review of selected programs concludes that market demand, irrespective of land constraints imposed by growth management programs, is the main determinant of housing price. Growth management programs do have effects, but they are difficult to isolate. Moreover, Nelson and coauthors note, traditional zoning and other local controls tend to drive up the price of housing; indeed, these regulations often are designed to exclude those of certain income levels. Growth management programs, by contrast, often increase housing supply and affordability, in many cases by design. In addition, even if housing prices rise, the land use patterns fostered by growth management programs may produce offsetting savings from lowered transportation, energy, and commuting costs. There are also the less tangible benefits of greater access to open space and greater local walkability.

A group of scholars contributing to a Brookings Institution project on the growth management/housing affordability question (Downs 2004a) and a recent review and analysis of Florida's situation (Jerry 2003) offer more mixed assessments. Much depends on definitions of "affordable" as well as specifics of program implementation. Downs (2004b) argues that there is not much of a constituency for affordable housing, but there is a powerful suburban constituency that opposes it, at least in their own communities. Smart growth advocates are reluctant to come out strongly in favor of affordable housing for fear of alienating these bread-and-butter suburban supporters. If affordable housing is to be ensured, says Downs

(2004b), then regionwide approaches and increased public spending are essential. The National Neighborhood Coalition (n.d.) and Smart Growth Network (Arigoni 2001) press the point that affordable housing will not just happen when smart growth programs are implemented. They feel that affordable housing must be a deliberate and important part of smart growth efforts.

Summary

Federal, state, and local growth management, environmental, and livability programs all have enormous potential to shape and reshape land use patterns. Common to most federal and state initiatives are targeted incentives, directed investments, and limited financial penalties. Place-based collaborative planning itself usually is organized at the regional and local levels. State and federal funds and technical assistance can support these projects, which are described in this chapter as well as chapters 4 and 6. But the federal government, in particular, is very wary of appearing to be directly involved in the planning process. State governments are more prone to be proactive about planning—though, even here, emphasis usually is on providing incentives and resources.

The quieter revolution approaches described above are constrained by their modest regulatory horsepower and limited funding appropriations. What emerges is a highly uneven landscape, with some states, regions, and localities doing much more than others to manage sprawl and protect farmland, open space, and other valued lands. None of these efforts—even a major federal one like TEA, which reallocates highway funds toward nonroad projects—will systemically influence land use patterns in the ways that the interstate highway system and subsidized home mortgages have done. Efforts to "nationalize" many of the current crop of smart growth and livability programs, by bringing them under a nurturing national umbrella, have sputtered. Congress failed to embrace the Clinton-Gore Livability Agenda and has not been able to move the Community Character Act. But the many quieter revolution initiatives collectively being put into place by governments, NGOs, foundations, and corporations are creating infrastructure that can be called up in the future, perhaps to help meet carbon emissions targets or implement a reinvigorated livability agenda.

CHAPTER SIX
LET A THOUSAND LOCAL INITIATIVES BLOOM

Local action is the lifeblood of progressive environmental democracy (Gottlieb 2001, 2005; Dowie 1996; Shabecoff 2003; Shellenberger and Nordhaus 2004). It is highly inspired and impassioned, close to the issues, and—to the extent that a place-based sense of environmental stewardship is passed from generation to generation—an enduring foundation for civic engagement. Yet no action is really local, in that every activity—at least in part—is the outcome of multiple forces working at various scales. Just as the problems of haphazard development, traffic congestion, and ecological degradation result from complex, overlapping forces and processes, the responses, too, are set within an infrastructural web of opportunities and constraints. Local land trusts, for example, are supported by state and federal tax structures that treat their activities favorably; conservation easements are governed by state and federal laws; and funding and cooperative working arrangements often link local government actions with state and federal agencies, as well as nonprofit organizations.

As a consequence, clarity and consistency about what constitutes "local" can be frustratingly elusive. For this chapter's purposes, at least, we consider mainly those activities that yield local-level results. If, for example, a town government spends money for land acquisition or to support land trust projects within its jurisdiction, then this would fit the bill. Of course, these projects may contribute to or be supported by regional-, state-, or national-level initiatives. But if the decisions are made at the local level—not simply in pursuit of funds from some higher level of government but as a genuinely local endeavor—then they are appropriate for consideration in this chapter. For the sake of the book's organizational convenience, exceptions are made for the following: statewide ballot questions, national land trust organizations, regional-scale land trusts and watershed associations, and a few of the more devolved federal and state funding programs that support local projects.

Not all local-level land use decision making can be covered here; to even attempt to do so would go well beyond the book's scope and intent. Indeed, as we have already noted, localities today take advantage of many more planning tools than they did thirty-five years ago (Daniels and Daniels 2003). This, too, is part of the quieter revolution narrative. But in many ways, local governments still lag or only act when prompted by NGOs and higher levels of government to act. It is this cajoling, collaborative nexus of local and extralocal that defines the quieter revolution. Local governments, in many places, work with a much different array of stakeholders than they did three or four decades ago—and they do so more transparently. Today's municipalities also bring more of their own laws and ordinances, funding, expertise, and political clout to collaborative ventures than was the case in decades past. In turn, they receive funds, comply with mandates, and are guided by incentives from higher levels of government; they also work with businesses and foundations. One of their most effective bargaining chips is threat; they can stimulate collaborative, place-based planning by standing ready to enact stronger, more regulatory alternatives if it fails.

This chapter's focus is on four areas where locally based activity has grown very appreciably in recent years: local land trusts, watershed conservancies, greenways, and ballot issues. Each holds significant potential for expanding civic engagement, improving local environmental quality, and amplifying those local changes through their connectedness with programs working at broader scales and employing complementary strategies. Each also raises important questions about distribution of benefits and costs.

These four categories are invoked so that a reasonable range of consequential local activities is covered. Additional types of local efforts are included in chapter 3. The boundaries separating these different types of activities—for example, watershed organization versus land trust—are highly permeable, and in some instances the distinctions are minimal or nonexistent. But by laying out these four categories, and examining additional local initiatives in other chapters, we can cover nearly the full range of local-level land use endeavors.

Land Trusts

At the end of the nineteenth century, when John Muir and Gifford Pinchot were staking out their positions on federal lands management, Boston landscape architect Charles Eliot was acting locally. Largely through his efforts, the Trustees of Reservations was created in 1891; this state-chartered corporation is generally regarded as the country's first land trust. Its express purpose was to acquire and protect natural, scenic, and historic sites. Tax-exempt status was granted by the Massachusetts legislature, and the trustees allowed public access to the lands they owned (Brewer 2003). Though Trustees of Reservations grew and prospered from the turn of the century onward, it was not until well after World War II that the national land trust movement would become something more than a scattering of small projects.

Land trusts generally are defined as nongovernment organizations that purchase land and/or conservation easements to protect lands. Land and easement donors enjoy tax deductions, and in most cases, land trusts are not assessed property taxes. Landowners and land trusts have before them a multitude of options, ranging from limited development to a full or partial land sale. Individual land protection deals can involve very complex legal and financial negotiations; these aspects are described in some detail on the "resources" section of the Land Trust Alliance (LTA) website (Land Trust Alliance 2007b) and in several books and reports (Randolph 2004; Land Trust Alliance 2007a).

From about 50 land trusts in 1950, the numbers soared past the 500 mark by the mid-1980s, hit 1,000 in the early 1990s, and reached 1,663 in 2005 (Land Trust Alliance 2006). A more telling measure may be acreage protected; here recent growth has approached exponential proportions. In 2000, 6.1 million acres were protected via ownership or easement; by 2005, that figure had leapt to 11.9 million acres. Conservation easements, especially, have found enormous favor over that same period: in 2000, easements were held on 2.5 million acres; the figure in 2005 was

6.25 million acres. Though it is often argued that nothing surpasses outright public ownership in ensuring security and permanence of land protection, conservation easements can be far more cost-effective. And, if carefully monitored, they may provide virtually the same surety of protection as ownership. But nothing is guaranteed, of course—not only easements but also conservation lands in outright ownership can be reevaluated, reclassified, or perhaps condemned by government. But the land trust movement has matured to the point where it has the skills, resources, and allies it needs to minimize most such risks.

All that said, a note of caution is in order in appraising the movement's accomplishments and potential. The LTA, heavily invested as it is in private land conservation's success, is ever eager to trumpet achievements, focusing on the best possible news represented in the upward-trending numbers of organizations and acreages protected from development. Even with this proviso in mind, though, there is no denying the movement's vitality. Former LTA president Jean Hocker attributes land trusts' rapid ascension to general growth in environmental awareness in the 1960s and 1970s, rapid real estate development and associated loss of open space in the 1980s, and government downsizing of the 1990s (Hocker 1996). Richard Brewer (2003) points to Reagan-era abdication of federal responsibility for land conservation as a leading causal factor. Because land trusts are nongovernment entities, they encounter fewer political minefields and can act more swiftly than public agencies in acquiring land and easements. Still, as discussed in chapter 7, property rights organizations critical of the tax advantages enjoyed by land trusts are vigorous opponents.

What does today's land trust community look like? Peak activities are in the areas experiencing greatest conflicts between metropolitan expansion (sprawl) and protection of farmland, forests, and other open spaces. As figure 6.1 shows, this is especially evident in the northeastern megalopolitan corridor, adjacent areas of the New England and Middle Atlantic regions, and the West Coast states, Great Lakes regions, and parts of the Rocky Mountains. These are not necessarily the most ecologically critical places (though clearly places of high ecological value are involved) but the places where threats are most immediate and visible and where the capacity to react is best developed (Mason and Mattson 1990).

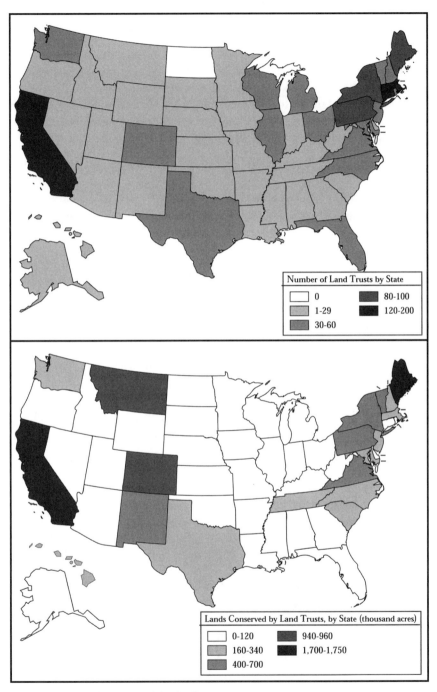

Figure 6.1. Land Trust Activity by State
Source: Land Trust Alliance (2006)

Most land trusts are modest operations; many do not even have a full-time staff member or dedicated office space. But some are quite large and act as regional, statewide, and even national players. The Nature Conservancy (TNC) and Trust for Public Land (TPL) are national giants, towering over the multitudes of local and regional land trusts. Brewer (2003, 34) points out that TNC and TPL at one time acted as models for local-level land trusts; they provided the impetus and the locals followed up. TPL did more than TNC, however, to incubate those local groups, particularly in the West. Working with government agencies, local NGOs, and individual landowners, TPL claims to have protected more than two million acres (Trust for Public Land 2007a). TNC, which by 1980 had moved toward a regional landscape approach, takes credit for protecting fifteen million acres in the United States (The Nature Conservancy 2007). TNC is now a leading example of a "big green" enterprise; as a consequence, it has faced intense criticism in recent years. Among the charges leveled in a *Washington Post* (2003) series are these:

- Fund-raising and collaborative amity trump science in guiding land management.

- Corporate board members wield undue influence over TNC's positions on major environmental issues.

- TNC is complicit in corporate "greenwashing," putting its logo up for sale to all corporate bidders.

- Enormous tax benefits go to wealthy individuals—including TNC board members and trustees—who retain limited development rights on their lands.

- "Compatible development" policies have allowed incompatible development, such as oil drilling and megahomes, on ecologically sensitive TNC lands.

- Stewardship on ranchlands where TNC holds easements is insufficient, despite assurances about "conservation beef" raised on those lands.

- Accounting and land-valuation practices are sometimes suspect.

- Public access is denied on some lands protected via public tax subsidies.

- TNC is not suited to running for-profit (environmentally compatible) ventures.

- Excessive compensation has been paid to employees and contractors ($420,000 to the TNC president in 1992).

In 2003, TNC acted to reform several practices identified in the *Washington Post*'s critique.

TPL and TNC are not the only national players. The Conservation Fund, working with government, foundations, and the private sector, claims credit for protecting 5.4 million acres since 1985 (Conservation Fund 2007). The American Farmland Trust provides planning and technical assistance to government agencies and NGOs and also lobbies for legislation supportive of land conservation. The American Land Conservancy focuses on large tracts of land, mostly in the West, and is responsible for protecting 195,000 acres through 332 projects (American Land Conservancy 2006). The National Audubon Society, through its many chapters, maintains a system of sanctuaries and preserves.

Given limited financial resources, staff time, and ability to monitor lands over the long term, land trusts often are faced with strategic dilemmas about what lands or easements to acquire and when to take action. In an orderly, rational world—a world that does not suddenly dangle in front of the Last Chance Land Trust a large parcel of ecologically critical land at a bargain price that if not immediately acquired will be turned into a housing estate and golf course—land trusts first ask if the potential acquisition is a good fit with the organization's mission and priorities. But while land trusts try to have in place strategies to deal with all contingencies, they can hardly be expected to anticipate everything that may come their way.

What are the overarching goals that drive land trusts? This is not an easy question, because most fill multiple roles. Prioritizing those roles is challenging, since there can be so much overlap among them. Still, recent survey data from the Land Trust Alliance give at least some sense of what most motivates local land trusts. According to the LTA's most recent census (Land Trust Alliance 2006), habitat protection is the primary purpose for land protection for 39 percent of land trusts, while open space protection was named by 38 percent and water resources (especially wetlands) by 26 percent. These data do not, however, represent a forced prioritization, since respondents could list more than one priority.

Clearly, habitat and open space are major motivators for land trusts. While they are not necessarily competing priorities, they certainly can come into sharp conflict in some places. Richard Brewer (2003), a biologist active in the local land trust movement, makes a strong case for an ecosystem perspective, for protecting large patches of land that represent natural ecosystems. And his priorities are in synch with the priorities of many local land trusts, perhaps the majority. Indeed, many land trusts not only are active in "preserving" land but also are interventionists, overseeing ambitious ecological restoration projects.

But there are other approaches. While few land trusts are likely to be stewards of suburban soccer fields, many are involved with working farms and forests, as well as urban parks and playgrounds. In some instances, aesthetic protection requires continuing land trust intervention. At an LTA annual meeting in New Hampshire some years ago, for example, one of the field trips included a small village where fields were kept mowed not for hay production so much as to maintain the historic rural landscape pattern of forest and field.

Land trust priorities are shaped by local environmental issues and perceived needs as much as they are guided by lofty general principles. Some land trusts are very specific in their missions; Alaska's Nushagak-Mulchatna Wood-Tikchik Land Trust (2007), for example, is dedicated to protecting local wild salmon runs. Initiated by the Choggiung Ltd. Native Corporation, the trust is acquiring lands and easements and thus precluding development on small parcels of land over a vast watershed area. Most of the lands are native allotments reluctantly put on the market by families facing financial ruin brought on by depressed salmon prices. While much of the region is protected via public ownership, many of these critical small pieces are not protected—and this is what prompted the trust to define its particular mission. It is a simple mission, but its execution requires the land trust to involve itself in a wide range of challenging activities, over an enormous and rugged area.

The Rocky Mountain Elk Foundation's (2007) name says it all—it is about elk and their habitats. The mission is clear and simple, but the area of concern is vast and the work complex and multifaceted. This is a land trust that acts locally but over a huge region encompassing eastern states as well as the Rocky Mountain West. Vital Ground (2007) is another land trust whose mission is centered on a species; its focus is the North American grizzly bear. The Civil War Preservation Trust, by contrast, has as its mission preservation of cultural landscapes. Along with its educational activities, it seeks to permanently protect hallowed ground—important battlefields—from commercial and residential development, as well as other uses deemed inappropriate.

In contrast with the rural/wildlands focus of most conservation land trusts, community land trusts (CLTs) are active in cities and towns (Institute for Community Economics 2007). They work on affordable housing, neighborhood revitalization, business development in underserved communities, historic preservation, and urban parks. Housing affordability is fostered by removing the cost of land from the cost of owning a home; CLTs own land but usually not the homes and businesses occupying that land. Environmental and economic sustainability together define many CLTs' missions. The CLT movement's growth through the 1980s and 1990s was quite sensational, with the state of Vermont standing out as a leader.

The limiting factor looming largest for most local land trusts is finances. Even if the operation is run on an administrative shoestring, as many are, land and easement acquisition is costly. Can the land trust afford the deal, especially if it is an expensive one? The organization must find funds, sometimes very quickly, when a critical land parcel is up for sale. Some land trusts have revolving funds they can draw upon; others are adept at rapid-response fund-raising. Still, cliffhanger situations are not at all uncommon, and in some instances—despite the best efforts—the deal falls off the cliff. But even a successful acquisition is not the end of the financial story. Brewer (2003) hits home with his concerns about long-term monitoring. When land trusts are acquiring easements, especially, they need to provide not only a means to pay for ongoing assessment of the land's ecological health but also to ensure full compliance with easement conditions.

Land trusts are successful at what they do in part because they are unobtrusive. They are nongovernment actors—even though many cooperate very closely with government agencies. Indeed, land trusts often step into the breach to acquire lands when agencies cannot act quickly enough.

Later, when public financing becomes available, the land may be sold to the agency. None of this has been lost on property rights and wise use advocates. They see the land trust movement as a thinly veiled part of the state planning apparatus. In recent years, some of these organizations have become quite adept at checkmating individual land trust actions and denouncing the movement generally (chapter 7).

So, how significant, really, is the land trust phenomenon? In the greater scheme of things, the acreages involved are rather miniscule. They only seem so impressive because of their near exponential growth in recent years. When we begin with a small base number, as was the case with acres protected by land trusts in 1960, then exponential growth is easily achieved, at least for a few years, or decades. The question is, when and where will that growth level off? We can hardly expect the exponential trend to continue to a point where land trust activity overspreads the whole of the American landscape like an algal bloom. But even if we limit our interest just to those lands of high ecological or cultural value—however we might define them—it still is exceedingly unlikely that land trusts will ever oversee substantial portions of any of the great ecoregions mentioned in chapter 4. They will manage patches and pieces—granted more and larger patches and pieces than in the past—yet still just a small proportion in sum. But from their "thousand points of land protection action," they just may be able to bring a regional sense of purpose and inspire other stakeholders—government agencies, NGOs, foundations, and private industry—to become major land protection players.

Indeed, acreage figures tell only a part of the land trust story. Equally important are the ways land trusts amplify the importance of their land purchases and easement acquisitions (Mason 1992b, 1995b). For example, land trusts can strategically direct their resources toward critically situated "keystone" parcels that act as ecological core, buffer, or corridor lands, and/or lands facing greatest threats from development or other disturbances.

Central New Jersey's D&R Greenway Land Trust is an interesting example; it directs its efforts mainly toward building a network of protected greenways (figure 6.2). D&R controls scattered but strategically situated parcels through the watershed region defined by two canals—the Delaware and the Raritan—as well as numerous streams and rivers. Its lands fit within a regional patchwork of protected farms, parklands, and other pre-

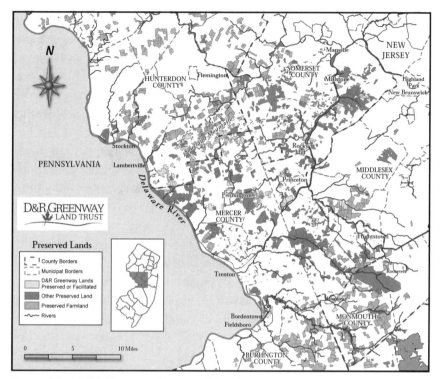

Figure 6.2. D&R Greenway Preserved Lands
Source: D&R Greenway Land Trust

serves. D&R's counterpart in adjacent Bucks County, Pennsylvania, has adopted similar strategies that complement D&R's efforts in neighboring parts of both New Jersey and Pennsylvania. In situations like this one, land trust tracts can act as anchors in a larger program that combines land acquisition, conservation easements, regulation, tax incentives, and other inducements that support regional land protection. Land trusts also expand their presence by working in concert with governments, doing everything from having their members and officers sit on planning boards to providing consulting services to localities.

Richard Brewer (2003), writing generally about land trusts in America, urges local conservancies to become more broadly involved in place-based planning, and especially to promote new urbanist and other development approaches that use land with greater care and efficiency than is typical of conventional practices. Pennsylvania's Natural Lands Trust (NLT), based outside the city of Philadelphia, is doing just that.

NLT acts basically as a local land trust in the Delaware Valley region of southeastern Pennsylvania and southern New Jersey, in that it acquires land and easements. But it also brings a regional coherence to its work, through its "Keystone" landscape and watershed programs. These efforts are guided by scientific assessments of ecological health and watershed dynamics. Though urban areas are not explicitly a part of NLT's efforts, its watershed programs affect heavily urbanized downstream areas. NLT cooperates with a suite of other local land trusts and conservation organizations. And the organization works directly with governments, as an open space planning consultant and in promoting conservation subdivisions (Natural Lands Trust 2007).

Conservation planning is still a tough sell, as most localities are reluctant to seriously alter the subdivision regulations they have on the books (Willmer 2006). Moreover, many suburban communities are fiercely opposed to higher-density development anywhere within their borders. But what has recently caught on, like wildfire in a lot of these same places, is open space acquisition (see discussion of ballot questions below); this is a leading local policy arena within which NLT and similar organizations elsewhere consult with localities. NLT also is active at the statewide scale: in conjunction with the Pennsylvania Department of Conservation and Natural Resources, Governor's Center for Local Government Services, and various NGOs, NLT is promoting its "Conservation by Design" approach to local conservation planning. This effort is part of Pennsylvania's Growing Greener program, a package of land use incentives and funding programs initiated in 1999 and expanded in 2005 by voter approval of "Growing Greener 2" (chapter 5). NLT also is a key player in the coalition of organizations supporting the Highlands study, which covers an area stretching from Pennsylvania to Connecticut (chapter 4). Several of NLT's land acquisition projects, some quite deliberately, are situated within the designated Highlands region (Natural Lands Trust 2005).

Granted, NLT's amplified regional efforts may be making only very limited headway in dealing with rapidly spreading regional sprawl (figure 6.3), but they are helping ensure protection for at least some critical areas. While their impact on larger regional development patterns may indeed seem very small, empirical evidence that would allow for meaningful assessment—in the Philadelphia region as in most other areas—is in short supply. We can say, though, that NLT's experience seems to support one

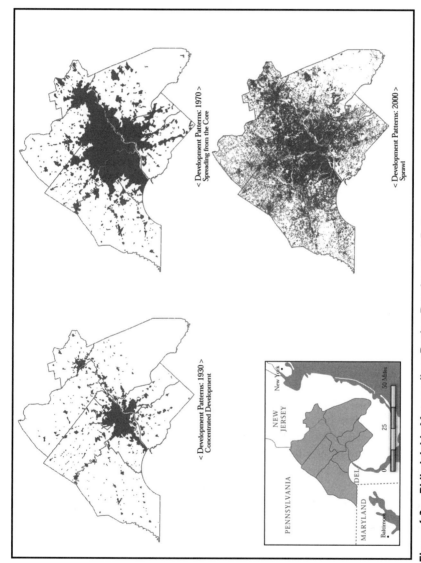

Figure 6.3. Philadelphia Metropolitan Region Development Patterns
Source: Delaware Valley Regional Planning Commission

of chapter 9's conclusions: the quieter revolution is succeeding in remaking local places, but so far, at least, it is meeting with only the most limited success in taking on the sprawl juggernaut at broader scales.

In some places, though, land trusts are reshaping sizeable regions. California's Marin County Agricultural Trust (MALT), for example, is doing much more than just protecting scattered parcels of farmland. When it was founded in 1980, during the era of the National Agricultural Lands Study (chapter 5) and farmland protection's ascendance on policy agendas, MALT became the first land trust dedicated exclusively to agricultural land protection. With its focus on dairy farms and ranchlands, MALT has become a national model for local farmland protection. It takes credit for permanent protection of thirty-eight thousand acres of land on fifty-seven family farms and ranches (Marin Agricultural Land Trust 2007).

MALT's efforts are part of a larger, countywide approach to growth management (figure 6.4). In the 1960s, a huge residential/commercial development was planned for Point Reyes, in the coastal part of the county. That plan energized local opposition, led to election of officials opposed to the plan, and ultimately prompted federal establishment of Point Reyes National Seashore in 1962. The National Park Service, which manages the area, is able to buy ranchlands and lease the lands back to the farmers who occupy them (National Parks Conservation Association 2002). Outside the National Seashore, California's Williamson Act plays a critical role in land conservation. Passed in 1965 and amended in 1998, the act allows farmers and ranchers who enter into Farmland Security Zone contracts, and keep their land in agriculture for twenty years, to become eligible for deeply reduced land valuations and property taxes. Under the state's 1971 Open Space Act, local governments receive payments in compensation for the lost tax revenues.

Innovative and far-reaching agricultural protection programs thus cover virtually all of Marin County's federal and nonfederal lands. And in this case, there was wide support from the farm and ranch community early on, rather than the intense hostility with which landowners so often greet such initiatives. In part, this is because metropolitan expansion posed a clear threat to a viable, sustainable, established way of life (Hart 1991).

Marin County is one of the places that helped inspire the American Farmland Trust's "Farming on the Edge" project (Sorensen, Greene, and

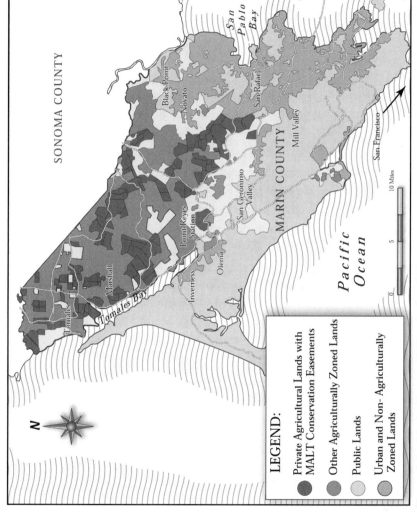

Figure 6.4.   Marin County, California, Land Management
Source: Marin Agricultural Land Trust (MALT)

Russ 1997) (see figure 5.1). Though Marin's rural character is constantly threatened by an expanding Bay Area population, the county has stood up to the challenge, keeping sprawl at bay and adaptively sustaining a traditional way of life. Major development is being concentrated mostly in the southeastern part of the county, where remaining rural spaces serve as attractive recreation venues within short driving distance of the city. Since its formation, MALT has been a local leader, working not only on its own projects but also with government agencies and NGOs to sustain its vision of an attractive, accessible working landscape.

The New Jersey Conservation Foundation (NJCF) is regarded by the Land Trust Alliance as a land trust. But its mission actually is much larger than that of the typical local land trust. NJCF is a statewide organization, well connected with New Jersey state government. That relationship—and associated movement of personnel between government and NGO—may be more pronounced when Democrats are in power, as has been the case for some years. But even with Republican administrations, NJCF and other members of the environmental community have a strong voice. This stands in contrast to many western and especially southern states, where land conservation is not so tightly woven into the conventional political fabric.

Hundreds more such highly proactive land trusts dot the national map. While many, perhaps most, are quite content to think locally as well as act locally—and clearly, their activities do make important differences locally—others have greater ambitions. And they are finding ways to play leading parts in advancing these larger agendas.

Land trusts' greatest achievements, then, often are strategic in nature: protecting critically situated parcels of land, working with government agencies, and helping develop larger regional visions and plans. With respect to environmental justice and equity, things are more mixed. The community land trust movement, briefly described above, has as its mission social equity, especially in urban areas. But much land trust activity is in exurban and rural locales, directed toward ecological and open space protection. The net effect in many places may be exclusionary, limiting opportunities for those of lesser means to live in these areas and increasing real estate values generally. As yet, though, evidence to support or refute such a broad conclusion is too scattered. It would behoove us to structure future investigations that can at least inform us about land trusts' cumulative economic and social impacts—as well as ecological and land protection accomplishments—at the metropolitan and ecoregional scales.

Local Watershed Conservancies

If the quieter revolution were to adopt a poster child, it might well be watershed planning. The "watershed approach" (U.S. Environmental Protection Agency [EPA] 1993; National Academy of Sciences Commission on Geosciences, Environment, and Resources 1999) is place-based; addresses a wide range of interrelated physical, social, and economic concerns; relies on public-private partnerships; and—at least by the National Academy of Science's (1999) reckoning—is meant to be cost-effective. Because watersheds include lands that drain into water bodies, this approach is well suited to dealing with nonpoint sources of pollution, such as farms, city streets, and suburban residential and commercial developments. Not every watershed council or conservancy will embrace all elements listed above, but all should have the potential to do so. To the extent that it builds long-term institutional capacity, enhances civic infrastructure, and promotes collaboration, the watershed approach is front and center in sustaining the place-based, collaborative face of the quieter revolution. Indeed, it seems that watershed management is now coming of age, with interest rising almost as fast as floodwaters in a suburban stormwater retention basin. Of course, actions on the ground can lag well behind the conceptual embrace and buzz of participatory enthusiasm.

Like land trusts, watershed conservancies have enjoyed remarkable recent growth. EPA's database included more than 4,000 local groups as of late 2006 (U.S. EPA 2007b), with nearly as many listed by the River Network as of 2003 (River Network 2007). Konisky and Beierle (2001) put the number at 2,500, based on a personal communication. Although it might seem that watershed conservancies are more singular in purpose than land trusts, the full picture really is more complex. Watershed groups concern themselves with water quality, land use, recreation, history, culture, public education, and more. Often, they are called upon to broker among an assortment of competing and conflicting interests interwoven through scales ranging from very local up to regional, state, interstate, national, and even international. Indeed, a downstream watershed group, acting in isolation, will have little influence with those who use and abuse water upstream; in turn, activities within its spatial domain will have their own downstream impacts. To be truly effective, the small, local group must be engaged in a planning process that covers the larger watershed of which it is but a wee part. Yet one study of western watershed management (Kenney 1997) found few institutional links in place to connect these nested watersheds across spatial scales.

Here, though, the focus is limited mainly to discrete local groups, where potential for place-based civic engagement is at its peak. Of course, the boundary between local and regional is never cleanly drawn; some of the "local" groups referred to below really do cover rather expansive regions. But as long as we recognize these multiple and overlapping scales, we need not be overly concerned, just now, with sorting each and every watershed association by size.

Generally, watershed organizations have little or no power to regulate land use, even within their own catchment areas. But they may be able to appreciably influence government policy—through lobbying, direct negotiations, public education programs, media events, and as working partners (Thomas 1999). Often, in addition to their responsibilities defined within conventional political boundaries, government officials will play a formal role at the bioregional scale, as members—for example—of a watershed association. In some places, as in Massachusetts in the 1990s, watershed councils receive strong support from state government (Michaels 1999).

An average small watershed organization might include members representing local businesses, farmers, students, residents, educational institutions, government agencies, and environmental organizations (U.S. EPA, Office of Water 2001). Monthly meetings are typical, but some groups will have much more intensive meeting schedules, especially when they have demanding projects on their plates. Other groups will meet only sporadically. Organizational structure and formality differ widely; in some cases, for example, structure and procedures are strategically developed, in order to comply with conditions tied to eligibility for external funding. While often lauded as examples of direct democracy, watershed associations are so varied in representativeness, process, and influence as to render such broad generalizations almost meaningless (chapter 3).

Riverkeeper organizations also have come into their own over the past few decades. The riverkeeper movement began in New York's Hudson Valley in the early 1960s, when the Hudson River was severely polluted.

Officially launched in 1966, the Hudson Riverkeeper's early membership was weighted toward blue-collar fishermen, factory workers, carpenters, and lathers (Riverkeeper 2007). Today's organization, while open and inclusive, is tilted more toward the elite; besides environmental activist Robert F. Kennedy Jr., the board of directors includes a movie star, tennis pro, and corporate leaders. Linked with the Riverkeeper is the historic sloop *Clearwater*. Launched in 1969 by folksinger and political activist Pete Seeger, the *Clearwater* serves as floating classroom, laboratory, and Hudson River icon. Several popular Clearwater festivals take place at the river's edge each year.

The Hudson Riverkeeper's main foci are restoring the riverine ecosystem, protecting New York City's drinking water supply, and improving public access to the river. Robert Kennedy is the organization's chief prosecuting attorney, and much of its work involves investigation and subsequent legal action against polluters. Successful settlements often mean funds for the Riverkeeper. Indeed, because they bring definitive results and needed funds, legal strategies are embraced by a great many of the riverkeepers now patrolling waterways across the country. Also critical to their missions are research, education, and monitoring.

One of the Riverkeeper functions is to promote river awareness. While watershed consciousness may well be on the rise, rather little empirical evidence is available to affirm this. What has become apparent in recent years are signs on highways marking watershed boundaries, often with appealing, regionally appropriate graphics; an infusion of watershed education programs into many school curricula; and adoption of the watershed concept as a tool by local citizens opposed to new residential and commercial development. In some cases, at least, these growth management crusades amount to little more than an appropriation—a hijacking, perhaps—of the watershed concept in support of narrowly defined ends. As with many other faces of the quieter revolution, critical questions can be raised about social justice and environmental equity (i.e., how evenly or unevenly are costs and benefits associated with watershed management distributed?). At the same time, though, some of these actions that spring from pure self-interest can in the end complement and bring greater acceptance to watershed-based planning. And once watershed-wide planning takes on a life of its own, equity and justice questions often are taken very seriously.

Potential for co-optation notwithstanding, watershed management—at least at the small, subbasin scale—is well suited to grassroots, locally inspired environmental action. Larger watersheds—the Upper Mississippi and Delaware River basins, for example—are more appropriately regarded at the macro level, since the federal government and/or multiple states oversee regional management. But local watershed efforts may need a jump start or mechanisms to assure that they actually make progress in reducing pollutant loadings and improving the general physical health of the watershed. Although multistakeholder, cooperative approaches are lauded as flexible alternatives to the conventional command-and-control regulatory model, we have little assurance of their potential for improving watersheds' physical states—unless, perhaps, collaborative goodwill is channeled toward meaningful action by the threat of increased regulation or enforcement of water quality or land use standards (Kenney 1997). This is especially the case when it comes to diffuse-source pollution, such as that from farm and urban runoff.

Nonpoint source pollution has had a place on the national environmental agenda at least since passage of the 1972 Clean Water Act (CWA) amendments. But it was much easier to subsidize construction of wastewater treatment facilities than deal with widely diffused problems such as urban and agricultural runoff. Indeed, only through regulation of industrial and domestic point-source pollution have CWA amendments made laudable strides in improving water quality for some of America's most vital waterways. Decades ago, through its Section 208 areawide planning requirements, the CWA amendments also recognized nonpoint sources as significant pollution contributors. But progress in dealing with them, as it turns out, has been very limited. Until quite recently, the EPA and the states were unable—or unwilling—to even begin to require costly, contentious actions to regulate development, improve farmers' management of cropland and disposal of manure, and deal with airborne transport of pollutants.

Before the CWA amendments, basinwide planning was promoted in the 1950s and 1960s, as described in chapter 2. Most of these efforts were supply-side and technology focused, relying on dams and other structural approaches for meeting water needs. Land use planning was not emphasized, though it is given much greater attention today by the few river commissions that remain. The Delaware River Basin Commission

(DRBC), chastened by the defeat of the proposed Tocks Island dam in the 1970s, turned toward nonstructural approaches to watershed management. Though the DRBC produces excellent educational programs and even regulates land use via groundwater withdrawal limits in parts of eastern Pennsylvania, its ability to shape overall watershed land use patterns remains very limited. In other regions, where there is no basinwide agency at all, the need to "grow" a collaborative watershed infrastructure becomes all the more critical.

For the EPA, the watershed approach is a winner. It makes enormous sense not only environmentally but also from political and public relations standpoints. While the EPA may come under fire for backsliding on many regulatory programs (Vig 2006), watershed planning is a way to present a good face to constituencies such as educators, local officials, and the general public. The EPA's watersheds website maintains an online directory of watersheds, provides course modules through its "watershed academy," allows access to water-quality data, offers resources for teachers, and directs users to EPA and external funding sources (U.S. EPA 2007g). EPA's "Adopt Your Watershed" and "Surf Your Watershed" features are web-based information portals, designed to kindle citizen interest in local watersheds (U.S. EPA 2007b).

But EPA does more than maintain watershed websites. Since the mid-1990s, watershed management has been promoted by way of inducements to states that embrace it. Among the potential benefits to adoptees are reduced water quality reporting requirements, with EPA requiring reports only every five years rather than biennially under Section 305(b) of the Clean Water Act; simplified wetlands permitting; more flexible NPDES (National Pollution Discharge Elimination System) permitting and water quality standard setting; and eligibility for more watershed planning and management grant funding (U.S. EPA 1997, 2002). Other laws and programs also are embracing watershed perspectives. The 1996 Safe Drinking Water Act amendments' Source Water Assessment Program (SWAP) is meant to foster a locally based approach to watershed health and water quality (Trust for Public Land and American Water Works Association 2004). The EPA's American Heritage Rivers Initiative assists river communities in securing funds from relevant federal programs (Hartig 2002; U.S. EPA 2007c). In all, according to McGinnis, Woolley, and Gamman (1999), at least eighteen federal agencies support watershed management. Among the laws and programs promoting watershed activities—beyond those already mentioned—are the North American Wetlands Conservation Act, Forest Legacy Program, and TEA (chapter 5). Yet demand for funds from the EPA and other agencies' suites of programs far outstrips supply (Leach and Pelkey 2001; U.S. EPA, Office of Water 2001).

Funding shortfalls notwithstanding, none of these national watershed initiatives ensures that land use patterns and land planning practices will be substantially altered or that interests of diverse stakeholders will be addressed. These are critical concerns for Connecticut's Quinnipiac River watershed, where government agencies, NGOs, and citizens are spending EPA grant monies for data gathering, planning, and improving watershed awareness (National Academy of Sciences Commission on Geosciences, Environment, and Resources 1999). This is a strong collaborative program—but what is it accomplishing? The project's next phase will examine outcomes, assessing the extent to which good intentions and earnest collaboration translate into improved water quality and land use management.

The greatest infusions of funds and other assistance for watershed planning come not from Washington but from the states. A recent EPA report (U.S. EPA 2002) reveals that twenty states have adopted a statewide watershed approach, which by the EPA's definition includes regulatory and nonregulatory measures, stakeholder involvement, and assessment of environmental results. Though state programs vary widely, most of them are very much quieter revolution initiatives. The Massachusetts Watershed Initiative (Michaels 1999), seen as a model among such programs, was funded to the tune of $3.5 million, mostly for education, outreach, and technical assistance. Though the commonwealth-level program is no longer active, it spawned many local initiatives that are now flying on their own. Other states with very active watershed programs include Oregon, Washington, Wisconsin, Pennsylvania, and California (Sabatier et al. 2005).

While watershed organizations do provide a means for grappling with important problems at appropriate spatial scales, and are able to exert some influence over allocation of state and federal monies that affect watershed development, most have little real power. Watershed councils and/or multiagency teams may produce watershed plans, but such plans usually lack teeth of their own; they can only seek to influence what is compulsory under legislation already in place. At best, watershed organizations do have some influence over allocation of state funding (U.S. EPA 2002) and can increase their effectiveness through coordination with state and local open space and agricultural preservation programs (Meridian Institute 2001).

But in certain instances (e.g., in the wake of major flooding or where EPA wields the prospect of costly new water quality requirements), a policy window opens and the responses can be dramatic. In the past, major structural responses at the large watershed scale followed Mississippi River flooding and were deployed to provide cheap electricity and foster regional economic development in the Tennessee Valley. The response to Hurricane Katrina's destruction in Louisiana and Mississippi, briefly covered in chapter 4, is still taking shape. But nonstructural, as well as structural, responses *can* emerge in the wake of major events: in New York State's Catskill region (chapter 4) land use and acquisition programs are being directed toward maintaining the high quality of New York City's drinking water. This regional-scale watershed protection program has gained New York City an exemption from federal requirements for filtration of public drinking water supplies, saving the city billions of dollars.

More typically, at the local as well as the larger scale, watershed managers must content themselves with expanded options for dangling carrots, but they have few opportunities to wield sticks. Nor is the United States about to emulate New Zealand's integrative approach. Its 1991 Resource Management Act, taking environmental sustainability to unprecedented administrative heights, reorganized and devolved political units to conform with watershed boundaries (Furuseth and Cocklin 1995; Michaels and Furuseth 1997; National Academy of Sciences Commission on Geosciences, Environment, and Resources; Ericksen et al. 2004). New Zealand is a small country, with a high level of environmental consciousness and far fewer built-in constraints to innovation than are present in the U.S. system. Still, New Zealand's successes with watershed and ecosystem management provide exemplary models—greatly downscaled though they would have to be in the U.S. context—for American policymakers.

What does hold real promise in this country are the total maximum daily load (TMDL) provisions of the federal Clean Water Act:

> Under the precepts of Section 303(d) of the Clean Water Act (CWA), states must identify pollution-impaired streams and develop plans to reduce pollutant loads. They then set TMDLs for individual water bodies that account for both point and nonpoint sources of pollutants. Development of TMDLs requires a broad understanding of point and nonpoint sources, the processes that influence their magnitude, timing, transport to bodies of water, and attenuation en route, and how they affect aquatic biota. This procedure tends to be highly site-specific, and watershed managers are challenged by frequent gaps in data, information, and modeling in their efforts to comply with this section of the CWA. (National Academy of Sciences Commission on Geosciences, Environment, and Resources 1999, 134)

In a separate report, the National Research Council Committee on Assessing and Valuing the Services of Aquatic and Related Terrestrial Ecosystems (2001) calls for the TMDL process to include regular assessment and adaptive implementation.

Data, adaptivity, and assessment challenges notwithstanding, the TMDL approach calls on federal and state government to do much more than is now entailed in regulation of point-source pollution. If we are to effectively deal with nonpoint sources—including farms, urban streets, housing developments, shopping malls, and office complexes—more nuanced, diverse, and innovative approaches will be required. Watershed organizations' missions can, conceivably, mesh very nicely with TMDL goals. And at the larger watershed scale, TMDL goals can be synched with broader regional land use concerns. TMDL is based on a simple set of physical parameters, yet to ensure that the approach is fully effective, it may have to be calibrated with additional physical measures, such as macroinvertebrate health in streams and timing and intensity of local flood regimes. Social and economic dimensions, too—including environmental justice questions—can be addressed by local and regional watershed organizations.

For all its potential benefits, TMDL is not a panacea for watersheds. One of the lessons from the 2001 National Watershed Forum (Meridian Institute 2001) is that TMDLs are interpreted and implemented inconsistently among the states. Water quality standards are not necessarily well integrated into the TMDL approach, and in many specific cases TMDLs seem to lack the appropriate scope, scale, focus, and time frame needed for effective watershed management (U.S. EPA, Office of Water 2002).

What more can be done to advance watershed management? Beyond the inventories, assessments, funding programs, local organizing, and adoption of TMDL approaches, participants at the 2001 National Watershed Forum called for creation of a quasi-public trust fund or endowment (Meridian Institute 2001). But perhaps the best way of ensuring a sustainable future for the watershed approach is to enshrine it in federal legislation. The National Academy of Sciences Commission on Geosciences, Environment, and Resources (1999) watershed strategy report suggested it be made an integral part of the federal Clean Water Act. Depending on how such legislation is configured, though, these added provisions might be interpreted as new regulation—to be vigorously opposed by wise use and property rights groups and their allies (chapter 7). Moreover—again depending on program structure—it could mean a loss of local autonomy and flexibility, perhaps constricting local watershed programs' adaptability.

The appropriate balance among local adaptability, a secure legal and financial foundation, and clear accountability protocols can be an exceedingly difficult one to strike. While local watersheds are very fitting venues for adaptive experimentation, we also want assurances about environmental outcomes, equity, and cost-effectiveness. Washington State's approach is an interesting one; it tries to balance multiple concerns by building adaptability into its evaluation procedures (National Academy of Sciences 1999). A good generic evaluation scheme, which incorporates several of the dimensions discussed in chapter 8, is provided by the National Academy of Public Administration. As part of a larger analysis of innovative environmental programs, the academy studied six watersheds of small to moderate size, four of which are part of the National Estuary Program, one a coastal-zone management program, and one (Lake Tahoe) a federal-state compact (Imperial and Hennessey 2000); six small watersheds, two each in Washington State, Wisconsin, and North Carolina (Born and Genskow 2000); and four large, basinwide programs, with a focus on the Colorado River Basin Salinity Control Program (Adler, Straube, and Green 2000). These analyses examine environmental outcomes, cost-effectiveness, project efficacy, equity issues, and monitoring protocols.

Sabatier et al.'s (2005) detailed empirical research—which examines mainly process and gives little attention to environmental outcomes—helps us assess the long-term prospects for collaborative watershed management. Sabatier et al. found that participants may initially be motivated to join the collaborative enterprise because they distrust other participants' motives, but—as trust is built over the longer term—their participation is sustained. They also hypothesized that if potential benefits outweigh transaction costs of participating in a watershed management program, then the process will be successful. Their analysis of participant cooperation in National Estuary Program (NEP) sites versus non-NEP sites supported this hypothesis.

In the end, watershed partnerships are an important tool for building social capital, sense of community, and adaptable local institutions (Sabatier et al. 2005; National Academy of Sciences 1999). Indeed, one of their greatest assets is their potential for experimentation and adaptive management. But if the collaborative watershed approach is to yield significant accomplishments through multiple and overlapping spatial scales, then it is important to have a dense national network of watershed organizations, endowed with the ability to effect significant local change and also tightly interwoven into progressively wider watershed communities and management structures. While there is no denying the value of amicable relations among diverse stakeholders, it is only the first step in tapping the full potential of collaborative watershed management.

A New Generation of Greenways

Local parks and public recreation areas have been with us for generations now (President's Commission on Americans Outdoors 1987). What has emerged recently are opportunities for new kinds of parks, differently configured from city and county parks of the past (Little 1990; Fabos 2004). They occupy abandoned rail rights-of-way, canal towpaths, riverbanks, and former roadways; receive funds and technical assistance from ballot measures (discussed below), local land trusts (discussed above), and federal and state grant programs (chapter 5); and are coordinated and promoted not only by multiple levels of government but also NGOs, such as The Nature Conservancy, Conservation Foundation, Trust for Public Land, and Rails to Trails Conservancy.

These linear protected areas—or greenways—serve multiple purposes, at a variety of spatial scales. Perhaps they are most widely recognized in local places as recreation corridors, used for hiking, biking, school education programs, and the like. Searns (1995) describes a historical progression for greenways that begins with axes, boulevards, and parkways, pre-1960. The second act, 1960–1985, features recreation trails defined by rivers, ridgelines, rail corridors, canals, and other, mostly linear features. Generation three, post-1985, is one of "multi-objective greenways."

Those objectives can be quite diverse. Some greenways act as buffers to protect water quality or windbreaks to reduce soil erosion. Others serve strategic functions as parts of metropolitan greenbelts or "firebreaks" to development. New Jersey's D&R Greenway Land Trust (D&R refers to the Delaware and Raritan canals) sees itself as just such a control on development. While the greenway itself is a linear canal system and lands immediately adjacent, the D&R Greenway Land Trust has made it into something more. D&R acquires strategic land parcels within the canals' larger watershed system (figure 6.2) and also works with government agencies and other NGOs over a fairly large area. It is a serious player in regional planning and open space protection.

Modern greenways, in Searns's (1995) view, are part of our environmental infrastructure, addressing such needs as habitat, hazard management, and education. Though our focus here is mainly on local and regional greenways, others see greenways mainly as long-distance hiking trails and ecological corridors (Fabos 2004; Ryan, Fabos, and Allan 2006); their perspective builds on Benton MacKaye's early vision of the Appalachian Trail as a critical linkage between urban populations and working farms and forests (chapter 2). Several recent observers envision an expanded role for greenways in local and regional planning. They are seen as part of the metropolitan fabric, as well as corridors that link metropolitan regions and ecological areas over considerable distances. This green infrastructural vision, in promoting systematic conservation over regions large and small, contrasts with as well as expands prevailing practices of protecting isolated green spaces (Beatley 1999; Bryant 2006; Walmsley 2006). The more optimistic supporters of such expansive views see greenways playing increasingly important roles in shaping urban growth and supporting smart growth planning strategies (Walmsley 2006). And some leading state and regional greenways programs are trending in just such integrative directions. Among the exemplars are Maryland's Green Print Program, Florida's Greenways Commission, New Jersey's Garden State Greenways Plan, Oregon's Greenspaces program, the Minneapolis-St. Paul regional initiative, the D.C. region's greenway systems, and the Regional Plan Association's greensward initiative for the New York metropolitan region, which includes the Highlands area that is examined in chapter 4 (Yaro and Hiss 1996; Fabos 2004; Bryant 2006).

But greenways may not yet be ready for prime time, at least not insofar as having the capacity to form dense networks that in turn organize urban and regional settlement patterns. On the ground, greenways must confront several troubling issues. For example, consider the environmental values of a linear park such as a community hike/bike path. It may promote environmental awareness among users and lead to enhanced protection of lands adjacent to it (presuming there are lands near it worthy of protection), but it may also create new environmental impacts. Not the least of these might be the fuel consumed by SUV-driving bicyclists carting their bikes to trails not connected to residential areas by bike-friendly corridors and not designed with bicycle commuting in mind. In some instances, the environmental advisability of converting a rail corridor to a recreation trail in the first place is questioned. If there is the possibility of restoring rail service to that line, what is the appropriate threshold of future uncertainty and transportation needs that tells us we should keep that option open? A trail could, of course, be converted back to a rail line, but if it is a popular trail, that could be a near impossibility, politically.

Despite greenway promoters' best intentions, these corridors act as more than ecological corridors and low-intensity recreation trails. In some locales, they are used for motorized vehicles, such as ATVs and snowmobiles. But user conflicts abound even when motorized use is not an issue. Competition among trail-bike, equestrian, and Vibram-soled constituencies can be intense. User conflicts, as well as greenway use itself, often are linked with questions of social class and race. Furuseth and Altman (1991), in a study of Raleigh-area greenways, learned that users tend to have high education and income levels and disproportionately are members of environmental organizations. Another source of conflict involves use of eminent domain power. Usually, this is limited to provision of public access and trail completion needs, especially in areas where private landowners vigorously resist having public trails in their backyards.

Several broad barriers stand in the way of integrated greenway networks—networks that might shape regional planning, enable smart growth, and begin to attend to the inter- and intraregional equity issues. Among these are limited coordination across government agencies and other organizations, absence of regional governance mechanisms, lack of funding, and limited public understanding of regional greenway projects (Erickson 2004; Ryan, Fabos, and Allen 2006).

Greenways are full of potential, much of it yet unrealized, as urban and regional connective tissue, buffers against development and natural hazards, and bicycle and pedestrian commuter ways. They also are splendid venues for fostering local and regional environmental stewardship. But to reach that full potential, we must move beyond popular conceptions of greenways as simply pleasing recreational frills; that perceptual transformation is, at best, proceeding only slowly and unevenly.

Ballot Measures

Though Robert Putnam (2000) questions the value of ballot measures as widespread indicators of civic engagement, there is little question about their importance in advancing the quieter revolution. Ballot questions often are used to secure funds for major initiatives, particularly when legislators are reluctant to earmark large sums for programs that do not fit neatly within conventional categories of health, human services, education, and transportation. Ballot measures also help fill gaps created by reductions in federal land conservation funding. As noted in chapter 5, federal allocations to states and localities from the signature federal program—the Land and Water Conservation Fund—have been very meager in recent years.

For land use decisions, referenda are far more common than ballot initiatives. The former are placed on the ballot by a legislative body, while the latter are proposed by voters directly. Environmental ballot measures are nothing new; indeed, statewide open space questions have been on ballots in New Jersey since 1961, when voters approved a $60 million bond issue that launched the state's Green Acres program. Two-thirds of the initial Green Acres funds were for state land acquisition, with the rest going to localities in the form of matching grants (Foresta 1981; Solecki, Mason, and Martin 2004). Green Acres, which subsequently authorized $1.42 billion through eight additional ballot questions (New Jersey Department of

Environmental Protection 2007b), stands as an exemplar and leads us to some general observations about ballot measures. First, the ballot measure model is one of intergovernmental partnership, providing state funds to support local-level actions—and increasingly, as we see below, local funds to support local projects. It is very much a quieter revolution model. Second, it raises important equity issues regarding the spatial character of open space spending. Which regions are favored by direct state expenditures and support to localities, and which are neglected? Are some places privileged users of ballot measures because they can afford them, whereas other places cannot? Both questions help guide this analysis of quieter revolution programs; indeed, equity issues have been raised in support of as well as to attack open space programs in New Jersey and elsewhere.

Ballot measures have become immensely popular over the past decade or so, with voters passing approximately three-quarters of them. Between 1988 and 2005, 1,986 land conservation measures were on ballots across the country; 1,519 were passed. Approval was given for $109.1 billion in funding, but because many of the measures include funds for infrastructure, waste management, and pollution control projects, total approved land conservation funding is pegged at $44.0 billion (Trust for Public Land 2007b). A dramatic surge in ballot question numbers is evident in 1996 and subsequent years. While the vast majority of these are municipal- and county-level measures, the small number of statewide questions passed account for almost half the funding total. Bond issues and tax increases are the prime funding sources. Funds directed toward watershed and farmland protection account for more than half of all land conservation funding secured via the ballot box. With their relatively dense populations, New England, New York, and the mid-Atlantic region are far and away the leaders in numbers of ballot measures. But some rapid-growth areas in the Sun Belt have witnessed a lot of activity as well. These data come from the "LandVote" database maintained by the Trust for Public Land (TPL). Using this information, TPL and the Land Trust Alliance (LTA) jointly produce annual summary reports (Trust for Public Land and Land Trust Alliance 2006). TPL and LTA do not have direct roles in sponsoring or promoting ballot questions, but their advising and data-gathering roles are illustrative of the synergistic relationship among the nongovernment land conservation community, government agencies, and the electorate. Of course, land trusts stand to benefit from new funds directed their way, by at least some of the ballot questions, for land and easement acquisition. This collaborative approach is quite in contrast to that of the conventional national-level environmental NGOs, which work toward many of the same goals but often in highly competitive fashion (Bosso 2005). While there is, inevitably, considerable competition for resources and credit even at the local level, it is not generally as fierce as that at the national scale.

The LandVote database does not include regulatory measures. Though such measures are relatively few, they do reach the ballot on occasion. More typically, though, regulatory measures are matters for legislatures and administrative bodies rather than direct votes. Also relatively rare are direct state-level—and to a lesser extent local-level—tax levy questions. An early analysis of the ballot box phenomenon, by land use analyst Phyllis Myers (1999), concludes that voters are tax averse, at least when it comes to new state-level taxes. They are more receptive to bond issues and earmarking of existing tax revenues. Unlike the LandVote database, Myers's analyses did include regulatory measures, though only for the years 1998 and 1999. During those two years, according to Myers, "a slew of urban growth boundaries were handily approved in California's Bay Area and Ventura County" (Myers and Puentes 2000, 3).

California, with its combination of intense growth pressures and a well-established tradition of citizen ballot initiatives, is the place where policymaking via local-level direct democracy has gained greatest traction (Caves 1990). Development moratoria, controls on rates of development, lot size regulations, zoning plans, conservation regulations, and even approval or disapproval of specific projects are typical matters that voters have decided directly. California may have done the most, but it is not the only place where policy decisions are made at the ballot box; Maine, Maryland, Massachusetts, and Washington are among the other citizen-initiative states where large numbers of land use decisions have been taken directly by voters (Caves 1990).

Equity and environmental justice issues are part and parcel of environmental ballot questions. In what locales, for instance, do measures appear on ballots in the first place? Do financial and political wherewithal play lead roles in determining where open space is protected? While some of the most threatened land parcels may indeed be found in more wealthy locales, it does not necessarily follow—on ecological or cost-effectiveness grounds—that they are the most worthy of protection. More generally, something of a mismatch is evident between local objectives—such as open space, recreation, and agricultural land preservation—and ecological/biodiversity goals. Very small protected parcels, especially those not connected to larger reserves or ecological corridors, may do little to meet conservation ecology goals (Brewer 2003). Yet those conservation purists whose top priority is ecosystem protection often will go along with protecting some of these smaller parcels, in the interest of keeping the larger land protection mission healthily afloat. Other conservation advocates, however, may argue against these small-bore actions, making the case that limited resources must be deployed in an ecologically strategic manner.

Additional questions about physical and economic value of the lands, as well as public access to protected lands, need to be asked. So, too, do questions about the lands' public uses. In some instances, land or easement acquisition will preclude hunting and fishing on lands that have hosted these uses for many decades, often with the landowner's tacit consent. In recent years, especially, questions of snowmobile, off-road vehicle, mountain bike, and horse access on protected lands have been hotly debated. In suburban locales, stakeholders often clash over use of acquired lands: ballparks, soccer fields, golf courses, and even Frisbee golf compete with more natural landscape options, such as ecological restoration.

It is not at all clear that ballot question voting, despite intuitive expectations, is mainly a matter of self-interest, socioeconomic standing, or political allegiance. The Trust for Public Land and Land Trust Alliance (2005), in reporting on the results of 2005 voting, highlight a tale of two New Jersey counties. Conservative Sussex County, in the northern part of the state, approved a property tax increase to support a $45 million open space and farmland acquisition program, by a margin of 57 to 43. Democratic Camden County, in southern New Jersey, passed a similar measure, 68 to 42. Though there is a clear difference in strength of support, the point being made by the land conservation organizations is that support for land protection spending often is quite bipartisan. Indeed, this is not all that surprising; well-to-do Republicans have long supported conservation, especially in their own backyards. This is not usually the case with libertarian-leaning voters, nor is it necessarily in keeping with the Republican Party's current character—especially at the national level (Bosso 2005).

The literature on support for growth management paints a more nuanced picture. Van Liere and Dunlap's (1980) widely cited analysis reveals that relationships between socioeconomic status and support for environmental protection generally are positive, but rather weakly so. Research directed specifically toward support for growth controls is even more ambiguous in its findings. Baldassare and Wilson's (1996) study in Orange County, California, showed that high incomes were a predictor of growth control support in the early 1980s, but this was no longer the case in the early 1990s. Chapin and Connerly's (2004) Florida analyses found only partial support for the social class hypothesis. They found both liberal and conservative support for growth management and that blacks are less likely than whites to support growth controls. Neiman and Loveridge (1981) learned that the predictive value of social class is greatest when the issues are specific, tangible, and highly contested. Baldassare (1990) and Baldassare and Wilson (1996) found that residence in a high-growth area was a predictor of support for growth management.

Anglin's (1990) research in New Jersey indicates high overall levels of support for growth management and that most respondents are willing to give up home rule in order to achieve more orderly future growth. But while it seems that voters are capable of transcending narrow self-interest in at least some cases, the issue is, in fact, rather murkier than this would imply. The darker side of "self-interest" may include exclusionary impulses, racist attitudes, and a selfish devotion to one's own peace and property. While these sentiments may indeed drive voters' choices on at least some local ballot questions, the same cannot necessarily be said for statewide measures.

For the sake of topical cohesiveness, a few words regarding state-level ballot questions are in order in this section about local initiatives. At the state level, a positive vote usually reflects support for open space protection in the abstract. The more selfish impulses, described above, may emerge as detailed plans for open space acquisition and management are put into effect in specific local places. Questions have been raised, for example, about the degree to which New Jersey's land acquisition programs favor wealthy, politically connected hobby farmers, offering compensation in many instances to folks whose lands face only minimal development threats (Mansur 2000).

In New Jersey in the late 1990s, Governor Christine Todd Whitman initially sought legislative approval of a dedicated fund for open space acquisition. When the legislature balked, a different tack was taken: voters were presented with a $1 billion bond issue question. As already noted, New Jersey has a history of approving open space ballot measures. This one was no exception; it passed by about a two-thirds vote. Solecki, Mason, and Martin (2004) found that socioeconomic status was an important determinant of ballot-measure voting patterns. Support for the ballot measure was particularly strong in north-central New Jersey's "wealth belt," where suburban and exurban land use futures are hotly debated. By contrast, support lagged in areas that already have significant proportions of protected open space, and also in core urban areas. Although the measure was approved in central urban tracts, the approval margins were much lower than in the rest of the state. What is not clear is the extent to which this may be attributed to general disinterest, low interest in the specific issue, and/or "ballot fatigue" sometimes associated with "down-ballot" voting behavior.

Even though the political cost of putting a question to voters may seem negligible, settling on the question's precise wording can be a critical and highly contested matter. Language and the sentiments it tapped into were very important in ensuring passage of Oregon's Measure 37 (chapter 7). Pennsylvania provides another recent illustration of the significance of ballot measure details. Shortly after taking office in 2003, Democratic governor Edward Rendell proposed an $800 million ballot question, to be funded by a tax on waste generation (Mason 2005). His attempts to get the question on the 2004 ballot failed; instead, a $625 million bond issue—to be funded by borrowing rather than the waste tax— was agreed to by the legislature and added to the May 2005 primary ballot. Though voter turnout was low, the question passed handily, by about a two-thirds vote. But it seems likely that Pennsylvania's voters would have approved Rendell's initial proposal, or perhaps even a more costly and/or regulatory measure. In this instance, legislative politics determined the ballot question's final form. In citizen-initiative states, where voters themselves can place measures on the ballot, matters can become quite complicated; voters sometimes are presented with multiple versions of the same question.

Summary

Local land use actions play a critical part in shaping the larger quieter revolution. As already noted, localities across the country are far more able and willing to do serious environmental planning than they were in the quiet revolution years. But in many places, growth—especially commercial growth—is still held sacred (Berke, Godschalk, and Kaiser 2006). In other locales, antigrowth sentiments dominate. And there are ever-present concerns about government intrusiveness and the effects of land use restrictions on property values.

These diverse interests and concerns are, at least in some measure, accommodated by the tools and strategies described in this chapter. Compared with governments, land trusts can act relatively quickly and unobtrusively to acquire land and conservation easements. Watershed conservancies, while usually possessing little political power of their own, do work at environmentally appropriate scales. And they can amplify their effectiveness by forging relationships with governments, land trusts, and other environmental NGOs. Most greenways are highly valued as local and regional environmental amenities. But they can also foster wider environmental awareness and act as linear loci, defining and attenuating environmental protection activities over watersheds and other regions. Ballot measures permit voters to make land use planning decisions directly. Most authorize funding for open space protection, but some give voice to deeper land management philosophies, running the range from ecocentric to libertarian.

What we have, then, is reinforcement of the phenomenon described elsewhere in this book: an uneven landscape featuring some local places that are making extraordinary efforts to protect and remake their proximate environments, contrasted with others for whom this is not a high priority. While the federal and state programs described in chapter 5 do iron out some of this unevenness, they can also exacerbate it. Much depends on local initiative—as well as local political capacity. Those places that cannot afford to invest heavily in land preservation and place-remaking may simply be left behind. This does not mean they are any less "livable" than the more advantaged locales—but their financial, planning, and decision-making options may be more limited.

CHAPTER SEVEN
COUNTERREVOLUTIONARIES

Election Day 2004: Oregon voters, by a 60–40 margin, pass a ballot measure requiring local governments to compensate landowners—at least those who held title to the land before Oregon's 1973 land use legislation was passed—when environmental or zoning regulations detract from the value of their investments (Barringer 2004a). And in February 2006, Oregon's Supreme Court unanimously upholds Measure 37, overturning a lower court decision that had invalidated it. This one simple measure may be able to undo many of the Beaver State's successes of the past several decades in reining in urban sprawl (chapter 5). Indeed, Oregon is widely regarded as a smart growth visionary; its statewide planning goals, in combination with urban growth boundaries, make it one of only a few places to confront sprawl in a comprehensive, legally enforceable manner (Abbott, Howe, and Adler 1994; Weitz 1999; DeGrove 2005; Judd and Beach 2003). So it is no surprise that an organized, vocal opposition has been hard at work since the 1970s. But while opponents have won concessions over the years, they could not persuade the state legislature to overturn the Land Use Planning Law. Nor had they succeeded, until 2004, at the ballot box.

What happened in 2004? No particular moment or event seems to have galvanized public opinion. Indeed, opponents of regulation simply may have learned how to play smarter. While stressing their broad support for environmental protection, they framed the issue at hand as one of fairness and equity. And opponents of statewide planning were well funded, supported by major timber interests and real estate companies that stand to benefit from subdivision of their landholdings (Harden 2005). Though a majority of Oregonians continue to express support for the land use law (Egan 2006), younger voters have no direct experience, and perhaps little awareness, of the development trends that prompted its passage thirty-five years ago. The land use law, it seems, is partly a victim of its own success.

A majority of 2004's voters may have been quite satisfied with the general condition of Oregon's environment and land. So when faced with basic questions about fairness—and presented with examples of cases where the little guy (or, more accurately, the little old lady featured in television commercials) lost out because of big government regulation—a majority voted to add new checks to that regulatory process. The spatial character of the vote is quite interesting. While it comes as no surprise that the measure enjoyed strong support in the state's rural and small-town locales, the bulk of Oregon's population resides in urban regions. Why had these voters not prevailed? Most of them actually supported the measure; only in the Corvallis area was it defeated. Even in the city of Portland, it passed by a small margin (Barringer 2004a). In large part, the measure's success may be attributed to a populist campaign that focused on the excesses of regulation. This goes to the heart of the American dilemma about planning, discussed at the outset of this book: Americans may appreciate many of the outcomes but feel that the process itself is unfair and intrusive.

Despite the favorable court ruling, it is still too early to know how the Oregon measure will play out. Will the state and/or localities be able to pay claims? Will proposed development have to be permitted in some or most cases? Do rights established by Measure 37 carry with sale of the land? While these and other matters are yet to be fully resolved, already there is some evidence of buyers' remorse; recent polling shows that voters did not anticipate the measure's negative landscape effect, and a majority may be ready to repeal it (Kitch 2007).

One thing, however, is very clear: Measure 37 is a dream come true for wise use and property rights (hereafter referred to as "WUPR") advocates (Gilroy 2006). What better place to successfully press their vision of equity and fairness than in Oregon, symbol of growth management success. Resources were poured into the campaign to pass this measure, which some proponents see as the appetizer for an even more important national project: repealing or greatly weakening the federal Endangered Species Act. While that goal may have become much more elusive with the 2006 election of a Democratic Congress, Oregon's victory remains iconic. Indeed, WUPR advocates in other states have taken notice. Neighboring Washington State put a measure similar to Oregon's before the voters in 2006. As they did with a similar measure in 1995, Washington's voters gave it a thumbs down. Washington's awareness of Oregon voters' regrets over Measure 37 undoubtedly played a part in the rejection. "Measure 37 clones," as the American Planning Association describes them, appeared on the ballot in 2006 in several other states, as well. In Idaho and California, they were defeated, but Arizona's ballot question passed by a wide margin. In Napa County, California, a regulatory takings measure was soundly defeated. Constitutional amendments and/or legislative measures were removed from the ballot in Colorado, Missouri, Montana, Nevada, and Oklahoma (American Planning Association 2006c).

These results may indicate that the tide is starting to turn. If so, Measure 37 may be remembered by land use policy historians as just one of a small number of outlier victories for a movement that peaked in the 1990s. But it is not at all clear that the WUPR movements are in remission—and if more measures like Oregon's are passed in coming years, and more Supreme Court decisions follow on the ones noted below, then the movement's star may again be ascending. If this turns out to be the case, then implied legal and regulatory "threats" may take on a distinctly different character than they did in the recent past. Whereas the mere possibility of a species listing under the Endangered Species Act often brings reluctant property owners to the collaborative table, in the near future it may be environmentalists who are more motivated to negotiate.

Regulation is an easy target for the WUPR opposition; witness, for example, the regulatory impact assessment (RIA) procedures initiated during the Reagan era. These RIAs can help us methodically assess economic efficiency—but this, of course, is not necessarily the perspective or intent of those who would reflexively oppose environmental regulation. Even as alternatives to the command-and-control regulatory model make their way into the mainstream—as quieter revolution approaches—they are challenged and redefined, every step of the way, by private property rights advocates, timber and mining interests, and farm organizations.

Incentive-based approaches do not escape any of antitax crusader Grover Norquist's scorn, as he speaks of

> coercive utopians who want to get the government to give them grants and then tell the rest of us you have to separate the green glass from the clear glass, and our toilets have to be too small to flush, and our cars have to be too small to have kids in, and you can't wear leather, and you can't date girls. (*American Prospect* editors 2006)

Let us place Measure 37 and related developments in context.

The Wise Use and Property Rights Movements (WUPR)

When Newt Gingrich and company rolled out the "Contract with America" in 1994, nothing was said directly about redefining environmentalism. But implicit in the contract's feel-good language was the imperative to do just that, by eliminating unfunded mandates, weakening or doing away with the Environmental Protection Agency, compensating property owners for losses in land value attributable to environmental regulations, eliminating or dramatically scaling back the Endangered Species Act, and opening up more public lands for resource extraction. Although Republican revolutionaries of the 1990s did not succeed in enacting all that much of their agenda, they did manage to create environmental gridlock, precluding passage of any significant environmental initiatives.

Though the 1990s may have witnessed one of the more prominent and public of them, environmental backlashes were nothing new. Ronald Reagan led one in the 1980s—and even during the tenures of Jimmy Carter and Gerald Ford in the 1970s, environmental protections were rolled back in deference to economic and energy priorities. And Sagebrush Rebellions, premised on the notion that the federal government owns and controls too much land, have a history that goes back more than a century (Switzer 1997).

One of the leading early architects of the current (approximately 1990 to present) opposition movement is policy entrepreneur Charles Cushman (Switzer 1997), known to some as "Rent-a-Riot" Cushman. As with so many leading individuals on all sides of land use policy debates, his national-level involvement grew from a defining personal experience. His cabin, situated on a private "inholding" within Yosemite National Park, came under threat from a National Park Service (NPS) policy adopted in the late 1970s. NPS was seeking to reduce inholdings, which it regards as incompatible with park scenic, recreational, and wilderness values. NPS's past actions in ejecting residents from such places as the Shenandoah region (Virginia), Delaware Water Gap (New Jersey/Pennsylvania), and Cuyahoga Valley (Ohio) make the agency an easy target. Although NPS had by the late 1970s moved mainly to a willing-seller policy, Cushman still felt threatened. Outraged, but also skilled in organizing, he reached out to thirty thousand inholders across the country and formed the National Parks Inholders Association. This was quite a feat in the pre–World Wide Web era, but Cushman was up to the task. The organization subsequently expanded its membership base and changed its name to the National Inholders Association. Cushman went on to organize several other property rights organizations and become a leading light in a larger movement that wants to undo most government land use programs, regulatory and nonregulatory alike.

The 1988 Multiple Use Strategy Conference, held in Reno, Nevada, and sponsored by the Center for the Defense of Free Enterprise (CDFE), is widely regarded as the birthplace of the wise use movement (Ramos 1995). Prime movers included CDFE president Alan Gottlieb and executive vice president Ron Arnold. Arnold, in particular, brought years of experience as an industry writer on resource issues, biographer of Reagan's secretary of the interior James Watt, and even one-time publicist for a local environmental group in the state of Washington. While the emerging movement did have considerable grassroots appeal, it was—and continues to be—underwritten by major timber harvesters and petroleum companies, resource-related trade associations, and conservative legal foundations and think tanks. Among its major supporters are the National Rifle Association; American Farm Bureau Federation; American Mining Congress; Petroleum Institute; Mountain States and Pacific Legal Foundations; Blue Ribbon Coalition, an off-road-vehicle group; Western States Public Lands Coalition, which later disbanded; and People for the West!, a subsidiary of the Western States Public Lands Coalition formed in 1989 by mining companies but dissolved in 2000 (Helvarg 1994; Ramos 1995; Layzer 2006). Following the Reno meeting, a twenty-five-point wise use agenda was produced (Gottlieb

1989). Its main points, as summarized by Helvarg (1994, 77–78), are as follows:

- Immediate development of the petroleum resources of the Arctic National Wildlife Refuge in Alaska

- Logging three million acres of the Tongass National Forest in Alaska

- Conversion of "all decaying and oxygen-using forest growth on [sic] the National Forests into young stands of oxygen-producing carbon dioxide–absorbing trees to help ameliorate the rate of global warming" (cutting down all old-growth trees to solve a problem that the anti-environmentalists deny exists)

- A foreign policy that "takes steps to insure raw material supplies for global commodity industries on a permanent basis"

- Exempting from the Endangered Species Act "non-adaptive species such as the California Condor, and endemic species lacking the biological vigor to spread in range"

- The right of prodevelopment groups "to sue on behalf of industries threatened or harmed by environmentalists"

- Opening up seventy million acres of federal wilderness to commercial development and motorized recreational use

- Opening all public lands "including wilderness and national parks" to mining and energy development

- Expanding national park concessions under the management of private firms, "with expertise in people-moving such as Walt Disney"

What was accomplished in Reno and follow-on meetings was a consolidation of WUPR thinking and a channeling of energy into nongovernment organizations. In 1991, over four hundred groups came together to form the Alliance for America, which lists as its constituencies farmers, ranchers, loggers, miners, harvesters, hunters, fishermen, trappers, landowners, recreationalists, teachers, nurses, homemakers, and citizens (Alliance for America 2006). Though loosely organized, the alliance came into being just as modern instantaneous electronic communication capabilities were becoming widely available. The ability to mobilize a large, far-flung membership by fax, e-mail, and websites has profoundly influenced the scope and scale of the alliance's many activities.

The WUPR movements developed quietly during "environmental president" George H. W. Bush's tenure. WUPR organizations stood ready to work hand in hand with their newly empowered compatriots when the 1994 Republican revolution propelled the Gingrich Congress to power. They were again there to support a movement-friendly executive branch under President George W. Bush. The 1990s brought a parade of legislative activity. Numerous anti-environmental riders were attached to federal budget bills, though President Clinton's vetoes and veto threats largely neutralized this strategy. In 1995, the House passed the Private Property Rights Act. Like Oregon's Measure 37, the act would have made landowners eligible for compensation for reductions in property value due to environmental regulations. The Senate, however, failed to pass a companion bill. Still, every state in the union took up property rights measures in the early 1990s; by late 1995, eighteen had enacted laws, most of which required a "takings impact assessment." Some went further, building compensation provisions into the legislation. But in many states, environmentalists mounted successful campaigns to derail or severely constrain these state legislative efforts (Layzer 2006). Legislation also was passed at the local level, much of it under the county-supremacy banner. Catron County, in southwestern New Mexico's ranching country, sought to assert its authority over federal lands and environmental programs in 1991 (Chaloupka 1996). Somewhere between thirty-five and one hundred additional counties, mostly in the rural west, made similar moves in the early to mid-1990s (Switzer 1997, 234). But the movement had no legal leg to stand on and lost much of its traction after the mid-1990s.

The current backlash, nurtured during the Gingrich era and reinvigorated by the Bush presidency, is the quieter revolution's fellow traveler. Each phenomenon represents a reaction to prevailing political circumstances and each embraces adaptive learning. They have not only reacted to but also helped shape our current land use regulatory climate. Of course, they are adversaries; the more extreme of the WUPRs, at least, are as opposed to the quieter revolution as they are to more intrusive forms of environmentalism. While it may seem that the quieter revolution is less vulnerable to attack than its more regulatory counterparts, to some opponents its relative unobtrusiveness makes it all the more insidious. WUPRs can and do counter the quieter wave at the ballot box by working to defeat environmental ballot issues or placing their own questions on the ballot. They also participate in collaborative endeavors, working directly with their enemies as they seek to redefine or undermine collaborative processes and products. Strategic media campaigns, too, can be highly effective in getting out the WUPR message.

Indeed, the WUPR opposition has been smart and adaptive in many ways. It is responsive to local conditions, working in the West mainly on public lands and resource issues, and in the East more on private property rights matters (Helvarg 1994). Its members co-opt the environmental movement's techniques and strategies and brand its enemies using confounding terminology like "radical preservation" (Ramos 1995, 83). WUPR groups act locally in communities as well as more centrally in the corridors of power in state capitals and Washington, D.C.; express support for broad environmental goals while seeking to undermine specific approaches to achieving those goals; structure the debate so as to simplify and dramatize the issues, draw sympathy to their positions, and vilify their opponents (Lange 1996); frame the debate in terms of equity, justice, and fairness (Emerson 1996); make the case that people must be brought back into the environmental management equation; and craft wide-ranging, convincing educational campaigns. WUPR proponents seize on the most egregious examples of bureaucratic bungling and red tape, as well as cases of agency personnel overzealously enforcing regulations, to assail everything environmental. Little people—the guy being pursued by regulators for filling in a wetland that is really an old tire dump—star in many a WUPR campaign (Switzer 1997). Moreover, smart naming strategies are deployed; WUPR groups take deceptive names like the National Wetlands Coalition, Environmental Conservation Association, Californians for Food Safety, Friends of Eagle Mountain, Northwesterners for More Fish, and the Wilderness Institute (Lewis 1995; Switzer 1997). Legal strategies also are employed, with conservative legal foundations supporting many local lawsuits. Some cases, noted below, have gone all the way to the Supreme Court. SLAPPs (strategic lawsuits against public participation) are effective in some circumstances in wearing down and depleting the finances of small NGOs that oppose development, mining, and timber interests (Layzer 2006). And some movement members, directly or by implication, support violence and intimidation in furtherance of their cause (Helvarg 1994; Switzer 1997; Layzer 2006).

Over the past two decades, Supreme Court rulings on the takings issue have lent limited support—though hardly a ringing endorsement—to the WUPR perspective. The Fifth Amendment to the U.S. Constitution states that just compensation must be provided when private property is taken for public use. Most state constitutions have similar provisions. But what constitutes a taking? Of particular concern to WUPR proponents are the issues surrounding environmental regulation. For much of the twentieth century, zoning, nuisance, and other environmental regulations were not regarded as takings. But in the 1987 *Nollan v. California Coastal Commission* case, the Supreme Court ruled that the state, in requiring a public access easement as a condition for granting a rebuilding permit for a beachfront home, must compensate Nollan (Platt 2004). The 5–4 majority opinion was written by Justice Antonin Scalia. Subsequent decisions further affirmed the rights of individual property owners.

In 1992, the *Lucas v. South Carolina* case attracted numerous amicus curiae briefs and garnered wide public attention. Lucas was challenging the prohibition on beachfront building on the seaward side of a defined baseline, imposed by South Carolina's 1988 Beachfront Management Act. The 6–3 majority, again led by Justice Scalia, argued that there is a taking when all economically beneficial or productive use of land is precluded. The implication is that if some value remains, then the state action is not necessarily a taking. Furthermore, Scalia stated that if a regulation is based on principles of nuisance, then a taking is not involved (Platt 2004). The Lucas decision, while supporting the property owner's rights in this particular case, did not establish a clear and simple precedent for ruling on subsequent takings challenges.

In its 1994 *Dolan v. City of Tigard* decision, the Supreme Court ruled on a local business's challenge to development conditions. Tigard was requiring Dolan to dedicate part of his land to floodplain open space and a bikeway. In calling for "rough proportionality" between public benefit and the burden placed on the landowner, the 5–4 decision expanded on the Lucas judgment. In this case, the Court ruled, the burden was out of proportion to the benefit and thus there was a taking. But in a 2002 ruling—*Tahoe-Sierra Preservation Council v. Tahoe Regional Planning Agency* (TRPA)—the court seemed to reaffirm, 6–3, that regional growth-control programs generally stand on solid legal ground. Two shoreline development moratoria, imposed by TRPA in the early to mid-1980s—were upheld; the court regarded them as a routine government action that does not constitute a taking (Platt 2004). In sum, then, recent Supreme Court rulings have supported property owners' rights but have not—at least not yet—hamstrung land use planning programs to the point where they become prohibitively costly or unwieldy.

In the related realm of direct use of the state's authority to take private lands, a rather different story is unfolding. Government use of eminent domain power—long a hot-button issue for WUPR advocates—is now under much broader critical scrutiny. Eminent domain power, also known as condemnation, allows the government to "take," or acquire, lands for public purposes. Compensation payments, often determined by courts, must be made to affected landowners. Condemnations of properties not only for recreation trails and transit-oriented developments, but also for big-box stores, luxury condominiums, and other controversial private and public uses (Berliner 2003), have captured much media and political attention in recent years.

In June 2005, public interest in eminent domain issues was galvanized by the Supreme Court's Kelo ruling (*Kelo v. City of New London*). In a 5–4 decision, the court upheld New London, Connecticut's right to condemn unwilling sellers' homes in an older neighborhood to make way for a new, mixed-use development (Dreher and Echeverria 2006). The American Planning Association supports the decision, arguing that New London's comprehensive economic development plan constitutes a valid public purpose (American Planning Association 2005). But the court's decision prompted a firestorm of outrage, opening a policy window for states to take action aimed at curbing use of eminent domain powers. In 2006 alone, twenty-seven states enacted eminent domain laws, while voters in ten states approved eminent domain ballot measures. Orange County, California voters passed their own local measure (American Planning Association 2006a). While some of these actions are largely symbolic, others seriously restrict governments' scope and ability to use the eminent domain power. Some legislatures are thoughtful and measured in their attempts to balance public and private interests; others act impulsively, with little more than rhetorical regard for fairness (Broder 2006). Texas, for example, quickly passed a law in 2005 affirming private landowners' rights while making a special exception for building a new Dallas Cowboys stadium. Of wider concern, though, is that some states have restricted use of eminent domain power to "blighted" areas; this means condemnation would take place almost exclusively in poor, minority, urban areas (Barron 2006).

Congress and the president, too, have felt compelled to react to Kelo. One year after the decision—on June 23, 2006—President Bush signed an executive order restricting federal agency use of eminent domain to public purposes, such as roads and hospitals. But this is largely a symbolic effort, since the federal government rarely condemns lands. In recent decades, especially, federal land managing agencies have been very reluctant to exercise eminent domain power. Federal funds do, however, support state and local projects that invoke this power. In 2005, the final House-Senate conference agreement on the Housing and Urban Development annual spending bill included an amendment prohibiting use of federal funds for many nonpublic projects that would involve eminent domain proceedings. This action was effective for only a year. While the House did pass legislation—the Private Property Rights Protection Act—barring use of federal funds for a wider range of economic development projects, the Senate failed to move a companion bill out of committee (American Planning Association 2006b).

WUPR and allied organizations may be strengthened by the Kelo decision. At the very least, it has put many of them—including some of the more extreme among them—on the same page with more mainstream interest groups. Perhaps the enhanced stature and credibility will only be temporary, but the effects—including legislative successes scored by post-Kelo political coalitions, as well as subtle shifts in public opinion—could be much more enduring.

Indeed, the Kelo decision hands WUPR and allied organizations a golden opportunity to broaden their appeal. Though Kelo was not about environmental regulations, it may help usher into place a climate more receptive to ballot questions like Oregon's. WUPR proponents are taking full advantage of this opening, deliberately conflating two distinct issues: 1) perceived overreach or government abuses of the eminent domain power and 2) the notion that anyone who is affected by any diminution in land value associated with environmental regulation must be compensated. Inspired by the Oregon vote and hostility toward Kelo, WUPRs are deploying this issue-muddying strategy to gain support for the Measure 37 copycat efforts (Cooper 2006). As noted earlier, though, regulatory compensation measures did not fare nearly as well in 2006 as those regulating eminent domain practices.

Environmentalists often are admonished to develop big-tent alliances with labor and civil rights interests; recently, several organizations have begun to do so (Apollo Alliance 2006; Gottlieb 2001, 2005; Greenhouse 2006). Similarly, WUPR groups can benefit from new bridges to the mainstream, moving beyond their symbiotic relationship with the resource-extractive sector. What better time for them to do so than now, while the post-Kelo policy window remains open? Public anger over Kelo has yielded a wider, more receptive audience for WUPR messages. Those messages are broadcast via op-ed pieces, letters to the editor, radio and television interviews, and websites. Calling attention to eminent domain excesses and promoting fairness and equity at the ballot box are winners for WUPRs, far better for their public image than virulently and potentially violently opposing environmental protection programs.

Kelo's full implications for quieter revolution initiatives are difficult to project. To the extent that states are circumscribing the use of eminent domain power, collaborative planning strategies may find greater favor. Most quieter revolution land transactions are, almost by definition, conducted on a willing-seller/donor basis. This is what land trusts and watershed organizations do and do well; thus their wisdom, skills, and strategies may be in greater demand post-Kelo. The quieter revolution's smart growth wing may also find its standing enhanced—not just because it favors soft, incentive-based approaches to growth management but also on account of its opposition to megamalls, housing projects, sports complexes, and other sprawling developments that increasingly are associated with eminent domain abuses.

So far, the post-Kelo era is shaping up to be one of new limits on what governments can do in the name of comprehensive planning, environmental protection, and economic development. And this may indeed benefit quieter revolution programs, which often serve as politically palatable alternatives to more regulatory approaches—approaches that may include exercise of eminent domain power. But there is a competing scenario: with governments and citizens racing to place new limits on use of these powers, quieter revolution options may lose some of their attractiveness. Without the threat of eminent domain or other strong regulatory measures hanging over their heads, participants in collaborative planning projects may be less motivated to work toward mutually satisfactory outcomes. Indeed, some may no longer want to participate at all.

The WUPR Movements and the Quieter Revolution

Prevailing wisdom holds that in a political climate skeptical of land use regulation, options like land trusts, collaborative planning, ballot measures and other nonregulatory programs will be the most favored planning strategies. This was especially true, it seems, when these approaches were in their formative stages and mostly slipped under the radar screens of potential opponents. Today's quieter revolution efforts, by contrast, rarely go unchallenged. WUPR proponents now track almost every move, actively monitoring, influencing, and redirecting quieter revolution initiatives.

The WUPR movements, at best, are a check on land use regulation generally and a form of civic engagement and empowerment that brings skeptical, libertarian-leaning stakeholders into the planning process (Boston 1999). At worst, it is a popular front manipulated and funded by timber, mining, and other resource extraction industries. In practice, it is both; broad generalizations obviously cannot capture its full texture and diversity.

Do WUPR organizations tend to thrive when sympathetic legislatures and executives are in power? Again, generalizations are elusive and perhaps deceptive. But it is apparent that a supportive governmental climate offers at least some political cover for WUPRs. The quieter revolution's ascendance also has implications for the WUPR movements. To the extent that quieter approaches seem sensible to the general public, the WUPR movements may be rendered less potent and their ability to grab headlines seriously diminished. Much of this boils down to an ongoing, low-level public relations battle, with outcomes dependent not only on respective political and media skills but also a wider set of political, social, and cultural circumstances. The bottom line, at present, seems to be that the quieter revolution is meeting with modest success, at best, in neutralizing WUPR's ascendancy.

WUPR and other forces opposed to environmental regulation have managed to stymie some major regional land use programs. As described in chapter 4, the Greater Yellowstone Ecosystem visioning exercise was torpedoed, largely through WUPR efforts. Although much of the antiplanning activity is in the western states, the movement supports local opponents of eastern initiatives, such as the Northern Forest Lands regional plan and expanded state planning in the Adirondack Park. Indeed, it has links with individuals and groups fighting environmental initiatives in all parts of the country.

In sum, then, how significant are these countervailing forces that strongly oppose most land use management programs? While the WUPR movements have scored many apparent victories, the net effect is rather difficult to gauge; sometimes programs are halted for economic or logistical reasons and in other cases support may never have been strong enough in the first place to sustain them. A WUPR group may claim victory, but often we cannot know just how much, if any, of the victory came from their efforts.

It is relatively easy for WUPR advocates to oppose regulation. But they also have to figure out how to contend with quieter revolution approaches to planning. While they have before them an array of possible responses, their choices are guided by political circumstances and adapted to different spatial and temporal scales. One option is total rejection. They can simply opt out of the planning process, or if they opt in, they can be obstructionists. Opting out is a course chosen not only by WUPRs, but—as noted in chapter 3—by some environmental organizations as well. Utah Wilderness Alliance issues director Ken Rait, for example, takes a hard line: "Our time is better spent filing appeals rather than sitting around the table trying to talk to a bunch of people who aren't interested in listening ... the collaborative approach takes people's focus off the land. I think our track record using NEPA and the ESA is better than it has been in sitting down and trying to seek collaborative solutions" (Jones 1996). Just as some environmentalists rejected the Applegate partnership (chapter 3), principled WUPRs will act likewise. They also can sabotage the process. In the 1980s, for example, one of the county representatives to New Jersey's Pinelands Commission taped closed commission sessions and then released the recordings to the press (Mason 1992a). In California's Santa Ynez watershed, in 1996, a coalition of recalcitrant property owners, farmers, and ranchers caused a collaborative watershed planning project to implode. The coalition favored flood control over habitat restoration and succeeded in pressing its interests to the point where federal agencies withdrew funding. Even a professional facilitator's intervention failed to get the project back on track (McGinnis, Woolley, and Gamman 1999).

WUPR representatives often find themselves faced with difficult choices. On the one hand, their antiplanning convictions may compel them to denounce collaborative initiatives from the outside. Or they may choose to participate, at the risk of being co-opted—or at least perceived by their supporters as having sold out. Finally, participation with intent to sabotage the planning process is an option.

Opposing National Programs

WUPR opponents have been there almost every step of the way, countering not only environmental regulation but also many quieter revolution initiatives. What follows are some recent examples of WUPR opposition in action. In some instances, these efforts are purely home grown and grassroots, while in others they are supported by powerful, well-financed national interests. In most cases, it seems, they are hybrids of local action and larger support systems. But it would be unfair to ascribe every comment and view reported below to the amorphous "WUPR opposition." Issue salience and views about specific issues vary widely among the diverse interests huddled together under that umbrella. Still, widely held WUPR beliefs in the sanctity of private rights and superiority of individual decision making implies that there is much more common ground than divisive fractures within the WUPR community. At the very least, its members seem adept at downplaying internal disagreements in the pursuit of larger goals.

Wetlands protection and the Endangered Species Act (ESA) are the hot-button issues that perhaps have done more than any others to sustain the WUPR opposition. Section 404 of the Clean Water Act, until recently very broadly interpreted to include even isolated small ponds and wetlands under the act's "navigable waters" provision, has enraged and energized opponents of government regulation. Though repeal or drastic scaling back of the act may be out of reach, WUPR proponents may find some limited comfort in the form of an ambiguous 2006 Supreme Court decision that seems to rein in federal jurisdiction over wetlands. It is not yet clear, however, to what extent this convoluted decision really does so. The ESA, because it imposes restrictions on use of private property, is seen as fundamentally unfair. And there are highly publicized, richly symbolic cases that the WUPR opposition continually trots out: the snail darter, a tiny fish in Tennessee that blocked a waterway for a time; the spotted owl controversy in the Pacific Northwest's old-growth forests; and even the development-blocking endangered snakes in New Jersey's Pinelands.

Several of the quieter revolution's central elements are vigorously opposed. The more organized WUPR opposition elements have successfully lobbied Congress, year after year, to severely limit appropriations under the Land and Water Conservation Fund (LWCF). Though the fund has long enjoyed bipartisan support, congressional allocations in most years remain well under the authorized level of $900 million (chapter 5). Those opposed to increased LWCF allocations argue that critical maintenance needs on exiting public lands should take priority over acquisition of new lands, that private ownership is preferable to public ownership, and that increased public ownership reduces revenues by taking lands off the tax rolls. And in recent years these arguments have had some sway, with an increased share of LWCF's very limited funding allocation directed toward maintenance, historic preservation, and payment-in-lieu-of-taxes programs.

The various farm bills (see chapter 5), even though they mainly attach new environmental conditions to existing subsidies, come under criticism (Zinn 1995). In fairness, it must be said that the more libertarian groups oppose all subsidies, whether or not they advance environmental objectives. The crux of the concerns is about the federal government having a say in the use of private land—even when the government is already subsidizing that land's agriculturally productive (or nonproductive) use. At least some WUPR opposition elements are fearful of government imposition of an environmental agenda—even one that is purely voluntary, backed only with some funding—upon private landowners.

Americans should be allowed to sprawl, if that is their desire, say philosophical opponents of smart growth. Samuel and O'Toole (1999), writing for the Cato Institute, see the government's antisprawl campaign as centralized social engineering, a regulatory challenge to American lifestyles. They especially take aim at the EPA and its associated Smart Growth Network (chapter 5). The EPA's smart growth activities, while scaled back by the Bush administration, continue to occupy an important place in the agency's constellation of activities. Samuel and O'Toole do acknowledge that American cities face serious traffic congestion, pollution, open space, and affordable-housing problems. But they believe that these issues should be dealt with at the local and state levels. The Lone Mountain Compact, a set of principles developed by conservative scholars and writers, affirms that people should be allowed to live and work how and where they like, densities and land uses should be market driven, planning controls should not increase burdens on lower-income groups, and private property rights should be a fundamental element of development controls (Lone Mountain Coalition 2000). Though federal policies may have facilitated sprawled development, new federal initiatives—even small-bore efforts—are seen as misguided, intrusive, and unfair.

ISTEA (Intermodal Surface Transportation Efficiency Act) and its successors (chapter 5) also come under fire. Cato Institute scholar Randall O'Toole (1997) depicts ISTEA as partially well intentioned but economically inefficient, anti-automobile, and likely to increase rather than reduce traffic congestion. Its support for new urbanism and neotraditionalist planning visions, he argues, runs counter to what most Americans desire and people will continue to drive even if they do live in denser, mixed-use developments. What rankles ISTEA's WUPR detractors most, it seems, is that the federal government would be presuming to support policies that have impacts on individual lifestyle choices.

Formal regional recognition—whether as world heritage areas, international biosphere reserves, heritage rivers (National Academy of Sciences Commission on Geosciences, Environment, and Resources 1999), or national heritage areas (chapter 5; Vincent and Whiteman 2006)—is viewed as the thin edge of a wedge that opens the way for an eventual federal, or even international, takeover of the protected areas. In the mid-1990s, Congress was considering legislation to establish a national heritage areas program. In contrast to the current National Park Service program described in chapter 5, this would have been a systematic program, with national standards, procedures, and funding in place. But that effort failed, in part because WUPR interests had exercised their influence with the recently elected Republican Congress to fundamentally alter the program originally proposed. Had the modified legislation passed, it could have been counterproductive, perhaps even fatally weakening national historic preservation programs (Williams 1999). WUPR proponents may not have been able to undo the Endangered Species Act, but as the fate of the heritage areas legislation demonstrates, they have scored some important victories. Congress continues to consider a formal heritage areas program—but even if the latest proposals fail, as happened in the 108th Congress, we still have something of a heritage areas program in place (chapter 5). And it continues to evoke WUPR opposition. A recent proposal to designate an individual heritage area—the "Journey Through Hallowed Ground National Heritage Area" defined by Route 15 between Charlottesville, Virginia, and Gettysburg, Pennsylvania—is seen by some opponents as federal land use planning at the expense of road improvements needed to accommodate a smoother flow of traffic (Knight 2006).

Given its mission of supporting local planning and smart growth, the Community Character Act was a natural for attenuating the opposition in 2002. Though the act never did emerge from congressional committee, the associated hearings brought wide disdain and strongly worded testimony from WUPR opponents. As already noted in chapter 5, the National Association of Home Builders and the Bush administration opposed the act; additional opponents included the Heritage Foundation (Cox 2002), American Farm Bureau Federation, National Cattlemen's Beef Association, National Association of Manufacturers, and Outdoor Advertising Association. In referring to the act, WUPR groups came up with names like the "Federal Zoning Act" and "APA (American Planning Association) Full Employment Act" (Taylor 2002). The Community Character Act also has been described as a backroom deal, federal bribe, and hostile takeover of local zoning.

Smart growth planning, while embraced by much of the mainstream development community (chapter 5), is a prime WUPR target. Various WUPR organizations urged the Department of Housing and Urban Development (HUD) to not release the *Growing Smart Legislative Guidebook* (Meck 2002) that had been commissioned during the Clinton years. One of the more sensational rebuttals of *Growing Smart* comes from the organization called Demographia. Its colorful website proclaims that "you could lose your home," minorities will be deprived of housing opportunities, and government will be sanctioning architectural taste. And New Zealand's land development rules are cited as an example of regulation resulting in unaffordable housing (Demographia n.d.). Surprisingly, given the Bush administration's proclivity for manipulating research findings, *Growing Smart* was released intact by HUD. It was, however, accompanied by a disclaimer stating that HUD neither supported nor endorsed the report's contents (Taylor 2002).

The campaigns against the Community Character Act and *Growing Smart* are not dissimilar to the ones waged against a national land use policy act in the early 1970s (chapter 2). But in today's deeply polarized climate, the opposition may be far more effective. Had the Nixon administration not imploded thirty-five years ago, we likely would have had a national land use law. Today, it is remarkable that the community-character legislation even made it beyond the starting line.

Given global climate change's current high profile, it comes as no surprise that WUPR and broader-based opposition groups are deeply involved with this issue. Though this crusade is separate from the land use antiregulatory campaigns, many of the same key actors are involved with both. The Global Climate Coalition, organized by Exxon and other industry giants, is at the forefront. Funding for research that counters prevailing climate change forecasts, television and newspaper advertisements, websites, and even the posting of a faux amateur, anti–Al Gore video on the popular YouTube website are among the strategies employed. This "anti–climate crisis movement" has spawned a slew of "counter anti–climate crisis" websites, sponsored by environmental and other citizen organizations.

Opposing Regional and Local Initiatives

The Property Rights Foundation of America (PRFA), based in New York State's Adirondack Park but with interests extending to the national and global scales, staunchly opposes not only most government land regulation and acquisition but also conservation easements. Easements, most of them held by NGOs, are seen as too intertwined with government planning agendas and too inflexible, since many of them seek to protect lands in perpetuity. Land trusts themselves, PRFA argues, need to be regulated. But PRFA and allied organizations have not had much success in containing the growth of land trusts and conservation easements. For one thing, this is not a simple partisan issue. While the Republican Party's more libertarian wing in Congress and many state houses often view easements with critical disdain, other Republicans do not. Easements help protect many landscapes of privilege and wealth, in the process providing substantial tax benefits to easement donors and sellers.

The issues that motivate PRFA and allied organizations are complex and tangled, often revealing a deep clash of cultures (McCarthy 2002). For example, WUPRs are battling to sustain traditional "hunting-camp culture" in New York's Adirondacks. For many years, hunting camps have occupied lands leased to them by timber companies, providing access to the woods for folks of modest means. But with New York State's late 1990s acquisitions of Champion Timber Company lands, as well as subsequent state timberland acquisitions, that culture is under threat. Not only potential hunting bans but also new restrictions on all-terrain vehicles and snowmobiles are highly contentious local issues. The narrative line put forth by PRFA is one of the rights of working-class citizens being trampled by legions of backpacking yuppies who have access to the levers of power in Albany's capitol complex.

But the issue, of course, is more nuanced. If left entirely to market forces, some of the lands in question might well be destined for resort and second-home development, within limits imposed by the Adirondack Private Land Use and Development Plan. But there is absolutely no assurance that hunting and off-road vehicle access would be allowed on such subdivided lands. Easements, though often opposed by WUPR advocates, could be written so as to allow certain traditional activities. But landowners unencumbered by such deed restrictions may simply opt for a "keep out" strategy.

In some instances, where New York State has acquired lands, longterm leases for hunting camps have been maintained, allowing for a gradual phase-out over one to two decades. The choice of a ten- to twenty-year time horizon is an interesting one, reflecting as it does rural cultural trends. Given recent declines in numbers of hunters—though not participants in many other outdoor pursuits—WUPR advocates may find some of their more strident positions becoming increasingly irrelevant. And that irrelevance will not be entirely the creation of governments and backpackers.

Ballot questions are a potentially fruitful front for antiplanning activists. WUPR organizations often direct or participate in campaigns aimed at defeating local and statewide measures for open space and easement acquisition. One high-profile defeat, achieved largely through the well-funded efforts of a coalition of opposition groups, was California's rejection of Proposition 128 (Switzer 1997). Known as "Big Green," the 1990 ballot question contained a wide-ranging suite of environmental measures. In 1997, Maine presented its voters with a rather complex set of forest management choices, including the compromise "Compact for Maine's Forests" (chapter 4). All options were voted down, leaving things just as they were before the vote. Another strategy, until recently rather rarely employed by WUPRs, is to place their own questions on the ballot. In citizen-initiative states this can be done directly by voters, while in other cases state and local governing bodies are lobbied to do so. Eminent domain and property rights questions are the leading ones that WUPRs sponsor. In Oregon, for example, voters regularly have faced measures aimed at weakening the state's Land Use and Development Plan (Myers 1999; Myers and Puentes 2000). Until the 2004 vote noted at the start of this chapter, these measures all were voted down.

Contemporary WUPR groups may well be more effective at stymieing regional planning efforts than their pre-1980s counterparts. The Greater Yellowstone Ecosystem Vision and a regional regulatory plan for the Northern Forest Lands, noted above and in chapter 4, are cases in point. To credit WUPR organizations solely and entirely, pleasing as it may be to their leaders to do so, would be to credit them too much. But they did play a major role, working very effectively within the prevailing political infrastructure.

People for the West!, the Wyoming Heritage Society, and other organizations mounted a vigorous campaign against the Yellowstone Vision for the Future (chapter 4). Much of that campaign's success may be attributed to issue framing: the vision was cast as an assault on private property rights. Opposition groups distributed "fact sheets" that were a much easier read than the vision document. As a consequence, many concerned citizens did not even try to work their way through the vision report. At the same time, Charles Cushman's National Inholders Association and allied organizations sent out thousands of informational packets that included mail-in postcards for obtaining a copy of the vision report. All those requests overwhelmed agency offices, giving the opposition more time to work its campaign. And citizens turned out in large numbers, delivered on buses hired by opposition organizations, at rallies that opposed the vision.

A few years later, regional WUPR groups again mobilized, this time around the wolf reintroduction issue. Wolves had become a potent symbol in the continuing wars between competing nature-society perspectives: ecosystem management versus supremacy for ranching culture and private property rights. It seems that Greater Yellowstone opponents have strategically moved beyond the myth of wolf as evil predator, with some spokespeople arguing that the real, bedrock concerns are about expansion of federal power and removal of people, or at least their property rights, from the land (Wilson 1997). But in some places, unlikely as it may at first seem, strategic alliances between ranchers and environmentalists have begun to emerge. Where second-home developments are threatening their way of life, some ranchers have learned that maintaining wolf habitat is a way to keep new human immigrants at bay. As a result, they are willing to invest in "training" wolves to avoid livestock, monitoring their behavior and using noisemakers and rubber bullets to scare them off (McMillion 2006). To the extent that such strategies succeed, WUPR proponents are likely to find their position diminished.

WUPR forces were not so successful in contesting designation of the Columbia River Gorge National Scenic Area (chapter 4). Charles Cushman did make an appearance in the Northwest in 1981, rallying local gorge opponents by citing federal disruptions of local communities in Ohio's Cuyahoga National Recreation Area. Though the scenic area did come into being, some of the compromises along the way came in response to pressure brought by the Committee to Preserve Property Rights and other opposition groups (Abbott, Adler, and Abbott 1997).

In New Jersey, as noted in chapter 4, the Highlands Conservation Act was passed by the legislature in 2004, but not without encountering spirited WUPR resistance. At one hearing, at a high school in the small town of High Bridge, a very imposing "tractor-cade" was assembled close to the school's main entrance. Also stationed near the doors were perhaps fifteen individuals with signs bearing the message: "New Jersey wants to take our property rights away." The atmosphere was quite peaceful, with environmentalists chatting with property rights advocates. But the WUPRs were adamant, if resigned to the likelihood that they would lose this one.

Extreme Environmental Opposition

Not all quieter revolution opposition is allied with the WUPR movements. First of all, there is the "friendly fire" coming from those who support broad planning goals but disagree with specific strategies. As noted
in chapter 3, former Sierra Club president and executive director Michael
McCloskey is a leading voice against collaborative projects. Though he
does not reject all collaboration, he believes that in most cases greater environmental gains can be realized through principled adversarialism. But
even when organizations agree on both goals and strategies, they often
compete for the lion's share of the credit for positive environmental outcomes. Some groups will play down—if not outright oppose—their kin-
dred spirits' efforts. But this is internecine wrangling, characteristic of
almost any advocacy movement, political party, or bureaucracy. It may be
counterproductive—but not nearly as destructive to the larger cause as
deep ideological opposition.

That deep opposition can come not only from WUPR groups but
also, in some instances, from radical environmental organizations. These
groups often regard quieter revolution approaches, as well as more regulatory structures, as entirely ineffective and even counterproductive. Environmental stewardship, as Merchant (1992) characterizes it, is
inherently homocentric, privileging humans over other species. Deep
ecologists (Devall and Sessions 1985; Naess 1989) take a biocentric approach, going so far in some cases as to call for relocation of human populations. And there are organizations that act decisively on this
philosophy. Tactics variously described as civil disobedience, "monkey-
wrenching" (Abbey 1975), and "ecotage" are embraced by these groups
(Foreman 1991; Foreman and Haywood 1993; List 1993). Tree spiking,
tree sitting, pouring sand into gas tanks of earth-moving machinery, and
removing structures deemed detrimental to ecological integrity are
among the direct actions supported. More established groups, such as
Greenpeace and Earth First!, have been merging into the mainstream in
recent years, moderating their positions, conducting peer-reviewed research, and engaging in prime-time policy debates. Earth First!, while
still proclaiming "No Compromise in Defense of Mother Earth," increasingly finds such intransigence, and some of the rhetoric used to but-
tress it, untenable. In the late 1970s, Greenpeace cofounder Paul Watson

became convinced that his organization was too inclined toward compromise, so he broke from it to form the Sea Shepherd Conservation Society (Scarce 2006).

Earth First! and Greenpeace continue to sponsor direct, sometimes unlawful actions (Manes 1990), but more radical organizations, such as the Animal Liberation Front and Earth Liberation Front, have no qualms about engaging in highly destructive activities. Like the extreme wing of the WUPR movements (Helvarg 1994), these organizations engage in terrorist acts. They have no tolerance and little patience for quieter revolution approaches, never mind regulatory or legal actions. The Earth Liberation Front is perhaps the most notorious among them, having torched SUVs, housing developments, and a partially built ski lodge that infringed on lynx habitat in Vail, Colorado (Barringer 2004b; Scarce 2006). Arguing that it is an ecological resistance movement rather than a radical organization, the Earth Liberation Front (2007) describes itself as "an underground movement with no leadership, membership, or official spokesperson."

Wise Use/Property Rights Future?

In the end, the quieter revolution can bring into its tent, or at least mollify or make irrelevant, some traditional opponents of environmentalism and land use planning. But as this chapter demonstrates, this hardly is true for all adversaries. There are enough unflinching opponents out there to collectively create a swift quieter revolution countercurrent. Even market-based approaches and those not supported by any government subsidies or benefits at all still must compete in the marketplace of ideas, publicity, image making, and funding. By all indications, we can expect that competition to remain fierce.

The wise use/property rights (WUPR) movements have benefited not only from a conservative president and Congress in recent years but also from the Supreme Court's Kelo decision. This decision, supporting a small Connecticut city's right to use eminent domain power to make way for a mixed-use development, has engendered wide public outrage and opened a strategic policy window for WUPR proponents and their allies. They not only are getting their message out through the media but have spearheaded legislative and ballot measure drives in many states as well.

Their greatest successes, so far, are with those measures and laws that restrict use of eminent domain power; attempts to require states and localities to compensate landowners for loss of value associated with environmental regulations have not fared so well. Whether or not the WUPR tide is beginning to turn remains to be seen.

CHAPTER EIGHT
EVALUATING THE REVOLUTION

To suggest that each and every quieter revolution initiative undergo comprehensive evaluation would be to suggest the impossible. But most programs already are assessed in whole or in part. Environmental impact statements may be required by the National Environmental Policy Act (NEPA) or a state-level counterpart, federal or state regulatory or fiscal impact assessment may be mandated, and relevant legislation—such as the Endangered Species Act—may contain additional evaluation requirements. Moreover, agencies, foundations, and other NGOs evaluate their programs usually as a matter of course. But most such appraisals are limited in various ways: they may examine only a part of the larger program, they may not cover the full temporal range from before to after the program, and they may not speak to the initiative's full physical, social, and cultural dimensions. What is offered here is a set of questions—questions to be considered before, during, and after program implementation. While these "dimensions" need not necessarily become rigorous evaluation protocols—indeed, their applicability will vary from program to program, place to place, and time to time—they can guide us toward a better understanding of quieter revolution initiatives and their consequences.

NEPA and many of its counterparts were designed to make us think about environmental consequences before actions get under way (Caldwell 1998; Cullingworth and Caves 2003; Randolph 2004). But this NEPA-style thinking, commendable as it is, should be adaptively extended. It can be deployed well beyond the preproject phase, ensuring that a wide range of implications is examined at all project and policy stages. But the temporal dimension is not the only one where many appraisals fall short. All too often, particularly in the literature, quieter revolution projects are regarded only, or mainly, from one viewpoint. It may be ecological effects, economic feasibility, political practicality, or any of a number of other perspectives. While political and public relations concerns may dictate narrowly constructed program rationales, it is incumbent upon the larger planning, academic, and civic communities to see the bigger picture. Only through our willingness to do so will we be able to better define and understand the emerging quieter revolution.

Though a wide range of dimensions is included in the inventory that follows, the listing should not be viewed as exhaustive. Rather, it might be seen as a work in progress, a checklist that can be adapted—expanded or contracted—to different situations and different needs.

Ecosystem Indicators

Clearly, ecosystem monitoring is not relevant to all the quieter revolution programs included in preceding chapters. But ecosystem protection is a principal, if not exclusive, rationale for many of them. And while ecosystem integrity often occupies a central place in evaluation efforts, its assessment can be enormously challenging. We are on a steep learning curve about how ecosystems work and evolve, what ecosystem restoration means, and how best to measure progress and change (Stein and Gelburd 1998). The single-species indicator approach, while relatively cost-effective, is not sufficient for understanding ecosystem processes and landscape change; a more complex suite of indicators is needed (Knight 1998). Yet politicians and policymakers often demand quick and least-cost answers, while most ecological processes compel us to take the long-term, and usually costlier, view. For political, public relations, and financial—if not scientific— purposes, it is often to the advantage of environmentalists to focus on the health of charismatic megafauna, or other iconic species, as proxies for ecosystem biodiversity.

Though the details of ecological monitoring are well beyond the scope of this chapter, extensive information, discussion, and guidance on monitoring ecological integrity, biodiversity, productivity, native species, water quality, and other indicators of ecological health are abundantly available through a wealth of sources (McAllister 1980; Vogt et al. 1997; Peck 1998; National Research Council Committee to Evaluate Indicators for Monitoring Aquatic and Terrestrial Environments 2000; Busch and Trexler 2003; Randolph 2004; France 2006). Perhaps most critical is that a fully planned and funded ecological monitoring program cover the project planning, design, and implementation stages. Prospective—or predictive or stress-oriented—monitoring can be as important, or in some instances more important, than retrospective monitoring (Noon 2003). Issues of uncertainty and the need for long-term perspective, difficult as they may be to incorporate into some quieter revolution programs, must be dealt with from the outset. And ecological benefits may come from projects not designed mainly to protect ecosystems; it is important that these benefits be recognized and understood. Of course, project proponents are unlikely, in most places at least, to neglect to trumpet such ancillary benefits. By the same token, caution should be exercised in attribution of benefits that may not be generated by the program being evaluated. If economic pressures stop destructive logging in a fragile watershed, and watershed health improves, then watershed managers and their allies can point to the ecological benefits. They can study long-term changes in forest health. But they cannot necessarily claim credit for environmental improvements.

In 1995, the National Biological Service was established, after proposals for a National Biological Survey were defeated. The latter would have systematically collected data nationwide, with a mission similar to that of the U.S. Geological Survey. The former, according to Twiss (1997), is more akin to a "fire station," dispatching biologists to crisis spots so they can make individual assessments. But even the crisis-oriented National Biological Service was short-lived; only a year after it started, it became the Biological Resource Division of the U.S. Geological Survey (USGS). The service, despite its constrained mission, might have provided at least some support for ecological appraisals of quieter revolution programs. But after it was folded into USGS, the project was reduced to little more than a resource-starved information portal that provides some very valuable, but very limited, information.

While we lack a National Biological Service, we do have regional indicators projects that collect ecological and other data. And they can focus in on quieter revolution projects at a variety of scales. The EPA's Regional

Vulnerability Assessment Program (U.S. Environmental Protection Agency [EPA] 2007e) and Mid-Atlantic Integrated Assessment (U.S. EPA 1997, 2007a) are exemplary of such programs; among other things, they are developing sets of ecosystem indicators and establishing benchmarks and protocols for monitoring ecosystem health.

Environmental Services

Ecosystems provide us with a multitude of services, among them climate regulation, hazard mitigation, air and water purification, soil protection, waste decomposition, pollution neutralization, pollination, and seed dispersal. Indeed, enormous economic benefits can be realized from healthy ecosystems. Economists continue to refine their protocols for putting dollar values to environmental services, but these methodologies remain contentious, laden as they are with assumptions about individual behavior and willingness to pay. While specifics of those methodologies are beyond this book's scope, reviews of ecosystem valuation approaches, uncertainties, and limits are provided by Salzman (1997), as well as in a very thorough National Research Council (National Research Council Committee of Assessing and Valuing the Services of Aquatic and Related Terrestrial Ecosystems 2001) report. Though geared toward aquatic systems, the NRC report's findings are widely applicable; it suggests that no single evaluation approach fits all circumstances. Perhaps the most sensible advice for the environmental services appraisal is that which applies to the evaluation enterprise more generally: it should strive to be comprehensive, but given economic and technical constraints, it must be selective, adaptive, experimental, and cognizant of its limits.

Development Patterns

Many quieter revolution programs are designed to influence residential and commercial development patterns. They seek to prohibit development in some areas, encourage it in others, and guide its timing and character overall. By their very nature, most quieter revolution programs cannot be expected to ensure specific, prescribed outcomes; instead, they try to guide development by providing targeted incentives, disincentives, information, and advice. These quieter approaches provide far less assurance than their more regulatory counterparts, in most instances, that desired outcomes will materialize. But they may bring the results that they do at lower economic and political cost than the more intrusive methods. It is imperative, therefore, that we view development outcomes in broader evaluatory contexts—but before we can begin to do that, we must have reliable temporal data that describe development trends.

Some of the larger, regional quiet revolution programs systematically collect data on development patterns; this is the case, for example, with New York State's Adirondack Park Commission (Harris and Jarvis 2004) and New Jersey's Pinelands Commission (Mason 2004). Similarly, large quieter revolution regional programs—such as the Chesapeake Bay Program and some state efforts described in chapter 4—maintain development-trends data. The many smaller projects are rarely assessed comprehensively, even though there is much that could be learned about the effectiveness of these approaches, if only we had more data. Even when we do have the requisite data, attributing development outcomes to specific land use programs—especially nonregulatory ones—often is risky, if not impossible.

A further, if frequently neglected, level of interrogation also is relevant here. The 2001 National Watershed Forum report puts it very simply, admonishing watershed organizations to answer this question: "If we control sprawl, is our watershed healthy?" (Meridian Institute 2001, 31). If a watershed group succeeds in reforming development patterns, then it may justifiably take pride. But if we want to know whether or not—or the extent to which—that change is responsible for improving watershed ecological health, then rigorous examination of the area in question, and comparison with control areas, is necessary. This is not to deny potential additional benefits, beyond ecological health, from controlling sprawl; some of those benefits are contained within this very list. The bottom line, though, is that the program evaluation should not claim more than what the available evidence permits.

Recreational, Aesthetic, and Health Benefits

A considerable body of research addresses the recreational and aesthetic benefits of open space; a good review, focusing on Minnesota, is provided by Anton (2005). Though these benefits might be incorporated into an assessment of environmental services, it will often make sense to separate them out, since they act as central rationales for so many projects and programs. This is particularly the case with farmland and open space protection. But the protection of open spaces is not the same as appreciation or use. Questions of public access and the land's aesthetic character will play important parts in assessing program value. And the assessments are not necessarily simple, especially when a protected land's fate becomes contentious. Is a golf course or baseball field, for example, comparable in recreational and aesthetic value to a forest preserve? How do we compare an inaccessible ecological treasure with a heavily used area? As with all the evaluation components described here, there is no one-size-fits-all methodology. But to the extent that aesthetic and use values can be agreed upon and reasonably assessed, we can in turn use this information to examine program cost-effectiveness.

Health benefits of concentrated development—provided through increased opportunities for walking, bicycling, and other outdoor activities— are just beginning to receive attention (McCann and Ewing 2003; Frumkin, Frank, and Jackson 2004). Smart growth advocates have quickly caught on to the notion that promoting smart growth's health benefits is a good way to get positive attention. To fully understand the potential benefits, we need to conduct more research in a variety of places. We will want to know, for example, the extent to which "walkability" actually means that people walk more than if they live in more sprawled settings. And how much driving do they give up, not just involving local errands and transporting children to school but also for going to outdoor recreation venues distant from their homes?

Cost-Effectiveness

What results are we getting in exchange for money spent? Cost-effectiveness assessments pose several challenges. Some are methodological, while others are definitional and contextual. Administrative scale plays an interesting part in determining how costs are distributed. Let's say, for example, that a locality receives a federal or state grant and only has to pay 20 percent of the total cost for acquiring a parcel of land. If this is a valued piece of land, and there is strong public and political support for buying it, then this is likely to be seen as a wonderful deal. Indeed, from the local standpoint, it is highly cost-effective. The same may not necessarily be said at the state or federal level, where the other 80 percent of the acquisition cost is borne. Perhaps that money could be better spent on land purchases elsewhere, for acquiring easements instead of buying land, or for some other environmental (or nonenvironmental) purpose.

In a similar vein, land trusts receive government subsidies via favorable tax treatment. This, of course, provokes outrage from the wise use/property rights movements. Resource-exploitative activities have received and continue to receive massive government assistance, especially from the federal government; this is rarely acknowledged by those who direct their wrath at subsidies enjoyed by land protection organizations. By the same token, those who see themselves as stewards of the land will keep quiet about their synergistic fiscal and other relationships with government agencies, when it is politically expedient to do so, and trumpet the relationship when it is to their benefit. The bottom line is that government subsidies—direct and indirect—should not escape scrutiny. When the objective is judged to be a sound and worthy one, we still need to ask whether the subsidy is bringing a reasonable return. The same level of scrutiny should also apply to NGO and corporate expenditures, especially when they are part of a larger collaborative effort.

An additional issue has to do with the oft-heard argument that "the money could be better spent elsewhere." Even if that elsewhere is relatively narrowly defined—limited, let's say, to land protection activities—we often have no assurance that if action is not taken, then the money will go to the "better purpose elsewhere." A locality applying for grant funds, especially, may be faced with a "use it or lose it" choice. If the land acquisition is popular locally, and sometimes even if it is not, cost-effectiveness may give way to economic expedience. It is hard to turn away "free," or almost free, money. At the state and federal levels, more rigorous cost accounting often is mandated. Still, state and federal programs are far from models of cost efficiency, especially when political actors exert their influence.

Finally, there is the matter of accounting for the full costs of monitoring and assessment, which often are underplayed or ignored. This applies especially to land and easement acquisitions, which generally incur long-term stewardship costs (Brewer 2003).

Civic Engagement

As a conceptual and evaluatory frame, civic engagement subsumes many questions about participatory process, outcome, and accumulation of social capital. Can these questions be reasonably incorporated into a program evaluation, without then having to monitor a long list of civic indicators? Conley and Moote's (2003) list of process and socioeconomic criteria, included as table 3.1, is a good basis for developing a civic-engagement evaluation. And they include with their list some eminently sensible and practical advice. Rather than employ a comprehensive set of indicators for each and every project, Conley and Moote suggest that evaluators develop an appropriately targeted set of criteria, weightings, and methods for the project at hand—and explain their choice.

Perhaps the most compelling process questions to be addressed are those of representativeness and transparency. Key outcome questions involve the relevance of public participation in shaping program outcomes, as well as fostering an enduring civic culture. It should not be taken as a given, as often seems to be the case, that civic engagement improves environmental and social outcomes. If, for example, wise use/property rights representatives are actively engaged, their efforts may detract from ecosystem quality goals. General environmental and social equity outcomes should, in the first instance at least, be assessed separately from the civic engagement. Let's suppose that proponents of collaboration wish to credit the collaborative process for improved ecosystem health. In many cases, perhaps even a great majority, that credit would be due. But this cannot be presumed. Causal linkages between civic engagement and ecosystem improvement would need to be clearly demonstrated. And even if it turns out that civic engagement is not responsible for particular outcomes in particular cases, its ancillary benefits still may justify the effort, expense, and complexity it adds to the process.

Many evaluations of collaborative planning (Selin and Myers 1995) rely entirely on stakeholder perceptions. Perception-based assessments do enhance our understanding of participation programs and broader development of civic culture. Positive perceptions about the process and participants' effectiveness are meaningful indicators of program success. But they only tell part of the story and should not be used as surrogates for assessing environmental, economic, and social outcomes. Valuable—indeed indispensable—information can be gleaned from careful analysis of participant perceptions, but it must be understood within the appropriate contexts.

Even when we can demonstrate that a program has fostered meaningful civic engagement, we need to inquire further about the sustainability of that civic engagement. Has social capital been accumulated? Has civic culture been enhanced? Press (1998, 37) characterizes "local environmental policy capacity" broadly, to include social capital, political leadership and commitment, economic resources, administrative resources, and environmental attitudes and behavior. This framework includes, but goes well beyond, basic civic culture as it is depicted here. Still, elements that contribute to local policy capacity also support, indirectly as well as directly, development of civic culture. Press lists indicators that may be used to measure each of these dimensions. His "social capital" and "environmentalism" indicators include issue awareness, voting behavior, interest group membership, and financial donations.

A healthy environmental civic culture depends on citizen understanding, or at least recognition, of the central issues. Today's communications technologies put all sorts of information at citizens' fingertips and facilitate very rapid mobilization around specific issues (Levitt 2002). Indeed, watershed and bioregional consciousness may be fostered via widely disseminated environmental information, especially through schools and other educational networks. Yet the same technologies that are so enabling may also have a role in limiting general awareness and understanding of specific issues. A generation or so ago, when news options were limited, there was much more of a common culture built around the daily newspaper and a limited number of television and radio news outlets. Now, with almost limitless information options, it is easy to simply tune out individual news items. How, then, do civic leaders engage those who are not already among the converted? While local cable access stations allow for wide dissemination of local environmental information, who actually watches? The Internet permits on-demand access to information, obviating the need to watch or record educational radio or television programming. But those unfortunate citizens on the wrong side of the digital divide are unable to access the rich assortment of information available via the World Wide Web; this is particularly a problem in impoverished inner-city and poor rural areas.

Institutional Capacity Building

Institutional capacity can contribute mightily to civic culture and environmental policy capabilities. But it can also come at their expense. If government agencies use NGOs simply to expand their own capacity, then citizens are being manipulated or co-opted. No doubt, this is a bargain some members of the public—those who see a net gain, for example, in environmental quality—are quite content to accept. While genuine power sharing is part of the ideal collaborative model (figure 3.1), it may not always be in the perceived best interests of participants. Devolved decision making *is*, however, in almost all instances critical to development of local civic culture.

We can ask to what extent specific quieter revolution projects build institutional capacity. How much better is an agency able to fulfill its statutory obligations and to what extent has it expanded its decision-making domain? In an era of decreasing federal and state environmental budgets, government agencies are increasingly motivated to work with nongovernment stakeholders. And those stakeholders often reap benefits in the form of environmental and social outcomes otherwise beyond either their own or the agencies' reaches.

Several variables measured by Selin, Schuett, and Carr (2000), in their study of collaborative initiatives involving the U.S. Forest Service, are useful for gauging institutional capacity building. Among the most relevant are "better interagency coordination," "enhanced resource sharing (information, labor, money)," "better communication," "leveraging of outside resources," "implementation of resource decisions," "reduction in litigation over management decisions," and "increased political support for decisions" (Selin, Schuett, and Carr 2000, 741).

Environmental Justice/Equity

Much of the concern about environmental justice has been directed toward toxic chemical emissions and noxious facility siting (Ringquist 2006). While environmental justice scholars have long recognized that the range of issues is much wider—indeed, some argue that we should be challenging institutionalized patterns of environmental injustice and racism rather than focusing on discrete injustices—this broader perspective has only slowly begun to diffuse beyond the literature.

In 1994, President Clinton issued an executive order requiring federal agencies to guarantee that their activities, programs, and policies not produce disproportionately high and adverse impacts on minority and low-income communities. Several states similarly sought to bring environmental justice concerns explicitly into the policy process. But in recent years, at least at the federal level, environmental justice has not been high on the policy agenda. For quieter revolution programs, though, equity and justice questions come up in many different contexts and ways. This is especially true of smart growth initiatives (National Governors Association Center for Best Practices 2001).

For example, who is involved? If a relatively narrow set of interests is highly engaged, is this desirable? It may well be, in that it makes sense for those stakeholders with deepest interests to be most active. But it also raises questions about equity and environmental justice, especially when the most engaged stakeholders are among the wealthier, more skilled, and more influential members of society. We need to ask, as chapter 3 proposes, much more about the equity aspects of participatory, collaborative processes.

We can also ask questions about outcome. Who gains from specific initiatives—and how are benefits and costs distributed program wide? While these are rather elusive questions, examining geographic distribution of program funds and other resources can be very revealing. This applies especially to open space acquisition and other programs described in chapters 5 and 6. Rather little such work has been done, though concerns about inequity often do rear their heads when citizens and lawmakers believe that particular policies and programs are patently unfair.

And there is the issue of huge sums received by private landowners merely because their land has development potential. Our system of land rights, premised on the notion that landowners are entitled to do as they wish with their land, allows them to profit handsomely from its development potential (Salkin 2003). Because we are so politically constrained in our ability to prescribe land use and determine land value with respect to environmental criteria, we are forced, time and again, to pay exorbitant sums to protect even very small pieces of land. While these funds arguably might be better spent elsewhere—perhaps for protecting remote parts of Alaska, fragile marine habitats, or city parks—the spatial stages on which these decisions are made do not allow for consideration of such a wide range of options. The issues are fought over in places where people live, and some places can afford to do much more within their local boundaries—even at exorbitant cost—than other places. One of the driving forces of early 1970s environmentalism was that playing fields, at least for pollution management, needed to be leveled across states and the nation, so that the more polluting industries would not thrive in areas where regulation and enforcement lagged. Perhaps, given land use management's devolved nature, these kinds of equity questions should be raised anew. In this case, we would examine variations in resources, civic capacity, and opportunity structures as they affect land management capabilities across localities and regions.

Another macroquestion for environmental planning initiatives is this: to what extent are we creating playgrounds and preserves for a leisure class? This is often the way protected areas are viewed by opponents of regional planning—especially local people who see resource-based economies being replaced by environmental utopias. While the more extreme opposing views kindle intense conflict and make for good news stories, in most regions there is a vast middle ground where the issues are less salient, where there is less posturing, and where more nuanced conceptions of local places are the norm. We need to develop better conceptions of what quieter revolution projects mean—economically, socially, perceptually—to the majorities who inhabit these places.

Carbon Production and Energy Consumption

Energy consumption and carbon impacts are closely linked with development patterns and trends (Benfield, Raimi, and Chen 1999). In many states and localities, as well as public and private institutions, these questions have come center stage in recent years. Household-level analyses of carbon and energy impacts, as well as calculation of ecological footprints more generally, are facilitated by web-based calculators. Solutions ranging from energy-efficient building designs to reduced food miles (a surrogate measure for environmental impacts incurred by our food production and distribution system) are being advanced by states and localities. There are signs, even, that the federal government will get into the game in a serious way in the relatively near future.

If only there were simple, unambiguous methods for calculating impacts of land use projects. In reality, these impacts can become quite complex and convoluted. Let us briefly consider carbon. First of all, there are uncertainties about carbon sequestration values of different types of land cover, even different forest types. Then there are the imponderables of what happens as the project is implemented. Consider as an example a small local project, the conversion of a neglected, grassy parcel of suburban open space into forested parkland. To begin with, there may be competing local demands for ball fields, soccer grounds, and other spaces with few trees. If trees are to be planted, questions about aesthetics, maintenance, biodiversity, and carbon sequestration potential may all be relevant. But setting aside issues of land cover, we also have questions associated with usership. Will sports fields bring an increase in auto trips to deliver children—and adults—to the park? Would there not be a comparable increase in auto trips to a forested park? Do these impacts matter all that much at such a small scale? They do, of course, as many communities seek to remake themselves as sustainable communities. But trying to work all of these questions into an analysis of a small quieter revolution project may simply be too controversial, costly, and fraught with uncertainties to be practical. A more feasible, if not entirely satisfactory, approach for local sustainability advocates may be to rally around activities that are demonstrated, generically at least, to reduce carbon and energy impacts.

Compared with our example, other carbon benefits may be easier to calculate, if not entirely free of methodological complications. The U.S. Department of Agriculture's Conservation Reserve Program (chapter 5), though not designed with carbon sequestration in mind, can tout it as a program benefit. In recent testimony before Congress, a USDA official claimed that the average acre of CRP land keeps 0.85 metric tons of carbon dioxide out of the atmosphere each year (Smith 2001).

Energy and carbon impacts are important indeed, and increasingly so at multiple spatial scales, as localities, states, and the federal government become more serious about addressing climate change and resource issues. Some states and localities have already done a great deal. As more and more quieter revolution initiatives are advanced, it is imperative that their carbon and energy impacts be considered. The more refined our assessment capabilities, the better positioned we will be to enlist the quieter revolution in the service of energy sustainability and adaptation to environmental change.

Sustainability/Ecological Footprint

This is in large part an extension of the energy and carbon analyses. Generally expressed as the amount of land and water needed to sustain a given lifestyle, the ecological footprint works well as an engaging educational tool (Chambers, Simmons, and Wackernagel 2000). Students can see just how wide the gulf is between the industrialized and nonindustrialized worlds, as well as within individual countries. These sorts of analyses can be put to more immediate, applied use as well. Take, for example, ethanol. While the ethanol boom might at first blush seem to be very beneficial for the Corn Belt and Great Plains (chapter 4), we need to ask about environmental implications overall. This is more complex than a simple footprint calculation, but some of the same principles can be invoked as we ask about energy inputs versus outputs and ecological impacts of associated land conversions. Similar questions are being asked about the sustainability of local food production versus our system that is so heavily based on long-distance transport of foodstuffs. Footprint and sustainability arguments frequently are cited by those who support farmland protection near metropolitan areas.

Quieter revolution program evaluations can take better account of project impacts by adapting footprint calculations and carbon impact analyses to local- and regional-level projects, as well as statewide growth management efforts. They can also begin to account for "environmental shadows"—that is, the impacts created in one area but imposed upon another. Those shadows can fall within local areas but can also reach across regions, states, and even the globe. If improved land use practices in one place impose costs upon another, this should be understood, valued, and accounted for.

Vulnerability Reduction

Vulnerability has many dimensions, and they range across several evaluation criteria already discussed. But vulnerability reduction merits separate mention, because it is about the resilience and adaptability of places, individually as well as collectively. Vulnerability questions mirror those about environmental and land use impacts. Rather than asking about a project or proposal's effects, vulnerability analysis considers its ability to buffer against externally generated risks and hazards—or, conversely, its role in amplifying risk and hazard impacts. At a broad scale, quieter revolution initiatives may help build up a sort of resiliency capital, by acting as part of a larger, interconnected bulwark against any of a number of risks. Vulnerability reduction, in short, is a form of anticipatory adaptive management; it provides the capacity to respond to the anticipated as well as the unexpected.

Vulnerability reduction can be an amorphous, catch-all evaluatory element. It has to be more narrowly defined in specific cases if it is to be a practical program evaluation component. And a thorough evaluation should account for increases, as well as reductions, in vulnerability. In some instances, increased vulnerability may well be outweighed by environmental or social benefits. Planning proponents, in such cases, may be tempted to downplay or ignore the vulnerability issue. Over the long term, though, it is important that researchers give vulnerability questions their proper due.

Again, vulnerability analysis is most readily examined on a case-by-case basis. But some plausible larger dimensions include the following.

Agricultural self-sufficiency

As stated in chapter 5, America is not suffering from a shortage of farmland. But environmentalists, planners, and other sustainability advocates increasingly are calling for greater local self-sufficiency in food production, in part because it offers a measure of protection against a dramatic increase in energy and transport costs. And farmland preservation programs can contribute immensely to reducing "food miles" and building such local food-system resiliency.

Hazard protection

Protecting Louisiana's coastal marshes (chapter 5) provides obvious benefits in buffering against hurricanes and other tropical storms. So, too, do many other local quieter revolution projects play a part in reducing hazard impacts (Randolph 2004). Protection of watershed lands, for instance, can reduce flood intensity—though just how much so is a matter of considerable contention. Maintaining water quality ensures that diverse water sources—including backup sources—can be tapped to meet household and other water needs.

Protection against resource shortages and surges in energy prices

Livable, walkable, bikable communities provide alternatives to automobile dependence and increase our capacity to respond collectively to energy and materials shortages. Not only is the social fabric likely to be more tightly woven than in sprawled developments; the physical proximity of neighbors, businesses, and civic facilities makes collective action more logistically practicable.

Evaluation in Context

It makes sense to regard most quieter revolution initiatives as experimental and adaptive. To the extent that it is practical, it can be advantageous to incorporate this into their basic rationales. But if those rationales are to be proved, we must be prepared to monitor and evaluate over the long term. To fail to do so, in the interest of cutting costs, may be false economy.

A final general caution: as particular indicators are adapted for assessing specific programs, evaluators should be cautious about cause and effect. A classic example is a reduction in greenhouse gasses and other pollutants in an area experiencing deindustrialization. Though it may not be possible to precisely determine the separate contributions of deindustrialization, conservation initiatives, land use trends, productivity changes, and even physical dynamics like climate patterns in explaining the trends, the full complement of factors must be recognized. All too often, for example, those promoting urban and regional sustainability are eager to latch onto indicators of success and claim credit for the good news. But if we are to achieve meaningful, long-term environmental improvement, and move beyond mere burden shifting, then it is essential that results be deconstructed and fully analyzed.

The criteria presented here can be employed as a project evaluation checklist, with items being accepted or rejected as appropriate for the case at hand. But each item should at least be considered. And the list can be expanded, so that it suits an even wider range of projects. Cultural resources (including archaeological) impacts and educational and outreach values are among the additional items that might be included.

The items listed are neither mutually exclusive nor entirely mutually supportive. Indeed, in particular instances, some may contradict others. This is to be expected and should not be a justification for constraining the evaluation. The evaluatory process might be viewed as taking a series of snapshots of a set of gauges, or instruments. Its value is both informational and diagnostic.

The checklist of criteria is meant to be used before, during, and after a project. It is only the most basic of guides, requiring much more detail and specificity before it can be applied in specific cases. Moreover, these criteria cannot cover all contingencies. Surprises should be expected and accommodated. Place-based, collaborative planning advocates make compelling arguments for adaptive management, for making course corrections that hone in on desired outcomes, and for good reason—the way toward those desired ends may become clear only as the process unfolds.

Chapter 9 brings this book to a close by summing up what we know about the quieter revolution, what we do not know, and the revolution's place in the larger land use management, environmental planning, and sustainability contexts.

CHAPTER NINE
A QUIETER FUTURE?

What is the quieter revolution's significance? Though its contributions to the making and remaking of American landscapes clearly are immense, they are uneven, inconsistent, and often difficult to define and impractical to quantify. In other words, the quieter revolution is enormously significant, but boiling that significance down into a short summary is a hugely demanding task. In part, this is because we have cast such an inclusive conceptual net. Part of the reason for doing so is that these individual quieter revolution elements have the potential to expand tremendously—individually as well as synergistically—as we increasingly confront issues of climate change, resource depletion, vulnerability, resilience, immigration, environmental injustice, and more.

The quieter revolution, almost by definition, is an evolution rather than a full-fledged revolution. "Evolution" is the term Michael Heiman (1988) used to describe state-level planning in New York State—and the characterization is fitting here as well. The quieter revolution, especially, is evolutionary because it embraces notions of adaptive management. At present, it seems fair to say, the quieter revolution is in a rather early evolutionary stage. It also is devolutionary, in that much of the policy entrepreneurship is at the local and state levels. As larger environmental and land use issues finally begin to receive the federal attention due them, as seems very likely in the very near future, the quieter revolution may be in for a major readaptation, with its trend toward devolution perhaps being arrested or even reversed.

Indeed, the quieter revolution may trend in any of several directions. We may move toward a stronger federal land management presence that fully embraces the notion of states and localities as laboratories that inform national policies. This is the controversial model in some ways already in place for welfare and health care policy reforms. We may see the bar raised by the federal government, with state and local governments forced to meet minimum standards for greenhouse gas emissions, hazard preparedness, reduced ecological footprints, and the like. Local governments may also have some of their policy and planning options constricted by federal and state laws—particularly when certain local actions are considered obstructionist. For example, federal and state laws may override local laws that impede construction of nuclear power plants, reject utility line corridors, or severely limit options for affordable housing in suburban communities.

The quieter revolution is more than simply a set of activities and processes that devolves existing decision-making authority and replaces regulatory practices. Indeed, new quieter revolution programs and projects are addressing land use concerns that were hardly addressed at all in the 1970s and 1980s. New avenues for civic engagement are opening, as are new, environmentally appropriate spatial scales for land use management. Communications technologies are fostering the formation of rapid-response networks that were inconceivable little more than a decade ago. And new funding, if only modest in most instances, is being made available to support many quieter initiatives.

In the scenarios sketched above, the quieter revolution likely has a secure place. But countervailing perspectives on nonregulatory approaches hold that they are of very limited effectiveness, that land and easement acquisitions are simply too expensive to be a sustainable land management strategy, that the quieter revolution is elitist, and that much of what it is achieving is rather low on the general public's priority list. In reality, the quieter revolution is multidimensional and complex, more than just a devolution of power or a platform for launching local land use strategies. It is perhaps best summed up as a malleable, innovative, adaptive phenomenon, whose most visible effects are at the local level—but which is also capable of effecting systemic change at wider scales. Let us begin with a final comparative look at the quiet revolution, before moving on to present and future prospects for the quieter revolution.

Then Versus Now

The original quiet revolution was buoyed by a rising tide of environmental awareness, coming as it did during a time when pollution problems were very much in the public eye. So, too, were concerns about rapid residential and commercial growth, second-home developments, access to recreation lands, and protection of wilderness areas. As already discussed in chapter 2, the imperative for public policy approaches—regulatory approaches—was powerful. The thinking then was that local governments could not adequately cope with these mounting pressures and more central oversight was needed.

But much has changed in the decades since. Local environmental planning, whatever its inadequacies, has become institutionalized. Economic development is still hotly sought after by most municipalities, but residential growth—even when it brings mainly middle- and upper-class residents—is no longer welcomed everywhere. Floodplains, steep slopes, aquifer recharge areas, farmland, and critical habitats are recognized and protected in ways that were inconceivable a few decades ago. At the same time, urban sprawl has become much more pervasive. Mobility has expanded dramatically. Even though Americans increasingly communicate electronically, annual per-capita vehicle miles have not decreased. In fact, the figure has ascended sharply, from 3,979 miles in 1960 to 9,220 miles in 1995, according to the Natural Resources Defense Council (Benfield, Raimi, and Chen 1999). By most reckonings, residential and commercial sprawl also have accelerated spectacularly (Benfield, Raimi, and Chen 1999), with many metropolitan regions actually "de-densifying." We experienced two major oil crises and occasionally flirt with a third. NIMBY-(not in my backyard)ism became a more potent force, influencing facility siting, as well as growth and development patterns more generally. Environmental education is now institutionalized in school systems across the country—though the content and comprehensiveness of environmental curricula vary widely. And state governments, as well as local, are much more attuned to environmental concerns than they were thirty-five years ago, as many environmental values introduced in the 1970s have become mainstream.

Although it would seem that the country now more than ever needs strong government intervention to regulate and rationalize land use, especially at the larger-than-local scale, the political climate has so changed that such approaches are unthinkable in many places. Is the quieter revolution filling the gap, at least in some measure? And what are the beneficial and detrimental consequences of quieter revolution activities? These questions have been addressed through this book, but we return to them here as we assess the quieter revolution's overall character. First let us ask if the quieter revolution is indeed a movement and then proceed to several additional questions about its significance.

Is the Quieter Revolution a Movement?

As conceptualized in this book's pages, the quieter revolution is a loose confederation of activities—something less than a movement yet more than the sum of its parts. Indeed, choices about what to include as quieter revolution endeavors are guided by a rather wide casting of the net, and this alone virtually ensures that it is too diffuse to be considered a social movement. It is a web too loosely connected, with too many divergent interests and strategies, to be regarded as a movement. It lacks the overall solidarity and unity of purpose that would allow it to meet prevailing definitions for a social movement (Tarrow 1998; Tilly 2004).

If it is any kind of movement, the quieter revolution is one of strategy, style, and techniques rather than broad mobilization around a single cause. And while it does not lend itself to two-sentence mission statements, its varied parts do interact and support one another in many more ways than they counteract and offset each other. Moreover, the quieter revolution embraces discrete bundles of activities, some of which may reach the definitional thresholds for social movements. Among them are grassroots ecosystem management, the new urbanism, smart growth, and perhaps even antigrowth activism. And the quieter revolution's contrarian counterpart—represented by the combined wise use/property rights movements—is indeed widely regarded as such.

Should the nation choose to focus, with a real unity of purpose, on climate, energy, and resource issues, then the quieter revolution—or something closely akin to it—might emerge as a full-fledged movement. This movement might be about social, ecological, and political adaptivity and resilience. It has its antecedents in the regionalism of the 1920s and the more recent bioregionalist movement.

Quieter Revolution Accomplishments and Issues

To fully assess the individual and collective value of the many and diverse quieter revolution activities would be an immense, and perhaps ultimately futile, undertaking. Instead, this chapter's summary comments are limited to quieter revolution responses to several critical issues: urban sprawl, ecological security, civic culture, cost effectiveness, and social and environmental justice.

Managing Sprawl and Transforming Development Patterns

If the goal is to control sprawl by promoting urban infill and density, protecting farmland and open space, developing greenfields efficiently when they must be developed, and reducing traffic congestion and economic burdens associated with metropolitan development patterns, then the quieter revolution has yet to live up to its potential. At the macro scale, greatest successes have come to places that implemented regulatory approaches during or shortly after the quiet revolution: Oregon is the leading state-level example; other cases are reviewed in chapter 2. Oregon's leadership status, as noted in chapter 7, is in question in the wake of voter-approved Measure 37, which requires that landowners be compensated for losses in property value attributable to environmental or land use regulations.

Quieter revolution initiatives do significantly influence land use patterns over larger landscapes, even if not with the same certainty and consistency as their more regulatory counterparts. Their greatest achievements, though, tend to be more local, in places willing and able to take full advantage of quieter revolution financing, incentive, technical assistance, and other programs. The result, even for many of the state and regional efforts described in chapters 4 and 5, is highly uneven patterns of policy innovation and physical outcomes across the larger landscapes. Marin County, California (chapter 4), is exceptional, in that a consistently high degree of land protection has been achieved across a rather large area. More realistically, across complex and expansive landscapes like the state of Maryland (chapter 5), New York and New England's Northern Forest, Southern California's Sage Scrub Region, the Sierra Nevada, the Chesapeake Bay Watershed, and the like (chapter 4), we should not expect such consistent outcomes unless comprehensive, quiet revolution regional plans are put in place.

Some of the greatest potential for quieter revolution programs is in older suburban areas, where revitalization is being promoted as part of the smart growth agenda; in small towns that remake themselves as attractive residential and commercial places; in localities and regions that have the resources—marshaled through ballot questions and taxes on developers—to buy or otherwise protect valued lands; and in transfer and purchase-of-development programs where the market is sufficiently strong and the trading fast paced enough to meaningfully guide larger development and landscape patterns.

Localities today have at their disposal a far greater range of options than they did in the quiet revolution years. Or, perhaps more importantly, they are more knowledgeable and willing to adopt planning techniques that they would not have even considered three and a half decades ago. Among them are steep slope, habitat, open space, farmland, and other critical areas protections; performance zoning; clustered development; and conservation subdivision design. Many localities are positioning themselves as sustainability leaders, linking land use planning with municipal-level Kyoto Protocol endorsement and other initiatives. Boulder, Colorado, may be the leading national example here, but many larger cities and metropolitan areas, as well, are now on board. Examples from Chicago, Pittsburgh, Cleveland, Portland, and Seattle are considered in chapter 4.

Good local planning can bring us exceptional local places, though not necessarily well-planned larger regions. But metropolitan regions, counties, and states are increasingly tending to larger landscapes. Pennsylvania, for example, is promoting multimunicipal planning, Washington State's Growth Management Act is concentrating development in urban regions, and Maryland is supporting smart growth statewide.

The new urbanism, a burgeoning movement in its own right, is also a quieter approach to land use planning. It provides a template, as well as the tools and cumulative expertise, to remake suburban and urban landscapes. But so far, the new urbanism has mainly filled niche demands and its orientation is principally toward the elite. New urbanist projects, like many other quieter revolution initiatives, are vital experiments that teach us a great deal and serve as models for larger-scale change. It is imperative that we continue to support these experiments—and greatly increase government, NGO, and corporate backing for them. Large segments of the public are not averse to new urbanist designs; this is affirmed by survey data and consumer behavior. But in most instances, limited inducements and constrained consumer choices act against wider diffusion of new urbanist development patterns. Still, they are increasingly being adopted by older localities, by public housing providers, and in government and private support for transit-oriented communities—thus putting into wider practice new urbanism ideals of diversity and affordability. But to take these landscape design principles up a level will require sustained political, institutional, and corporate commitments. And those commitments may, in the not-too-distant future, be spurred by rising gasoline prices and mandatory carbon emission reductions.

Protecting Ecosystems and Environmental Services

Quieter revolution approaches will rarely satisfy deep ecologists, earth liberationists, and other biocentrists. As we saw in chapter 3, even mainstream environmental organizations, such as the Sierra Club, are at times prone to reject collaborative planning. Land acquisition, by contrast, is almost universally supported by environmentalists—contingent, of course, on the land's use and management after acquisition. Conservation easements are regarded more skeptically; there are always fears that easements will be undone or compromised. Publicly owned lands—however badly managed—bring a greater sense of security, since they are unlikely to return to private hands. Those concerns aside, though, land trusts, watershed organizations, and local and state governments have made substantial progress in protecting valued local and regional lands. As with sprawl containment, though, what is the effect at wider scales? Generally, it is limited at best, and inconsistent across large spatial expanses (Weber 2000a). The cases reviewed in chapter 4—ranging from the Greater Yellowstone Ecosystem to the New York/New Jersey/Pennsylvania/Connecticut Highlands—point to the quieter revolution's ecoregional potential and mixed results.

Though The Nature Conservancy (TNC) seeks to protect large landscapes across the country and has made some enormous land purchases, its efforts still amount, in sum, to only a small part of what it would ideally want to achieve. Strategic and leveraged land and easement acquisitions do increase the importance and effectiveness of these individual activities. And initiatives such as TNC's Last Great Places campaign and the Sierra Club's Critical Ecoregions program do bring systematic attention and resources to large critical areas (chapter 4). The Buffalo Commons, perhaps, is further along than other large regional quieter revolution efforts—but we are still far from crossing over a Great Plains ecological restoration threshold. While collaborative accomplishments in places like the Highlands, Northern Forest, and Buffalo Commons are impressive, resources are too limited—and costs too high—to make these efforts into full-blown, quieter regional planning schemes.

The most vigorous land acquisition and easement activity is at the local, small-region, and state levels. Land trusts, watershed associations, and local and state governments—via ballot questions and general appropriations—are the key players. Some federal support comes from various programs described in chapter 5, but the traditional mother lode for such support—the Land and Water Conservation Fund—has been grossly underfunded for years. Land and easement acquisitions are costly and, given funding constraints, must be done strategically, in coordination with other government and nonprofit land protection activities. An example of how this can work is provided by central New Jersey's D&R (Delaware and Raritan) Greenway Trust, which works with several other government and nongovernment land conservation programs to produce a patchwork of protected lands at the small-watershed scale (figure 6.2).

The same observations about scale apply for environmental services, especially vulnerability reduction. Local, watershed-level success stories abound—and larger coastal and inland wetland restoration projects in the Everglades and along Louisiana's Gulf Coast are poised to join them. If environmental vulnerability reduction and local resilience can be successfully framed as a national security issue, then the potential for new initiatives, at a variety of spatial scales, could expand exponentially. Vulnerability reduction allows us to respond to climate threats not only prospectively by reducing carbon impacts but also adaptively to rising sea levels and greater incidences of floods and other severe weather events.

Civic Culture

Weber (2000a) paints a bright picture for "grass roots ecosystem management" (GREM)'s future, going so far as to depict it as a new environmental movement. But at the same time as he cites two hundred plus success stories, he also acknowledges uncertainty about GREM's long-term durability. Civic engagement is fundamental to GREM, just as it is to many quieter revolution endeavors. Yet, as Weber acknowledges with reference to southwest Washington's Willapa watershed case (chapter 3), most participants come from the upper rungs of the socioeconomic ladder. While this is hardly the case for all land use management initiatives, it is characteristic enough to make it a critical concern in assessing the quieter revolution's civic character.

While collaborative planning's proponents ardently support citizen engagement in the planning process, it is not an unalloyed blessing. A more active civic culture does not necessarily yield better ecological, social, or economic outcomes. Indeed, civic engagement can bring with it costly obstruction and delays. While that obstruction may be used to stymie environmentally harmful projects, it can also hinder environmentally beneficial ones. Of course, few projects are entirely environmentally beneficial or harmful in the first place; the point here is that civic engagement's consequences can play more than one way. Moreover, if wise use/property rights advocates and other parties not strongly supportive of environmental conservation are active participants, then environmental proponents may question the value of the entire participation enterprise. This is already the way some local collaborative ventures are being regarded, as we have seen in chapter 3, by the Sierra Club, Wilderness Society, and other environmental NGOs. And in most of those cases, the local participants to which they so object do not even come from the rabidly anti-environmental fringe of the property rights and wise use movements.

These issues aside, civic culture is beneficial in its own right, regardless of its effects on collaborative planning outcomes. To the degree that quieter revolution initiatives bring about a more informed citizenry, higher voting rates, deeper sense of place, and more community discussion and interaction, generally, we may regard them as positive civic influences. While it would appear that this is generally the case with quieter revolution civic engagement, it does—as we have seen—come under critical scrutiny for its tendencies toward elitism, toward bringing together communities of relatively high educational and financial status. To the extent that quieter programs become more diverse and inclusive—and some of them, at least, do work across the full socioeconomic spectrum—the stronger is their civic character.

Cost-Effectiveness

The quieter revolution is expensive, particularly when it involves purchases of lands and easements. Because of constitutional, cultural, and political limits on our ability to regulate land use, we often must pay landowners not just when we acquire their land outright but also when we restrict their land use options. This is not the case in the United Kingdom and parts of continental Europe, where land use and development rights are more centrally controlled (Cullingworth 1994; Kayden 2002; Bruegmann 2003). Oregon now finds itself in a situation where its pioneering land use program may become prohibitively expensive, given that property owners impacted by environmental regulations will have to be compensated. And Oregon's program is not even a quieter revolution program to begin with. Because quieter revolution programs rely so heavily on payments and incentives, they can be very costly, and their overall effectiveness may be very much constrained by funding availability. Take as an example agricultural preservation programs; in most instances, far more applicants are lined up to participate than there are funds available for land and easement purchases.

States, localities, and NGOs often pay dearly to protect lands, especially when those lands are ripe for commercial or residential development. Not all quieter revolution initiatives are so costly, of course; some incentive-based programs and planning innovations actually save money. There is a rather extensive literature, reviewed in chapter 5, attesting to enormous cost savings that can be achieved at the local, state, and national levels through effective containment of sprawl. Those quieter revolution efforts that do bring big bangs for the buck by successfully managing growth are among the most important ones, in that their cost efficiency can justify some of the large expenditures for land and easement purchases.

As noted in chapter 8, cost-effectiveness may be determined, in great degree, by the place or perspective from which it is calculated. Quieter revolution programs can bring very high returns on small local investments. Local governments and NGOs often secure substantial funding, having only to invest their required—let's say for the sake of example here—10 percent match. This subsidy system serves to amplify the quieter revolution's local value.

Given the enormous costs associated with sprawl management, ecological restoration, and other projects that quieter revolution approaches support, competition for funding often is intense. Some places will be winners; other will be losers—or at least they will not win as much. The reasons some are more favored than others have to do with political savvy, luck, and timing—as well as with local environmental and economic factors. This takes us on to the quieter revolution's equity and justice dimensions.

Environmental Justice

It is relatively simple, it seems, to make a strong case for the multiple benefits provided by urban gardens and green spaces—a topic only lightly addressed in this book. But are the benefits of suburban and rural open space as easily justified? Given the sometimes exorbitant cost, limited numbers of beneficiaries, and equity questions associated with closing off residential opportunities for those "late ones in" to the suburbs and exurbs, the case can be harder to make. This is where the smart growth agenda has tremendous potential: it can bring a regional perspective into play, although often it does not.

Most quieter revolution initiatives have not made environmental justice a priority. Issues of affordable housing, economic impacts of environmental protection in rural locales, and availability of funds for land protection in and near major metropolitan regions are among the justice and equity issues invoked by quieter revolution programs. To be sure, some quieter revolution efforts are deeply attuned to, or even have been prompted by, environmental and social equity concerns. Many small, collaborative programs, especially in the West, are very much about local economies. And smart growth programs do advocate affordable housing, though this dimension of growth management often is drowned out, if not outright opposed, by growth control advocates. But it appears that the quieter times are changing, with equity concerns at all levels increasingly finding places on land management agendas. Chapter 3 pointed to the role of civic culture, in earlier decades, in sustaining local inequalities. Contemporary environmental civic culture, with sufficient collective interest and will, can take an entirely different approach to environmental and social justice issues. And this is where quieter revolution programs hold perhaps the greatest potential.

It is fair to say that many quieter revolution programs thrive in more wealthy, elite locales. These are the places where ample civic capacity generally is in place. Extending it to new land use management programs—and paying for those programs—is well within reach. Building this capacity in poorer, less privileged places is one of the greatest challenges that the quieter revolution faces. Though affordable housing, infill development, and brownfields redevelopment all are planks in many a quieter revolution platform, how much priority are they being given? And when state and federal funds, or even local funds, are disbursed in support of quieter revolution programs, how equitable is that distribution? Land and easement acquisition programs have a built-in bias, in many places, toward relatively well-off areas where low-density sprawl threatens valued environments. This structural inequity may to some degree be redressed by giving equal attention to affordable-housing issues and access across the socioeconomic spectrum to protected areas. These are very troublesome questions, however, that many communities receiving quieter revolution benefits would prefer to avoid entirely.

Quieter Revolution Accomplishments in Summary

With respect to all the issues described here, more information is needed. Many more analyses of individual programs, as well as collective efforts, are called for. This work need not—and very often will not—be part and parcel of the quieter revolution framework developed here; instead, program appraisals will be conducted through a multiplicity of frameworks. But the questions posed here—especially in this chapter and chapter 8—should be asked by diverse evaluators and observers. They are directed toward critical, if too often neglected, themes that are shaping our communities, lands, and landscapes.

In summary, we can say that the quieter revolution has spawned a great many programs and projects, probably far more than a continuation of the quiet revolution would ever have given us. In part, of course, this is a matter of definition, since we have included here a great many small, diverse, collaborative efforts. Beyond these, there are the initiatives that never were launched. For all the success stories—or at least stories—there are the projects, solutions, collaborations, and innovations that failed to materialize. These are the stories that rarely get written. It might behoove us to learn more about opportunities that the quieter revolution managed to miss—and what it would have taken to push them over the implementation threshold—or whether we were better off without them.

Collectively, it seems, quieter revolution initiatives and their successors hold much potential. But if we were to generalize from Bateson and Smith's (1994, 195) assessment of the northern New York and New England situation—that land trusts "collectively have not made a splash on our Northern Forest map"—then we would have to conclude that the quieter revolution's overall impacts are minimal. But this is a rather extreme view. It would be hard to estimate—at the individual project or collective scales—how conditions would have differed had these quieter revolution initiatives not been launched—or, alternatively, had stronger, more regulatory measures been in place. But it does seem that the quieter revolution, thus far, has mattered—and mattered significantly. There would be no denying this on the part of its wise use/property rights opponents (chapter 7).

Looking Ahead

Future climate and resource crises could compel us to adopt more regulatory approaches to land use management, taking us well beyond the bounds of current political acceptability. But whatever the future holds, quieter revolution approaches are likely to play an important part. Should the political climate trend further in the direction of individual rights and away from collective-interest mandates, then unobtrusive quieter approaches will have their niche defined for them. If, on the other hand, we move to a more regulatory system, there will still be a secure place for quieter initiatives. Perhaps they would seep in to fill the gaps in states and communities that reject more regulatory approaches. Places that now find even quieter revolution approaches beyond their thresholds of tolerance may in the future be swept into adopting them as a larger wave of regulatory activity builds around them. Whatever the future holds, regulatory and less regulatory approaches—just as they do now—can coexist and even be mutually supportive.

There will always be quieter revolution tension between place-based action and stewardship of larger, interconnected landscapes. Indeed, even the bioregionalists—whose horizons are almost exclusively local and regional—still must come to terms with questions of multiple, overlapping scales (Mason, Solecki, and Lotstein 1987). Creative solutions can and do emerge to fill spatially complex niches; Duane (1998), for example, speaks of the Sierra Nevada's "middle landscape," where ecoregional solutions are crafted over coffee and breakfast at the local level, rather than in Sacramento or Washington. While it is wildly unrealistic to expect scale-spanning quieter revolution initiatives to work smoothly and in seamless integration, they can be made to work. We have already seen that they do work in many cases, in many places.

To the degree that quieter revolution "superstructures" are in place—in the form of policy guidance and resources disbursed from central sources—there are overarching structural issues. Quite conceivably, superstructural resources may expand in future years, in response, for example, to national-level carbon and energy policies. Some of the greatest challenges will be situated at the nexus between the quieter revolution's centralized infrastructure and local needs, priorities, and programs. One way to handle this might be a modified block grant approach. Modeled after federal education, health care, housing, and transportation programs, this entails grants to states and localities, with wide local discretion in spending the monies. The Better America Bonds program (chapter 5) and Community Character Act (chapter 5) each sought, in their own ways, to distribute central funds to local places. Both these initiatives died, the first during the Clinton years and the second in more recent congressional committee deliberations. But these or similar funding programs may find new life in the near future—and they can be fashioned so as to keep most of the decision authority devolved, at the local and regional levels. We could still have in place accountability standards, to ensure that local initiatives are in synch with regional and state interests, as well as broader environmental sustainability and justice criteria. More rigorous and consistent program evaluations that address the points raised in this chapter and chapter 8 would be a constructive first step toward creating a credible multiscale accountability system.

Environmental sustainability themes, in particular, compel wider discussions about goals and priorities. If, for example, we promote afforestation for its carbon sequestration value, what kinds of trees are being planted in restored local forests? Are biodiversity and ecological resilience taken fully into account? Similarly, we might ask about local and regional ecological impacts of increased biofuel production. A more pervasive environmental issue, perhaps, is how much sense it makes to try to protect as many local ecosystems as possible, whatever the expense. Should we consider "writing off" some areas and focusing more energy and resources on others? Such an approach may be shown to yield greater ecological benefits overall, as well as greater economic efficiencies. But this may come at a price. Local stewardship programs bring with them civic engagement, educational value, and enriched sense of place. Caring for a distant watershed simply does not have the same meaning and value as local stewardship.

Then there are questions about local impacts from projects that bring wider environmental benefits. Transit-oriented development (TOD) is a prime example. TOD proposals often face strong local resistance. Much of that resistance may be based on local misperceptions, but pressing that point will not necessarily bring project success. And if eminent domain is invoked, then more issues are raised (chapter 7). Planned-unit developments have long faced such challenges, and in many instances, localities are reluctant to support nonconventional subdivision practices—such as narrowed residential streets and elimination of cul-de-sacs—of any kind.

In the end, the quieter revolution, as currently structured, cannot stop sprawl, ensure consistent ecological protection, or guarantee local resiliency. With respect to sprawl, at least, it is already too late in many places. What we can do is better plan future development, promote infill, reclaim ghost malls and other abandoned spaces, and modify our resource footprint in a great many ways. We can also reshape some of our existing sprawled and strip-developed landscapes. New urbanist planners have done just that in many locales, making them more walkable and aesthetically pleasing, and less energy consumptive. And we can creatively and adaptively protect valued farm, recreation, and ecological lands inside as well as outside our metropolitan areas. While such harmonious and sustainable visions will not flourish everywhere, there is much that can be done.

Some of these sustainable redevelopment and smart growth initiatives will encounter fierce opposition: it's un-American, too costly, too European, interferes with free choice, and so on. But in all likelihood, we will soon be contending much more seriously than we are now with climate and energy concerns. Quieter revolution infrastructure already in place can help us do so in an orderly way. We might set central goals and targets, with creative and adaptive implementation devolving to local-, regional-, and state-level collaborative endeavors. Federal and state funds might reward those initiatives, based first on their promise for meeting targets and then their actual success in doing so.

Barring such catastrophic future events as sustained terrorist attacks, World War III, huge increases in petroleum prices, or a series of crippling natural or technological disasters—and none of these can be ruled out, of course—draconian new environmental and planning regulations probably will not be put into place. Evolutionary approaches can be expected to prevail, with the quieter revolution poised and ready to ride new waves of concern over climate change, resource scarcity, and food security.

Even evolutionary approaches, as we have already observed, will draw intense opposition from wise use/property rights advocates and other "anti-environmental" activists (chapter 7). Federal involvement, in particular, will come under heavy fire. But consider, for a moment, carbon emission targets. This is not so extraordinary, as we already have emissions-trading schemes, most notably in support of national sulfur dioxide targets. Countries that have ratified the Kyoto Protocol are already trading carbon credits. Even in the United States, where the treaty has been rejected, carbon trading is starting to take place, without the federal government's involvement. The innovators are state and local governments, NGOs, and the corporate sector. We could argue that the quieter revolution, like these trading schemes, simply does not need the federal government, at least not all that much.

But if we are to do the big things, even if in relatively quiet and gentle ways, then a national commitment is necessary. Quieter revolution approaches will be most effective when there is national oversight (Talen 2005)—oversight that rewards innovation but discourages laggardness. Should we eventually determine, collectively, that healthy forests, properly functioning ecosystems, affordable housing, energy-efficient living, efficient public transit, and accessible recreation spaces are our priorities, then quieter revolution approaches will be well positioned to step up. Southern California, perhaps, will be one of the places leading the way (chapter 4). In the interim, we continue to test, appraise, experiment with, adapt, and cull these approaches.

This book, it is earnestly hoped, can help guide us. Its examples are meant to inspire as well as strike the appropriate cautionary notes. The last two chapters, in particular, offer some suggestions for thinking rigorously and comprehensively about the quieter revolution's potential and pitfalls. If we can make serious, yet adaptive, progress toward protecting valued places and allocating resources in sensible, fair, and economically and ecologically efficient ways, then we will be on a hopeful path toward a more livable, environmentally sustainable society.

REFERENCES

Abbey, Edward. 1975. *The monkey wrench gang*. Philadelphia: Lippincott.

Abbott, Carl, Sy Adler, and Margery Post Abbott. 1997. *Planning a new west: The Columbia River Gorge National Scenic Area*. Corvallis: Oregon State University Press.

Abbott, Carl, Deborah Howe, and Sy Adler, eds. 1994. *Planning the Oregon way: A twenty-year evaluation*. Corvallis: Oregon State University Press.

Adler, Robert W., Michele Straube, and Heather Green. 2000. *Lessons from large watershed programs: A comparison of the Colorado River Basin salinity control program with the San Francisco Bay-Delta program, central and south Florida, and the Chesapeake Bay program*. Washington, DC: National Academy of Public Administration. www.napawash.org/pc_economy_environment/epafile10.pdf (accessed 12 April 2007).

Alanen, Arnold R., and Robert Z. Melnick. 2000. *Preserving cultural landscapes in America*. Baltimore: Johns Hopkins University Press.

Alliance for America. 2006. Home page, www.allianceforamerica.org (accessed 14 August 2006).

Alliance for the Wild Rockies. 2007. Home page, www.wildrockiesalliance.org (accessed 12 April 2007).

Almond, Gabriel A., and Sidney Verba. 1963. *The civic culture: Political attitudes and democracy in five nations*. Boston: Little, Brown.

American Farmland Trust. Farmland Information Center. 2001. *Fact sheet: Transfer of development rights*. Northampton, MA: Farmland Information Center. www.farmlandinfo.org/documents/27746/FS_TDR_1-01.pdf (accessed 12 April 2007).

———. 2002. *Fact sheet: The farmland protection toolbox.* Northampton, MA: Farmland Information Center. www.farmlandinfo.org/documents/27761/FS_Toolbox_10-02.pdf (accessed 12 April 2007).

———. 2005. *Fact sheet: Status of local PACE programs.* Northampton, MA: Farmland Information Center. www.farmland.org/about/mission/documents/AFT_Pace_state_8-05.pdf (accessed 12 April 2007).

———. 2006. *Fact sheet: Agricultural conservation easements.* Northampton, MA: Farmland Information Center. www.farmlandinfo.org/documents/27762/ACE_06-10.pdf (accessed 12 April 2007).

American Land Conservancy. 2006. Home page, www.alcnet.org (accessed 12 April 2007).

American Planning Association. 2001. House reintroduces bill to help states practice smart growth. News release, www.planning.org/newsreleases/2001/ftp040901.htm (accessed 14 August 2006).

———. 2002. Senate committee supports smart growth planning legislation. News release, www.planning.org/newsreleases/2002/ftp0425.htm (accessed 14 August 2006).

———. 2005. Kelo Supreme Court decision emphasizes the importance of planning. News release, 23 June, www.planning.org/newsreleases/2005/ftp062305.htm (accessed 12 April 2007).

———. 2006a. Eminent domain legislation across America. www.planning.org/legislation/eminentdomain/index.htm (accessed 12 April 2007).

———. 2006b. *Federal eminent domain legislation in the 109th Congress: Fact sheet.* www.planning.org/policyconference/pdf/eminentdomainfederalfacts.pdf (accessed 12 April 2007).

———. 2006c. Regulatory takings ballot measures across America. www.planning.org/legislation/measure37/index.htm (accessed 12 April 2007).

American Prairie Foundation. 2007. Home page, www.americanprairie.org (accessed 12 April 2007).

American Prospect editors. 2006. The world according to Grover. Web exclusive, 6 July 2006, www.prospect.org/web/page.ww?section=root&name=ViewWeb&articleId=11699 (accessed 12 April 2007).

America's Wetland. 2007. America's wetland: Campaign to save coastal Louisiana. Home page, www.americaswetland.com (accessed 12 April 2007).

Amy, Douglas J. 1987. *The politics of environmental mediation.* New York: Columbia University Press.

Anderson, Jeremy, and Steven Yaffee. 1998. *Balancing public trust and private interest: Public participation in habitat conservation planning: A summary report.*

Ann Arbor: University of Michigan School of Natural Resources. www.snre .umich.edu/ecomgt/pubs/hcp.pdf (accessed 12 April 2007).

Anderson, Larry. 2002. *Benton MacKaye: Conservationist, planner, and creator of the Appalachian Trail.* Baltimore: Johns Hopkins University Press.

Andrews, Richard N. L. 2006a. *Managing the environment, managing ourselves: A history of American environmental policy.* 2nd ed. New Haven, CT: Yale University Press.

———. 2006b. Risk-based decision making: Policy, science, and politics. In *Environmental policy: New directions for the twenty-first century*, eds. Norman J. Vig and Michael E. Kraft, 6th ed., 215–38. Washington, DC: CQ Press.

Anglin, Roland. 1990. Diminishing utility: The effect on citizen preferences for local growth. *Urban Affairs Quarterly* 25:684–96.

Anton, Paul A. 2005. *The economic value of open space: Implications for land use decisions.* St. Paul, MN: Wilder Research. www.embraceopenspace.org/ stream_document.aspx?rRID=2998&pRID=2997 (accessed 12 April 2007).

Apollo Alliance. 2006. About the alliance, www.apolloalliance.org/about_the_ alliance (accessed 12 April 2007).

Arendt, Randall. 1996. *Conservation design for subdivisions: A practical guide to creating open space networks.* Washington, DC: Island Press.

Arigoni, Danielle. 2001. *Smart growth and affordable housing: Making the connection.* Washington, DC: Smart Growth Network and National Neighborhood Coalition. www.neighborhoodcoalition.org/pdfs/AH%20and%20SG.pdf (accessed 12 April 2007).

Arnstein, Sherry. 1969. A ladder of citizen participation. *Journal of the American Institute of Planners* 35 (4):216–24.

Babbitt, Bruce. 2005. *Cities in the wilderness: A new vision of land use in America.* Washington, DC: Island Press.

Babcock, Richard F. 1966. *The zoning game: Municipal practices and policies.* Madison: University of Wisconsin Press.

Babcock, Richard F., and Charles L. Siemon. 1985. *The zoning game revisited.* Cambridge, MA: Lincoln Institute of Land Policy.

Baldassare, Mark. 1990. Suburban support for no-growth policies. *Journal of Urban Affairs* 12:197–206.

Baldassare, Mark, and Georjeanna Wilson. 1996. Changing sources of suburban support for local growth controls. *Urban Studies* 33:459–71.

Baltimore Ecosystem Study. 2006. Home page, www.beslter.org (accessed 12 April 2007).

Banach, Melissa, and Denis Canavan. 1987. Montgomery County agricultural preservation program. In *Managing land-use conflicts: Case studies in special area management*, eds. David J. Brower and Daniel S. Carol, 244–68. Durham, NC: Duke University Press.

Bank of America. 1995. *Beyond sprawl*. www.bankofamerica.com/environment/ index.cfm?template=env_reports_speeches&context=sprawl&state=IT#skip-nav (accessed 12 April 2007).

Barker, Paul D., Jr. 1990. The Chesapeake Bay Preservation Act: The problem with state and local regulation of interstate resources. *William and Mary Law Review* 31:735–72.

Barnett, Jonathan, ed. 2000. *Planning for a new century: The regional agenda*. Washington, DC: Island Press.

Baron, Jill S., ed. 2002. *Rocky Mountain futures: An ecological perspective*. Washington, DC: Island Press.

Barringer, Felicity. 2004a. Property rights law may alter Oregon landscape. *New York Times*, 26 November.

———. 2004b. Neighbors of burned homes pained by suburban sprawl. *New York Times*, 12 December.

Barron, David. 2006. Eminent domain is dead! (long live eminent domain!). *Boston Globe*, 16 April.

Bartsch, Charles, and Bridget Dorfman. 2002. *Brownfields "State of the states": An end-of-session review of initiatives and program impacts in the 50 states*. Washington, DC: Northeast-Midwest Institute. www.nemw.org/brown_stateof.pdf (accessed 12 April 2007).

Bateson, Emily, and Nancy Smith. 1994. Making it happen: Protecting wilderness on the ground. In *The future of the Northern Forest*, ed. Christopher Mc-Grory Klyza, 182–210. Hanover, NH: University Press of New England.

Bean, Michael J. 2006. Second-generation approaches. In *The Endangered Species Act at thirty: Renewing the conservation promise*, eds. Dale D. Goble, J. Michael Scott, and Frank W. Davis, vol. 1, 274–85. Washington, DC: Island Press.

Beatley, Timothy. 1994. *Habitat conservation planning: Endangered species and urban growth*. Austin: University of Texas Press.

———. 1999. *Green urbanism: Learning from European cities*. Washington, DC: Island Press.

Beatley, Timothy, David J. Brower, and William H. Lucy. 1994. Representation in comprehensive planning: An analysis of the Austin plan process. *Journal of the American Planning Association* 60:185–96.

Beatley, Timothy, David J. Brower, and Anna K. Schwab. 2002. *An introduction to coastal zone management*. Washington, DC: Island Press.

Beatley, Timothy, and Kristy Manning. 1997. *The ecology of place: Planning for environment, economy, and community*. Washington, DC: Island Press.

Beierle, Thomas C. 1999. Using social goals to evaluate public participation in environmental decisions. *Policy Studies Review* 16:75–103.

———. 2002. The quality of stakeholder-based decisions. *Risk Analysis* 22:739–49.

Beierle, Thomas C., and Jerry Cayford. 2002. *Democracy in practice: Public participation in environmental decisions.* Washington, DC: Resources for the Future.

Beierle, Thomas C., and David M. Konisky. 2000. Values, conflict, and trust in participatory environmental planning. *Journal of Policy Analysis and Management* 19:587–602.

———. 2001. What are we gaining from stakeholder involvement? Observations from environmental planning in the Great Lakes. *Environment and Planning C: Government and Policy* 19:515–27.

Belden, Russonello & Stewart. 2004. *2004 American communities survey: National survey on communities.* Washington, DC: Belden, Russonello & Stewart. www.commutesolutions-hou.com/resources/NAR-SGA%20Commuter%20 Survey.pdf (accessed 12 April 2007).

Benfield, F. Kaid, Matthew D. Raimi, and Donald D. T. Chen. 1999. *Once there were greenfields: How urban sprawl is undermining America's environment, economy and social fabric.* New York: Natural Resources Defense Council.

Benfield, F. Kaid, Jutka Terris, and Nancy Vorsanger. 2001. *Solving sprawl: Models of smart growth in communities across America.* New York: Natural Resources Defense Council.

Bengston, David N., George Xu, and David P. Fan. 2001. Attitudes toward ecosystem management in the United States, 1992–1998. *Society and Natural Resources* 14:471–87.

Berger, Jonathan, and John W. Sinton. 1985. *Water, earth, and fire: Land use and environmental planning in the New Jersey pine barrens.* Baltimore: Johns Hopkins University Press.

Berke, Philip R., David R. Godschalk, and Edward J. Kaiser with Daniel A. Rodriguez. 2006. *Urban land use planning.* 5th ed. Urbana: University of Illinois Press.

Berliner, Dana. 2003. *Public power, private gain: A five-year, state-by-state report examining the abuse of eminent domain.* Arlington, VA: Institute for Justice. www.ij.org/private_property/connecticut/ED-Report-DBerliner.doc (accessed 12 April 2007).

Bernard, Ted, and Jora Young. 1997. *The ecology of hope: Communities collaborate for sustainability.* Gabriola Island, BC, Canada: New Society Publishers.

Bingham, Gail. 1986. *Resolving environmental disputes: A decade of experience.* Washington, DC: Conservation Foundation.

REFERENCES

Blumbert, Louis, and Darrell Knuffke. 1998. Count us out: Why the Wilderness Society opposed the Quincy Library Group legislation. *Chronicle of Community* 2(2):41–44.

Blumm, Michael C. 1997. The amphibious salmon: The evolution of ecosystem management in the Columbia River Basin. *Ecology Law Quarterly* 24:653–76.

Born, Stephen M., and Kenneth D. Genskow. 2000. *The watershed approach: An empirical assessment of innovation in environmental management.* Washington, DC: National Academy of Public Administration. www.napawash.org/pc_economy_environment/epafile0701.pdf (accessed 12 April 2007).

Bosselman, Fred P. 1986. State and local plans in Hawaii: Lessons for Florida. In *Perspectives on Florida's Growth Management Act of 1985*, eds. John M. De-Grove and Julian Conrad Juergensmeyer, 1–14. Cambridge, MA: Lincoln Institute of Land Policy.

Bosselman, Fred, and David Callies. 1971. *The quiet revolution in land use control.* Washington, DC: Council on Environmental Quality.

Bosso, Christopher J. 2005. *Environment, Inc.: From grassroots to beltway.* Lawrence: University of Kansas Press.

Bosso, Christopher J., and Deborah Lynn Guber. 2006. Maintaining presence: Environmental advocacy and the permanent. In *Environmental policy: New directions for the twenty-first century*, eds. Norman Vig and Michael E. Kraft, 6th ed., 78–99. Washington, DC: CQ Press.

Boston, Tim. 1999. Exploring anti-environmentalism in the context of sustainability. *Electronic Green Journal*, 11 December, egj.lib.uidaho.edu/egj11/boston1.html (accessed 12 April 2007).

Botshon, Ann, Lisa Botshon, and Michael Botshon. 2007. *Saving Sterling Forest: The epic struggle to preserve New York's Highlands.* Albany: State University of New York Press.

Box, Richard C. 1998. *Citizen governance: Leading American communities into the 21st century.* Thousand Oaks, CA: Sage Publications.

Brandenburg, Andrea M., and Matthew S. Carroll. 1995. Your place or mine? The effect of place creation on environmental values and landscape meanings. *Society and Natural Resources* 8:381–98.

Breckenridge, Lee P. 1995. Reweaving the landscape: The institutional challenges of ecosystem management for lands in private ownership. *Vermont Law Review* 19:367–422.

———. 1999. Nonprofit environmental organizations and the restructuring of institutions for ecosystem management. *Ecology Law Quarterly* 25:692–706.

Brewer, Richard. 2003. *Conservancy: The land trust movement in America.* Hanover, NH: University Press of New England.

Brick, Philip, Donald Snow, and Sarah Van de Wetering. 2001. *Across the great divide: Explorations in collaborative conservation and the American West.* Washington, DC: Island Press.

Broder, John M. 2006. States curbing right to seize private homes. *New York Times*, 21 February.

Brody, Samuel D. 2003. Measuring the effects of stakeholder participation on the quality of local plans based on the principles of collaborative ecosystem management. *Journal of Planning Education and Research* 22:407–19.

Brookings Institution. Center on Urban and Metropolitan Policy. 2003. *Back to prosperity: A competitive agenda for renewing Pennsylvania.* Washington, DC: Brookings Institution. www.brookings.edu/es/urban/publications/pa.htm (accessed 12 April 2007).

Bruegmann, Robert. 2003. *Sprawl: A compact history.* Chicago: University of Chicago Press.

Brunner, Ronald D., Toddi A. Steelman, Lindy Coe-Juell, Christina M. Cromley, Christine M. Edards, and Donna W. Tucker. 2005. *Adaptive governance: Integrating science, policy, and decision making.* New York: Columbia University Press.

Bryant, M. Margaret. 2006. Urban landscape conservation and the role of ecological greenways at local and metropolitan scales. *Landscape and Urban Planning* 76:23–44.

Burby, Raymond J. 2003. Making plans that matter: Citizen involvement and government action. *Journal of the American Planning Association* 69:33–49.

Burchell, Robert W., Naveed A. Shad, David Listokin, Hilary Phillips, Anthony Downs, Samuel Seskin, Judy S. Davis, Terry Moore, David Helton, and Michelle Gall. 1998. *The costs of sprawl–revisited.* Washington, DC: National Academy Press. trb.org/news/blurb_detail.asp?id=2578 (accessed 12 April 2007).

Burke, Edmund M. 1968. Citizen participation strategies. *Journal of the American Institute of Planners* 34:287–94.

Busch, David E., and Joel C. Trexler, eds. 2003. *Monitoring ecosystems: Interdisciplinary approaches for evaluating ecoregional initiatives.* Washington, DC: Island Press.

Buttimer, Anne. 1978. Charism and context: The challenge of La Geographie Humaine. In *Humanistic geography: Prospects and problems*, eds. David Ley and Marwyn S. Samuels, 58–76. London: Croom Helm.

Caldwell, Lynton K. 1970. The ecosystem as a criterion for public land policy. *Natural Resources Journal* 10:203–21.

———. 1998. *The National Environmental Policy Act: An agenda for the future.* Bloomington: Indiana University Press.

REFERENCES

Callenbach, Ernest. 1996. *Bring back the buffalo: A sustainable future for America's Great Plains.* Berkeley: University of California Press.

Callies, David L. 1984. *Regulating paradise: Land use controls in Hawaii.* Honolulu: University of Hawaii Press.

Calthorpe, Peter. 1993. *The next American metropolis: Ecology, community, and the American dream.* New York: Princeton Architectural Press.

Calthorpe, Peter, and William Fulton. 2001. *The regional city: Planning for the end of sprawl.* Washington, DC: Island Press.

Caro, Robert A. 1974. *The power broker: Robert Moses and the fall of New York.* New York: Knopf.

Carson, Rachel. 1962. *Silent spring.* Boston: Houghton Mifflin.

Carter, Luther J. 1974. *The Florida experience: Land and water policy in a growth state.* Baltimore: Johns Hopkins University Press.

Cattaneo, Andrea, Daniel Hellerstein, Cynthia Nickerson, and Christina Myers. 2006. *Balancing the multiple objectives of conservation programs.* ERR-19. Washington, DC: U.S. Department of Agriculture, Economic Research Service. www.ers.usda.gov/publications/ERR19/ERR19.pdf (accessed 12 April 2007).

Caves, Roger W. 1990. Determining land use policy via the ballot box: The growth initiative blitz in California. *Land Use Policy* 79:70–79.

Center for American Places. 2007. Home page, www.americanplaces.org (accessed 12 April 2007).

Center for Natural Lands Management. 2004. *Natural lands management cost analysis: 28 case studies.* Fallbrook, CA: Center for Natural Lands Management.

Chaloupka, William. 1996. The county supremacy and militia movements: Federalism as an issue on the radical right. *Publius* 26:161–75.

Chambers, Nicky, Craig Simmons, and Mathis Wackernagel. 2000. *Sharing nature's interest: Ecological footprints as an indicator of sustainability.* London: Earthscan.

Chapin, Timothy S., and Charles E. Connerly. 2004. Attitudes towards growth management in Florida: Comparing resident support in 1985 and 2001. *Journal of the American Planning Association* 70:443–52.

Chase, Alston. 1986. *Playing god in Yellowstone: The destruction of America's first national park.* Boston: Atlantic Monthly Press.

Checkoway, Barry, and Jon Van Til. 1978. What do we know about citizen participation? A selective review of research. In *Citizen participation in America: Essays on the state of the art*, ed. Stuart Langton, 25–42. Lexington, MA: Lexington Books.

Cheng, Antony S., and Steven E. Daniels. 2003. Examining the interaction between geographic scale and ways of knowing in ecosystem management: A case study of place-based collaborative planning. *Forest Science* 49:841–54.

Chesapeake Bay Commission. 2005. *2007 federal Farm Bill: Concepts for conservation reform in the Chesapeake Bay region.* Annapolis, MD: Chesapeake Bay Commission. www.chesbay.state.va.us/Publications/Farm%20Bill%20Report.pdf (accessed 12 April 2007).

———. 2006. *2006 state of the bay.* Annapolis, MD: Chesapeake Bay Foundation. www.cbf.org/site/DocServer/SOTB_2006.pdf?docID=6743 (accessed 12 April 2007).

———. 2007. Chesapeake Bay Foundation: Saving a national treasure. Home page, www.cbf.org (accessed 12 April 2007).

Chess, Caron, Billie Jo Hance, and Ginger Gibson. 2000. Adaptive participation in watershed management. *Journal of Soil and Water Conservation* 55:248–52.

Claassen, Roger. 2003. Emphasis shifts in US agri-environmental policy. *Amber Waves* 1(5):39–44. www.ers.usda.gov/AmberWaves/November03/Features/emphasis_shifts.htm (accessed 12 April 2007).

———. 2004. Have conservation compliance incentives reduced soil erosion? *Amber Waves* 2(3):30–37. www.ers.usda.gov/AmberWaves/June04/Features/HaveConservation.htm (accessed 12 April 2007).

Clarion Associates. 2000. *The costs of sprawl in Pennsylvania.* Denver: Clarion Associates.

Clark, Tim W., and David L. Gaillard. 2001. Organizing an effective partnership for the Yellowstone to Yukon conservation initiative. *Yale School of Forestry & Environmental Studies Bulletin* 105:223–39.

Clark, Tim W., and Ann H. Harvey. 1990. The greater Yellowstone ecosystem policy arena. *Society and Natural Resources* 3:281–84.

Clawson, Marion. 1981. *New Deal planning: The NRPB.* Baltimore: Johns Hopkins University Press.

———. 1983. *The federal lands revisited.* Baltimore: Johns Hopkins University Press.

Coalition for a Livable Future. 2007. Home page, www.clfuture.org (accessed 12 April 2007).

Coggins, George C. 1999. Regulating federal natural resources: A summary case against devolved collaboration. *Ecology Law Quarterly* 25:602–10.

Collins, Beryl Robichaud, and Emily W. B. Russell, eds. 1988. *Protecting the New Jersey Pinelands: A new direction in land-use management.* New Brunswick, NJ: Rutgers University Press.

Columbia River Gorge National Scenic Area. 2007. *Management plan for the Columbia River Gorge National Scenic Area.* www2.co.multnomah.or.us/Community_Services/LUT-Planning/urban/CRGNSAPlan/Home/NSAMP_Home.html (accessed 12 April 2007).

REFERENCES

Commission on the Adirondacks in the Twenty-First Century. 1990. *The Adirondack Park in the twenty-first century.* Albany: State of New York.

Confessore, Nicholas. 2006. Cities grow up, and some see sprawl. *New York Times,* 6 August.

Conley, Alexander, and Margaret A. Moote. 2003. Evaluating collaborative natural resource management. *Society and Natural Resources* 16:371–86.

Connor, Desmond M. 2001. *Constructive citizen participation: A resource book.* 8th ed. Victoria, BC, Canada: Development Press.

Conservation Fund. 2007. Land conservation. www.conservationfund.org/?article=2031 (accessed 12 April 2007).

Constantini, Edward, and Kenneth Hanf. 1973. *The environmental impulse and its competitors: Attitudes, interests, and institutions at Lake Tahoe.* Davis: University of California at Davis Institute of Governmental Affairs.

Cooper, Christopher. 2006. Court's eminent-domain edict is a flashpoint on state ballots. *Wall Street Journal,* 7 August.

Corbett, Marjorie R., ed. 1983. *Greenline parks: Land conservation trends for the eighties and beyond.* Washington, DC: National Parks and Conservation Association.

Cortner, Hanna J., Sam Burns, Lance R. Clark, Wendy Hinrichs Sanders, Gus Townes, and Martha Twarkins. 2001. Governance and institutions: Opportunities and challenges. In *Understanding community-based forest ecosystem management,* eds. Gerald J. Gray, Maia J. Enzer, and Jonathan Kusel, 65–95. Binghamton, NY: Food Products Press.

Cortner, Hanna J., and Margaret A. Moote. 1994. Trends and issues in land and water resources management: Setting the agenda for change. *Environmental Management* 18:167–73.

———. 1998. *The politics of ecosystem management.* Washington, DC: Island Press.

Cox, Wendell. 2002. *Forfeiting the American dream: The HUD-funded smart growth guidebook's attack on homeownership* (Backgrounder #1565). Washington, DC: Heritage Foundation. www.heritage.org/Research/SmartGrowth/BG1565.cfm (accessed 7 April 2007).

Creighton, James L. 2005. *The public participation handbook: Making better decisions through citizen involvement.* San Francisco: Jossey-Bass.

Cronin, John, and Robert F. Kennedy Jr. 1997. *The Riverkeepers: Two activists fight to reclaim our environment as a basic human right.* New York: Scribner.

Cronon, William. 1983. *Changes in the land: Indians, colonists, and the ecology of New England.* New York: Hill and Wang.

Crowfoot, James, and Julia Wondolleck. 1990. *Environmental disputes: Community involvement in conflict resolution.* Washington, DC: Island Press.

Cullingworth, Barry. 1994. Alternate planning systems: Is there anything to learn from abroad? *Journal of the American Planning Association* 60:162–73.

Cullingworth, Barry, and Roger W. Caves. 2003. *Planning in the USA: Policies, issues and processes*, 2nd ed. New York: Routledge.

Cunningham, James V. 1972. Citizen participation in public affairs. *Public Administration Review* 32:589–602.

Dahl, Robert A. 1989. *Democracy and its critics*. New Haven, CT: Yale University Press.

Daniels, Steven E., and Gregg B. Walker. 2001. *Working through environmental conflict: The collaborative learning approach*. Westport, CT: Praeger.

Daniels, Tom. 1999. *When city and country collide: Managing growth in the metropolitan fringe*. Washington, DC: Island Press.

Daniels, Tom, and Deborah Bowers. 1997. *Holding our ground: Protecting America's farms and farmland*. Washington, DC: Island Press.

Daniels, Tom, and Katherine Daniels. 2003. *The environmental planning handbook for sustainable communities and regions*. Chicago: American Planning Association Planners Press.

Dardick, Samuel. 1999. The changing politic of the Northern California Sierra. *Ecology Law Quarterly* 25:659–64.

Davidson, Steven G., Jay G. Merwin Jr., John Capper, Garret Power, and Frank R. Shivers Jr. 1997. *Chesapeake waters: Four centuries of controversy, concern and legislation*. 2nd ed. Centreville, MD: Tidewater Publishers.

Day, Diane. 1997. Citizen participation in the planning process: An essentially contested concept. *Journal of Planning Literature* 11:421–34.

Dean, Cornelia. 2006. Home on the range: A corridor for wildlife. *New York Times*, 23 May.

Dean, Howard. 1996. Growth management plans. In *Land use in America*, eds. Henry L. Diamond and Patrick F. Noonan, 135–54. Washington, DC: Island Press.

DeGrove, John M. 1984. *Land, growth & politics*. Washington, DC: American Planning Association.

———. 1989. Growth management and governance. In *Understanding growth management: Critical issues and a research agenda*, eds. David J. Brower, David R. Godschalk, and Douglas R. Porter, 22–42. Washington, DC: Urban Land Institute and University of North Carolina at Chapel Hill Center for Urban and Regional Studies.

———. 2005. *Planning policy and politics: Smart growth and the states*. Cambridge, MA: Lincoln Institute of Land Policy.

DeGrove, John M., and Julian Conrad Juergensmeyer, eds. 1986. *Perspectives on Florida's Growth Management Act of 1985*. Cambridge, MA: Lincoln Institute of Land Policy.

Deitrick, Sabina, and Cliff Ellis. 2004. New urbanism in the inner city: A case study of Pittsburgh. *Journal of the American Planning Association* 70:426–42.

DellaSala, Dominick A., and Jack E. Williams, eds. 2006. Special section: The Northwest Forest plan: A global model of forest management in contentious times. *Conservation Biology* 20:274–76.

Demographia. n.d. *The "growing smart" legislative guidebook: Model legislation threatens opportunity*. www.demographia.com/db-grsmart.htm (accessed 12 April 2007).

Denworth, Joanne R. 2002. *Planning beyond boundaries: A multi-municipal planning and implementation manual for Pennsylvania municipalities*. Philadelphia: 10,000 Friends of Pennsylvania. www.10000friends.org/downloads/Planning_Beyond_Boundaries_excerpt_032906.pdf (accessed 12 April 2007).

Devall, Bill, and George Sessions. 1985. *Deep ecology: Living as if nature mattered*. Salt Lake City: Peregrine Smith.

Diamond, Henry L., and Patrick F. Noonan. 1996. *Land use in America*. Washington, DC: Island Press.

Dickinson, Robert E. 1964. *City and region: A geographical interpretation*. London: Routledge and Kegan Paul.

Dimond, Paul R. 2000. Empowering families to vote with their feet. In *Reflections on regionalism*, ed. Bruce Katz, 249–71. Washington, DC: Brookings Institution Press.

Dobbs, David, and Richard Ober. 1996. *The Northern Forest*. White River Junction, VT: Chelsea Green Publishing Company.

Doremus, Holly. 2006. Lesssons learned. In *The Endangered Species Act at thirty: Renewing the conservation promise*, eds. Dale D. Goble, J. Michael Scott, and Frank W. Davis, vol. 1, 195–207. Washington, DC: Island Press.

Dowie, Mark. 1996. *Losing ground: American environmentalism at the close of the twentieth century*. Cambridge, MA: The MIT Press.

Downs, Anthony. 1972. Up and down with ecology—The "issue-attention cycle." *Public Interest* 28:38–50.

———. 2001. What does "smart growth" really mean? *Planning* 67(4):20–25.

———, ed. 2004a. *Growth management and affordable housing: Do they conflict?* Washington, DC: Brookings Institution Press.

———. 2004b. Growth management, smart growth, and affordable housing. In *Growth management and affordable housing: Do they conflict?* ed. Anthony Downs, 264–74. Washington, DC: Brookings Institution Press.

Dreher, Robert G.,and John D. Echeverria. 2006. *Kelo's unanswered questions: The policy debate over the use of eminent domain for economic development.* Washington, DC: Georgetown Environmental Law & Policy Institute, Georgetown University Law Center. www.law.georgetown.edu/gelpi/current_research/documents/GELPIReport_Kelo.pdf (accessed 12 April 2007).

Duane, Timothy P. 1997. Community participation in ecosystem management. *Ecology Law Quarterly* 24:771–97.

———. 1998. *Shaping the Sierra: Nature, culture, and conflict in the changing West.* Berkeley: University of California Press.

Duany, Andres, Elizabeth Plater-Zyberk, and Jeff Speck. 2000. *Suburban nation: The rise of sprawl and the decline of the American dream.* New York: North Point Press.

Duerksen, Christopher J., Donald L. Elliot, N. Thompson Hobbs, Erin Johnson, and James R. Miller. 1997. *Habitat protection planning: Where the wild things are.* Planning Advisory Service Report Number 470/471. Chicago: American Planning Association.

Dunlap, Riley E. 1992. Trends in public opinion toward environmental issues: 1965–1990. In *American environmentalism: The U.S. environmental movement, 1970–1990,* eds. Riley Dunlap and Angela Mertig, 89–116. New York: Taylor and Francis.

Dunlap, Riley. 2002. An enduring concern: Light stays green for environmental protection. *Public Perspective* 13:10–14.

Dyballa, Cynthia D. 1979. *Regionalism in the Catskills: A political analysis.* Ithaca, NY: Cornell University, Center for Environmental Research.

Dyballa, Cynthia D., Lyle S. Raymond Jr., and Alan J. Hahn. 1981. *The Tug Hill program.* Syracuse, NY: Syracuse University Press.

Earth Liberation Front. 2007. Home page, www.earthliberationfront.com (accessed 12 April 2007).

Echeverria, John D., and Jon T. Zeidler. 1999. *Barely standing: The erosion of citizen "standing" to sue to enforce federal environmental law.* Washington, DC: Georgetown University Environmental Policy Project. www.law.georgetown.edu/gelpi/research_archive/standing/BarelyStanding.pdf (accessed 12 April 2007).

Ecocity Cleveland. 2006. Home page, www.ecocitycleveland.org (accessed 12 April 2007).

EDAW Inc. 2006. *Big Darby Accord watershed master plan.* San Francisco: EDAW Inc. assets.columbus.gov/Council/initiative/BigDarbyAccordFinalReport.pdf (accessed 12 April 2007).

Egan, Timothy. 2006. Oregon's property rights law kicks in, easing rigid rules. *New York Times,* 25 July.

Emerson, Kirk. 1996. Taking the land rights movement seriously. In *A wolf in the garden: The land rights movement and the new environmental debate*, eds. Philip D. Brick and R. McGreggor Cawley, 115–34. Lanham, MD: Rowman & Littlefield.

Endicott, Eve, ed. 1993. *Land conservation through public/private partnerships*. Washington, DC: Island Press.

Ericksen, Neil J., Philip R. Berke, Janet L. Crawford, and Jennifer E. Dixon. 2004. *Plan-making for sustainability: The New Zealand experience*. Aldershot, UK: Ashgate.

Erickson, Donna. 2004. Connecting lines across the landscape: Implementing metropolitan greenway networks in North America. In *Ecological networks and greenways: New paradigms for ecological planning*, eds. Rob H. G. Jongman and Gloria Pungetti, 200–221. Cambridge: Cambridge University Press.

Ernst, Howard R. 2003. *Chesapeake Bay blues: Science, politics, and the struggle to save the bay*. Lanham, MD: Rowman & Littlefield.

Ethridge, Marcus E. 1987. Procedures for citizen involvement in environmental policy: An assessment of policy effects. In *Citizen participation in public decision making*, eds. Jack DeSario and Stuart Langton, 115–31. New York: Greenwood Press.

Eugster, J. Glenn. 2003. Evolution of the heritage areas movement. *The George Wright Forum* 20(2):50–59.

Ewing, Reid. 1997. Is Los Angeles–style sprawl desirable? *Journal of the American Planning Association* 63:107–26.

Fabos, J. G. 2004. Greenway planning in the United States: Its origins and recent case studies. *Landscape and Urban Planning* 68:321–42.

Fagence, Michael. 1977. *Citizen participation in planning*. Oxford: Pergamon Press.

Fairfax, Sally K., Louise P. Fortmann, Ann Hawkins, Lynn Huntsinger, Nancy Lee Peluso, and Steven A. Wolf. 1999. The federal forests are not what they seem: Formal and informal claims to federal lands. *Ecology Law Quarterly* 25:630–46.

Fairfax, Sally K., Lauren Gwin, Mary Ann King, Leigh Raymond, and Laura A. Watt. 2005. *Buying nature: The limits of land acquisition as a conservation strategy, 1780–2004*. Cambridge, MA: The MIT Press.

Featherstone, Jeffrey P. 1996. Water resources coordination and planning at the federal level: The need for integration. *Water Resources Update* 104:52–54.

Fiorina, Morris P. 1999. Extreme voices: A dark side of civic engagement. In *Civic engagement in American democracy*, eds. Theda Skocpol and Morris P. Fiorina, 395–426. Washington, DC: Brookings Institution Press. Brookings.nap.edu/books/0815728093/html/index.html (accessed 12 April 2007).

Fischer, Michael L. 1985. California's coastal program: Larger-than-local interests built in to local plans. *Journal of the American Planning Association* 51:312–21.

Fisher, Robert A. 2000–2001. Better America Bonds: Better is in the eye of the beholder. *William & Mary Environmental Law and Policy Review* 25:233–60.

Fitzsimmons, Allan K. 1998. Why a policy of federal management and protection of ecosystems is a bad idea. *Landscape and Urban Planning* 40:195–202.

Florida, Richard L. 2005. *Cities and the creative class*. New York: Routledge.

Foreman, Dave. 1991. *Confessions of an eco-warrior*. New York: Harmony Books.

———. 2004. *Rewilding North America: A vision for conservation in the 21st century*. Washington, DC: Island Press.

Foreman, Dave, and Bill Haywood, eds. 1993. *Ecodefense: A field guide to monkey-wrenching*. Chico, CA: Abbzug Press.

Foresta, Ronald A. 1981. *Open space policy: New Jersey's Green Acres Program*. New Brunswick, NJ: Rutgers University Press.

———. 1984. *America's national parks and their keepers*. Washington, DC: Resources for the Future.

———. 1987. The transformation of the Appalachian Trail. *Geographical Review* 77:76–86.

Forester, John. 1999. *The deliberative practitioner: Encouraging participatory planning processes*. Cambridge, MA: The MIT Press

France, Robert L. 2006. *Introduction to watershed development: Understanding and managing the impacts of sprawl*. Lanham, MD: Rowman & Littlefield.

Freemuth, John, and R. McGreggor Cawley. 1998. Science, expertise, and the public: The politics of ecosystem management in the greater Yellowstone ecosystem. *Landscape and Urban Planning* 40:211–19.

Friedmann, John, and Clyde Weaver. 1979. *Territory and function: The evolution of regional planning*. Berkeley: University of California Press.

Frumkin, Howard, Lawrence Frank, and Richard Jackson. 2004. *Urban sprawl and public health: Designing, planning, and building for healthy communities*. Washington, DC: Island Press.

Fulton, William. 1991. The second revolution in land use planning. In *Balanced growth: A planning guide for local government*, ed. John M. DeGrove. Washington, DC: International City Management Association.

Fulton, William, Rolf Pendall, Mai Nguyen, and Alicia Harrison. 2001. Who sprawls most? How growth patterns differ across the U.S. Washington, DC: Brookings Institution Center on Urban & Metropolitan Policy. www.knowledgeplex.org/kp/facts_and_figures/facts_and_figures/relfiles/bi_fulton_sprawls.pdf (accessed 12 April 2007).

Funders' Network for Smart Growth and Livable Communities. 2007. Home page, www.fundersnetwork.org (accessed 12 April 2007).

Furuseth, Owen J., and Robert E. Altman. 1991. Who's on the greenway: Socio-economic, demographic, and locational characteristics of greenway users. *Environmental Management* 15:329–36.

Furuseth, Owen J., and Chris Cocklin. 1995. An institutional framework for sustainable resource management: The New Zealand model. *Natural Resources Journal* 35:243–73.

Furuseth, Owen J., and John T. Pierce. 1982. A comparative analysis of farmland preservation programmes in North America. *Canadian Geographer* 26:191–206.

Gale, Dennis E. 1992. Eight state-sponsored growth management programs: A comparative analysis. *Journal of the American Planning Association* 58:425–39.

Galston, William A., and Peter Levine. 1998. America's civic condition: A glance at the evidence. In *Community works: The revival of civil society in America*, ed. E. J. Dionne, 30–36. Washington, DC: Brookings Institution Press. brookings.nap.edu/books/0815718675/html/index.html (accessed 12 April 2007).

Garreau, Joel. 1981. *The nine nations of North America*. Boston: Houghton Mifflin.

———. 1991. *Edge city: Life on the new frontier*. New York: Doubleday.

General Services Administration. 2007. The Catalog of Federal Domestic Assistance. http://12.46.245.173/cfda/cfda.html 12.46.245.173/cfda/cfda.html (accessed 12 April 2007).

Gillham, Oliver. 2002. *The limitless city: A primer on the urban sprawl debate*. Washington, DC: Island Press.

Gilroy, Leonard C. 2006. *Statewide regulatory takings reform: Exporting Oregon's Measure 37 to other states*. Los Angeles: Reason Foundation. www.reason.org/ps343.pdf (accessed 12 April 2007).

Giuliano, Genevieve. 2004. Where is the "region" in regional planning? In *Up against the sprawl: Public policy and the making of Southern California*, eds. Jennifer Wolch, Manuel Pastor Jr., and Peter Dreier, 151–70. Minneapolis: University of Minnesota Press.

Glikson, Artur. 1971. *The ecological basis of planning*. Lewis Mumford, ed. The Hague: Martinus Nijhoff.

Godschalk, David E. 2004. Land use planning challenges: Coping with conflicts in visions of sustainable development and livable communities. *Journal of the American Planning Association* 70:5–13.

Godschalk, David R. 2003. Book review: Growing smart legislative guidebook: Model statutes for planning and the management of change. *Journal of the American Planning Association* 69:99–100.

Gordon, Peter, and Harry W. Richardson. 1997. Are compact cities a desirable planning goal? *Journal of the American Planning Association* 63:95–106.

Gordon, William R., Jr. 1984. The Coastal Barrier Resources Act of 1982: An assessment of legislative intent, process, and exemption alternatives. *Coastal Zone Management Journal* 12:257–86.

Gore, Al. 2006. *An inconvenient truth: The planetary emergency of global warming and what we can do about it.* Emmaus, PA: Rodale.

Gottlieb, Alan M., ed. 1989. *The wise use agenda.* Bellevue, WA: Free Enterprise Press.

Gottlieb, Robert. 2001. *Environmentalism unbound: Exploring new pathways for change.* Cambridge, MA: The MIT Press.

———. 2005. *Forcing the spring: The transformation of the American environmental movement.* Washington, DC: Island Press.

Governors' Task Force on Northern Forest Lands. 1990. *The Northern Forest lands: A strategy for their future.* No Location: Author.

Graham, Frank J., Jr. 1978. *The Adirondack Park: A political history.* New York: Knopf.

Grant, Jane A. 2003. *Community, democracy, and the environment.* Lanham, MD: Rowman & Littlefield.

Gray, Barbara. 1989. *Collaborating: Finding common ground for multiparty problems.* San Francisco: Jossey-Bass.

Gray, Gerald J., Maia J. Enzer, and Jonathan Kusel. 2001. Understanding community-based forest ecosystem management: An editorial synthesis. In *Understanding community-based forest ecosystem management*, eds. Gerald J. Gray, Maia J. Enzer, and Jonathan Kusel, 1–23. Binghamton, NY: Food Products Press.

Gray, Lewis C., et al. 1924. Utilization of our lands for crops, pasture and forests. In *Agriculture yearbook 1923*, U.S. Department of Agriculture, 415–506. Washington, DC: U.S. Government Printing Office.

Gray, Robert J., et al. 1981. *National agricultural lands study final report.* Washington, DC: U.S. Government Printing Office.

Great Plains Restoration Council. 2007. Home page, www.gprc.org (accessed 12 April 2007).

Greenhouse, Steven. 2006. Steelworkers and Sierra Club unite. *New York Times*, 8 June.

Gregory, Robin. 2000. Using stakeholder values to make Smarter environmental decisions. *Environment* 42(5):34–44.

Grima, A. P., and R. J. Mason. 1983. Apples and oranges: Toward a critique of public participation in Great Lakes futures. *Canadian Water Resources Journal* 8:22–50.

Grumbine, R. Edward, ed. 1994a. *Environmental policy and biodiversity.* Washington, DC: Island Press.

Grumbine, R. Edward. 1994b. What is ecosystem management? *Conservation Biology* 8:27–38.

——. 1997. Reflections on "What is ecosystem management?" *Conservation Biology* 11:41–47.

Grunwald, Michael. 2006. *The swamp: The Everglades, Florida, and the politics of paradise.* New York: Simon & Schuster.

Grunwald, Michael, and Susan B. Glasser. 2005. The slow drowning of New Orleans. *Washington Post*, 9 October.

Guber, Deborah Lynn. 2003. *The grassroots of a green revolution: Polling America on the environment.* Cambridge, MA: The MIT Press.

Gunderson, Lance H., C. S. Holling, and Stephen S. Light, eds. 1995. *Barriers & bridges to the renewal of ecosystems and institutions.* New York: Columbia University Press.

Gundry, Kathleen G., and Thomas A. Heberlein. 1984. Do public meetings represent the public? *Journal of the American Planning Association* 50:175–82.

Gurwitt, Rob. 1999. The state vs. sprawl. *Governing* 12(4):18–23.

Guttenberg, Albert Z. 1973. *The land use movement of the 1920s: A bibliographic essay.* Exchange Bibliography No. 462. Monticello, IL: Council of Planning Librarians.

Haeuber, Richard. 1996. Setting the environmental policy agenda: The case of ecosystem management. *Natural Resources Journal* 36:1–28.

Hall, Peter. 2002. *Cities of tomorrow: An intellectual history of urban design and planning in the twentieth century*, 3rd ed. Oxford: Blackwell.

Hamin, Elisabeth M. 2001. The U.S. National Park Service's partnership parks: Collaborative responses to middle landscapes. *Land Use Policy* 18:123–35.

Harden, Blaine. 2005. Anti-sprawl laws, property rights collide in Oregon. *Washington Post*, 28 February.

Hardin, Garrett. 1968. The tragedy of the commons. *Science* 162:1243–48.

Harper, Stephen C., Laura L. Falk, and Edward W. Rankin. 1990. *The Northern Forest lands study of New England and New York.* Rutland, VT: U.S. Department of Agriculture, Forest Service.

Harris, Glenn R., and Michael G. Jarvis. 2004. *A history of planning in the Adirondack Park: The enduring conflict.* In *Big places, big plans*, eds. Mark B. Lapping and Owen J. Furuseth, 139–77. Aldershot, UK: Ashgate.

Hart, John. 1991. *Farming on the edge: Saving family farms in Marin County, California.* Berkeley: University of California Press.

Hartig, John H. 2002. A river runs through it. *Water Environment & Technology* 14(11):35–38.

Harwell, Mark A., John H. Gentile, Ann Bartuska, Christine C. Harwell, Victoria Myers, Jayantha Obeysekera, John C. Ogden, and Stephen C. Tosini. 1999.

A science-based strategy for ecological restoration in south Florida. *Urban Ecosystems* 3:201–22.

Hayduk, Ronald. 2003. Race and suburban sprawl: Regionalism and structural racism. In *Suburban sprawl: Culture, theory, and politics*, eds. Matthew J. Lindstrom and Hugh Bartling, 137–70. Lanham, MD: Rowman & Littlefield.

Hays, Samuel P. 1959. *Conservation and the gospel of efficiency: The progressive conservation movement, 1890–1920*. Cambridge, MA: Harvard University Press.

———. 1987. *Beauty, health, and permanence: Environmental politics in the United States, 1955–1985*. New York: Cambridge University Press.

———. 2000. *A history of environmental politics since 1945*. Pittsburgh: University of Pittsburgh Press.

Healey, Patsy. 2006. *Collaborative planning: Shaping places in fragmented societies*. 2nd ed. Houndmills, London: Palgrave Macmillan.

Healy, Robert G., ed. 1978. *Protecting the golden shore: Lessons from the California coastal commissions*. Washington, DC: Conservation Foundation.

Healy, Robert G., and John S. Rosenberg. 1979. *Land use and the states*. 2nd ed. Baltimore: Johns Hopkins University Press.

Heeter, David G. 1976. The Vermont experience. In *Environmental and land controls legislation*, ed. Daniel R. Mandelker, 323–91. Indianapolis: Bobbs-Merrill.

Heiman, Michael K. 1988. *The quiet evolution: Power, planning, and profits in New York State*. New York: Praeger.

———. 1990. From "Not in my backyard!" to "Not in anybody's backyard!" *Journal of the American Planning Association* 56:359–62.

Helvarg, David. 1994. *The war against the greens: The "wise-use" movement, the new right, and anti-environmental violence*. San Francisco: Sierra Club Books.

Highlands Coalition. 2007. Home page, www.highlandscoalition.org/home.htm (accessed 12 April 2007).

Hill, Jason, Erik Nelson, David Tilman, Stephen Polasky, and Douglas Tiffany. 2006. Environmental, economic, and energetic costs and benefits of biodiesel and ethanol biofuels. *Proceedings of the National Academy of Sciences* 103:11206–10. www.pnas.org/cgi/reprint/0604600103v1 (accessed 12 April 2007).

Hirner, Dierdre K. 1985. *Public parks on private lands: Greenline parks protecting landscapes of national significance*. PhD dissertation, Texas Tech University.

Hiss, Tony. 1990. *The experience of place*. New York: Knopf.

Hocker, Jean W. 1996. Patience, problem solving, and private initiative: Local groups chart a new course for land conservation. In *Land use in America*, eds. Henry L. Diamond and Patrick F. Noonan, 245–59. Washington, DC: Island Press.

Holling, C. S. 1978. *Adaptive environmental assessment and management.* London: John Wiley.

Horton, Tom. 2003. *Turning the tide: Saving the Chesapeake Bay.* Washington, DC: Island Press.

House, John W. 1983. Regional and area development. In *United States public policy: A geographical view*, ed. John W. House, 34–79. Oxford: Clarendon House.

Hudson River Valley Greenway Communities Council Greenway Conservancy for the Hudson River Valley, Inc. 1997. *The Hudson River Valley Greenway Act of 1991 (revised as of November 1997).* Albany, NY: Hudson River Valley Greenway Communities Council Greenway Conservancy for the Hudson River Valley, Inc. www.hudsongreenway.state.ny.us/commcoun/HRVG%20 Legislation.pdf (accessed 12 April 2007).

Imperial, Mark T., and Timothy Hennessey. 2000. *Environmental governance in watersheds: The importance of collaboration to institutional performance.* Washington, DC: National Academy of Public Administration. www.napawash .org/pc_economy_environment/epafile08.pdf (accessed 12 April 2007).

Innes, Judith E. 1996. Planning through consensus building: A new view of the comprehensive planning ideal. *Journal of the American Planning Association* 62:460–72.

Innes, Judith E., and David E. Booher. 1999a. Consensus building and complex adaptive systems. *Journal of the American Planning Association* 65:9–26.

———. 1999b. Consensus building as role playing and bricolage: Toward a theory of collaborative planning. *Journal of the American Planning Association* 65:412–23.

———. 2004. Reframing public participation: Strategies for the 21st century. *Planning Theory & Practice* 5:419–36.

Innes, Judith E., and Jane Rongerude. 2006. *Collaborative regional initiatives: Civic entrepreneurs work to fill the governance gap.* Working Paper 2006–2004. Berkeley: Institute of Urban and Regional Development, University of California at Berkeley. www.irvine.org/assets/pdf/pubs/civic/insight_CRI.pdf (accessed 12 April 2007).

Institute for Community Economics. 2007. Community land trusts. www.iceclt .org/clt (accessed 12 April 2007).

Interagency Wild and Scenic Rivers Coordinating Council. 2004. *Wild & scenic rivers reference guide.* Washington, DC: National Park Service. www.rivers.gov/ publications.html (accessed 12 April 2007).

Irvin, Renée A., and John Stansbury. 2004. Citizen participation in decision making: Is it worth the effort? *Public Administration Review* 64:55–65.

Isenberg, Andrew C. 2000. *The destruction of the bison: An environmental history, 1750–1920.* Cambridge: Cambridge University Press.

Jackson, Kenneth T. 1985. *Crabgrass frontier: The suburbanization of the United States*. New York: Oxford University Press.

Jackson, Philip L., and Robert Kuhlken. 2006. *A rediscovered frontier: Land use and resource issues in the new west*. Lanham, MD: Rowman & Littlefield.

Jerry, Anthony. 2003. The effects of Florida's growth management act on housing affordability. *Journal of the American Planning Association* 69:282–95.

John, DeWitt. 1994. *Civic environmentalism: Alternatives to regulation in states and communities*. Washington, DC: CQ Press.

Johnson, Bart R., and Ronald Campbell. 1999. Ecology and participation in landscape-based planning within the Pacific Northwest. *Policy Studies Journal* 27:502–29.

Johnson, Denny, ed. 2002. *Planning for smart growth: 2002 state of the states*. Chicago: American Planning Association. www.planning.org/growingsmart/pdf/states2002.pdf (accessed 12 April 2007).

Jonas, Andrew E. G., and David Wilson. 1999. The city as growth machine: Critical reflections two decades later. In *The urban growth machine: Critical perspectives two decades later*, eds. Andrew E. G. Jonas and David Wilson. Albany: State University of New York Press.

Jones, Lisa. 1996. Some not-so-easy steps to successful collaboration. *High Country News* 28(9), 13 May. www.hcn.org/servlets/hcn.Article?article_id=1840 (accessed 12 April 2007).

Judd, Richard W., and Christopher S. Beach. 2003. *Natural states: The environmental imagination in Maine, Oregon, and the nation*. Washington, DC: Resources for the Future.

Kagan, Robert A. 1997. Political and legal obstacles to collaborative ecosystem planning. *Ecology Law Quarterly* 24:871–75.

Kahn, Matthew E. 2001. Does sprawl reduce the black/white housing consumption gap? *Housing Policy Debate* 12:77–86.

Katz, Bruce, ed. 2000. *Reflections on regionalism*. Washington, DC: Brookings Institution Press. www.brook.edu/es/urban/reflections.htm (accessed 12 April 2007).

Kauffman, Kris G., and Alice Shorett. 1979. A perspective on public involvement in water management decision making. *Public Administration Review* 37:467–71.

Kayden, Jerold S. 2002. The constitution neither prohibits nor requires smart growth. In *Smart growth: Form and consequences*, eds. Terry S. Szold and Armando Carbonell, 158–79. Cambridge, MA: Lincoln Institute of Land Policy.

Keiter, Robert B., and Mark S. Boyce, eds. 1991. *The greater Yellowstone ecosystem: Redefining America's wilderness heritage*. New Haven, CT: Yale University Press.

REFERENCES

Kemmis, Daniel. 1990. *Community and the politics of place.* Norman: University of Oklahoma Press.

KenCairn, Brett. 1996. Peril on common ground: The Applegate experiment. In *A wolf in the garden: The land rights movement and the new environmental debate,* eds. Philip D. Brick and R. McGreggor Cawley, 261–77. Lanham, MD: Rowman & Littlefield.

Kenney, Douglas S. 1997. *Resource management at the watershed level: An assessment of the changing federal role in the emerging era of community-based watershed management.* Boulder: Natural Resources Law Center, University of Colorado School of Law. repository.unm.edu/dspace/bitstream/1928/2794/1/RESOURCE.pdf (accessed 12 April 2007).

———. 1999. Historical and sociopolitical context of the western watersheds movement. *Journal of the American Water Resources Association* 35:493–503.

———. 2000. *Arguing about consensus: Examining the case against western watershed initiatives and other collaborative groups active in natural resources management.* Boulder: Natural Resources Law Center, University of Colorado School of Law. www.colorado.edu/Law/centers/nrlc/publications/RR23.pdf (accessed 12 April 2007).

Kenney, Douglas S., Sean T. McAllister, William H. Caile, and Jason S. Peckham. 2000. *The new watershed source book: A directory and review of watershed initiatives in the western United States.* Boulder: Natural Resources Law Center, University of Colorado School of Law. www.colorado.edu/law/centers/nrlc/publications/Watershed_Chapters/Cover.pdf (accessed 12 April 2007).

Kingdon, John W. 2002. *Agendas, alternatives, and public policies.* 2nd ed. New York: Longman.

Kitch, Mary Pitman. 2007. This land is whose land? *The Oregonian,* 11 February.

Kline, Jeffrey D. 2000. Comparing states with and without growth management analysis based on indicators with policy implications comment. *Land Use Policy* 17:349–55.

Klyza, Christopher McGrory. 1994. The Northern Forest: Problems, politics, and alternatives. In *The future of the Northern Forest,* ed. Christopher McGrory Klyza, 36–51. Hanover, NH: University Press of New England.

Klyza, Christopher McGrory, ed. 2001. *Wilderness comes home: Rewilding the Northeast.* Hanover, NH: University Press of New England.

Knight, Peyton. 2006. The journey through Hallowed Ground National Heritage Area: An example of how pork-barrel politics can threaten local rule and property rights. *National Policy Analysis* 540. www.nationalcenter.org/NPA540HallowedGround.html (accessed 12 April 2007).

Knight, Richard L. 1998. Ecosystem management and conservation biology. *Landscape and Urban Planning* 40:41–45.

Knight, Richard L., Wendell C. Gilgert, and Ed Marston, eds. 2002. *Ranching west of the 100th meridian: Culture, ecology, and economics.* Washington, DC: Island Press.

Knopman, Debra S., Megan M. Susman, and Marc K. Landy. 1999. Tackling tough land-use problems with innovative governance. *Environment* 24–32.

Knott, Catherine Henshaw. 1998. *Living with the Adirondack Forest: Local perspectives on land use conflicts.* Ithaca, NY: Cornell University Press.

Konisky, David M., and Thomas C. Beierle. 2001. Innovations in public participation and environmental decision making: Examples from the Great Lakes region. *Society and Natural Resources*: 14:815–26.

Koontz, Tomas M., Toddi A. Steelman, JoAnn Carmin, Katrina Smith Korfmacher, Cassandra Moseley, and Craig W. Thomas. 2004. *Collaborative environmental management: What roles for government?* Washington, DC: Resources for the Future.

Krueckeberg, Donald A. 1983. *Introduction to planning history in the United States.* New Brunswick, NJ: Rutgers University Center for Urban Policy Research.

Land Trust Alliance. 2006. *National land trust census report.* Washington, DC: Land Trust Alliance. www.lta.org/aboutlt/census.shtml (accessed 12 April 2007).

———. 2007a. *Publications.* www.lta.org/publications (accessed 12 April 2007).

———. 2007b. *Resources for land trusts.* www.lta.org/resources (accessed 12 April 2007).

Landy, Marc K., Megan M. Susman, and Debra S. Knopman. 1999. *Civic environmentalism in action: A field guide to regional and local initiatives.* Washington, DC: Progressive Policy Institute Center for Innovation and the Environment. www.ppionline.org/ppi_ci.cfm?knlgAreaID=115&subsecID=900025&contentID=1059 (accessed 12 April 2007).

Lange, Jonathan I. 1996. The logic of competing information campaigns: Conflict over old growth and the spotted owl. In *A wolf in the garden: The land rights movement and the new environmental debate*, eds. Philip D. Brick and R. McGreggor Cawley, 135–50. Lanham, MD: Rowman & Littlefield.

Langton, Stuart. 1978a. Citizen participation in America: Current reflections on the state of the art. In *Citizen participation in America: Essays on the state of the art*, ed. Stuart Langton, 1–12. Lexington, MA: Lexington Books.

———. 1978b. What is citizen participation? In *Citizen participation in America: Essays on the state of the art*, ed. Stuart Langton, 13–24. Lexington, MA: Lexington Books.

Layzer, Judith. 2006. *The environmental case: Translating values into policy.* 2nd ed. Washington, DC: CQ Press.

Leach, William D., and Neil W. Pelkey. 2001. Making watershed partnerships work: A review of the empirical literature. *Journal of Water Resources Planning and Management* 127:378–85.

League of Conservation Voters. 2006. *The national environmental scorecard.* www.lcv.org/scorecard (accessed 12 April 2007).

Lee, Kai N. 1989. The Columbia River Basin: Experimenting with sustainability. *Environment* 31(6):6–11, 30–33.

———. 1993. *Compass and gyroscope: Integrating science and politics for the environment.* Washington, DC: Island Press.

Lehman, Tim. 1995. *Public values, private lands: Farmland preservation policy, 1933–1985.* Chapel Hill: University of North Carolina Press.

Leo, Christopher, Mary Ann Beavis, Andrew Carver, and Robyne Turner. 1998. Is urban sprawl back on the political agenda? Local growth control, regional growth management, and politics. *Urban Affairs Review* 34 (2):179–212.

Leopold, Aldo. 1949. *A Sand County almanac, and sketches here and there.* New York: Oxford University Press.

Levitt, James N., ed. 2002. *Conservation in the Internet age: Threats and opportunities.* Washington, DC: Island Press.

Lewis, Thomas A. 1995. Cloaked in a wise disguise. In *Let the people judge: Wise use and the property rights movement,* 13–20. Washington, DC: Island Press.

Licht, Daniel S. 1997. *Ecology & economics of the Great Plains.* Lincoln: University of Nebraska Press.

Lichtman, Pamela, and Tim W. Clark. 1994. Rethinking the "Vision" exercise in the greater Yellowstone ecosystem. *Society and Natural Resources* 7:450–78.

Lindstrom, Matthew J., and Hugh Bartling, eds. 2003. *Suburban sprawl: Culture, theory, and politics.* Lanham, MD: Rowman & Littlefield.

Linowes, R. Robert, and Don T. Allensworth. 1975. *The states and land-use control.* New York: Praeger.

Lioz, Adam. 2001. *Land use in Pennsylvania: An analysis of changes to Pennsylvania's municipalities planning code in 2000.* Philadelphia: PennEnvironment.

Liroff, Richard A., and G. Gordon Davis. 1981. *Protecting open space: Land use controls in the Adirondack Park.* Cambridge, MA: Ballinger.

List, Peter C. 1993. *Radical environmentalism: Philosophy and tactics.* Belmont, CA: Wadsworth Publishing Company.

Litt, Jill S., Nga L. Tran, and Thomas A. Burke. 2002. Examining urban brownfields through the public health "Macroscope." *Environmental Health Perspectives* 110(Supplement 2):183–93.

Little, Charles E. 1990. *Greenways for America.* Baltimore: Johns Hopkins University Press.

Livable Communities. 2000. *Livable communities: Sustaining prosperity, improving quality of life, building a sense of community.* Washington, DC: Livable Communities. www.dnr.sc.gov/water/envaff/flood/img/report2knew.pdf (accessed 12 April 2007).

Locke, Harvey. 2000. The Wildlands Project: A balanced approach to sharing North America. *Wild Earth,* Spring:1–5.

Logan, John R., and Harvey Molotch. 1987. *Urban fortunes: The political economy of place.* Berkeley: University of California Press.

Lone Mountain Coalition. 2000. *The Lone Mountain Compact: Principles for preserving freedom and livability in America's cities and suburbs.* www.pacificresearch.org/pub/sab/enviro/lonemtn.html (accessed 12 April 2007).

Long, Frederick J., and Matthew B. Arnold. 1995. *The power of environmental partnerships.* Forth Worth, IN: The Dryden Press.

Louisiana Coast Wetlands Conservation and Restoration Task Force and the Wetlands Conservation and Restoration Authority. 1998. *Coast 2050: Toward A sustainable coastal Louisiana.* Baton Rouge: Louisiana Department of Natural Resources. coast2050.gov/2050reports.htm (accessed 12 April 2007).

Luccarelli, Mark. 1997. *Lewis Mumford and the ecological region: The politics of planning.* New York: Guilford Press.

Lyday, Noreen. 1976. *The law of the land: Debating national land use legislation 1970–75.* Washington, DC: Urban Institute.

Malmsheimer, Robert W., William R. Bentley, and Donald W. Floyd. 2000. *The implementation of the Northern Forest Lands Council's recommendations: An analysis six years later.* Syracuse: The State University of New York College of Environmental Science and Forestry. www.northernforestlands.org/publications/AssessmentReport_2.8.01.pdf (accessed 12 April 2007).

Mandelker, Daniel R. 1976. *Environmental and land use controls legislation.* Indianapolis: Bobbs-Merrill.

———. 1989. The quiet revolution—Success and failure. *Journal of the American Planning Association* 55:204–5.

Manes, Christopher. 1990. *Green rage: Radical environmentalism and the unmaking of civilization.* Boston: Little, Brown.

Manning, Richard. 1997. Working the watershed. *High Country News* 29(5), 17 March. www.hcn.org/servlets/hcn.Article?article_id=3357 (accessed 12 March 2007).

Mansur, Jean. 2000. Spending to save farmland draws critics. *Newark Star-Ledger,* 2 April.

Manzo, Lynne C., and Douglas D. Perkins. 2006. Finding common ground: The importance of place attachment to community participation and planning." *Journal of Planning Literature* 20:335–50.

REFERENCES

Marin Agricultural Land Trust. 2007. Home page, www.malt.org (accessed 12 April 2007).

Marsh, Elizabeth R. 1981. *Cooperative rural planning: A Tug Hill case study.* Watertown, NY: Temporary State Commission on Tug Hill.

Marston, Ed. 2000. Squishy soft processes—Hard results. *High Country News* 32 (16), 28 August. www.hcn.org/servlets/hcn.Article?article_id=5981 (accessed 12 April 2007).

Maryland Department of Natural Resources. 2007. Chesapeake Bay 2000: "The renewed Bay Agreement." dnrweb.dnr.state.md.us/bay/res_protect/c2k (accessed 12 April 2007).

Maryland Department of Planning. 2007. *Office of smart growth.* www.mdp .state.md.us (accessed 12 April 2007).

"Maryland Smart Growth Laws Having an Impact." 2002. *New Urban News* 5 (7). www.newurbannews.com/maryland.html (accessed 12 April 2007).

Mason, Robert J. 1992a. *Contested lands: Conflict and compromise in New Jersey's pine barrens.* Philadelphia: Temple University Press.

———. 1992b. Defining and protecting rural environments in the U.S. In *Contemporary rural systems in transition. Vol. 2: Economy and society*, eds. Ian R. Bowler, Christopher R. Bryant, and N. Duane Nellis, 129–40. Wallingford, UK: CAB International.

———. 1994. The greenlining of America. *Land Use Policy* 11:208–21.

———. 1995a. Sustainability, regional planning and the future of New York's Adirondack Park. *Progress in Rural Policy & Planning* 5:15–28.

———. 1995b. Saving place: Land trusts as conservators of local and regional landscapes. *Small Town* 26(2):14–19.

———. 2004. *The Pinelands.* In *Big places, big plans*, eds. Mark B. Lapping and Owen J. Furuseth, 27–51. Aldershot, UK: Ashgate.

———. 2005. Confronting sprawl in southeastern Pennsylvania: New options for communities. *Temple University Environmental Law & Technology Journal* 23:23–40.

Mason, Robert J., and Mark T. Mattson. 1990. *Atlas of United States environmental issues.* New York: Macmillan.

Mason, Robert J., William D. Solecki, and Enid L. Lotstein. 1987. Comment on "On 'bioregionalism' and 'watershed consciousness.'" *The Professional Geographer* 39:67–68.

Matthews, Anne. 2002. *Where the buffalo roam: Restoring America's Great Plains.* 2nd ed. Chicago: University of Chicago Press.

McAllister, Donald M. 1980. *Evaluation in environmental planning: Assessing environmental, social, economic, and political trade-offs.* Cambridge, MA: The MIT Press.

McCally, David. 1999. *The Everglades: An environmental history*. Gainesville: University Press of Florida.

McCann, Barbara A., and Reid Ewing. 2003. *Measuring the health effects of sprawl: A national analysis of physical activity, obesity, and chronic disease*. Washington, DC: Smart Growth America. www.smartgrowthamerica.org/report/ HealthSprawl8.03.pdf (accessed 12 April 2007).

McCarthy, James. 2002. First world political ecology: Lessons from the wise use movement. *Environment and Planning A* 34:1281–302.

McCarthy, John D., and Mayer Zald. 1973. *The trend of social movements in America: Professionalization and resource mobilization*. Morristown, NJ: General Learning Press.

McCloskey, Michael. 1999. Local communities and the management of public forests. *Ecology Law Quarterly* 25:624–29.

McComas, Katherine A., and Clifford W. Scherer. 1998. Reassessing public meetings as participation in risk management decisions. *Risk: Health, Safety and Environment* 9:347–60.

McCool, Stephen F., and Kathleen Guthrie. 2001. Mapping the dimensions of successful public participation in messy natural resource management situations. *Society and Natural Resources* 14:309–23.

McGinnis, Michael Vincent, ed. 1999. *Bioregionalism*. London: Routledge.

McGinnis, Michael Vincent, John Woolley, and John Gamman. 1999. Bioregional conflict resolution: Rebuilding community in watershed planning and organizing. *Environmental Management* 24:1–12.

McHarg, Ian. 1995. *Design with nature*. New York: John Wiley & Sons.

McKinney, Matthew, and William Harmon. 2004. *The western confluence: A guide to governing natural resources*. Washington, DC: Island Press.

McMartin, Barbara. 2002. *Perspectives on the Adirondacks: A thirty-year struggle by people protecting their treasure*. Syracuse, NY: Syracuse University Press.

McMillion, Scott. 2006. Wolf killings: Rancher, predator detente has limits. *Bozeman Daily Chronicle*.

McNeely, Jeffrey A., ed. 1995. *Expanding partnerships in conservation*. Washington, DC: Island Press.

Meck, Stuart, ed. 2002. *Growing smart legislative guidebook: Model statutes for planning and the management of change*. Chicago: American Planning Association.

Meffe, Gary K., Larry A. Nielsen, Richard L. Knight, and Dennis A. Schenborn. 2002. *Ecosystem management: Adaptive, community-based conservation*. Washington, DC: Island Press.

Melosi, Martin V. 1981. *Garbage in the cities: Refuse, reform, and the environment, 1880–1980*. College Station: Texas A&M University Press.

REFERENCES

Merchant, Carolyn. 1992. *Radical ecology: The search for a livable world*. New York: Routledge.

———. 2002. *The Columbia guide to American environmental history*. New York: Columbia University Press.

Meridian Institute. 2001. *Final report of the national watershed forum June 27–July 1, 2001, Arlington, Virginia*. Dillon, CO: Meridian Institute. www.epa.gov/owow/forum/finalrpt.pdf (accessed 12 April 2007).

Michaels, Joseph A., Robert L. Neville, David Edelman, Time Sullivan, and Leslie A. DiCola. 1992. *New York–New Jersey Highlands regional study*. Radnor, PA: U.S. Department of Agriculture Forest Service.

Michaels, Sarah. 1999. Configuring who does what in watershed management: The Massachusetts Watershed Initiative. *Policy Studies Journal* 27:565–77.

———. 2001. Making collaborative watershed management work: The confluence of state and regional initiatives. *Environmental Management* 27:27–35.

Michaels, Sarah, and Owen Furuseth. 1997. Innovation in environmental policy: The National Environmental Policy Act of the U.S. and the Resource Management Act of New Zealand. *The Environmentalist* 17:181–90.

Michaels, Sarah, Robert J. Mason, and William D. Solecki. 1999. Motivations for ecostewardship partnerships: Examples from the Adirondack Park. *Land Use Policy* 16:1–9.

———. 2001. Participatory research on collaborative environmental management: Results from the Adirondack Park. *Society and Natural Resources* 14:251–55.

Miller, Char. 2001. *Gifford Pinchot and the making of modern American environmentalism*. Washington, DC: Island Press/Shearwater Books.

Millersville University Center for Opinion Research. 2001. *Metropolitan Philadelphia policy survey: Summary of findings*. Millersville, PA: Millersville University Center for Opinion Research.

Mitchell, Alison E. 1992. *The New Jersey Highlands: Treasures at risk*. Morristown: New Jersey Conservation Foundation.

Mogulof, Melvin. 1975. *Saving the coast: California's experiment in intergovernmental land use control*. Lexington, MA: Lexington Books.

Montgomery, David R., Gordon E. Grant, and Kathleen Sullivan. 1995. Watershed analysis as a framework for implementing ecosystem management. *Water Resources Bulletin* 31:369–86.

Moore, C. Nicholas. 1995. *Participation tools for better land-use planning: Techniques & case studies*. Sacramento, CA: Center for Livable Communities.

Moote, Margaret A., Mitchel P. McClaran, and Donna K. Chickering. 1997. Theory in practice: Applying partcipatory democracy theory to public land planning. *Environmental Management* 21:877–89.

More, Thomas A. 1996. Forestry's fuzzy concepts: An examination of ecosystem management. *Journal of Forestry* 94(8):19–23.

Mullner, Scott A., Wayne A. Hubert, and Thomas A. Wesche. 2001. Evolving paradigms for landscape-scale renewable resource management in the United States. *Environmental Science & Policy* 4:39–49.

Myers, Phyllis. 1976. *Zoning Hawaii: An analysis of the passage and implementation of Hawaii's Land Classification Law.* Washington, DC: Conservation Foundation.

———. 1999. *Livability at the ballot box: State and local referenda on parks, conservation, and smarter growth, election day 1998.* Washington, DC: Brookings Institution Center on Urban and Metropolitan Policy. www.brookings.edu/es/urban/myersexec.pdf (accessed 12 April 2007).

Myers, Phyllis, and Robert Puentes. 2000. *Growth at the ballot box: Electing the shape of communities in November 2000.* Washington, DC: Brookings Institution Center on Urban and Metropolitan Policy. www.brookings.edu/es/urban/ballotbox/finalreport.pdf (accessed 12 April 2007).

Naess, Arne. 1989. *Ecology, community, and lifestyle: Outline of an ecosophy.* New York: Cambridge University Press.

Napier, Ted L. 1998. Conservation coalitions cannot overcome poor conservation programming. *Journal of Soil and Water Conservation* 53:300–303.

Napier, Ted L., and Eric. J. Johnson. 1998. Impacts of voluntary conservation initiatives in the Darby Creek watershed of Ohio. *Journal of Soil and Water Conservation* 53(1):78–84.

Nash, Roderick. 1982. *Wilderness and the American mind.* 3rd ed. New Haven, CT: Yale University Press.

National Academy of Sciences. Commission on Geosciences, Environment, and Resources. 1999. *New strategies for America's watersheds.* Washington, DC: National Academies Press. books.nap.edu/catalog.php?record_id=6020 (accessed 12 April 2007).

National Association of Home Builders. 2002. *Smart growth: Building better places to live, work and play.* Washington, DC: National Association of Home Builders. www.nahb.org/publication_details.aspx?sectionID=154&publicationID=192 (accessed 12 April 2007).

National Governors Association. 2000. *Where do we grow from here: New mission for brownfields: Attacking sprawl by revitalizing older communities.* Washington, DC: National Governors Association. www.nga.org/Files/pdf/REPORT 200010BROWNFIELDS.pdf (accessed 12 April 2007).

National Governors Association. Center for Best Practices. 2001. *Issue brief: How smart growth can address environmental justice issues.* www.nga.org/cda/files/052201ENVIROJUS.pdf (accessed 12 April 2007).

REFERENCES

National Neighborhood Coalition. 2000. *Connecting neighborhood and region for smarter growth.* www.neighborhoodcoalition.org/pdfs/Lit 2001.pdf (accessed 12 April 2007).

———. n.d. *Smart growth for neighborhoods: Affordable housing and regional vision.* www.neighborhoodcoalition.org/pdfs/hsg report copy2.pdf (accessed 12 April 2007).

National Parks Conservation Association. 2002. *State of the parks: A resource assessment. Point Reyes National Seashore.* Washington, DC: National Parks Conservation Association. www.npca.org/stateoftheparks/point_reyes/ptReyes.pdf (accessed 12 April 2007).

National Research Council. Commission on Behavioral and Social Sciences and Education. 1996. *Understanding risk: Informing decisions in a democratic society.* Washington, DC: National Academies Press. www.nap.edu/books/030905396X/html (accessed 12 April 2007).

———. Committee to Evaluate Indicators for Monitoring Aquatic and Terrestrial Environments. 2000a. *Ecological indicators for the nation.* Washington, DC: National Academies Press. www.nap.edu/catalog.php?record_id=9720 (accessed 12 April 2007).

———. Committee to Review the New York City Watershed Management Strategy. 2000b. *Watershed management for potable water supply: Assessing the New York City strategy.* Washington, DC: National Academies Press. books.nap.edu/catalog.php?record_id=9677 (accessed 12 April 2007).

———. Committee on Assessing and Valuing the Services of Aquatic and Related Terrestrial Ecosystems. 2001a. *Valuing ecosystem services: Toward better environmental decision-making.* Washington, DC: National Academies Press. www.nap.edu/catalog.php?record_id=11139 (accessed 12 April 2007).

———. Committee to Assess the Scientific Basis of the Total Maximum Daily Load Approach to Water Pollution Reduction. 2001b. *Assessing the TMDL approach to water quality management.* Washington, DC: National Academies Press. www.nap.edu/catalog.php?record_id=10146 (accessed 12 April 2007).

———. Committee on the Restoration and Protection of Coastal Louisiana. 2006. *Drawing Louisiana's new map: Addressing land loss in coastal Louisiana.* Washington, DC: National Academies Press. www.nap.edu/catalog.php?record_id=11476 (accessed 12 April 2007).

National Transportation Enhancements Clearinghouse. 2002. *Enhancing America's communities: A guide to transportation enhancements.* Washington, DC: National Transportation Enhancements Clearinghouse. www.enhancements.org/misc/TEGuide2002.pdf (accessed 12 April 2007).

———. 2007a. *National TE project lists.* www.enhancements.org/projectlist.asp (accessed 12 April 2007).

———. 2007b. *Transportation enhancements: Summary of nationwide spending as of FY 2005.* Washington, DC: National Transportation Enhancements Clearinghouse. www.enhancements.org/misc/tedatafy05.pdf (accessed 12 April 2007).

Natural Lands Trust. 2005. The Highlands: New federal funding will boost land protection. *Natural Lands* 131:3–4.

———. 2007. Home page, www.natlands.org (accessed 12 April 2007).

Natural Resources Defense Council. 2006. Biogems: Saving endangered wild places. Home page, www.savebiogems.org (accessed 12 April 2007).

Neiman, M., and R. Loveridge. 1981. Environmentalism and local growth control: A probe into the class bias thesis. *Environment and Behavior* 13:759–72.

Nelson, Arthur C. 1999. Comparing states with and without growth management: Analysis based on indicators with policy implications. *Land Use Policy* 16:121–27.

Nelson, Arthur C., and Terry Moore. 1996. Assessing growth management policy implementation: Case study of the United States' leading growth management initiative. *Land Use Policy* 13:241–59.

Nelson, Arthur C., Rolf Pendall, Casey J. Dawkins, and Gerrit J. Knaap. 2002. *The link between growth management and housing affordability: The academic evidence.* Washington, DC: Brookings Institution Center on Urban and Metropolitan Policy. www.brookings.edu/es/urban/publications/growthmang.pdf (accessed 12 April 2007).

Nelson, Robert H. 1995. *Public lands and private rights: The failure of scientific management.* Lanham, MD: Rowman & Littlefield.

New Jersey Department of Environmental Protection. 2007a. *DEP guidance for the Highlands Water Protection & Planning Act.* www.nj.gov/dep/highlands (accessed 12 April 2007).

———. 2007b. Green Acres Program. Home page, www.state.nj.us/dep/greenacres (accessed 12 April 2007).

New Jersey Future 2000. *Survey of registered voters in New Jersey on suburban sprawl* Washington, DC: Belden, Russonello & Stewart. www.brspoll.com/Reports/NJ%20Future%20summary.pdf (accessed 12 April 2007).

New Jersey Highlands Council. 2007. Home page, www.highlands.state.nj.us/njhighlands (accessed 12 April 2007).

New Jersey Pinelands Commission. 1980. *Comprehensive management plan for the Pinelands National Reserve and Pinelands Area.* New Lisbon: New Jersey Pinelands Commission. www.state.nj.us/pinelands/images/pdf%20files/CMP_8_21_06.pdf (accessed 12 April 2007).

REFERENCES

New Jersey State Planning Commission. 2001. *Communities of place: The New Jersey State Development and Redevelopment Plan.* Trenton: New Jersey State Planning Commission. www.nj.gov/dca/osg/plan/stateplan.shtml (accessed 12 April 2007).

Nickelsburg, Stephen M. 1998. More volunteers? The promise and limits of community-based environmental protection. *Virginia Law Review* 84:1371–1409.

Niles, Lawrence, and Kimberly Korth. 2006. State wildlife diversity programs. In *The Endangered Species Act at thirty: Renewing the conservation promise (Volume 1),* eds. Dale D. Goble, J. Michael Scott, and Frank W. Davis, 141–55. Washington, DC: Island Press.

Noon, Barry R. 2003. Conceptual issues in monitoring ecological resources. In *Monitoring ecosystems: Interdisciplinary approaches for evaluating ecoregional initiatives,* eds. David E. Busch and Joel C. Trexler, 27–71. Washington, DC: Island Press.

North East State Foresters Association. 2005. *Northern Forest Lands Council 10th anniversary forum final report.* Concord, NH: North East State Foresters Association. www.nefainfo.org/publications/nflc10thforumfinal.pdf (accessed 12 April 2007).

Northern Forest Alliance. 2007. Home page, www.northernforestalliance.org (accessed 12 April 2007).

Northern Forest Center. 2007. Home page, www.northernforest.org (accessed 12 April 2007).

Northern Forest Lands Council. 1994. *Finding common ground: Conserving the Northern Forest.* Concord, NH: Northern Forest Lands Council. www.northernforestlands.org/fcg.htm (accessed 12 April 2007).

Noss, Reed F., and Allen Y. Cooperrider. 1994. *Saving nature's legacy: Protecting and restoring biodiversity.* Washington, DC: Island Press.

Noss, Reed F., Michael O'Connell, and Dennis D. Murphy. 1997. *The science of conservation planning: Habitat conservation under the Endangered Species Act.* Washington, DC: Island Press.

Nushagak-Mulchatna Wood-Tikchik Land Trust. 2007. Home page, www.nmwtlandtrust.org (accessed 12 April 2007).

Ohio Environmental Protection Agency. Division of Surface Water. 2004. *Darby at the crossroads: A summary of Ohio EPA's work and collaboration to protect and restore an important water resource.* Columbus: Ohio EPA. www.epa.state.oh.us/dsw/documents/Darby%20Crossroads_june04.pdf (accessed 12 April 2007).

———. 2006. *Total maximum daily loads for the Big Darby Creek watershed.* Columbus: Ohio EPA. www.epa.state.oh.us/dsw/tmdl/DarbyTMDL_final_all_jan06.pdf (accessed 12 April 2007).

O'Leary, Rosemary, and Lisa B. Bingham, eds. 2003. *The promise and performance of environmental conflict resolution*. Washington, DC: Resources for the Future.

Omernik, James M. 2004. Perspectives on the nature and definition of ecological regions. *Environmental Management* 34:S27–S38.

1000 Friends of Oregon. 2007. About 1000 friends of Oregon. www.friends.org/about (accessed 12 April 2007).

Opie, John. 1998. *Nature's nation: An environmental history of the United States.* Fort Worth, TX: Harcourt Brace.

Oregon Department of Land Conservation and Development. 2007. Goals. www.oregon.gov/LCD/goals.shtml (accessed 12 April 2007).

O'Riordan, Timothy. 1981. *Environmentalism*. 2nd ed. London: Pion.

O'Toole, Randal. 1997. ISTEA: A poisonous brew for American cities. CATO Policy Analysis No. 287. www.cato.org/pubs/pas/pa-287.html (accessed 12 April 2007).

Overdevest, Christine. 2000. Participatory democracy, representative democracy, and the nature of diffuse and concentrated interests: A case study of public involvement on a national forest district. *Society & Natural Resources* 13:685–96.

Owens, David W. 1985. Coastal management in North Carolina: Building a regional consensus. *Journal of the American Planning Association* 51:322–29.

Ozawa, Connie P., ed. 2004. *The Portland edge*. Washington, DC: Island Press.

PA. 2007. Growing Greener. Home page, growinggreener2.com (accessed 12 April 2007).

Palmer, Time. 1993. *The wild and scenic rivers of America*. Washington, DC: Island Press.

Parsons, James J. 1985. On "bioregionalism" and "watershed consciousness." *Professional Geographer* 37:1–6.

Pastor, Manuel, Jr., Peter Dreier, J. Eugene Grigsby III, and Martina Lopez-Garza. 2000. *Regions that work: How cities and suburbs can grow together*. Minneapolis: University of Minnesota Press.

Pateman, Carol. 1970. *Participation and democratic theory*. Cambridge: Cambridge University Press.

Peck, Sheila. 1998. *Planning for biodiversity: Issues and examples*. Washington, DC: Island Press.

Pelham, Thomas G. 1979. *State land use planning and regulation: Florida, the Model Code, and beyond*. Lexington, MA: D.C. Heath and Co.

Pendall, Rolf, Robert Puentes, and Jonathan Martin. 2006. *From traditional to reformed: A review of the land use regulations in the nation's 50 largest metropolitan areas*. Washington, DC: Brookings Institution. www.brookings.edu/metro/pubs/20060802_Pendall.pdf (accessed 12 April 2007).

Pennsylvania Department of Community and Economic Development. Governor's Center for Local Government Services. 2001. *Local land use controls in Pennsylvania.* Harrisburg: Pennsylvania Department of Community and Economic Development. www.newpa.com/download.aspx?id=67 (accessed 12 April 2007).

———. 2003. 2002 annual report on land use. Harrisburg: Pennsylvania Department of Community and Economic Development. www.newpa.com/default.aspx?id=358#Annual (accessed 12 April 2007).

———. 2007. E-library. www.elibrary.state.pa.us/elibpub.asp (accessed 12 April 2007).

Pennsylvania Department of Conservation and Natural Resources. 2006. *News release: Governor Rendell announces investment of nearly $17 million to protect PA's natural resources, open space.* 23 May. www.dcnr.state.pa.us/news/newsreleases/2006/0506-landconservationgrants.htm (accessed 12 April 2007).

Pennsylvania 21st Century Environment Commission. 1998. *Report of the Pennsylvania 21st Century Environment Commission.* Harrisburg: Pennsylvania 21st Century Environment Commission. www.21stcentury.state.pa.us/2001/final.htm (accessed 12 April 2007).

Perlman, Janice E. 1978. Grassroots participation from neighborhood to nation. In *Citizen participation in America: Essays on the state of the art,* ed. Stuart Langton, 65–79. Lexington, MA: Lexington Books.

Pew Center for Civic Journalism. 2007a. *Research-straight talk from Americans-2000: National part 1.* www.pewcenter.org/doingcj/research/r_ST2000nat1.html (accessed 12 April 2007).

———. 2007b. *Research-straight talk from Americans-2000: Philadelphia part 1.* www.pewcenter.org/doingcj/research/r_ST2000phil1.html (accessed 12 April 2007).

Pfeffer, Max J., and Linda P. Wagenet. 1999. Planning for environmental responsibility and equity: A critical appraisal of rural/urban relations in the New York City watershed. In *Contested countryside: The rural urban fringe in North America,* eds. Owen J. Furuseth and Mark B. Lapping, 179–205. Aldershot, UK: Ashgate Publishing Company.

Phelps, Marcus G., and Martina C. Hoppe. 2002. *New York-New Jersey Highlands regional study: 2002 update (final report).* Newtown Square, PA: U.S. Department of Agriculture, Forest Service. www.na.fs.fed.us/highlands/maps_pubs/regional_study/regional_study.shtm (accessed 12 April 2007).

Pincetl, Stephanie, 2004. The preservation of nature at the urban fringe. In *Up against the sprawl: Public policy and the making of Southern California,* eds. Jennifer Wolch, Manuel Pastor Jr., and Peter Dreier, 225–51. Minneapolis: University of Minnesota Press.

Pires, Mark. 2004. Watershed protection for a world city: The case of New York. *Land Use Policy* 21:161–75.

Platt, Rutherford H. 1994. Evolution of coastal hazard policies in the United States. *Coastal Management* 22:265–84.

———. 2004. *Land use and society: Geography, law, and public policy.* Washington, DC: Island Press.

———, ed. 2006. *The humane metropolis: People and nature in the 21st century.* Amherst: University of Massachusetts Press.

Platt, Rutherford H., Paul K. Barten, and Max J. Pfeffer. 2000. A full, clean glass? Managing New York City's watersheds. *Environment* 42(5):9–20.

Plotkin, Sidney. 1980. Policy fragmentation and capitalist reform: The defeat of national land-use policy. *Politics and Society* 9:409–445.

Plummer, Ryan, and John FitzGibbon. 2004. Some observations on the terminology in co-operative environmental management. *Journal of Environmental Management* 70:63–72.

Poisner, Jonathon. 1996. A civic republican perspective on the National Environmental Policy Act's process for citizen participation. *Environmental Law* 26:53–94.

Pollard, Trip. 2001. Greening the American dream: If sprawl is the problem, is new urbanism the answer? *Planning* 67(9):10–15.

Pontier, Glenn. 1987. Impasse on the upper Delaware. In *Managing land-use conflicts: Case studies in special area management*, eds. David J. Brower and Daniel S. Carol, 231–43. Durham, NC: Duke University Press.

Popper, Deborah E., and Frank J. Popper. 1987. The Great Plains: From dust to dust. *Planning* 53(12):12–18.

———. 1998. The Buffalo Commons: Metaphor as method. *Geographical Review* 89:491–510.

———. 2006. The onset of the Buffalo Commons. *Journal of the West* 45(2): 29–34.

Popper, Frank J. 1981. *The politics of land-use reform.* Madison: University of Wisconsin Press.

———. 1988. Understanding American land use regulation since 1970: A revisionist interpretation. *Journal of the American Planning Association* 54:291–301.

Popper, Frank J., and Deborah E. Popper. 1994. Great Plains: Checkered past, hopeful future. *Forum for Applied Research and Public Policy* 9(4):89–100.

Porter, Douglas R., Robert T. Dunphy, and David Salvesen. 2002. *Making smart growth work.* Washington, DC: Urban Land Institute.

Porter, Douglas R., and David A. Salvesen. 1995. *Collaborative planning for wetlands and wildlife: Issues and examples.* Washington, DC: Island Press.

Porter, Douglas R., and Allan D. Wallis. 2002. *Exploring ad hoc regionalism.* Cambridge, MA: Lincoln Institute of Land Policy.

(City of) Portland, Oregon. 2007. Office of sustainable development. Home page, www.portlandonline.com/osd (accessed 12 April 2007).

Power, Thomas Michael. 1991. Ecosystem preservation and the economy in the greater Yellowstone area. *Conservation Biology* 5:395–404.

President's Commission on Americans Outdoors. 1987. *Americans outdoors: The legacy, the challenge.* Washington, DC: U.S. Government Printing Office.

President's Materials Policy Commission. 1952. *Resources for freedom: A report to the president.* Washington, DC: U.S. Government Printing Office.

Press, Daniel. 1998. Local environmental policy capacity: A framework for research. *Natural Resources Journal* 38:29–52.

Press, Daniel, and Daniel A. Mazmanian. 2003. Understanding the transition to a sustainable economy. In *Environmental policy: New directions for the twenty-first century*, eds. Norman J. Vig and Michael E. Kraft, 5th ed., 275–98. Washington, DC: CQ Press.

Pritchett, Laura, Richard L. Knight, and Jeff Lee. 2007. *Home land: Ranching and a West that works.* Boulder, CO: Johnson Books.

Putnam, Robert D. 2000. *Bowling alone: The collapse and revival of American community.* New York: Simon & Schuster.

Rabe, Barry G. 2006. Power to the states: The promise and pitfalls of decentralization. In *Environmental policy: New directions for the twenty-first century*, eds. Norman J. Vig and Michael E. Kraft, 6th ed., 34–56. Washington, DC: CQ Press.

Ramos, Tarso. 1995. Wise use in the West: The case of the northwest timber industry. In *Let the people judge: Wise use and the property rights movement*, eds. John Echeverria and Raymond Booth Eby, 82–118. Washington, DC: Island Press.

Randolph, John. 2004. *Environmental land use planning and management.* Washington, DC: Island Press.

Randolph, John, and Michael Bauer. 1999. Improving environmental decision-making through collaborative methods. *Policy Studies Review* 16:168–91.

Reading, Richard P., and Tim W. Clark. 1994. Attitudes and knowledge of people living in the greater Yellowstone ecosystem. *Society and Natural Resources* 7:349–65.

Reagan, Patrick D. 2000. *Designing a new America: The origins of New Deal planning, 1890–1943.* Amherst: University of Massachusetts Press.

Real Estate Research Corporation. 1974. *The costs of sprawl.* Washington, DC: Real Estate Research Corporation.

Reidel, Carl. 1994. The political process of the Northern Forest lands study. In *The future of the Northern Forest*, ed. Christopher McGrory Klyza, 93–111. Hanover, NH: University Press of New England.

Reilly, William K., ed. 1973. *The use of land: A citizen's guide to urban growth*. New York: Thomas Y. Crowell.

Reilly, William K. 1990. Aiming before we shoot: The quiet revolution in environmental policy. *Northern Kentucky Law Review* 18:159–74.

Reisch, Mark. 2002. *The brownfields program authorization: Cleanup of contaminated sites*. RL30972. Washington, DC: Congressional Research Service.

Renn, Ortwin, Thomas Webler, and Peter Wiedemann. 1995. A need for discourse on citizen participation. In *Fairness and competence in citizen participation: Evaluating models for environmental discourse*, eds. Ortwin Renn, Thomas Webler, and Peter Wiedemann, 1–16. Dordrecht: Kluwer.

———, eds. 1995. *Fairness and competence in citizen participation: Evaluating models for environmental discourse*. Dordrecht: Kluwer.

Resources for the Future. 1954. *The nation looks at its resources. Report of the mid-century conference on resources for the future*. Washington, DC: Author.

Restore: The North Woods. 2007. Home page, www.restore.org (accessed 12 April 2007).

Rewilding Institute. 2007. Home page, www.rewilding.org.

Riebsame, William E., ed. 1997. *Atlas of the new west: Portrait of a changing region*. New York: W.W. Norton & Company.

Ringquist, Evan J. 2006. Environmental justice: Normative concerns, empirical evidence, and government action. In *Environmental policy: New directions for the twenty-first century*, eds. Norman J. Vig and Michael E. Kraft, 6th ed., 239–63. Washington, DC: CQ Press.

Riverkeeper. 2007. Home page, www.riverkeeper.org (accessed 12 April 2007).

River Network. 2007. National directory of river and watershed conservation groups. www.rivernetwork.org/library/index.cfm?doc_id=116 (accessed 12 April 2007).

Rocky Mountain Elk Foundation. 2007. Home page, www.rmef.org (accessed 12 April 2007).

Rome, Adam W. 1996. Coming to terms with pollution: The language of environmental reform, 1865–1916. *Environmental History* 1:6–28.

———. 2001. *The bulldozer in the countryside: Suburban sprawl and the rise of American environmentalism*. New York: Cambridge University Press.

Rosenbaum, Walter A. 1976. The paradoxes of public participation. *Administration and Society* 8:355–83.

Rothman, Hal. 2000. *Saving the planet: The American response to the environment in the twentieth century*. Chicago: Ivan R. Dee.

Rottle, Nancy D. 2006. Factors in the landscape-based greenway: A mountains to sound case study. *Landscape and Urban Planning* 76:134–71.

Rowe, Gene, and Lynn J. Frewer. 2000. Public participation methods: A framework for evaluation. *Science, Technology, & Human Values* 25:3–29.

Runte, Alfred. 1997. *National parks: The American experience*. Lincoln: University of Nebraska Press.

Russell, Edmund P. 1997. Lost among the parts per billion: Ecological protection at the United States Environmental Agency, 1970–1993. *Environmental History* 2:29–51.

Ryan, Robert L., Julius Gyula Fabos, and Jessica Jo Allan. 2006. Understanding opportunities and challenges for collaborative greenway planning in New England. *Landscape and Urban Planning* 76:172–91.

Sabatier, Paul, and David Mazmanian. 1979. *Can regulation work: The implementation of the 1972 California Coastal Initiative*. Davis: University of California, Davis, Institute of Government Affairs and Pomona College Program in Public Policy Analysis.

Sabatier, Paul A., Will Focht, Mark Lubell, Zev Trachtenberg, Arnold Vedlitz, and Marty Matlock. 2005. *Swimming upstream: Collaborative approaches to watershed management*. Cambridge, MA: The MIT Press.

Sagoff, Mark. 2002. On the value of natural ecosystems: The Catskills parable. *Philosophy & Public Policy Quarterly* 22:10–16.

Sale, Kirkpatrick. 1985. *Dwellers in the land: The bioregional vision*. San Francisco: Sierra Club Books.

Salkin, Patricia. 2002a. Congress misses twice with the Community Character Act: Will three times be a charm? *Real Estate Law Journal* 31:167–82.

———. 2002b. Smart growth and sustainable development: Threads of a national land use policy. *Valparaiso University Law Review* 36:381–412.

———. 2003. Smart growth and the law. In *Suburban sprawl: Culture, theory, and politics*, eds. Matthew J. Linstrom and Hugh Bartling, 213–34. Lanham, MD: Rowman & Littlefield.

Salzman, James. 1997. Valuing ecosystem services. *Ecology Law Quarterly* 24:887–903.

Samuel, Peter, and Randal O'Toole. 1999. *Smart growth at the federal trough: EPA's financing of the anti-sprawl movement*. Washington, DC: Cato Institute. www.cato.org/pubs/pas/pa361.pdf (accessed 12 April 2007).

Sanford, Robert M., and Mark B. Lapping. 2003. The beckoning country: Act 200, Act 250 and regional planning in Vermont. In *Big places, big plans*, eds. Mark B. Lapping and Owen J. Furuseth, 5–27. Aldershot, UK: Ashgate.

Sanford, Robert M., and Hubert B. Stroud. 1997. Vermont's Act 250 legislation: A citizen-based response to rapid growth and development. *Land Use Policy* 14:239–56.

Santos, Susan L., and Caron Chess. 2003. Evaluating citizen advisory boards: The importance of theory and participant-based criteria and practical implications. *Risk Analysis* 23:269–79.

Sayen, Jamie. 1994. Northern Appalachian wilderness: The key to sustainable natural and human communities in the Northern Forests. In *The future of the Northern Forest*, eds. Christopher McGrory Klyza and Stephen C. Trombulak, 177–96. Hanover, NH: University Press of New England.

———. 2001. An opportunity for big wilderness in the northern Appalachians. In *Wilderness comes home: Rewilding the Northeast*, ed. Christopher McGrory Klyza, 124–56. Hanover, NH: University Press of New England.

Scarce, Ric. 2006, updated. *Eco-warriors: Understanding the radical environmental movement*. Walnut Creek, CA: Left Coast Press.

Scheiber, Harry N. 1997. From science to law to politics: An historical view of the ecosystem idea and its effect on resource management. *Ecology Law Quarterly* 24:631–51.

Schneider, Keith. 2006. To revitalize a city, try spreading some mulch. *New York Times*, 17 May.

Schneider, Mark, John Scholz, Mark Lubell, Denisa Mindruta, and Matthew Edwardsen. 2003. Building consensual institutions: Networks and the national estuary program. *American Journal of Political Science* 47:143–58.

Schulz, Florian, ed. 2005. *Yellowstone to Yukon: Freedom to roam*. Seattle: Mountaineers Books.

Searns, Robert M. 1995. The evolution of greenways as an adaptive urban landscape form. *Landscape and Urban Planning* 33:65–80.

Selin, Steve, and Deborah Chavez. 1995. Developing a collaborative model for environmental planning and management. *Environmental Management* 19:189–95.

Selin, Steve, and Nancy Myers. 1995. Correlates of partnership effectiveness: The Coalition for United Recreation in the eastern Sierra. *Journal of Park & Recreation Administration* 13:38–47.

Selin, Steve W., Michael A. Schuett, and Debbie Carr. 2000. Modeling stakeholder perceptions of collaborative initiative effectiveness. *Society and Natural Resources* 13:735–45.

Selznick, Philip. 1953. *TVA and the grass roots: A study in the sociology of formal organization*. Berkeley: University of California Press.

Sewell, W. R. Derrick, and J. T. Coppock, eds. 1977. *Public participation in planning*. London: John Wiley & Sons.

Sewell, W. R. Derrick, and Timothy O'Riordan. 1976. The culture of participation in environmental decisionmaking. *Natural Resources Journal* 16:1–21.

Sewell, W. R. Derrick, and Susan D. Phillips. 1979. Models for the evaluation of public participation programmes. *Natural Resources Journal* 19:337–58.

Shabecoff, Philip. 1983. Watt battled a rising tide. *New York Times*, 10 October.

———. 2003. *A fierce green fire: The American environmental movement*, rev. ed. Washington, DC: Island Press.

REFERENCES

Shafer, Craig L. 2004. A geography of hope: Pursuing the voluntary preservation of America's natural heritage. *Landscape and Urban Planning* 66:127–71.

Shear, Michael J. 2006. Kaine limits harvest of key fish. *Washington Post*, 1 August.

Sheikh, Pervaze A., and Nicole T. Carter. 2006. South Florida ecosystem restoration and the comprehensive Everglades Restoration Plan. RS20702. Washington, DC: Congressional Research Service. www.cnie.org/nle/crsreports/biodiversity/biodv-38.pdf (accessed 12 April 2007).

Shellenberger, Michael, and Ted Nordhaus. 2004. *The death of environmentalism: Global warming politics in a post-environmental world*. www.thebreakthrough.org/images/Death_of_Environmentalism.pdf (accessed 12 April 2007).

Sierra Business Council. 2007. Publications. sbcouncil.org/wiki/Category:Publications (accessed 12 April 2007).

Sierra Club. 1999. *Solving sprawl: The Sierra Club rates the states*. San Francisco: Sierra Club. www.sierraclub.org/sprawl/report99 (accessed 12 April 2007).

———. 2007a. Ecoregions. www.sierraclub.org/ecoregions (accessed 12 April 2007).

———. 2007b. Stopping sprawl. www.sierraclub.org/sprawl (accessed 12 April 2007).

Sierra Nevada Alliance. 2007. Home page, www.sierranevadaalliance.org (accessed 12 April 2007).

Sierra Nevada Ecosystem Project. 1996. *Sierra Nevada Ecosystem Project final report to Congress: Status of the Sierra Nevada*. Davis: University of California, Centers for Water and Wildland Resources. www.ceres.ca.gov/snep/pubs (accessed 12 April 2007).

Sies, Mary Corbin, and Christopher Silver, eds. 1996. *Planning the twentieth-century American city*. Baltimore: Johns Hopkins University Press.

Simon, Julian L. 1998. *The ultimate resource 2*. Princeton, NJ: Princeton University Press.

Simpson, John Warfield. 1999. *Visions of paradise: Glimpses of our landscape's legacy*. Berkeley: University of California Press.

Singleton, Sara. 2002. Collaborative environmental planning in the American West: The good, the bad and the ugly. *Environmental Politics* 11(3):54–75.

Sirianni, Carmen, and Lewis Friedland. 2001. *Civic innovation in America: Community empowerment, public policy, and the movement for civic renewal*. Berkeley: University of California Press.

Skocpol, Theda. 2003. *Diminished democracy: From membership to management in American civic life*. Norman: University of Oklahoma Press.

Slocombe, D. Scott. 1998. Defining goals and criteria for ecosystem-based management. *Environmental Management* 22:483–93.

Smart Communities Network. 2007. www.smartcommunities.ncat.org (accessed 12 April 2007).

Smart Growth America. 2007. Home page, www.smartgrowthamerica.org (accessed 12 April 2007).

Smart Growth Network. 2007. Home page, www.smartgrowth.org (accessed 12 April 2007).

Smith, Katherine R. 2001. Testimony of Katherine R. Smith, Director, Resource Economics Division, Economic Research Service, U.S. Department of Agriculture before the Senate Committee on Agriculture, Nutrition & Forestry, Feburary 28. agriculture.senate.gov/Hearings/Hearings_2001/February_28_2001/0228smi.htm (accessed 12 April 2007).

Smith, Patrick D., and Maureen H. McDonough. 2001. Beyond public participation: Fairness in natural resource decision making. *Society and Natural Resources* 14:239–49.

Sokolow, Alvin D., and Anita Zurbrugg, eds. 2003. *A national view of agricultural easement programs: Profiles and maps—Report 1.* Washington, DC: American Farmland Trust.

Solecki, William D., Robert J. Mason, and Shannon Martin. 2004. The geography of support for open space initiatives: A case study of New Jersey's 1998 ballot measure. *Social Science Quarterly* 85:624–39.

Solecki, William D., and Fred M. Shelley. 1996. Pollution, political agendas, and policy windows: Environmental policy on the eve of *Silent Spring*. *Environment and Planning C: Government and Policy* 14:451–68.

Sorensen, A. Ann, Richard P. Greene, and Karen Russ. 1997. *Farming on the edge.* Washington, DC: American Farmland Trust.

Soule, David C. 2006a. Defining and managing sprawl. In *Urban sprawl: A comprehensive reference guide*, ed. David C. Soule, 3–11. Westport, CT: Greenwood Press.

———, ed. 2006b. *Urban sprawl: A comprehensive reference guide.* Westport, CT: Greenwood Press.

Soulé, Michael E., and John Terborgh. 1999. *Continental conservation: Scientific foundations of regional reserve networks.* Washington, DC: Island Press.

Squires, Gregory D., ed. 2002. *Urban sprawl: Causes, consequences and policy responses.* Washington, DC: The Urban Institute.

SRA International Inc. 2005. *Brownfields federal programs guide.* Arlington, VA: SRA International Inc. www.epa.gov/brownfields/partners/2005_fpg.pdf (accessed 12 April 2007).

Stalley, Marshall, ed. 1972. *Patrick Geddes: Spokesman for man and the environment.* New Brunswick, NJ: Rutgers University Press.

Stein, Susan M. (Huke), and Diane Gelburd. 1998. Healthy ecosystems and sustainable economies: The Federal Interagency Ecosystem Management Initiative. *Landscape and Urban Planning* 40:73–80.

Steinberg, Philip E., and George E. Clark. 1999. Troubled water? Acquiescence, conflict, and the politics of place in watershed management. *Political Geography* 18:477–508.

Steinberg, Theodore. 2002. *Down to earth: Nature's role in American history.* New York: Oxford University Press.

Stokes, Samuel N., A. Elizabeth Watson, and Shelley S. Mastran. 1997. *Saving America's countryside: A guide to rural conservation.* Baltimore: Johns Hopkins University Press.

Strange, John H. 1972. The impact of citizen participation on public administration. *Public Administration Review* 32:457–70.

Streever, Bill. 2001. *Saving Louisiana? The battle for coastal wetlands.* Jackson: University Press of Mississippi.

Strong, Douglas H. 1984. *Tahoe: An environmental history.* Lincoln: University of Nebraska Press.

Susskind, Lawrence E., Paul F. Levy, and Jennifer Thomas-Larmer. 1999. *Negotiating environmental agreements: How to avoid escalating confrontation, needless costs, and unnecessary litigation.* Washington, DC: Island Press.

Susskind, Lawrence, Sarah McKearnan, and Jennifer Thomas-Larmer, eds. 1999. *The consensus building handbook: A comprehensive guide to reaching agreement.* Thousand Oaks, CA: Sage Publications.

Susskind, Lawrence E., Mieke van der Wansem, and Armand Ciccarelli. 2000. *Mediating land use disputes: Pros and cons.* Cambridge, MA: Lincoln Institute of Land Policy.

Sussman, Carl, ed. 1976. *Planning the fourth migration: The neglected vision of the Regional Planning Association of America.* Cambridge, MA: The MIT Press.

Sustainable Communities Network. 2007. Home page, www.sustainable.org (accessed 12 April 2007).

SustainableOregon.net. 2007. Home page, www.sustainableoregon.net (accessed 12 April 2007).

Sustainable Pittsburgh. 2004. *Southwestern Pennsylvania regional indicators report 2004.* Pittsburgh: Sustainable Pittsburgh. 203.147.150.6/docs/swpaindicators2002.pdf (accessed 12 April 2007).

Sustainable Seattle. 2007. Home page, www.sustainableseattle.org (accessed 12 April 2007).

Switzer, Jacqueline Vaughn. 1997. *Green backlash: The history and politics of environmental opposition in the U.S.* Boulder, CO: Lynne Rienner Publishers.

Szaro, R. C., W. T. Sexton, and C. R. Malone. 1998. The emergence of ecosystem management as a tool for meeting people's needs and sustaining ecosystems. *Landscape and Urban Planning* 40:1–7.

Talen, Emily. 2005. *New urbanism and American planning: The conflict of cultures.* London: Routledge.

Tarr, Joel A. 1996. *The search for the ultimate sink: Urban pollution in historical perspective.* Akron, OH: University of Akron Press.

Tarrow, Sidney G. 1998. *Power in movement: Social movements and contentious politics.* Cambridge: Cambridge University Press.

Taylor, Pat. 2002. Congress ponders "Federal Zoning Act": Critics of the Community Character Act say its passage would lead to federal infringement on the rights of state and local governments to manage growth on their own. newssearch.looksmart.com/p/articles/mi_m1571/is_27_18/ai_90114134 (accessed 12 April 2007).

10,000 Friends of Pennsylvania. 2007. Multi-municipal planning and implementation. www.10000friends.org/growth/mmp (accessed 12 April 2007).

Terborgh, John, and Michael Soulé. 1999. Why we need large-scale networks and megareserves: How to design them. *Wild Earth*, Spring 1999:66–72.

Terrie, Philip G. 1999. *Contested terrain: A new history of nature and people in the Adirondacks.* Syracuse, NY: Syracuse University Press.

The Nature Conservancy. 2004. Using the power of the Internet to protect great places everywhere. www.nature.org/pressroom/press/press1690.html (accessed 12 April 2007).

———, Government Relations Department. 2004. State level conservation funding mechanisms. Arlington, VA: The Nature Conservancy. www .biodiversitypartners.org/policy/Funding_Mechanism.pdf (accessed 12 April 2007).

———. 2007. How we work: Conservation methods. www.nature.org/aboutus/ howwework/conservationmethods/privatelands (accessed 12 April 2007).

Thomas, Craig W. 1999. Linking public agencies with community-based watershed organizations: Lessons from California. *Policy Studies Journal* 27:544–64.

———. 2003. *Bureaucratic landscapes: Interagency cooperation and the preservation of biodiversity.* Cambridge, MA: The MIT Press.

Thomas, William L., ed. 1956. *Man's role in changing the face of the earth.* Chicago: University of Chicago Press.

Thompson, Barton H. 2006. Managing the working landscape. In *The Endangered Species Act at thirty: Renewing the conservation promise (Volume 1)*, eds. Dale D. Goble, J. Michael Scott, and Frank W. Davis, 101–26. Washington, DC: Island Press.

Thompson, George F., and Frederick R. Steiner, eds. 1997. *Ecological design and planning*. New York: John Wiley & Sons.

Tilly, Charles. 2004. *Social movements, 1768–2004*. Boulder, CO: Paradigm Publishers.

de Tocqueville, Alexis. 1945. *Democracy in America*. Ed. Phillips Bradley. New York: Vintage Books.

Trombulak, Stephen C. 1994. A natural history of the Northern Forest. In *The future of the Northern Forest*, eds. Christopher McGrory Klyza and Stephen C. Trombulak, 11–26. Hanover, NH: University Press of New England.

———. 2003. An integrative model for landscape-scale conservation in the twenty-first century. In *Reconstructing conservation: Finding common ground*, eds. Ben A. Minteer and Robert E. Manning, 263–76. Washington, DC: Island Press.

Trust for Public Land. 2007a. About TPL. www.tpl.org/tier2_sa.cfm?folder_id=170 (accessed 12 April 2007).

———. 2007b. LandVote. www.tpl.org/tier2_kad.cfm?folder_id=2386 (accessed 12 April 2007).

Trust for Public Land and American Water Works Association. 2004. *Protecting the source: Land conservation and the future of America's drinking water*. San Francisco: Trust for Public Land. www.tpl.org/content_documents/protecting_the_source_04.pdf (accessed 12 April 2007).

Trust for Public Land and Land Trust Alliance. 2006. *LandVote 2005: Americans invest in parks & conservation*. Washington, DC: Trust for Public Land and Land Trust Alliance. www.tpl.org/download_landvote05_report.cfm (accessed 12 April 2007).

Tuan, Yi-Fu. 2001. *Space and place: The perspective of experience*. Minneapolis: University of Minnesota Press.

Tucker, William. 1982. *Progress and privilege: America in the age of environmentalism*. New York: Anchor/Doubleday.

Tug Hill Commission. 2007. Tug Hill Commission organization & approach. www.tughill.org/comm1.html (accessed 12 April 2007).

Tuler, Seth, and Thomas Webler 1999. Voices from the forest: What participants expect of a public participation process. *Society & Natural Resources* 12:437–53.

Turner, Frederick Jackson. 1920. *The frontier in American history*. New York: Henry Holt & Co.

Twiss, Robert H. 1997. New tools for building the future of ecosystem management. *Ecology Law Quarterly* 24:877–82.

———. 2004. Planning and land regulation at Lake Tahoe: Five decades of experience. In *Big places, big plans*, eds. Mark B. Lapping and Owen J. Furuseth, 83–95. Aldershot, UK: Ashgate.

United Nations Educational, Scientific, and Cultural Organization. 2007. World heritage list. whc.unesco.org/en/list (accessed 12 April 2007).

U.S. Army Corps of Engineers New Orleans District and State of Louisiana. 2004. *Louisiana Coastal Area, Louisiana: Ecosystem restoration study.* New Orleans: U.S. Army Corps of Engineers. www.lca.gov/final_report.aspx (accessed 12 April 2007).

U.S. Department of Agriculture. Forest Service. 2003. *Forest legacy program implementation guidelines.* Washington, DC: USDA Forest Service. www.fs.fed .us/spf/coop/library/flp_guidelines.pdf (accessed 12 April 2007).

———. 2005. Forest legacy program: Five-year strategic direction. Washington, DC: USDA Forest Service.

———. 2007. Forest legacy program: Protecting private forest lands being converted to non-forest uses. www.fs.fed.us/spf/coop/programs/loa/flp.shtml (accessed 12 April 2007).

———, Northeastern Area. 2007. The Highlands of Connecticut, New Jersey, New York, and Pennsylvania. www.na.fs.fed.us/highlands (accessed 12 April 2007).

U.S. Department of Agriculture, Forest Service, and U.S. Department of the Interior, National Park Service. 1990. *Vision for the future: A framework for coordination in the greater Yellowstone area.* Washington, DC: U.S. Government Printing Office.

U.S. Department of Agriculture, Natural Resources Conservation Service. 2002. *Farm Bill 2002: Conservation provisions overview.* Washington, DC: USDA Natural Resources Conservation Service. www.nrcs.usda.gov/Programs/ farmbill/2002/pdf/ConsProv.pdf (accessed 12 April 2007).

U.S. Department of the Interior, National Park Service. 2004. Total leveraging of NPS HPF appropriations to heritage areas 1:8. Washington, DC: U.S. National Park Service. www.cr.nps.gov/heritageareas/INFO/halev.pdf (accessed 12 April 2007).

———. 2007a. National heritage areas. www.cr.nps.gov/heritageareas (accessed 12 April 2007).

———. 2007b. Land & Water Conservation Fund. www.nps.gov/ncrc/programs/ lwcf (accessed 12 April 2007).

———. 2007c. National trails system. www.nps.gov/nts (accessed 12 April 2007).

———. 2007d. Rivers, trails, and conservation assistance program. www.nps.gov/ rtca (accessed 12 April 2007).

U.S. Department of the Interior and U.S. Army Corps of Engineers. 2005. *Comprehensive Everglades restoration plan: 2005 report to Congress.* Washington, DC: U.S. Department of the Interior and U.S. Army Corps of Engineers. www .evergladesplan.org/pm/program_docs/cerp_report_congress_2005.aspx#docs (accessed 12 April 2007).

REFERENCES

U.S. Environmental Protection Agency. 1987. *Unfinished business: A comparative assessment of environmental problems.* Washington, DC: U.S. Environmental Protection Agency.

———. 1993. *The watershed protection approach, annual report 1992.* USEPA 840-S-93-001. Washington, DC: Environmental Protection Agency.

———. 1996. *Why watersheds?* EPA800-F-96-001. Washington, DC: U.S. Environmental Protection Agency. www.epa.gov/owow/watershed/why.html (accessed 12 April 2007).

———. 1997. *An ecological assessment of the United States mid-Atlantic region: A landscape atlas.* Washington, DC: U.S. Environmental Protection Agency. www.srs.fs.usda.gov/pubs/misc/epa_600_r-97_130.pdf (accessed 12 April 2007).

———. 2002. Watershed-based national pollution discharge elimination system (NPDES) permitting policy statement. www.epa.gov/npdes/pubs/watershed-permitting-policy.pdf (accessed 12 April 2007).

———. 2005. *Community-based watershed management: Lessons from the national estuary program.* EPA-842-B-05-003. Washington, DC: U.S. Environmental Protection Agency.

———. 2007a. About the mid-Atlantic integrated assessment (MAIA). www.epa.gov/maia/html/about.html (accessed 12 April 2007).

———. 2007b. Adopt your watershed. Home page, www.epa.gov/adopt (accessed 12 April 2007).

———. 2007c. American heritage rivers. www.epa.gov/rivers (accessed 12 April 2007).

———. 2007d. Brownfields cleanup and redevelopment. Home page, www.epa.gov/brownfields (accessed 12 April 2007).

———. 2007e. Regional vulnerability assessment (ReVA) program. Home page, www.epa.gov/reva (accessed 12 April 2007).

———. 2007f. Smart growth. Home page, www.epa.gov/smartgrowth (accessed 12 April 2007).

———. 2007g. Watersheds. Home page, www.epa.gov/owow/watershed (accessed 12 April 2007).

———, Office of Water. 2001. *Protecting and restoring America's watersheds: Status, trends, and initiatives in watershed management.* EPA-840-R-00-001. Washington, DC: U.S. Environmental Protection Agency. www.epa.gov/owow/protecting/restore725.pdf (accessed 12 April 2007).

———, Office of Water. 2002. *A review of statewide watershed management approaches, final report.* Washington, DC: U.S. Environmental Protection Agency. www.epa.gov/owow/watershed/approaches_fr.pdf (accessed 12 April 2007).

———, Office of Water. 2005. *Community-based watershed management: Lessons from the National Estuary Program.* Washington, DC: U.S. Environmental Protection Agency. www.epa.gov/neplessons/documents/srNEPPrimer.pdf (accessed 12 April 2007).

———, Science Advisory Board. 1990. *Reducing risk: Strategies for environmental protection.* Washington, DC: U.S. Environmental Protection Agency.

U.S. Fish and Wildlife Service. 2007. Conservation plans and agreements database. ecos.fws.gov/conserv_plans/public.jsp (accessed 12 April 2007).

Van de Ven, Andrew H., and Diane L. Ferry. 1980. *Measuring and assessing organizations.* New York: John Wiley & Sons.

Van Liere, Kent D., and Riley E. Dunlap. 1980. The social bases of environmental concern: A review of hypotheses, explanations and empirical evidence. *Public Opinion Quarterly* 44:181–97.

Verba, Sidney, and Norman H. Nie. 1987. *Participation in America: Political democracy and social equality.* Chicago: University of Chicago Press.

Verba, Sidney, Kay Lehman Schlozman, Henry Brady, and Norman H. Nie. 1993. Citizen activity: Who participates? What do they say? *American Political Science Review* 87:303–19.

Vig, Norman J. 2006. Presidential leadership and the environment. In *Environmental policy: New directions for the twenty-first century,* eds. Norman J. Vig and Michael E. Kraft, 6th ed., 100–123. Washington, DC: CQ Press.

Vincent, Carol Hardy, and David L. Whiteman. 2006. *Heritage areas: Background, proposals, and current issues.* Washington, DC: Congressional Research Service, Resources, Science, and Industry Division. cnie.org/NLE/CRSreports/06Dec/RL33462.pdf (accessed 12 April 2007).

Vital Ground. 2007. Home page, www.vitalground.org (accessed 12 April 2007).

Vogt, Kristina A., John C. Goron, John P. Wargo, Daniel J. Vogt, Heidi Asbjornsen, Peter A. Palmiotto, Heidi J. Clark, Jennifer L. O'Hara, William S. Keeton, Toral Patel-Weynard, and Evie Witten. 1997. *Ecosystems: Balancing science with management.* New York: Springer-Verlag.

Vos, Jaap. 2004. The Everglades: Where will all the water go? In *Big places, big plans,* eds. Mark B. Lapping and Owen J. Furuseth, 97–113. Aldershot, UK: Ashgate.

Wald, Matthew L. 1999. Federal land deal protects Yellowstone herd and geysers. *New York Times,* 22 August.

Walker, Richard A., and Michael K. Heiman. 1981. Quiet revolution for whom? *Annals of the Association of American Geographers* 71:67–83.

Wallach, Bret. 1985. The return of the prairie. *Landscape* 28(3):1–5.

Walmsley, Anthony. 2006. Greenways: Multiplying and diversifying in the 21st century. *Landscape and Urban Planning* 76:252–90.

Washington Post. 2003. Series of articles about The Nature Conservancy. 4 March–21 December.

Weaver, Clyde. 1984. *Regional development and the local community: Planning, politics and social context.* Chichester, England: Wiley.

Weaver, Timothy. 1997. Litigation and negotiation: The history of salmon in the Columbia River Basin. *Ecology Law Quarterly* 24:677–87.

Weber, Edward P. 2000a. A new vanguard for the environment: Grass-roots ecosystem management as a new environmental movement. *Society & Natural Resources* 13:237–59.

———. 2000b. *Bringing society back in: Grass roots ecosystem management, accountability, and sustainable communities.* Cambridge, MA: The MIT Press.

Webler, Thomas, and Seth Tuler. 1999. Integrating technical analysis with deliberation in regional watershed management planning: Applying the National Research Council approach. *Policy Studies Journal* 27:530–43.

Weidner, Charles H. 1974. *Water for a city: A history of New York City's problem from the beginning to the Delaware River system.* New Brunswick, NJ: Rutgers University Press.

Weigel, Lori, John Fairbank, and David Metz. 2004. Memorandum to The Nature Conservancy/Trust for Public Land: Key findings from a national voter survey on conservation. Alexandria, VA: Public Opinion Strategies and Fairbank, Maslin, Maullin & Associates. www.nature.org/pressroom/files/pollmemo.pdf (accessed 12 April 2007).

Weitz, Jerry. 1999. *Sprawl busting: State programs to guide growth.* Chicago: American Planning Association.

Weitz, Jerry, and Terry Moore. 1998. Development inside urban growth boundaries: Oregon's empirical evidence of contiguous urban form. *Journal of the American Planning Association* 64:424–39.

Wengert, Norman. 1976. Citizen participation: Practice in search of a theory. *Natural Resources Journal* 16:24–40.

Wickham, J. D., K. B. Jones, K. H. Riitters, R. V. O'Neill, R. D. Tankersley, E. R. Smith, A. C. Neale, and D. J. Chaloud. 1999. Environmental auditing: An integrated environmental assessment of the U.S. mid-Atlantic region. *Environmental Management* 24:553–60.

Wildlands Project. 2007. Home page, www.wildlandsprojectrevealed.org (accessed 12 April 2007).

Wild Rockies Action Fund. 2007. Home page, www.wildrockies.org/nrepa (accessed 12 April 2007).

Williams, Florence. 2001. Frank and Deborah Popper's "Buffalo Commons" is creeping toward reality. *High Country News* 33(1), 15 January. www.hcn.org/servlets/hcn.Article?article_id=10194 (accessed 12 April 2007).

Williams, Patricia. 1999. Vice president for policy and programs, American Association of Museums. Personal communication, 2 June.

Willmer, Ralph. 2006. Planning framework: A planning framework for managing sprawl. In *Urban sprawl: A comprehensive reference guide*, ed. David C. Soule, 61–78. Westport, CT: Greenwood Press.

Wilson, Matthew A. 1997. The wolf in Yellowstone: Science, symbol, or politics? Deconstructing the conflict between environmentalism and wise use. *Society and Natural Resources* 10:453–69.

Wilson, William H. 1989. *The city beautiful movement*. Baltimore: Johns Hopkins University Press.

Wolch, Jennifer, Manuel Pastor Jr., and Peter Dreier, eds. *Up against the sprawl: Public policy and the making of Southern California*. Minneapolis: University of Minnesota Press.

Wolpert, Julian. 1976. Regressive siting of public facilities. *Natural Resources Journal* 16:103–15.

Wondolleck, Julia M., and Steven L. Yaffee. 2000. *Making collaboration work: Lessons from innovation in natural resource management*. Washington, DC: Island Press.

Wright, John B. 1993. *Rocky Mountain divide: Selling and saving the West*. Austin: University of Texas Press.

Yaffee, S. L., A. F. Phillips, I. C. Frentz, P. W. Hardy, S. M. Maleki, and B. E. Thorpe. 1996. *Ecosystem management in the United States*. Washington, DC: Island Press.

Yaro, Robert, Randall G. Arendt, Harry L. Dodson, and Elizabeth A. Brabec. 1988. *Dealing with change in the Connecticut River Valley: A design manual for conservation and development*. Cambridge, MA: Lincoln Institute of Land Policy.

Yaro, Robert, and Tony Hiss. 1996. *A region at risk: The third regional plan for the New York–New Jersey–Connecticut metropolitan area*. New York: Regional Plan Association.

Yellowstone to Yukon Conservation Initiative. 2005. *Yellowstone to Yukon Conservation Initiative annual report 2005*. Bozeman, MT: Yellowstone to Yukon Conservation Initiative. www.y2y.net/documents/Y2Y_AR_2005.pdf (accessed 12 April 2007).

Young, Dwight. 1995. *Alternatives to sprawl*. Cambridge, MA: Lincoln Institute of Land Policy.

Zinn, Jeffrey. 1995. *The Farm Bill: Soil and water conservation issues*. Washington, DC: Congressional Research Service. digital.library.unt.edu/govdocs/crs//data/1995/upl-meta-crs-174/IB95027_1995Dec29.html?PHPSESSID=9890619b795319d3b7316da7267339ab (accessed 12 April 2007).

REFERENCES

———. 2005. *Land and Water Conservation Fund: Current status and issues.* RS 21503 Washington, DC: Congressional Research Service. www.national aglawcenter.org/assets/crs/RS21503.pdf (accessed 12 April 2007).

Zinn, Jeffrey, and Tadlock Cowan. 2005. *Agriculture conservation programs: A scorecard.* RL32940.Washington, DC: Congressional Research Service. opencrs.cdt.org/getfile.php?rid=43792 (accessed 12 April 2007).

INDEX

activism, 56–57
adaptive behavior, 65–66, 279
Adirondack Park, 9, 27–34, 82,
    138–39, 196, 253
Adirondack Park Agency (APA), 80
Adirondack Park Commission, 265
Adirondack Private Land Use and
    Development Plan, 80, 254
Administrative Procedures Act
    (APA), 54
adversarialism, 257
advisory committees, 56, 62
agricultural subsidies, 31. See also
    farmland; subsidies
air quality, 171
Alaska National Interest Lands
    Conservation Act (1980), 31, 83
Alliance for America, 240–41
Alliance for the Wild Rockies, 120
American Farmland Trust, 157–58,
    205
American Institute of Architects, 193
American Planning Association, 171,
    179, 244–45; smart growth, 193
American Prairie Foundation, 138

Animal Liberation Front, 258
anti-environmental interests, 52
antigrowth sentiment, 46–47, 194
Anza-Borrego Desert State Park, 163
Apollo Alliance, 39
Appalachian Regional Development
    Act (1965), 24
Appalachian Trail, 23, 225
Appalachians, 121, 129
Applegate Partnership, 68–69, 182–83
Applegate Watershed, 68
Arctic National Wildlife Refuge, 36,
    240
Arnold, Ron, 239
Arnstein, Sherry, 60
Atlanta, 9
Atlanta's Atlantic Steel Project, 168

Babbitt, Bruce, 100, 103–4
ballot questions, 4–8, 14–15, 146, 200,
    227–32, 244–45; California, 255;
    Oregon, 235–37
Baltimore Ecosystem Study (2006),
    143
Baxter State Park, 132

Beachfront Management Act (1988), 243

beautification, 19

Better America Bonds, 13, 292

Bhopal tragedy (1984), 35

Big and Little Darby Creeks watershed, 70–71

Big Darby Accord, 71

bikeways, 37

biocentrism, 12

biodiesel, 139

biodiversity, 10, 65, 82

Biogems, 83

bioregionalism, 80

Blumenaeur, Earl, 171, 182

Boston Harbor, 36

boycotts, 51

Brandywine Valley, 82

Brewer, Richard, 202, 204, 206, 209

Brookings Institution, 193, 197

brownfields, 7–8, 14, 167–69, 194

Brownfields Voluntary Cleanup and Revitalization Program, 185

buffalo, 136, 139. *See also* ranching

Buffalo Commons, 79, 86, 135–38

Bureau of Forestry. *See* Forestry Service

Bureau of Reclamation, 159

Bush, George H. W., 3, 7, 36–37, 241

Bush, George W., 6–7, 38, 100, 117, 241, 251

Byrne, Brendan, 183, 186

California, 27–28, 104–8, 179; ballots, 229; land protection program, 111; Quincy Library Group, 67, 70

Callenbach, Ernest, 138

Candidate Conservation Agreements, 104

Cape Cod National Seashore (Massachusetts), 160

carbon emissions, 16, 38, 145, 153, 272–73

Carson, Rachel, 19

Carter, Jimmy, 117, 238

Carville, James, 188

Cato Institute, 250–51

Catskill Fund for the Future, 97

Catskill Park, 27, 86, 92, 93, 95–97

Center for American Places, 47

Center for the Defense of Free Enterprise (CDFE), 239

Chaffee, Lincoln, 171

Cheney, Dick, 62

Chernobyl nuclear disaster (1986), 35

Chesapeake Bay, 9, 46, 87–92, 103, 169, 184; agreement, 88

Chesapeake Bay Commission, 88, 91

Chesapeake Bay Foundation, 87–88

Chesapeake Bay Preservation Act (Virginia), 90

Chesapeake Bay Program, 31, 81, 90–91, 265

Church Universal and Triumphant, 116–17

Cie General Electricite, 131

Cienega, 163

civic engagement, 43, 45–46, 49–50; barriers, 105; chart, 61; citizen scientists, 51; culture, 48, 268–70, 283, 286–89; dark side, 53–54; definition, 50, 267–69; and education, 60–61; environmental, 51; evaluation, 266–69; mainstream, 56; participation, 56–60; types, 55. *See also* local action

Civil War Preservation Trust, 207

Civilian Conservation Corps, 19
clams, 87–88
Clean Air Act (1970), 31
Clean Air Act (1990), 36
Clean Water Act (1972), 31, 54, 71, 218, 222; opposition, 249–50
clear-cutting, 141–42
Clearwater, 217
Cleveland Ecovillage, 143–44
climate change, 77; global, 36
Clinton, Bill, 40, 67, 103, 117, 241, 252, 270
Clinton-Gore Livability Initiative, 170, 191, 198
Coalition for a Livable Future, 183
Coalition of Watershed Towns, 97
Coast 2050, 141
Coastal Barrier Resources Act (CBRA) (1982), 31
Coastal Wetlands Planning, Protection, and Restoration Act, 141
coastal zone management, 27, 30; Coastal Zone Management Act (CZMA) (1972), 30–31
Coates, Bill, 67
collaboration, 2–3, 63; cases, 67–69, 70–71; vs. cooperation, 44; in ecosystem management, 66; elements, 4; evaluation, 15; failed, 44–45, 76–77; future, 72; opinions about, 287; opportunity, 45; opposition to projects, 257; and the quieter revolution, 73–74; resistance to, 14–15; scale, 10, 12–13; against sprawl, 151; in the West, 72–73. *See also* new regionalism; place-based planning; smart growth
Collaborative Environmental Management, 73

collaborative land use planning. *See* collaboration
Colorado, 32; farmland, 157
Colorado River Basin Compact, 23
Colorado River Basin Salinity Control Program, 223
Columbia River Gorge National Scenic Area, 82, 86, 112–16, 256
Columbia Trust, 116
Commission on Environmental Justice and Sustainable Communities, 186
Commission on the Adirondacks in the Twenty-First Century, 133
Committee to Preserve Property Rights, 256
communities: character, 174; intentional, 196–97; mixed-income, 197; of place, 48
Community Character Act, 13, 172, 191, 198, 252, 292
community land trusts. *See* land trusts
Community Services Administration, 192
Comprehensive Environmental Response Compensation and Liability Act (Superfund) (1980), 35
Comprehensive Everglades Restoration Plan (CERP), 99–100, 103
Comprehensive Management Plan, 80
Comprehensive Plan and Zoning Ordinance (Philipstown, NY), 127
Conference on Environment and Development (1992), 20
conflict: reducing, 58; underrecognition, 48

Congress for the New Urbanism (CNU), 13, 193
Connecticut, 9
conservation, 17; easements, 112; planning, 210. *See also* preservation
conservation biology, 138
Conservation Fund, 120, 205
Conservation Reserve Enhancement Program, 97, 155
Conservation Reserve Program, 31, 125–26, 136–38, 154, 273
Conservation Security Program, 155
Consumer Reports, 93
cooperation, vs. collaboration, 44
Cooperative Conservation grants, 169
Corporate Average Fuel Economy (CAFE), 39
cost-effectiveness, 266–67, 288
The Costs of Sprawl, 152
crabs, 87–88, 92
crime, 170–71
critical area planning, 9
Critical Areas Act (CAA) (Maryland), 90, 184
Critical Ecoregions Program, 83
cultural resources management, 10
Cuomo, Mario, 33, 133
Cushman, Charles, 238–39, 255–56
Cuyahoga National Recreation Area, 256

D&R Greenway Land Trust, 208–9, 286
Daley, Richard J., 29
Daley, Richard M., 144
dams, 103
Darby Creek Partnership, 70–71
de Tocqueville, Alexis, 48
Delaware, 82

Delaware National Scenic River (New Jersey/New York/Pennsylvania), 160
Delaware River, 126
Delaware River Basin Agreement, 93
Delaware River Basin Commission, 25, 93, 218–19
democracy, 52–53; and collaboration, 75; environmental, 199. *See also* civic engagement
demographics, 55–56
Desert Act, 22
development: business, 207; high-density, 128, 194–96; and land use, 29–30; patterns, 264–65, 281–85
Diamond International Corporation, 131–32
disaster resistance. *See* hazard management
discrimination, 55
Dolan v. City of Tigard, 243
Doris Duke Foundation, 120
Douglas, Marjory Stoneman, 102
Downs, Anthony, 72, 176
Ducks Unlimited, 138

Earth Day, 19, 36
Earth First!, 82–83, 257–58
Earth Liberation Front, 258
easements, 131, 146, 157, 201–2, 230–33, 254; cost, 288
Ecocity Cleveland, 143–44
ecological footprint. *See* footprint, ecological
Economic, Growth, Resource Protection, and Planning Act (1992), 184–85
ecoregionalism, 9, 80
ecosystem management model, 64; CERP, 102; definition, 64–65;

failures, 119–20; goals, 65–66, 72; grassroots, 67, 72, 286–87; opposition, 119; and the quieter revolution, 73–74. *See also* collaboration

ecosystem monitoring, 262–64. *See also* evaluation

ecosystem representation, 82

Ecotopia, 138

ecotourism. *See* recreation; tourism

Ecotrust, 70

education, 5, 60–61

Ehrlich, Robert L., Jr., 186

electricity. *See* energy

Eliot, Charles, 201

eminent domain, 7, 15, 95, 98

empowerment, local, 46

Endangered Species Act (1973), 19, 31, 64, 71–72, 103, 105; evaluations, 261; exemptions, 240; opposition, 237–38, 249–50

energy: crisis (1970s), 19; efficiency, 19–20; independence, 39; renewable, 41, 171

engagement. *See* civic engagement

Environmental Block Grant Program, 190

Environmental Defense, 193

environmental footprint. *See* footprint, ecological

environmental justice, 7, 21, 270–71, 279–83, 289, 292; economics, 8; and place-based planning, 10–11; toxic issues, 35–36. *See also* smart growth; wealth

Environmental Protection Agency (EPA), 8, 19, 88, 95–96; opposition, 238; and smart growth, 250–51

environmental protection programs, 92

Environmental Quality Incentives Program, 126, 155

environmental racism, 35–36

environmental services, 264

Environmental Stewardship and Watershed Protection Act (Pennsylvania), 189

environmentalism: adversarial, 6–7; anger and, 40–41; civic, 12–14; and civic engagement, 43; "death of," 20; early, 17–18; elitist, 49; extremism, 15; future, 21; government-controlled, 2–3; grassroots, 49; "issue-attention" model, 20; local, 49; modern, 17–20; motivations for participation, 12

erosion, 31

ethanol, 274. *See also* biodiesel

evaluation, 261–66; context, 276–77; energy consumption, 272; environmental impact, 272–75; opportunities, 129; product-oriented, 58–59; social goals, 58; stakeholders, 271–72; of watershed management, 223–24. *See also* ecosystem monitoring

Everglades, 34, 86, 99–103

Everglades Forever Act, 100

Exxon Valdez, 36

Farm and Ranch Lands Protection Program, 155

Farm Bill (1985), 31, 154, 156

Farm Bill (1990), 133, 160–61

farmland, 13; erosion, 31; loss, 12; preservation, 153–54, 157–59, 174;

protection, 34; surpluses, 22. *See also* agricultural subsidies
Farmland Information Center, 157–58
Farmland Protection Policy Act (1981), 153
Farmland Security Zone, 212
farms, corporate, 190
Federal Advisory Committee Act (FACA), 69
Federal Housing Authority, 24
Federal Land Policy and Management Act (1976), 31
fertilizer, 19
filtration avoidance determination (FAD), 96
Finding Common Ground, 133–34
Fire Island, 125
fish, 87–92. *See also* salmon
Fish and Wildlife Service, 103, 159
fishing, 140
Flathead National Park, 120
Flood Disaster Protection Act (1973), 31
Florida, 26–27, 30, 179
footprint, ecological, 87, 110–12, 196–97, 273–74, 280, 293
Ford, Gerald, 238
Foreman, Dave, 82–83, 108
Forest Land Enhancement Program, 125
Forest Legacy program, 125, 133, 160–61, 220
Forest Service, 115–17, 159–61; studies, 123–24
Forest Service's Economic Action Program, 125
forestry, 129, 190. *See also* clear-cutting
Forestry Service, 18

Friends of the Columbia River Gorge, 114
frontier, 17–18
fuel economy, 39
Funders' Network for Smart Growth and Livable Communities, 193
funding, 200, 207–8, 271, 288–89; watersheds, 221; WUPR on, 250

Gallatin Valley Land Trust, 120
garden city, 18, 23
Geddes, Patrick, 22
general management area, 115–16
gentrification, 195
geographic scale. *See* scale, geographic
Georgia, 28, 32, 179
Gingrich, Newt, 14, 238, 241
Glendening, Parris, 183, 185–86, 192
Global Climate Coalition, 253
gnatcatcher, 105, 107
Goldsmith, James, 131
Gore, Al, 1, 5–6, 37–38, 100, 170, 253
government: agencies, 81; competing partners, 64, 280; environmental assistance, 2–3, 25, 30–31, 40; environmental control, 1–3, 19, 21; management of public land, 76; role in regional management, 133
Governors' Task Force, 133
Grassland Reserve Program, 136, 155
Great Lakes, 25, 56, 88; cleanups, 103
Great Lakes Revolving Fund, 162
Great Plains, 73, 135–36
Great Plains Restoration Council, 138
Greater Yellowstone Coalition, 110, 117

Greater Yellowstone Ecoregion, 117, 120, 248, 255–56; goals for, 119
Green Mountain National Forest, 128, 132
Green Mountains (Vermont), 82
greenbelt towns, 19
greenline, 114
greenline parks. *See* parks
Greenpeace, 257–58
greenways, 8, 14, 146, 224–26, 233; barriers, 227
grizzly bears, 119–20
Growing Greener, 2, 189–90, 210
Growing Smart Legislative Guidebook, 193, 252–53
Growing Smarter, 189
growth. *See* smart growth; sprawl
growth management, 198; government participation, 198; research, 231
Gulf Coast, 139–41

Habitat Conservation Planning, grants, 169
habitat conservation plans, 103–5, 107, 205
Hackensack Meadowlands, 38
Hardin, Garret, 66
Harvard University, 47
Hawaii, 25–26, 179
hazard management, 77, 139, 170–71, 275
Headwaters, 69
Heiman, Michael, 279
heritage areas, 163–64
Heritage Foundation, 193
Hetch Hetchy Dam, 18
Highlands, 38, 81, 86, 127–28; sprawl, 121–23

Highlands Coalition, 127
Highlands Conservation Act (NJ), 43–44
Highlands program, expansion, 129
Highlands Stewardship Act, 123
Highlands Trail, 126
Highlands Water Protection and Planning Council, 127–28
Highway Beautification Act (1965), 24
Highway Trust Fund, 37
highways. *See* interstate highway system
Historic Preservation Act (1966), 24
Hocker, Jean, 202
Homestead Acts, 22
housing, 13, 19, 171, 174, 185; affordable, 7, 23–30, 196–98, 207, 252–54; federal control, 28–29; post–WWII suburbanization, 23–24; second-home developments, 26, 27, 34
Hudson River, 92–93, 126; Hudson Riverkeepers, 216–17
Hudson River Valley Greenway, 123, 126
Hudson River Valley National Heritage Area, 123
Hurricane Katrina, 129–42, 221
Hurricane Rita, 142
Hussein, Saddam, 103

ideology, 48
Illinois, farmland, 155
incentives, 151; for eco-friendly practices, 145–46; against sprawl, 150
India, 35
indigenous peoples, 23

infill development, 195–97, 283
infrastructure turndowns, 178
institutional capacity, 215, 269–70
intentional communities, 196–97
Intermodal Surface Transportation
    Efficiency Act (ISTEA), 36–37,
    251. *See also* Safe, Accountable,
    Flexible, Efficient Transportation
    Equity Act (SAFETEA)
International City/County
    Management Association, 193
Interstate Commission on the
    Potomac River Basin, 25
Interstate Highway Act (1956), 24
interstate highway system, 23, 27,
    150, 172
issue-attention cycle, 72

Jackson, Michael, 67
Job Creation Tax Credit, 185
justice, 269–70

kangaroo rat, 105
Kean, Tom, 186
Kelo v. City of Nevada, 15
Kelo v. City of New London, 244–46,
    258
Kennedy-Townsend, Kathleen, 186
Kerry, John, 39
Kitzhaber, John, 182
Kyoto Protocol, 294

Lake Erie, 162. *See also* Great Lakes
Lake Okeechobee, 99
Lake Tahoe, 28, 196
Land Acquisition and Stewardship
    Program (New York), 127
Land and Water Conservation Fund,
    117, 132–34, 159, 227; and

funding, 269–70, 286; WUPR on,
    250
Land and Water Conservation Fund
    Act (1965), 24
land classification, 22–23
Land Grant Acts, 22
land scarcity, 22
Land Trust Alliance (LTA), 14,
    201–2, 206; research, 228, 230
land trusts, 4–5, 8, 14, 146, 200–201,
    205–6; community, 207; examples,
    210–14; funding, 228–29; and
    states, 208
land use planning: centralized
    oversight, 1–2; concerns, 48; conflict
    resolution, 62; evaluating impact,
    272–73; government, 2–3; growth
    of, 151; history, 11–12; local, 2–3,
    14; mixed-use, 174; national, 28–29;
    new varieties, 147; opposition, 30;
    public activities, 51–52, 53–54;
    public opinion, 38–39; regional, 19,
    22, 26; stakeholder networks,
    63–64, 175. *See also* civic
    engagement; collaboration; local
    action; regional planning
Land Use Planning Act, 181;
    opposition, 235
Lands Legacy Initiative, 171
Lassiter Properties, 131
Last Chance Land Trust, 205
Laurentide ecoregion, 82, 129
League of Conservation Voters, 50
legislation. *See* ballot questions; *specific
    bills*
Levitt, William, 23
Licht, Daniel, 138
Lily Tulip Plant Redevelopment
    Project, 168

linear greenways, 112. *See also* greenways
Little Darby Wildlife Refuge, 71
livable communities, 13, 21
Live Near Your Work Program, 185
local action, 199; definition, 199–200; land use, 233; opposition, 249; opposition to action, 254; stakeholder collaboration, 200; watersheds, 215–16. *See also* civic engagement
Local Government Commission, 193
Local Initiatives Support Corporation, 193
Lone Mountain Compact, 251
Louisiana Coastal Area Program, 141–42
Love Canal, 35
Lower Delaware River, 126
Lucas v. South Carolina, 243

MacKaye, Benton, 23, 225
Maine, 26, 32
Maine Forest Biodiversity Project, 75
Man and the Biosphere program, 99
Marin County Agricultural Trust (MALT), 212, 214
Marshall, Robert, 20
Maryland, 8–9, 13, 34, 90–92; farmland, 155, 157; smart growth, 184–85, 187
Maryland Association of Counties, 185
mass transportation, 37. *See also* transportation
Massachusetts, 26
McCall, Tom, 183
McCloskey, Michael, 66–67, 75–76, 257

McGreevey, James, 127–28
megascales, 82–87
Merrill Lynch, 195
Metropolitan Development Act (1966), 24
Michigan, 22, 59–60, 73
Middlesex School (Concord, MA), 46–47
migrants, ecological impact, 110–11
Million Acres Project, 138
mining, 119, 190
Minnesota, 155
minorities. *See* demographics; race
Mississippi River, 140
Missouri River Basin, 25
Model Cities Program, 60
Moses, Robert, 96
Muir, John, 17, 108, 201
multimunicipal planning, 8
Multiple Use Strategy Conference (1988), 239
multistakeholders, 3–4, 12
Myers, Phyllis, 229

National Academy of Sciences Commission of Geosciences, Environment, and Resources, 223
National Agricultural Lands Study, 212
National Association of Counties, 193
National Association of Home Builders, 13, 29, 171, 175, 194, 252
National Association of Realtors, 171, 191
National Audubon Society, 193
National Biological Service, 263
National Center for Appropriate Technology (NCAT), 192

National Center for Smart Growth Research and Education (University of Maryland), 193

National Environmental Policy Act (1969), 19, 54, 173; evaluations, 261

National Estuarine Research Reserve System, 31

National Estuary Program, 48, 71, 169, 223–24

National Flood Insurance Act (1968), 24

National Flood Insurance Program (NFIP), 140

National Forest Act (1976), 31

National Governors Association, 168

National Land Use Policy Act, 28–29

National Multi-Housing Council, 191

National Natural Landmarks program, 169

National Neighborhood Coalition, 191, 198

National Park Service, 117, 159, 164, 166–67, 239; grants, 161

National Parks Inholders Association, 239, 255–56

National Planning Board, 23

National Pollution Discharge Elimination System (NPDES), 219

National Research Council, 142

National Research Council Committee on Assessing and Valuing the Services of Aquatic and Related Terrestrial Ecosystems, 222

National Research Council Committee to Review the New York City Watershed Management Strategy, 97–98

National Resource Planning Board, 19

National Resources Commission, 23

National Resources Defense Council, 192–93, 281

National Science Foundation's Long-Term Ecological Research program, 143

National Smart Growth Council, 192

National Trails System, 167

National Trails System Act (1968), 24

National Trust for Historic Preservation, 47

National Watershed Forum (2001), 222–23

National Wild and Scenic Rivers System, 166–67

National Wildlife Federation, 135

Native Americans, 139

Natomas Basin Habitat Conservation Plan, 104–5

Natural Community Conservation Planning (NCCP), 105, 107

natural disasters. See hazard management

Natural Lands Trust, 210

Natural Resources Defense Council, 83

The Nature Conservancy (TNC), 70, 83–84, 107, 120; criticism, 204–5; goals and successes, 285–86; Northern Forest, 131; role in regional management, 138

neighborhood revitalization, 207

Nelson, Tom, 67

Nevada, 28

New Communities Act (1968), 24

New England Regional Commission, 23

New England River Basin
    Commission, 26
New England Rivers, 25
New Jersey, 3, 8–9, 13, 32–34;
    Delaware River, 126;
    environmental studies, 128;
    farmland, 157; greenways, 127;
    growth management, 38;
    Highlands, 81; Highlands
    Conservation Act, 43–44. *See also*
    New York/New Jersey Highlands;
    Pinelands National Reserve
New Jersey Conservation Foundation,
    123, 214
new regionalism, 2
new urbanism, 113, 151, 196, 251,
    282, 284–85, 308, 331, 339
New West, 67, 70, 73, 108, 110, 114,
    116
New York, 22, 27–28, 44, 79, 92–93,
    97; drinking water, 93–97, 221;
    Hudson River, 126; participation,
    56. *See also* Adirondack Park; Love
    Canal
New York City Board of Water
    Supply, 95
New York State Department of
    Environmental Conservation, 97
New York/New Jersey Harbor Estuary
    Program, 126
New York/New Jersey Highlands,
    8–9, 125
New York/New Jersey Palisades
    Interstate Park Commission, 125
New Zealand, 252
NIMBYism, 53, 281
Nixon, Richard, 28–29
*Nollan v. California Coastal
    Commission*, 243

nongovernmental organizations, 49,
    63, 70, 81, 84, 97; environmental,
    51; role, 134, 138; and sprawl, 150
Norquist, Grover, 238
North American Wetlands
    Conservation Act, 169, 220
North Carolina, 27
North East State Foresters
    Association, 134
Northeast-Midwest Institute, 193
Northern Forest, 79, 82, 86; attributes
    of region, 131; collaboration,
    131–32; exploitation, 129
Northern Forest Alliance, 134–35
Northern Forest Center, 135
Northern Forest Lands Council
    (NFLC), 133–34
Northern Forest Lands Study, 132
Northern Rockies Ecosystem
    Protection Act, 120
Northwest Forest Plan, 5, 103
Norton, Gale, 8
Nushagak-Mulchatna Wood-Tikchik
    Land Trust, 206

Ogallala Aquifer, 136
Ohio, 71, 74
Ohio Department of Natural
    Resources, 162
Ohio River, 25
Ohio Valley, 46
oil dependence, 77
Oil Pollution Act (1990), 36
oil spills: *Exxon Valdez* (1990), 20;
    Santa Barbara (1969), 19
Olmsted, Frederick Law, 18
open space, 38; benefits of, 265–66
Open Space Institute, 124–25
open-space protection, 34

Oregon, 8, 13, 26, 30–33, 68, 114–15, 179; land use, 288; Measure 37, 14–15, 30; Portland, 144–45; smart growth, 181–84
O'Toole, Randall, 251
outcomes, 271. *See also* evaluation
Outdoor Recreation Coordination Act (1963), 24
oysters, 69–70, 87–89, 140
ozone pollution, 36

Pacific Mega-Linkage, 108
Pacific Northwest, 46
Pacific Northwest Regional Planning Commission, 23
Pacific Northwest Rivers, 25
parks, 18, 34
Pataki, George, 97
Pennsylvania, 8–9, 13, 34, 90–92; farmland, 155, 157; smart growth, 187–90. *See also* Three Mile Island
People for the West!, 239, 255
Pequannock Watershed, 126–27
petitions, 51
Pictured Rocks National Lakeshore (Michigan), 160
Pinchot, Gifford, 18, 95, 117, 201
Pinelands, 3, 28, 128, 186
Pinelands Commission, 80–81, 265
Pinelands Comprehensive Management Plan, 80–81
Pinelands National Reserve, 33–34, 38, 81, 114
place-based planning, 2, 7, 9–12, 38–42, 112; economics, 10, 12; evaluation, 10–11; geographic scale, 45–46; global impact, 21; infrastructure, 77; origins, 35–38; public opinion, 39–40;

stakeholder networks, 48, 56–57; triggers, 34
planning: regional, 79, 146; statewide, 79
Poconos, 123
Point Reyes National Seashore, 212
political associations, 48; grassroots, 49; single-issue, 50
politicians, 57
pollution, 17–19, 41, 87–88, 91, 99–100; global impact, 21; regulation, 35
Popper, Deborah, 135–36, 138–39
Popper, Frank, 135–36, 138–39
poverty. *See* wealth
power. *See* energy
preservation, 17, 22; vs. conservation, 18; early, 17–18; farmland, 153. *See also* conservation
Preserve Appalachian Wilderness, 132–33
priority funding areas (PFAs), 185
private property, 250
Private Property Rights Act, 241
Private Property Rights Protection Act, 245
Private Stewardship grants, 169
Progressive Urban Real Estate, 144
property rights. *See* Wise Use and Property Rights Movements (WUPR)
Property Rights Foundation of America (PRFA), 253–54
Prophet, Elizabeth Clare, 116–17
public land: development, 22; management of, 76

quiet revolution, 25–30; accomplishments, 283–84, 290–91;

and civic engagement, 43, 49–51, 56; vs. conservation biology, 138; current status, 281; goals and successes, 291–95; as movement, 282; regulation, 80; significance, 279–81; and sprawl, 150. *See also* collaboration; place-based planning
Quincy Library Group (California), 67–68, 70
Quinnipiac River, 220

race, 55–56
racial segregation. *See* segregation
Rails-to-Trails Conservancy, 167
Rait, Ken, 248
ranching, 119, 136. *See also* buffalo
Ray, Dixie Lee, 115
Reading Prong, 123
Reagan, Ronald, 30, 55, 153, 192, 202, 237–38
Real Estate Research Corporation, 152
reclamation, land, 149
recreation, 129, 167, 254, 266. *See also* greenways
regional planning, 13; critics of, 23
Regional Planning Association of America (RPAA), 22–23
Regional Vulnerability Assessment Program, 263–64
regionalism, 22–23
regulation: centralized, 77; conventional approaches, 43; historic preservation, 178; of sprawl, 111–12, 149–52. *See also* subdivision regulations
Reilly, William K., 36
Rendell, Edward, 190, 232
Republican Party, 230, 253–54

research. *See* evaluation
Resettlement Administration, 19
residential development, 103
resource scarcity, 20, 275–76
restoration, ecological, 136, 138, 155
Restore, 135
rewilding, 138–39
Rewilding Institute, 83
Rhode Island, 32, 179
Ridge, Tom, 189
river basin planning, 25. *See also* Tennessee Valley Authority (TVA)
River Trails and Conservation Assistance Program, 126
River's Edge Project, 168
Rivers, Trails, and Conservation Assistance Program, 169
Rockies Prosperity Act, 120
Rocky Mountain Cordillera, 82
Rocky Mountain Elk Foundation, 206–7
Roosevelt, Theodore, 18
Royal Teton Ranch, 116

Safe Drinking Water Act (1974), 31
Safe Drinking Water Act (1996), 31–32
Safe Drinking Water Act Amendments (1986), 95
Safe Harbor Agreements, 104
Safe, Accountable, Flexible, Efficient Transportation Equity Act (SAFETEA), 162–63
salmon, 46, 69–70, 114
San Francisco Bay Conservation and Development Commission, 26
sanitation, 20
Santa Monica Mountains National Recreation Area, 160

Save Our Everglades, 99
scale, geographic, 55; megascales, 82–83; small, 46
Scalia, Antonin, 243
Schaefer, William Donald, 184
schools, 170, 185
Sea Shepherd Conservation Society, 258
seafood, 87–89
segregation, 46
self-sufficiency, agricultural, 275. *See also* sustainability
Senetec Canyon, 163
September 11 attacks (2001), 39
shad, 87–88
Shell Oil, 141
Shipley, Jack, 68
shortages, 275–76
Sierra Business Council, 110
Sierra Club, 17, 49, 66–68, 75, 83, 146, 257; goals and successes, 285–86; John Muir, 108; smart growth, 192
Sierra Nevada, 67, 86, 110, 112; subregions, 108
Sierra Nevada Alliance, 110
Sierra Nevada Ecosystem Project (SNEP), 109–10
Sierra Summit, 109
Simberloff, Daniel, 83
Simon, Julian, 149
Siskiyou Mountains, 68
Skocpol, Theda, 49
Sky Islands Wildlands Network, 83
Sleeping Bear Dunes National Lakeshore (Michigan), 160
Smart Communities Network, 192
smart growth, 3–9, 13–14, 21, 34, 153, 169, 171; agenda, 176–78;

boom, 179; and corporations, 29; definition, 173; and environmental justice, 7, 11; and housing, 175, 197; individual states, 179–81, 190; opposition, 174; opposition to term, 173; participants, 191–93; philosophical objections, 250–51; urban, 194–95. *See also* sprawl
Smart Growth America (SGA), 174, 191–92
Smart Growth and Neighborhood Conservation Initiative, 185
Smart Growth Leadership Institute, 192
Smart Growth Network, 191, 198, 250–51
social equity, 5, 12, 39–40, 44; environmental burdens, 20
Society for Protection of New Hampshire Forests, 131
Soil Conservation Service, 19
soil management, 19
Solving Sprawl: The Sierra Club Rates the States, 192
Souris-Red-Rainy Rivers, 25
special management area, 115
sprawl, 12–13, 41; adaptation, 149–50; analysis, 129; in Appalachians, 121; attempts to address, 150; California, 107–8; commitment to reversing, 173; control, 111–12; costs of managing, 288–89; definition, 152; failure to control, 149; management, 182; potential for solving, 283; vs. protection, 202; and race, 175; and urban living, 143; vertical, 196. *See also* smart growth

Spruce Run Reservoir (New Jersey), 127
Stapleton Airport (Denver), 169, 172
State Development and Redevelopment Plan (New Jersey), 126
state-run planning, 25–30; aftermath, 30–34; coercive vs. empowering, 32–33; triggers, 34
Sterling Forest, 125, 127
Sterling Forest Corporation (SFC), 124
stewardship, place-based, 199
Stewardship Incentive Program, 134
Stewardship Program, 125
Storm King Park, 126
subdivision regulations, 150
subsidies, 150, 156, 250–51; home mortgages, 172
sugar, 99–100
Superfund, 54. *See* Comprehensive Environmental Response Compensation and Liability Act
Superfund Amendments and Reauthorization Act (SARA) (1986), 35, 54
Surface Mine Control and Reclamation Act (1977), 31
Surface Transportation Policy Project, 193
Susquehanna River Basin Commission, 25
sustainability, 65, 80, 133, 136, 143, 273–74; grants, 97
Sustainable Development Commission, 145
Sustainable Pittsburgh, 144
Sustainable Seattle, 145
systems perspectives, 66

Tahoe Regional Planning Agency, 109
Tahoe-Sierra Preservation Council v. Tahoe Regional Planning Agency (TRPA), 244
taxes, 156–57; deductions for mortgages, 150
Temporary State Commission to Study the Catskills, 93
Tennessee Valley Authority (TVA), 19, 23
terminology, confusion, 79–80
Teton Regional Land Trust, 120
think tanks, 193
Thoreau Country Conservation Alliance, 47
Three Mile Island, 35
timber, 114, 119
Timber and Stone Act, 22
Timber Culture Act, 22
Tocks Island, 219
Tongass National Forest, 240
total maximum daily load (TMDL) rules, 222
tourism, 129, 136, 139–40, 164
toxic chemicals, 35
traffic, 34–37, 150
transferable development rights (TDRs), 128, 157–58
transportation, 162–63, 170, 174; detractors, 196; development, 196; transit-oriented development (TOD), 293
Transportation Efficiency Grants, 166, 171
Transportation Equity Act for the 21st Century (TEA-21). *See* Safe, Accountable, Flexible, Efficient Transportation Equity Act (SAFETEA)

Trust for Public Land, 14, 97, 107, 116, 120, 124–25; research, 228–30; scale, 204

Trustees of Reservations, 201

Tucker, Robert, 47

Tug Hill, 27–28, 81

Tugwell, Rexford, 19

Turner, Frederick Jackson, 17

Turner, Ted, 136

Twin Cities Metropolitan Council, 26

Udall, Morris, 29

United Nations, 37

United Nations Biosphere Reserve, 117

Upper Delaware River, watershed, 93

Upper Mississippi River, 25

Urban and Community Forestry Program, 125

urban areas, 143; reducing footprint, 150; revitalization, 5, 14, 170, 194–95

urban growth boundaries (UGBs), 181–82, 184

Urban Land Institute, 193

Urban Mass Transportation Act (1964), 24

U.S. Fish and Wildlife Service, 71

Utah Wilderness Alliance, 248

Vail, Colorado ski lodge burning, 15

Vermont, 26–27, 30, 32, 179; farmland, 155, 157

Veterans Administration, 24

Vital Ground, 207

Vitter, David, 141–42

vulnerability, 263, 274–75, 286. See also hazard management

Walden Woods, 47

walkability, 172, 174, 266, 275–76

Wallach, Bret, 139

Wal-Mart, 186

Washington (state), 28, 32–33, 53, 114–15, 179, 223; smart growth, 184; Willapa Bay, 69–70

Washington Landing (Pittsburgh), 168–69

waste management, 20

water, 10, 93, 96–97; standards, 127

Water Resources Planning Act (1965), 24–25

Watershed Agricultural Council, 97

Watershed Forum Report (2001), 265

watersheds, 65, 74, 82; associations, 14, 24–25, 200; Chesapeake, 91–92; conservancies, 146, 215–16, 218–21; Great Lakes, 88; management, 18–19, 22, 24–25, 98; Pequannock, 126–27; programs, 169; Upper Delaware River, 93

Watson, Paul, 257–58

Watt, James, 55, 239

wealth, 230–32, 272, 289–90; and civic engagement, 287; elitism, 284. See also environmental justice; housing

wetlands protection, 8, 31, 249–50

Wetlands Reserve Program, 31, 126, 154–55

Weyerhauser Corporation, 70

White Mountain National Forest, 129, 132

White Mountains (New Hampshire), 82

Whitman, Christine Todd, 192, 232

Wild and Scenic River designation, 126
Wild and Scenic Rivers Act (1968), 24
Wild Earth, 146
Wild Rockies Action Fund, 120
Wilderness Act (1964), 24
Wilderness Society, 68
Wildlands Project, 83, 108
Wildlife Habitat Incentive Program (WHIP), 155
Willapa Alliance, 69–70
Williamson Act (California), 212
Wisconsin, 22, 26, 56
Wisconsin Karner Blue Butterfly Habitat Conservation Plan, 105
Wise Use and Property Rights Movements (WUPR), 237–45, 247–48, 250, 254; current status, 258–59; and the Kelo decision, 245–46; as movement, 282; opposition to action, 249–52, 256–57

wise use movement, 95, 239, 246–47; agenda, 240
workplace hazards, 20, 41
Works Progress Administration, 19
World Heritage program, 47
World Wildlife Fund, 138
WUPR. *See* Wise Use and Property Rights Movements
Wyoming Heritage Society, 255

Year 2020 Panel, 184–85
Yellowstone National Park, 82, 86, 117. *See also* Greater Yellowstone Ecoregion
Yellowstone to Yukon program, 120–21
Yosemite National Park, 239
Yosemite Valley, 18
Yukon to Yellowstone project, 82

zoning, 146, 150, 176; and the Community Character Act, 252